GUNTHER™

MONSTERS AND MUSTACHES!

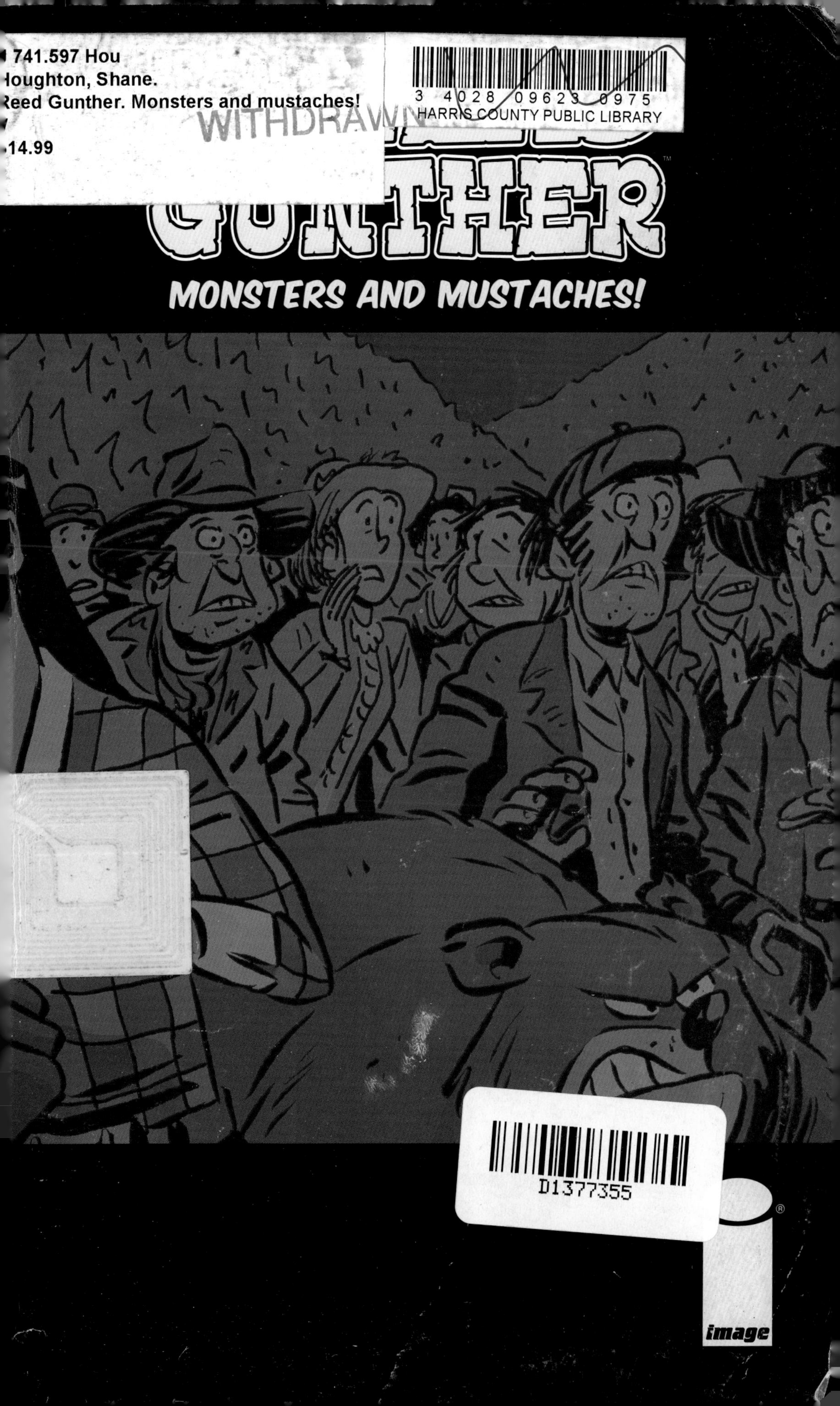

image®

SPECIAL THANKS TO KASSANDRA HELLER, KATIE SCOTT,
IAN BOOTHBY, KAZU KIBUISHI, CHRIS SCHWEIZER,
ANDY SURIANO, SCOTT SHAW!, VINCENT KUKUA,
RICHARD STARKINGS, ERIC STEPHENSON,
AND MOM & DAD HOUGHTON.

WWW.REEDGUNTHER.COM

WRITE US AT:
MAIL@REEDGUNTHER.COM
WE'D LOVE TO HEAR FROM YOU!

FIRST EDITION JULY 2012

ISBN: 978-1-60706-556-2

PRINTED IN SOUTH KOREA

THIS BOOK COLLECTS THE REED GUNTHER COMIC BOOK SERIES, ISSUES 6-10.
PUBLISHED BY IMAGE COMICS.

REED GUNTHER ™

CREATED BY
SHANE & CHRIS HOUGHTON

WRITTEN BY
SHANE HOUGHTON

DRAWN BY
CHRIS HOUGHTON

COLORED BY
JOSH ULRICH

COLOR FLATS BY
JOSE FLORES

INTRODUCTION
by Ian Boothby

It's a story about about a cowboy who rides a bear. If that isn't enough to get you interested in a comic book then we are very different people.

We've had decades of great cowboy stories from *High Noon* to *The Good the Bad and The Ugly*, but there's always been one element clearly missing, a bear. Likewise Winnie the Pooh, Yogi Bear and Paddington have been woefully short of cowboys. But with Reed Gunther the peanut butter has met the chocolate and we're all the better for it.

Fun has become a dirty word in comics. And not one of the good dirty words. Speaking of which, Reed Gunther has some of the best new swear words you'll ever read. Ones that people don't know yet so you can use them at school or work without getting kicked out. Shane and Chris Houghton have done something special here, creating an original all-ages book that's both a fun and funny action packed adventure. Where a cowboy rides a bear. Sorry to keep banging that nail, but it's worth re-banging.

Speaking of bears. Like the North American Grizzly, this comic has a dark underbelly. This is a world where death lurks around every corner, monsters from your creepiest nightmares lie in wait alongside mystical villains who would like nothing better than to steal your soul! But that's no reason to not have a good time. And our heroes Reed, Sterling, and Starla do just that!

One thing that impresses me about Reed Gunther is that it's an all-ages book that actually is for all ages. That's every age there is! As someone who writes for that market as well, let me tell you, that is a difficult task. The most difficult ages to write for? 47 and 82 years old. No idea why, but people who are those two ages are real jerks. And don't get me started on trying to hold a four month old's interest in your multi-issue subplot. They're all, "I can put my foot in my mouth." Meanwhile, 107 year olds say, "Leave the comic on the table next to my deathbed. I'll read it in a little while." But they never do. Selfish.

This is a comic book the whole family can read. But not at the same time. The couch is only so wide, and let's be honest, Dad's been putting on a few pounds. And since you've purchased it in a collection there are none of those potentially deadly staples you'd find in the comic version. I mean what if your little brother swallows them and then walks under a powerful electromagnet? If he's on a leash you might have a chance to pull him back down but... let's just be grateful you got this in collected form.

Now at this point you're saying, "Sounds good, but what makes Reed Gunther so unique?" Well, first of all, please stop talking out loud to a comic book collection. There's no way Shane or I can hear you. Chris has some mild telepathic powers, like all comic book artists, so it's better to just think your comments to him as hard as you can. Shane and I, like all comic book writers, have the ability to taste ice cream with our fingertips and breathe fire.

But back to what makes the book special. The first issue is an origin story. Sure, comic books run thick with origin stories but how many contain the origin of a mustache? Three at the most.

By buying this collection here's what you'll get; scary face contests, battle-field child births, wolf attacks, guff rebuffing, monster-hunting posses, pancake-loving reverse werewolves, arm wrestling, pretty dresses, face-eating mummies, human sacrifice, railway building, soul selling, possessed bears, attempted baby eating, machine guns, fire mustaches, mind battles, kissing, boat scuttling, the world's best pickles and much much more!

I know when most people say, "and much much more," they really mean, "and not much more." But there's a whole heap of more muchness in these here pages partner! Before you get reading you'd better loosen your brain belt because it's time for an imagination feast!

And did I mention a cowboy rides a bear? There's always room for one more, just grab a scruff of fur (not from the lower back please, Sterling is thinning a bit and is a little sensitive about it) and come along for the ride!

Ian Boothby
— *Eisner Award winning writer for The Simpsons and Futurama Comics. Co-host of the Sneaky Dragon podcast.*

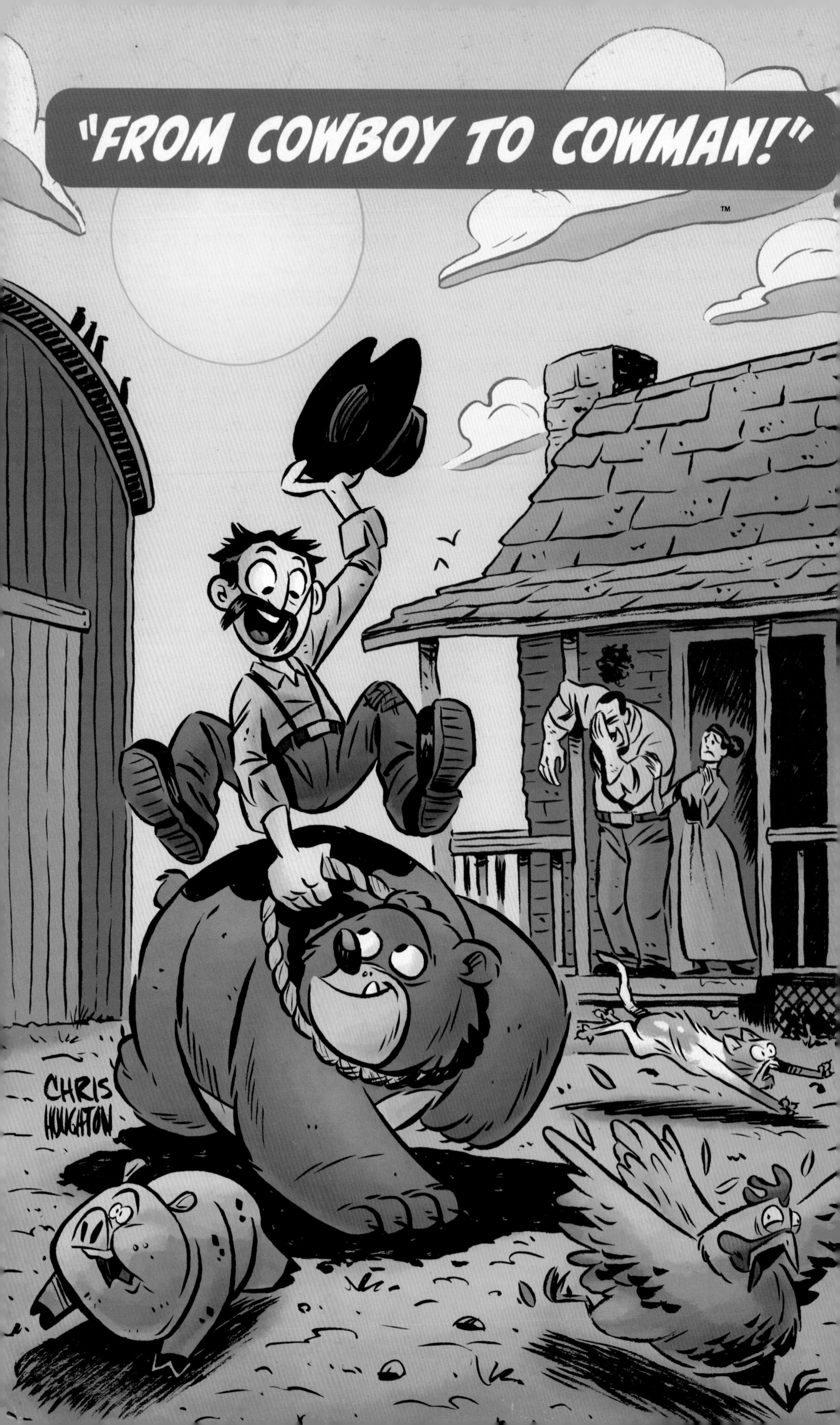
"FROM COWBOY TO COWMAN!"
™
CHRIS HOUGHTON

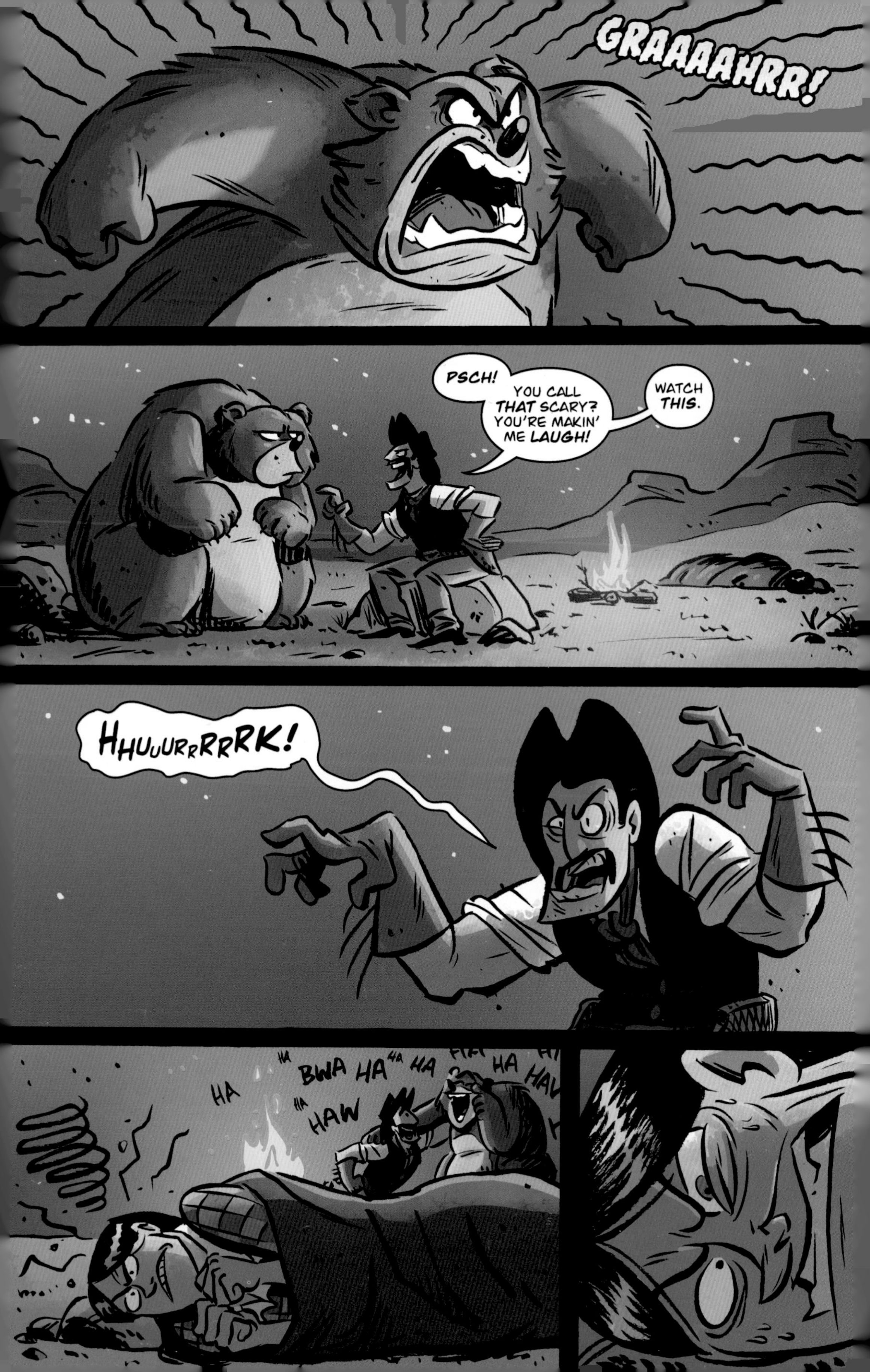
GRAAAAAHRR!
PSCH!
YOU CALL THAT SCARY? YOU'RE MAKIN' ME LAUGH!
WATCH THIS.
HHUUURRRRK!
HA
HA
BWA HA HA HA
HA
HAW
HA
HAW

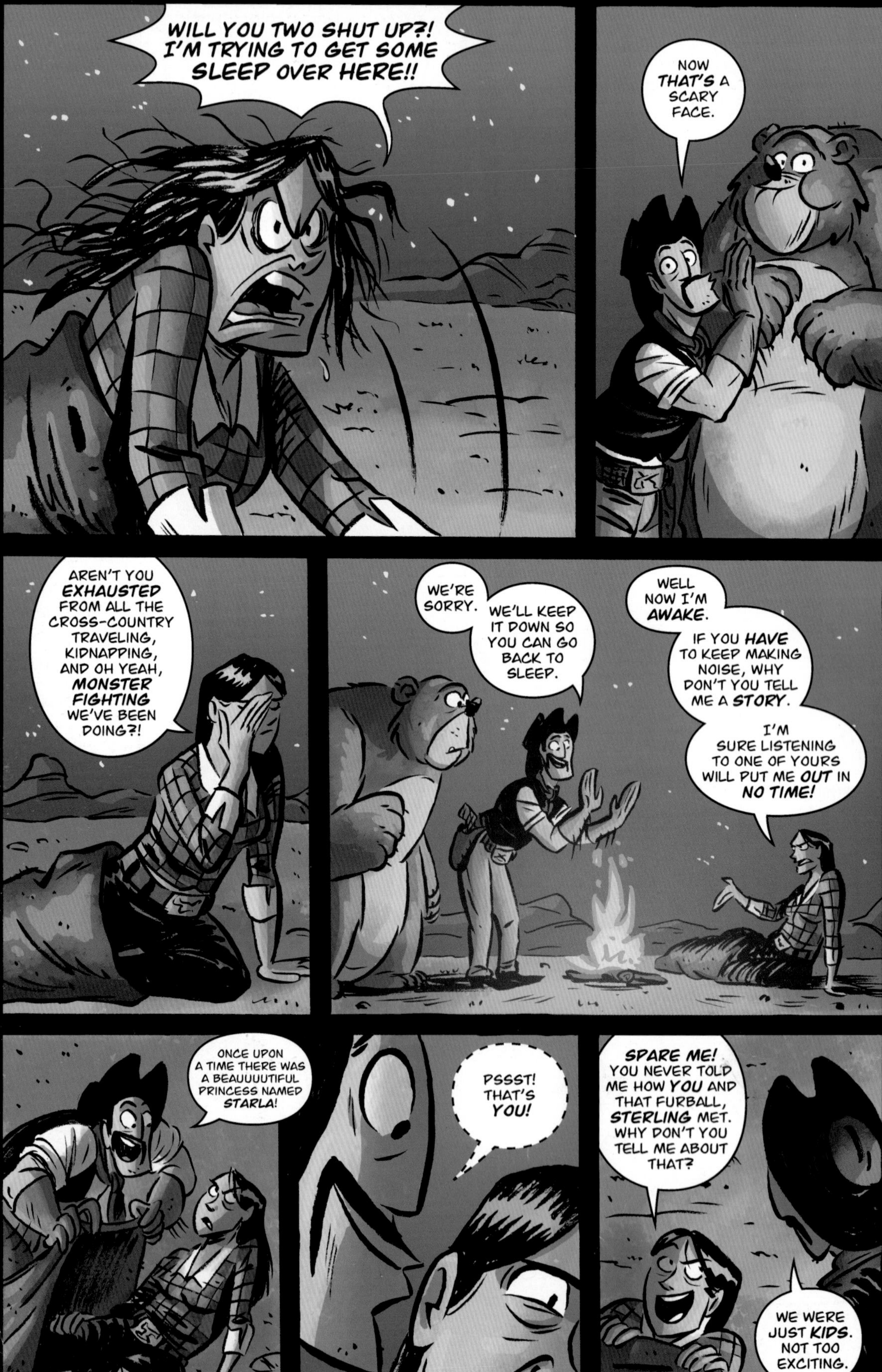
WILL YOU TWO SHUT UP?! I'M TRYING TO GET SOME SLEEP OVER HERE!!
NOW THAT'S A SCARY FACE.
AREN'T YOU EXHAUSTED FROM ALL THE CROSS-COUNTRY TRAVELING, KIDNAPPING, AND OH YEAH, MONSTER FIGHTING WE'VE BEEN DOING?!
WE'RE SORRY.
WE'LL KEEP IT DOWN SO YOU CAN GO BACK TO SLEEP.
WELL NOW I'M AWAKE.
IF YOU HAVE TO KEEP MAKING NOISE, WHY DON'T YOU TELL ME A STORY.
I'M SURE LISTENING TO ONE OF YOURS WILL PUT ME OUT IN NO TIME!
ONCE UPON A TIME THERE WAS A BEAUUUUTIFUL PRINCESS NAMED STARLA!
PSSST! THAT'S YOU!
SPARE ME! YOU NEVER TOLD ME HOW YOU AND THAT FURBALL, STERLING MET. WHY DON'T YOU TELL ME ABOUT THAT?
WE WERE JUST KIDS. NOT TOO EXCITING.

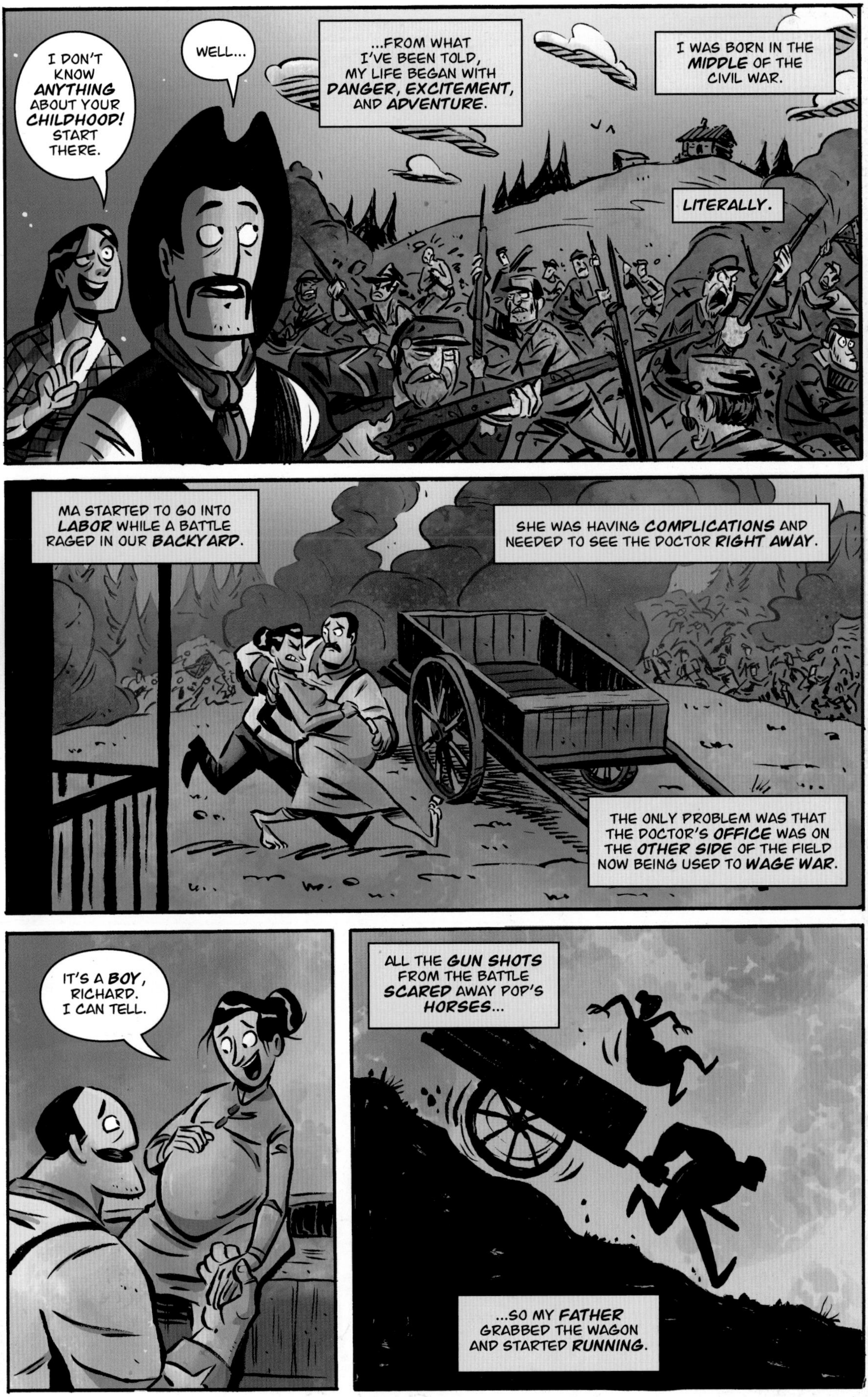
I DON'T KNOW ANYTHING ABOUT YOUR CHILDHOOD! START THERE.
WELL...
...FROM WHAT I'VE BEEN TOLD, MY LIFE BEGAN WITH DANGER, EXCITEMENT, AND ADVENTURE.
I WAS BORN IN THE MIDDLE OF THE CIVIL WAR.
LITERALLY.
MA STARTED TO GO INTO LABOR WHILE A BATTLE RAGED IN OUR BACKYARD.
SHE WAS HAVING COMPLICATIONS AND NEEDED TO SEE THE DOCTOR RIGHT AWAY.
THE ONLY PROBLEM WAS THAT THE DOCTOR'S OFFICE WAS ON THE OTHER SIDE OF THE FIELD NOW BEING USED TO WAGE WAR.
IT'S A BOY, RICHARD. I CAN TELL.
ALL THE GUN SHOTS FROM THE BATTLE SCARED AWAY POP'S HORSES...
...SO MY FATHER GRABBED THE WAGON AND STARTED RUNNING.

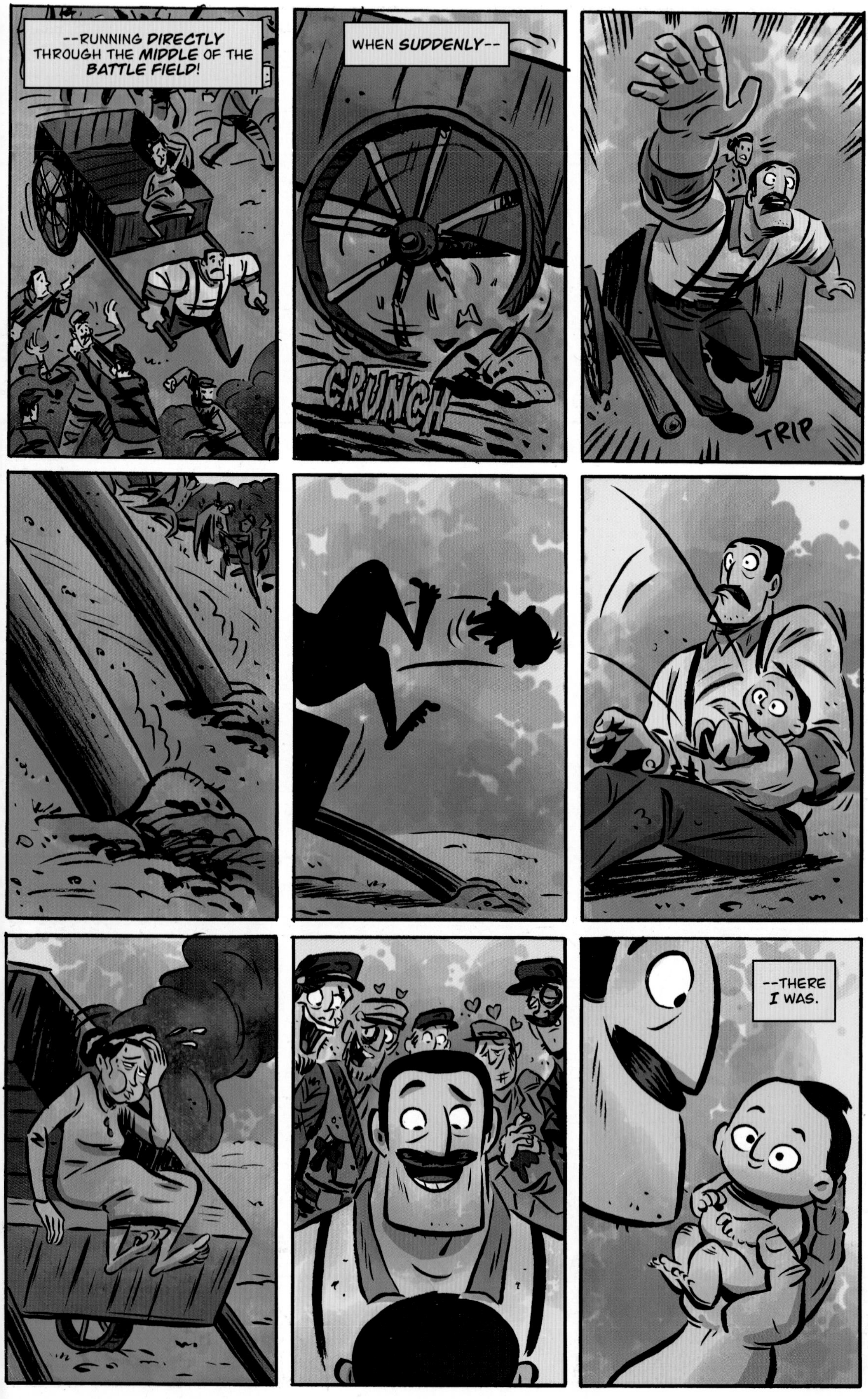
--RUNNING DIRECTLY THROUGH THE MIDDLE OF THE BATTLE FIELD!
WHEN SUDDENLY--
CRUNCH
TRIP
--THERE I WAS.

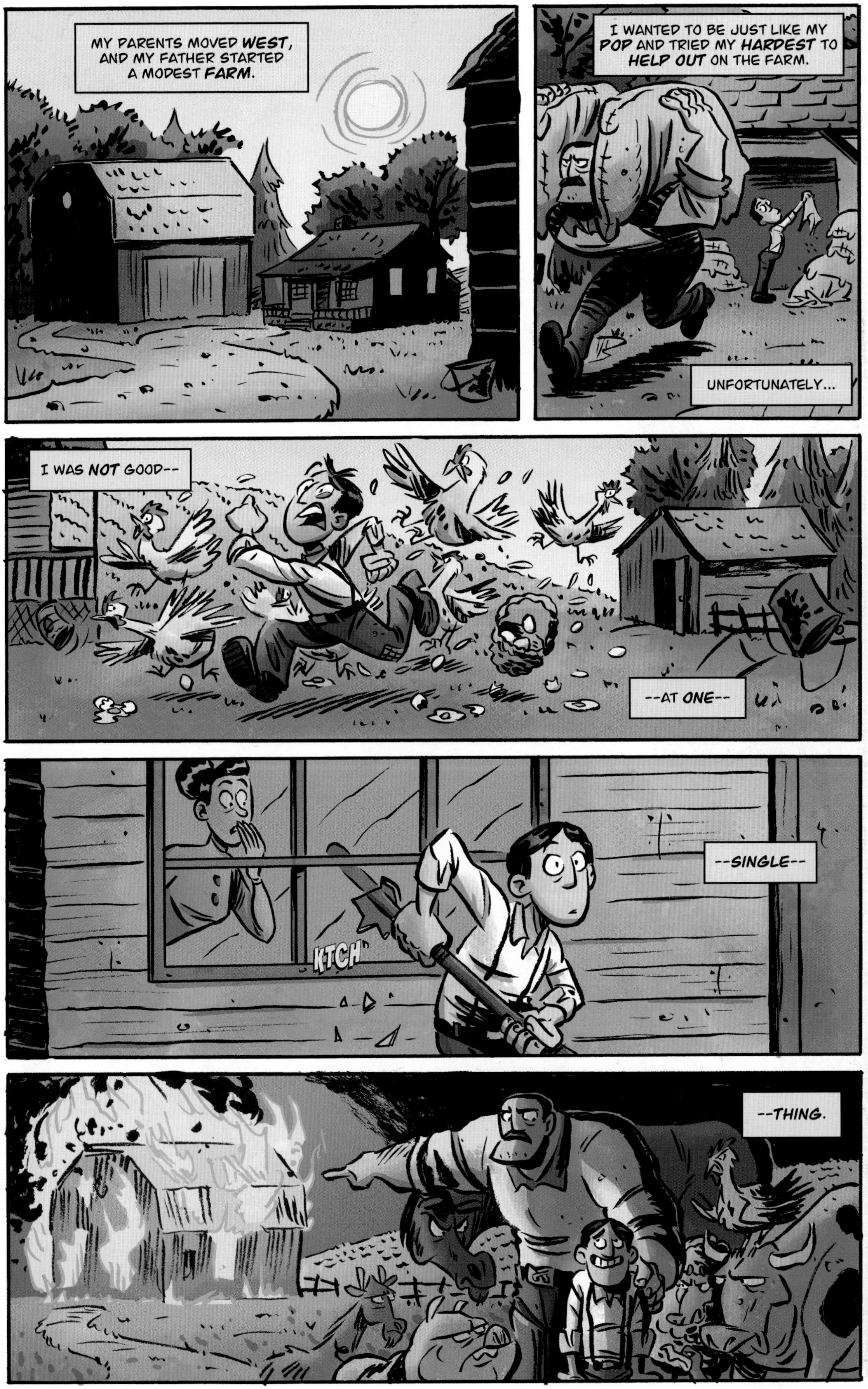
MY PARENTS MOVED WEST, AND MY FATHER STARTED A MODEST FARM.
I WANTED TO BE JUST LIKE MY POP AND TRIED MY HARDEST TO HELP OUT ON THE FARM.
UNFORTUNATELY...
I WAS NOT GOOD--
--AT ONE--
--SINGLE--
KTCH
--THING.

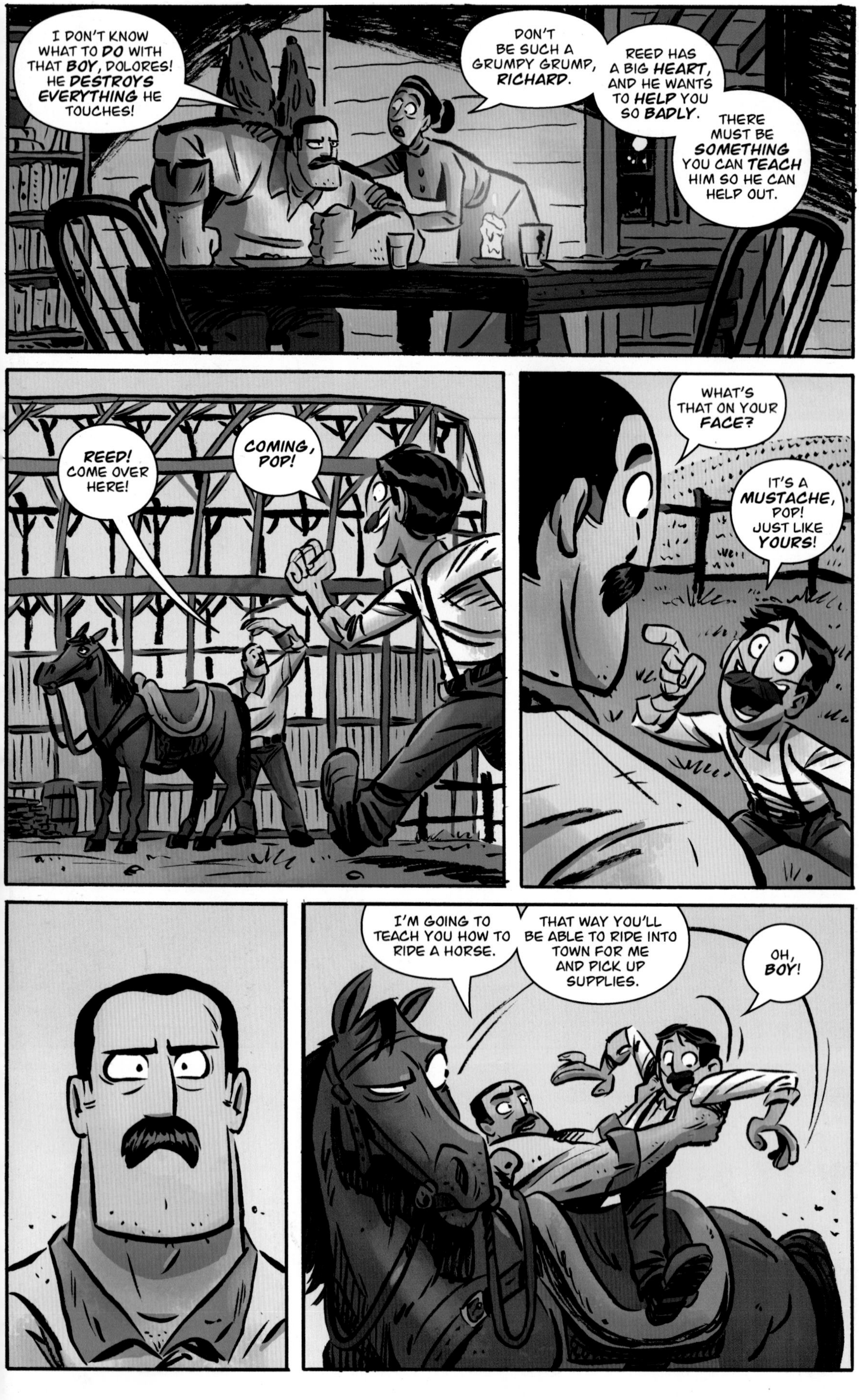

I DON'T KNOW WHAT TO DO WITH THAT BOY, DOLORES! HE DESTROYS EVERYTHING HE TOUCHES!
DON'T BE SUCH A GRUMPY GRUMP, RICHARD.
REED HAS A BIG HEART, AND HE WANTS TO HELP YOU SO BADLY.
THERE MUST BE SOMETHING YOU CAN TEACH HIM SO HE CAN HELP OUT.
REED! COME OVER HERE!
COMING, POP!
WHAT'S THAT ON YOUR FACE?
IT'S A MUSTACHE, POP! JUST LIKE YOURS!
I'M GOING TO TEACH YOU HOW TO RIDE A HORSE.
THAT WAY YOU'LL BE ABLE TO RIDE INTO TOWN FOR ME AND PICK UP SUPPLIES.
OH, BOY!

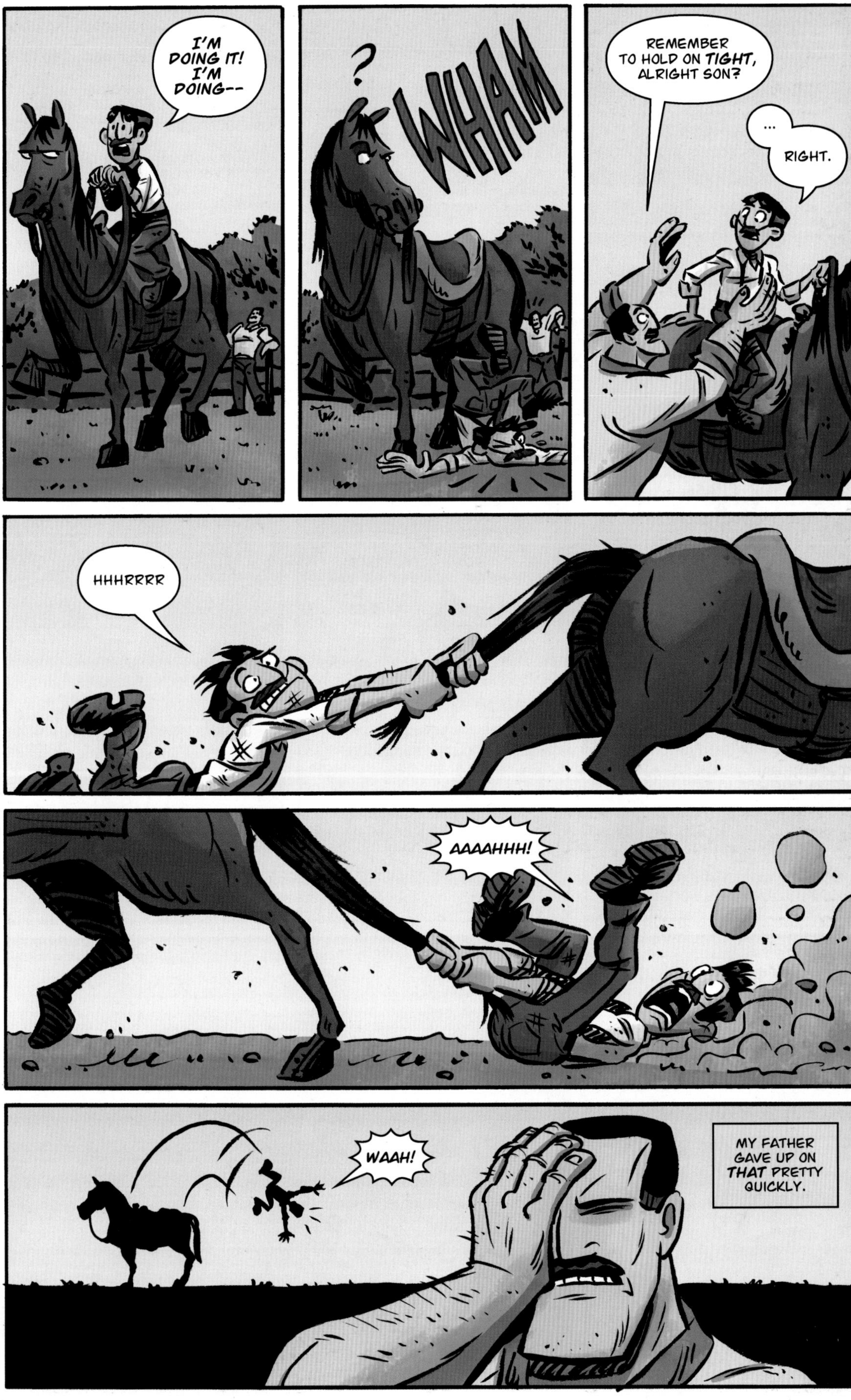
I'M DOING IT! I'M DOING--
?
WHAM
REMEMBER TO HOLD ON TIGHT, ALRIGHT SON?
...
RIGHT.
HHHRRRR
AAAAHHH!
WAAH!
MY FATHER GAVE UP ON THAT PRETTY QUICKLY.

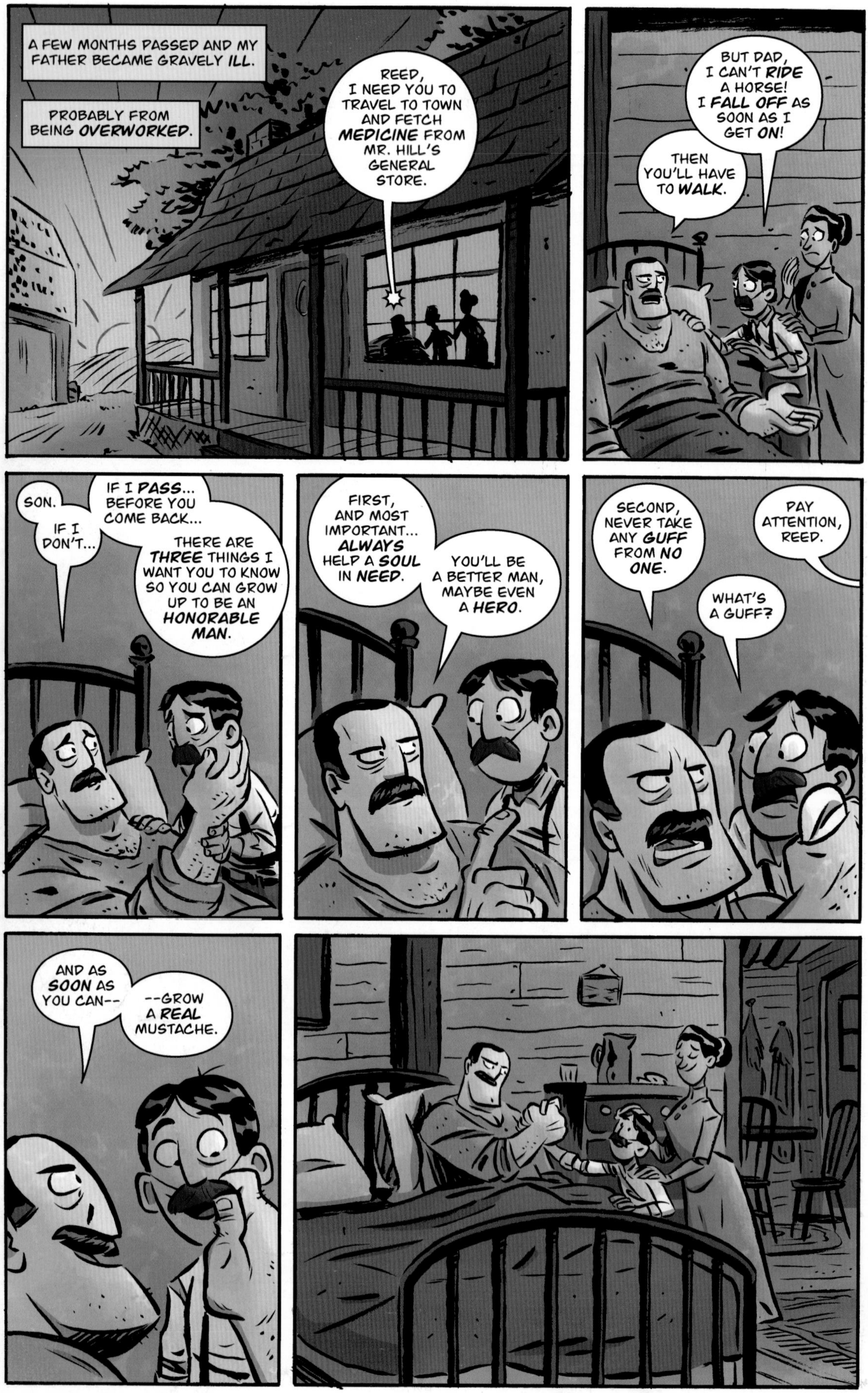

A FEW MONTHS PASSED AND MY FATHER BECAME GRAVELY **ILL**.
PROBABLY FROM BEING **OVERWORKED**.
REED, I NEED YOU TO TRAVEL TO TOWN AND FETCH **MEDICINE** FROM MR. HILL'S GENERAL STORE.
BUT DAD, I CAN'T **RIDE** A HORSE! I **FALL OFF** AS SOON AS I GET **ON**!
THEN YOU'LL HAVE TO **WALK**.
SON.
IF I DON'T...
IF I **PASS**... BEFORE YOU COME BACK...
THERE ARE **THREE** THINGS I WANT YOU TO KNOW SO YOU CAN GROW UP TO BE AN **HONORABLE MAN**.
FIRST, AND MOST IMPORTANT... **ALWAYS** HELP A **SOUL** IN **NEED**.
YOU'LL BE A BETTER MAN, MAYBE EVEN A **HERO**.
SECOND, NEVER TAKE ANY **GUFF** FROM **NO ONE**.
PAY ATTENTION, REED.
WHAT'S A GUFF?
AND AS **SOON** AS YOU CAN--
--GROW A **REAL** MUSTACHE.

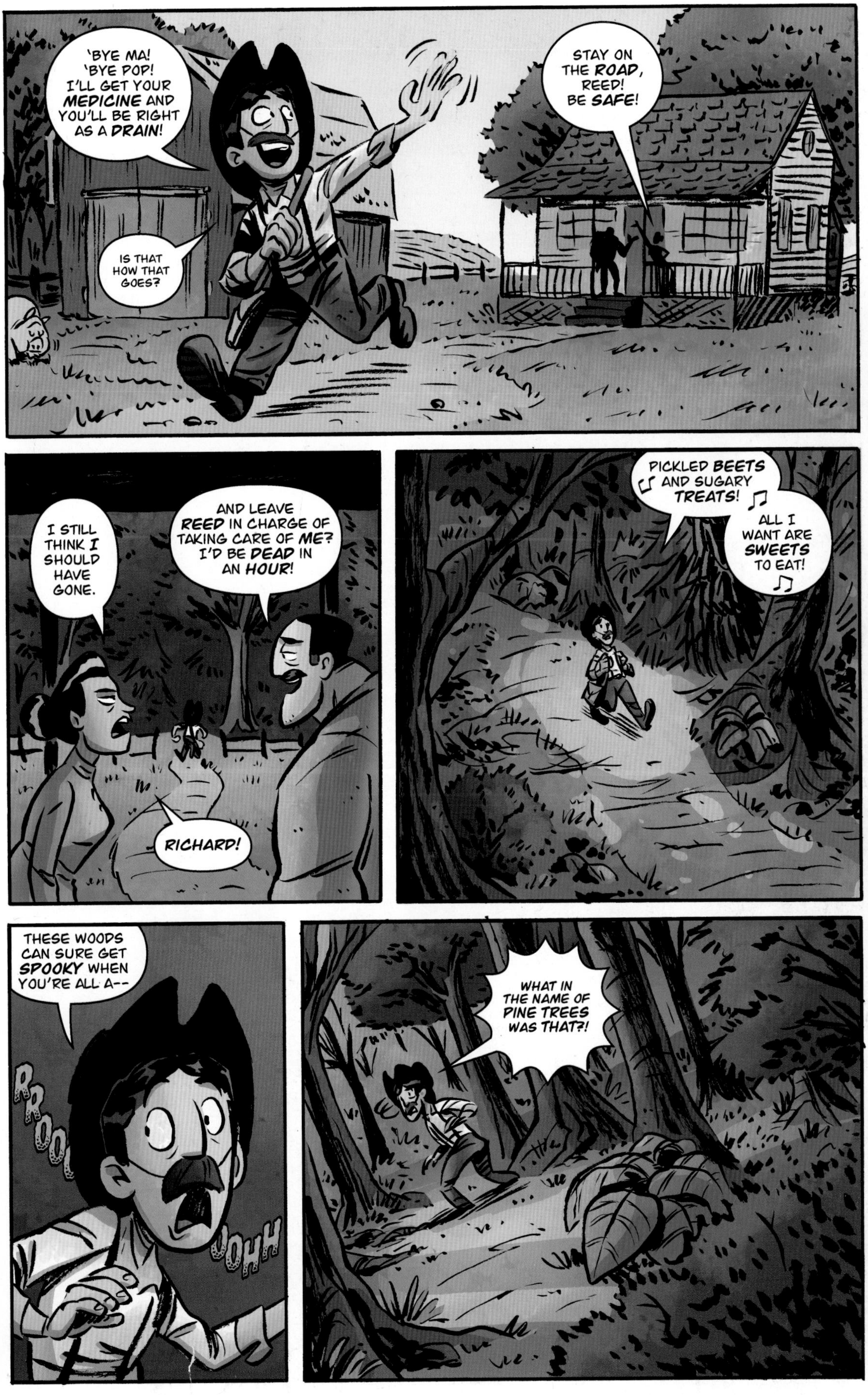
'BYE MA! 'BYE POP! I'LL GET YOUR MEDICINE AND YOU'LL BE RIGHT AS A DRAIN!
IS THAT HOW THAT GOES?
STAY ON THE ROAD, REED! BE SAFE!
I STILL THINK I SHOULD HAVE GONE.
AND LEAVE REED IN CHARGE OF TAKING CARE OF ME? I'D BE DEAD IN AN HOUR!
RICHARD!
PICKLED BEETS AND SUGARY TREATS!
ALL I WANT ARE SWEETS TO EAT!
THESE WOODS CAN SURE GET SPOOKY WHEN YOU'RE ALL A--
RROOOOOHH
WHAT IN THE NAME OF PINE TREES WAS THAT?!

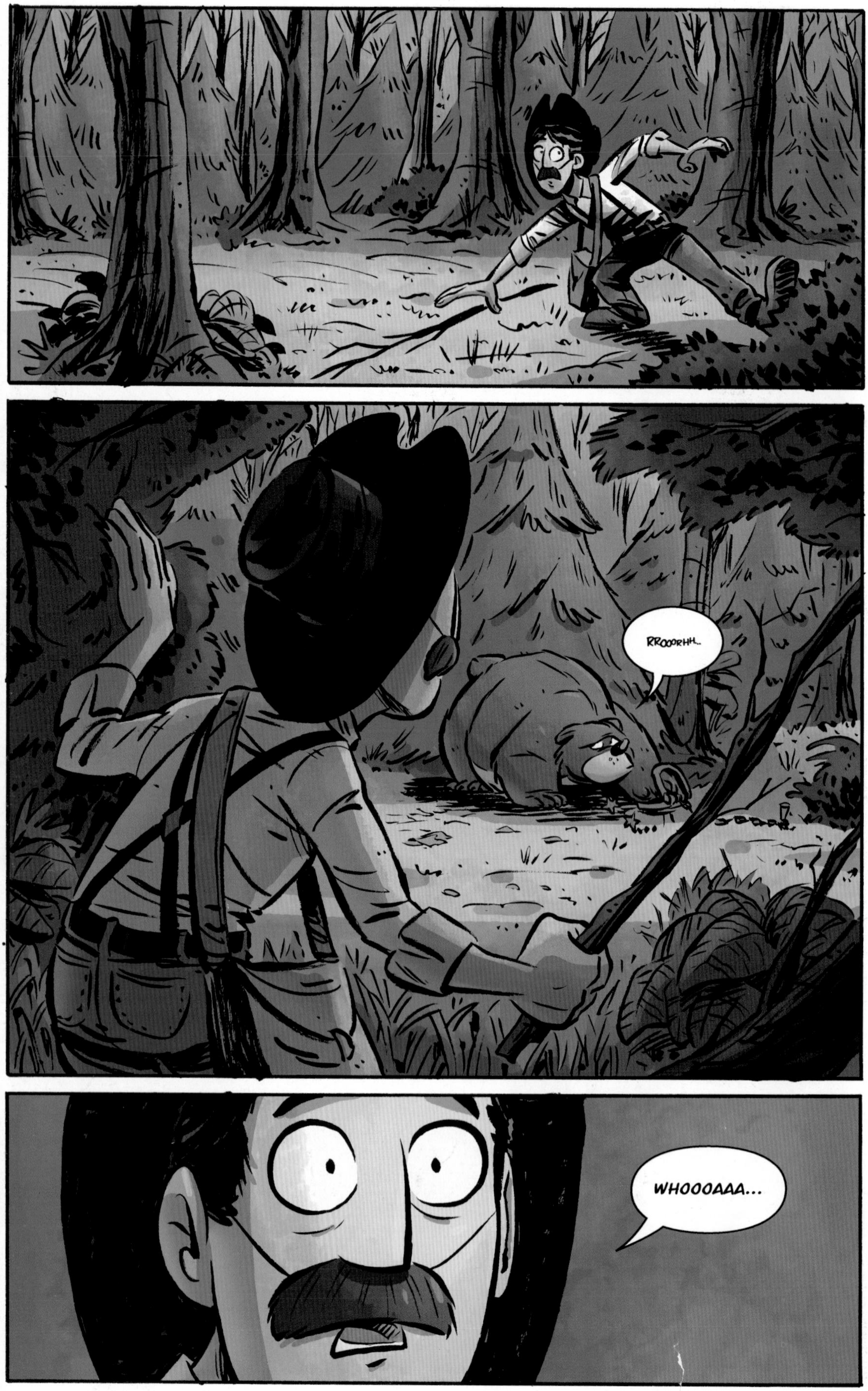
RROOORHH..
WHOOOAAA...

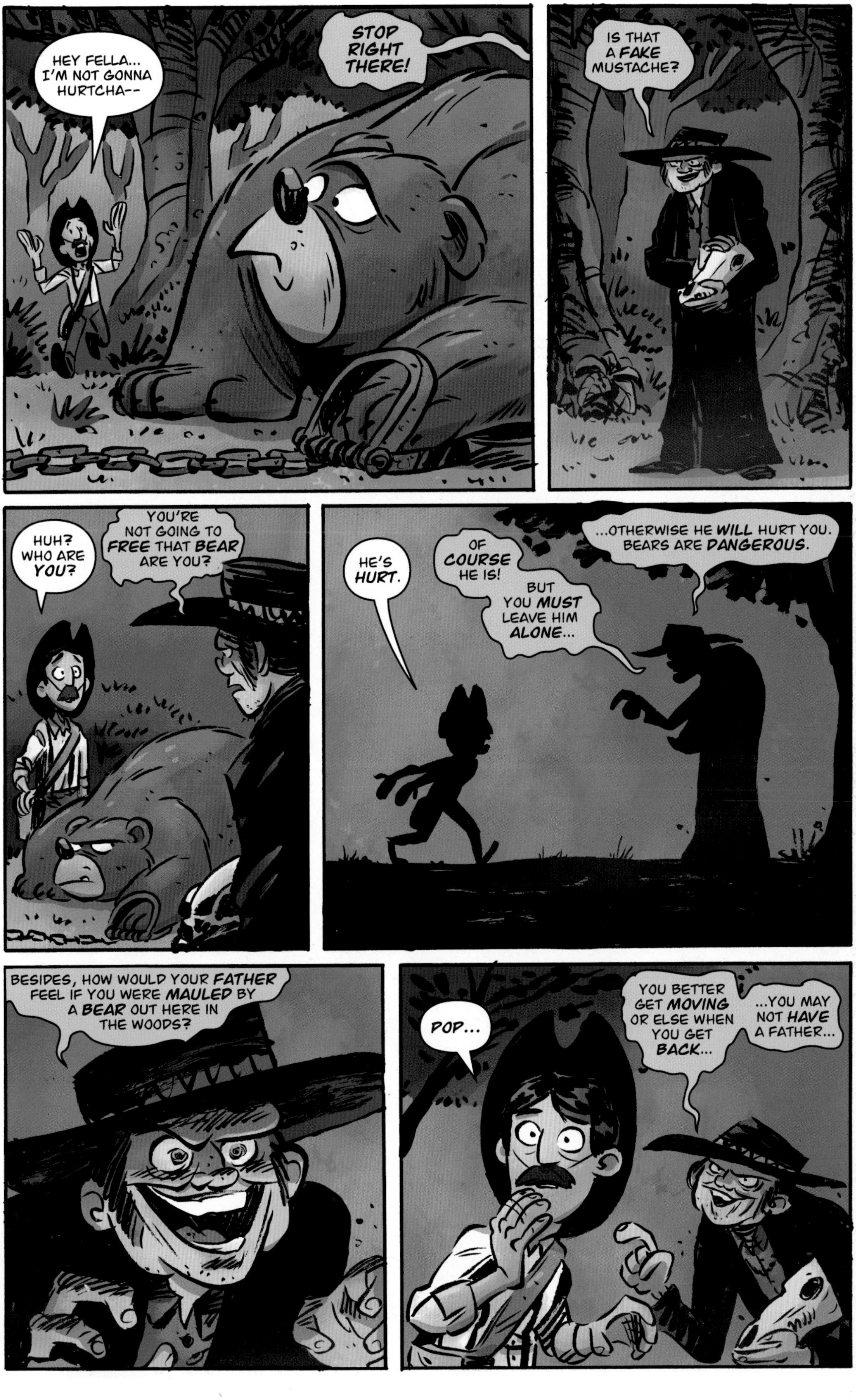
HEY FELLA... I'M NOT GONNA HURTCHA--
STOP RIGHT THERE!
IS THAT A FAKE MUSTACHE?
HUH? WHO ARE YOU?
YOU'RE NOT GOING TO FREE THAT BEAR ARE YOU?
HE'S HURT.
OF COURSE HE IS!
BUT YOU MUST LEAVE HIM ALONE...
...OTHERWISE HE WILL HURT YOU. BEARS ARE DANGEROUS.
BESIDES, HOW WOULD YOUR FATHER FEEL IF YOU WERE MAULED BY A BEAR OUT HERE IN THE WOODS?
POP...
YOU BETTER GET MOVING OR ELSE WHEN YOU GET BACK...
...YOU MAY NOT HAVE A FATHER...

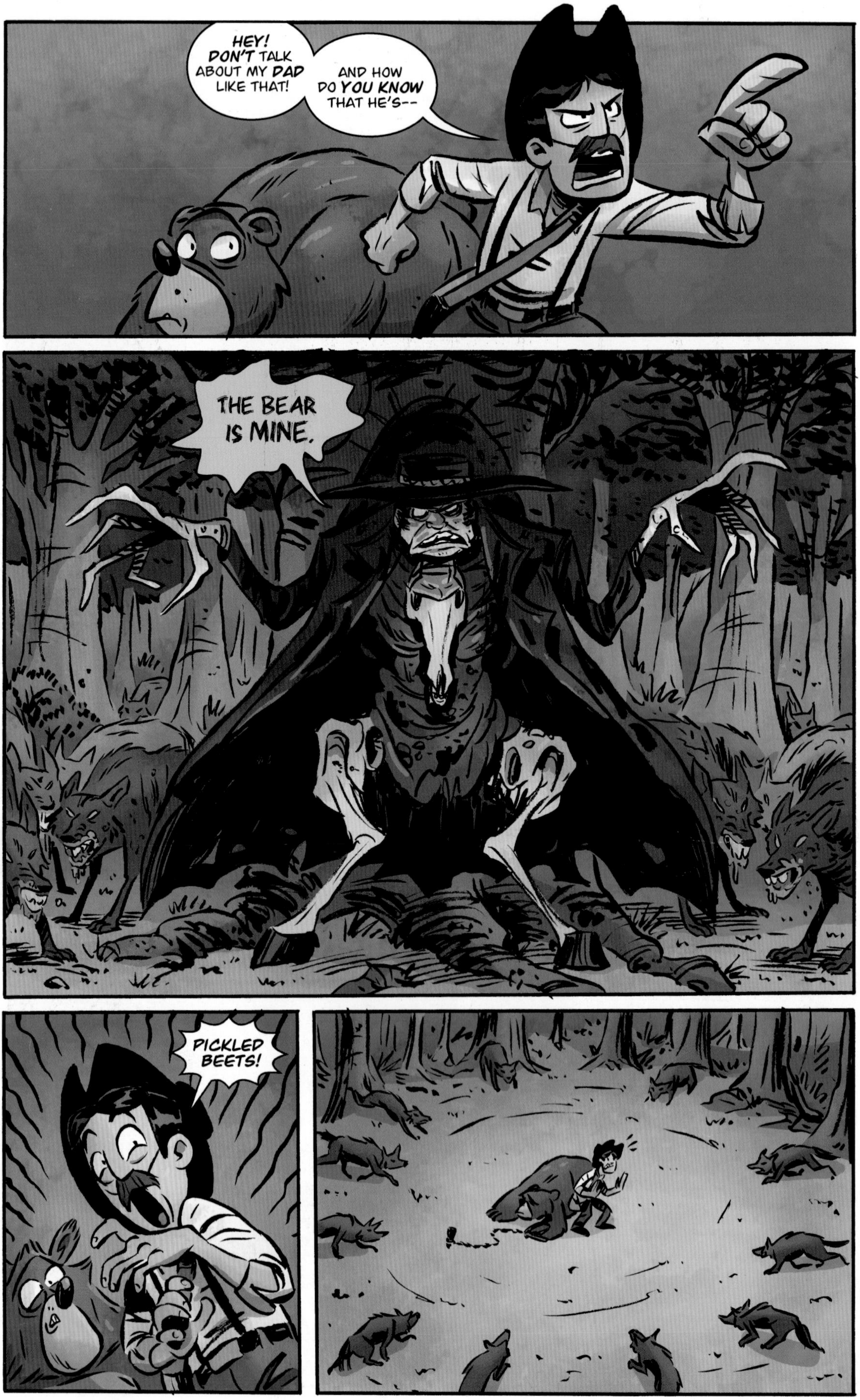

HEY! DON'T TALK ABOUT MY DAD LIKE THAT!
AND HOW DO YOU KNOW THAT HE'S--
THE BEAR IS MINE.
PICKLED BEETS!

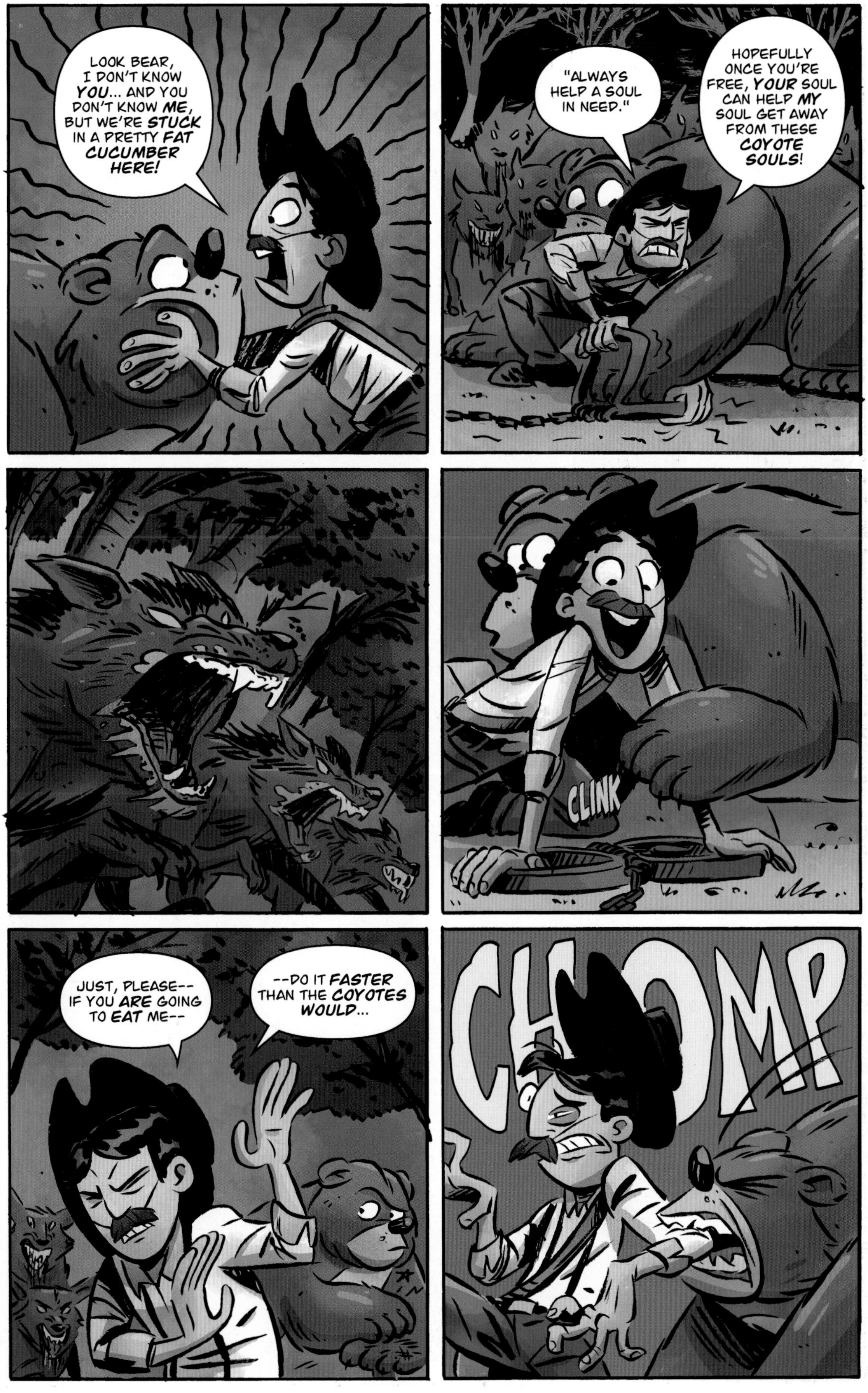

LOOK BEAR, I DON'T KNOW YOU... AND YOU DON'T KNOW ME, BUT WE'RE STUCK IN A PRETTY FAT CUCUMBER HERE!
"ALWAYS HELP A SOUL IN NEED."
HOPEFULLY ONCE YOU'RE FREE, YOUR SOUL CAN HELP MY SOUL GET AWAY FROM THESE COYOTE SOULS!
CLINK
JUST, PLEASE-- IF YOU ARE GOING TO EAT ME--
--DO IT FASTER THAN THE COYOTES WOULD...
CHOMP

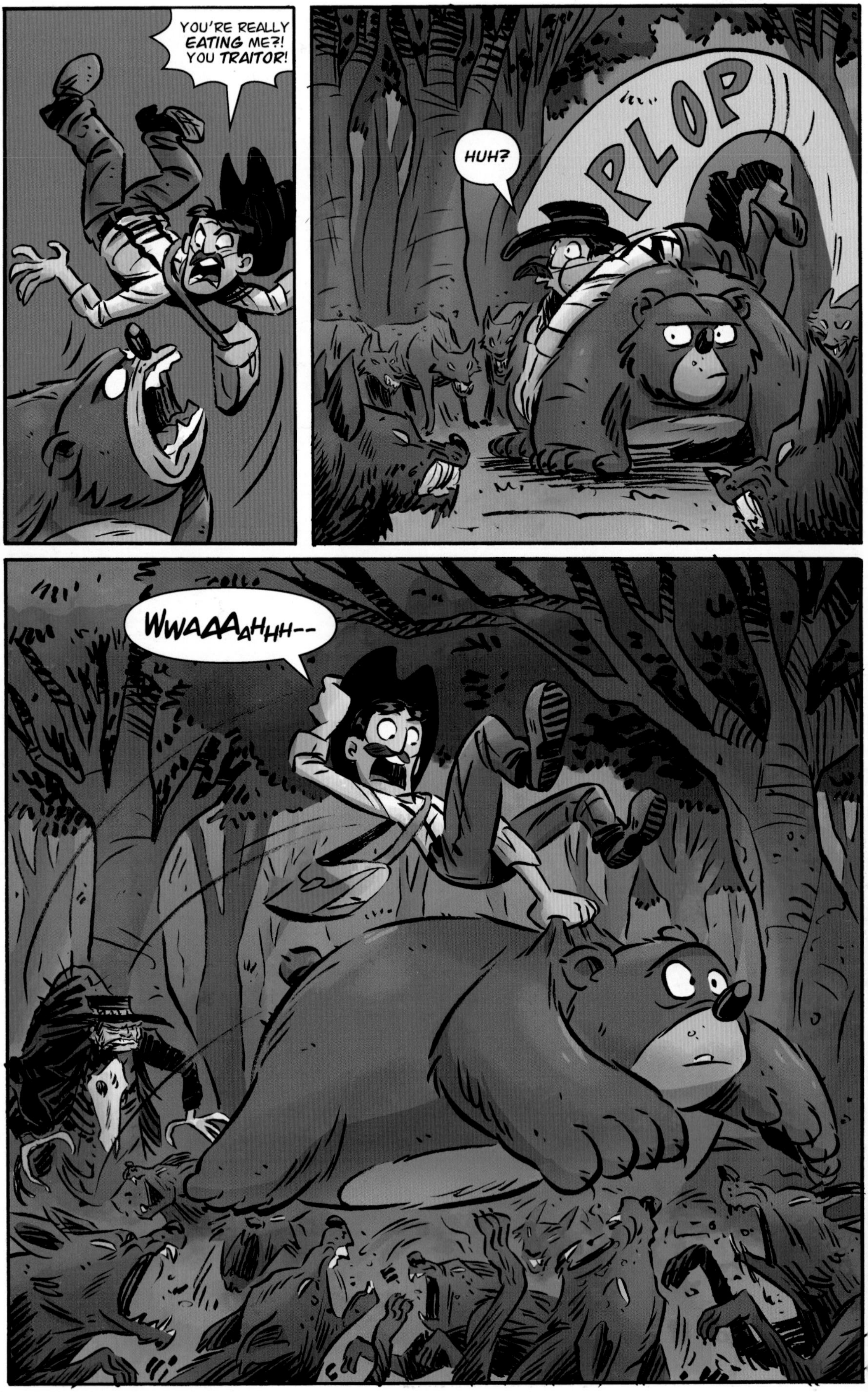
YOU'RE REALLY EATING ME?! YOU TRAITOR!
HUH?
PLOP
WWAAAAHHH--

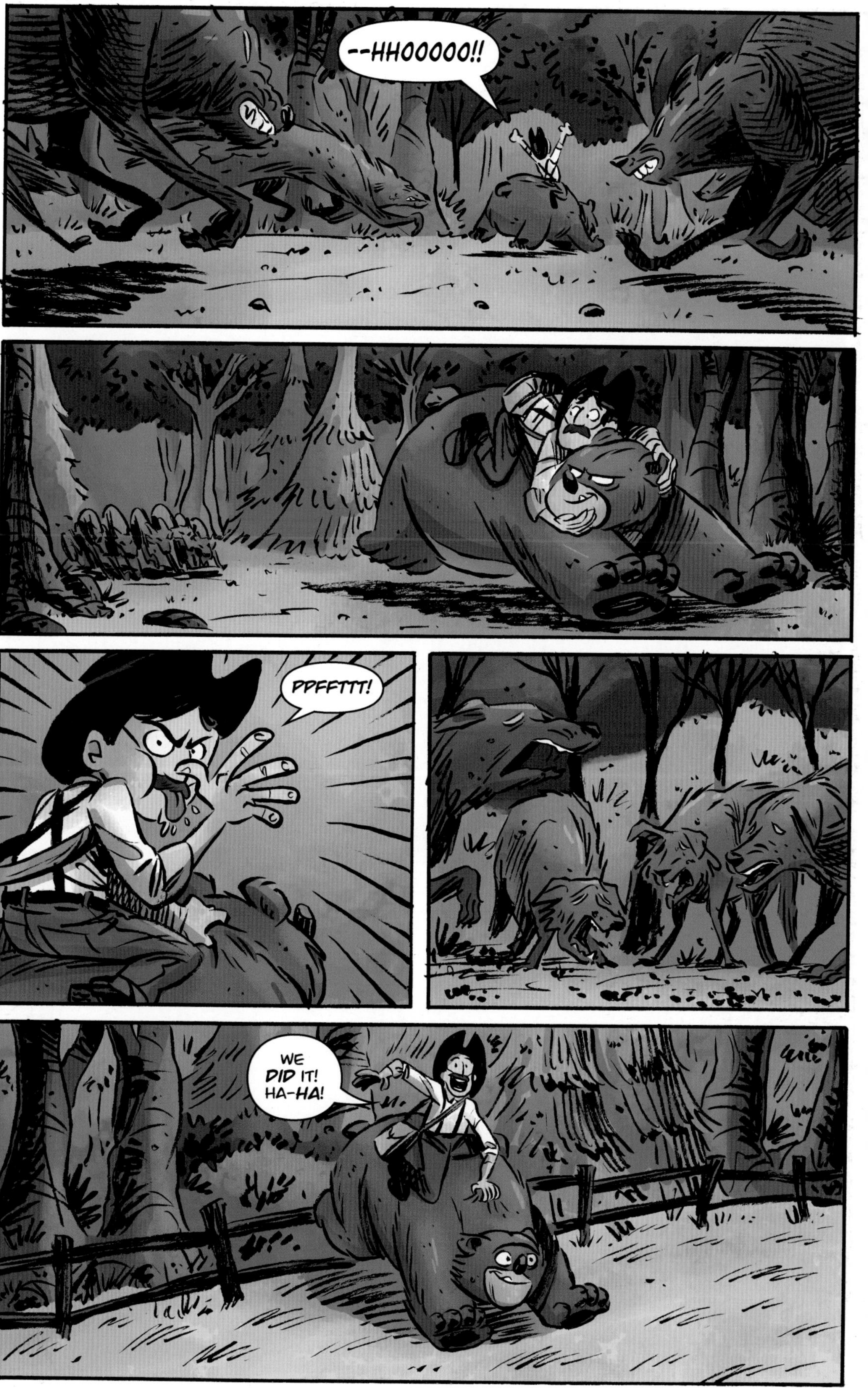
--HHOOOOO!!
PPFFTTT!
WE DID IT! HA-HA!

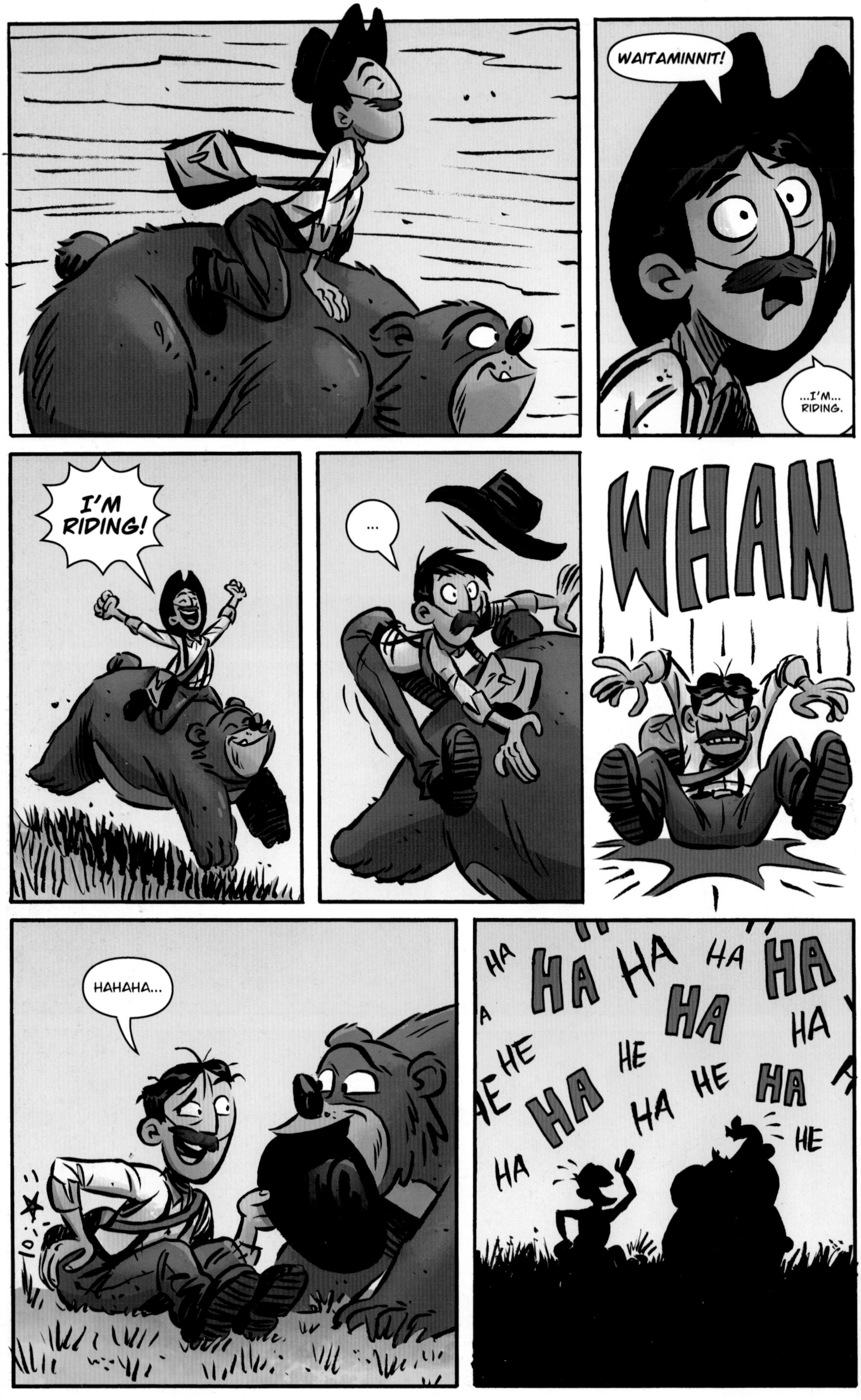
WAITAMINNIT!
...I'M... RIDING.
I'M RIDING!
...
WHAM
HAHAHA...
HA HA HA HA HA HA
HA HA
HE HE HA
HE HA HA HE HA
HA HE

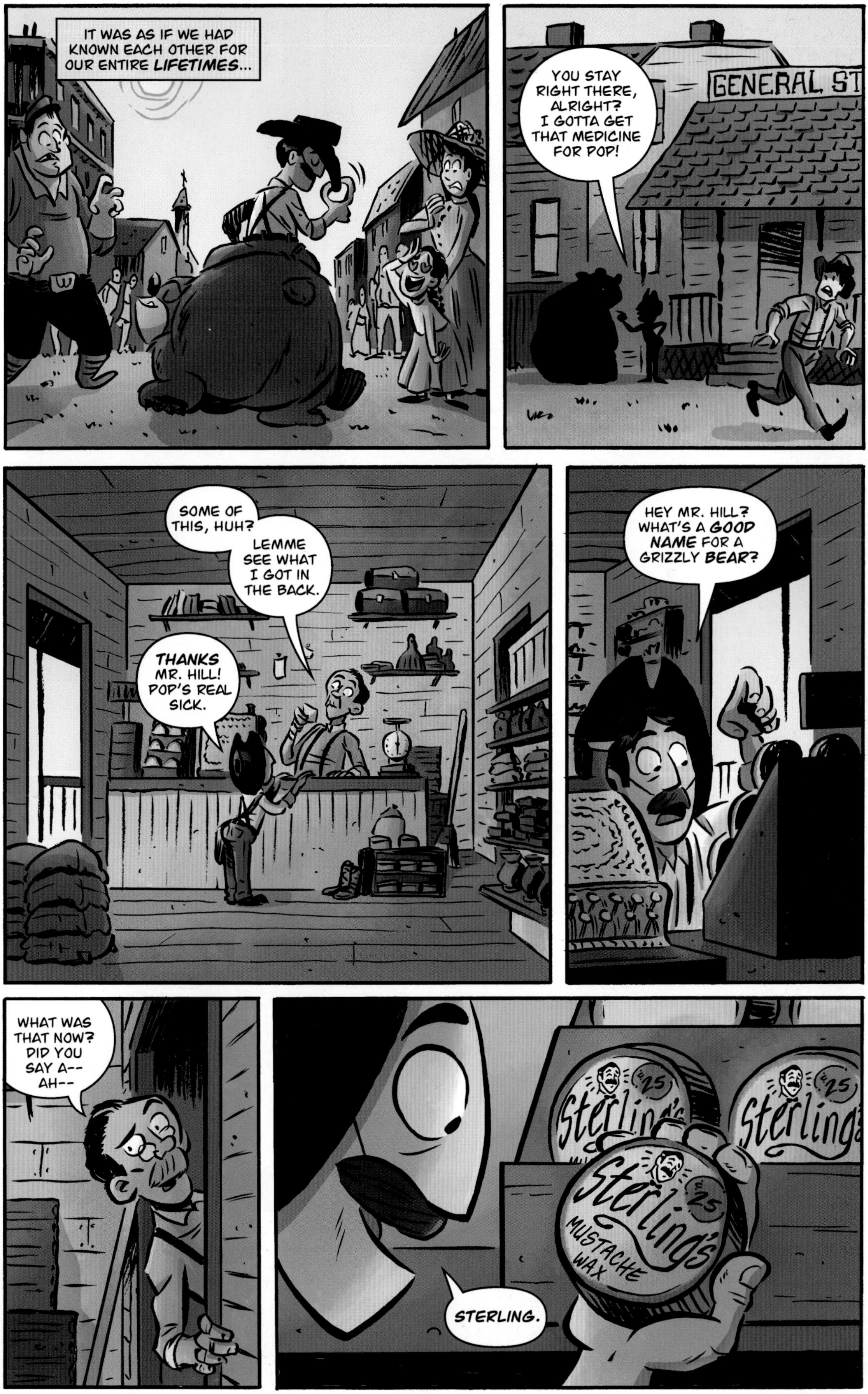
IT WAS AS IF WE HAD KNOWN EACH OTHER FOR OUR ENTIRE LIFETIMES...
YOU STAY RIGHT THERE, ALRIGHT? I GOTTA GET THAT MEDICINE FOR POP!
GENERAL ST
SOME OF THIS, HUH?
LEMME SEE WHAT I GOT IN THE BACK.
THANKS MR. HILL! POP'S REAL SICK.
HEY MR. HILL? WHAT'S A GOOD NAME FOR A GRIZZLY BEAR?
WHAT WAS THAT NOW? DID YOU SAY A-- AH--
Sterling's MUSTACHE WAX
25
STERLING.

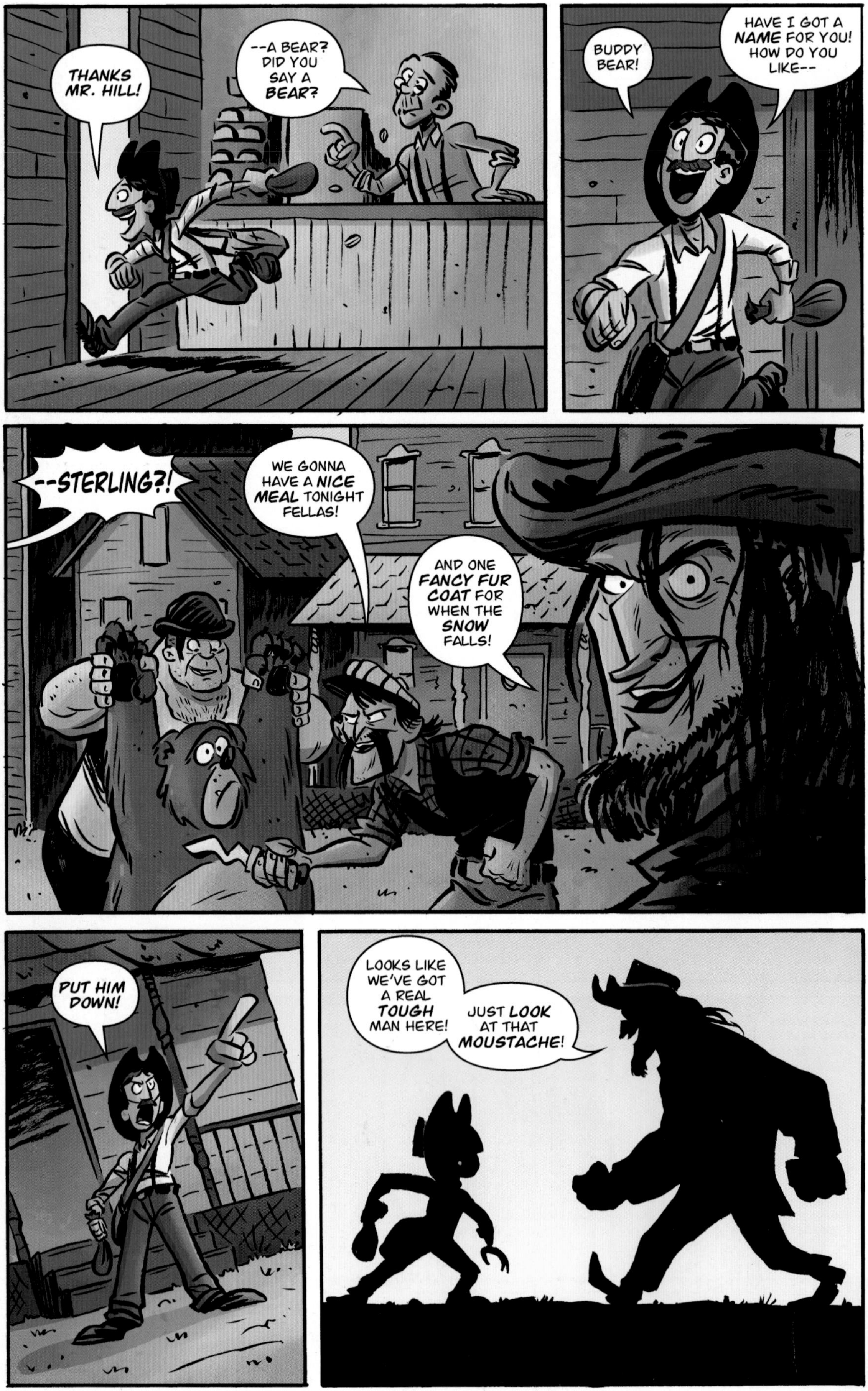
THANKS MR. HILL!
--A BEAR? DID YOU SAY A BEAR?
BUDDY BEAR!
HAVE I GOT A NAME FOR YOU! HOW DO YOU LIKE--
--STERLING?!
WE GONNA HAVE A NICE MEAL TONIGHT FELLAS!
AND ONE FANCY FUR COAT FOR WHEN THE SNOW FALLS!
PUT HIM DOWN!
LOOKS LIKE WE'VE GOT A REAL TOUGH MAN HERE!
JUST LOOK AT THAT MOUSTACHE!

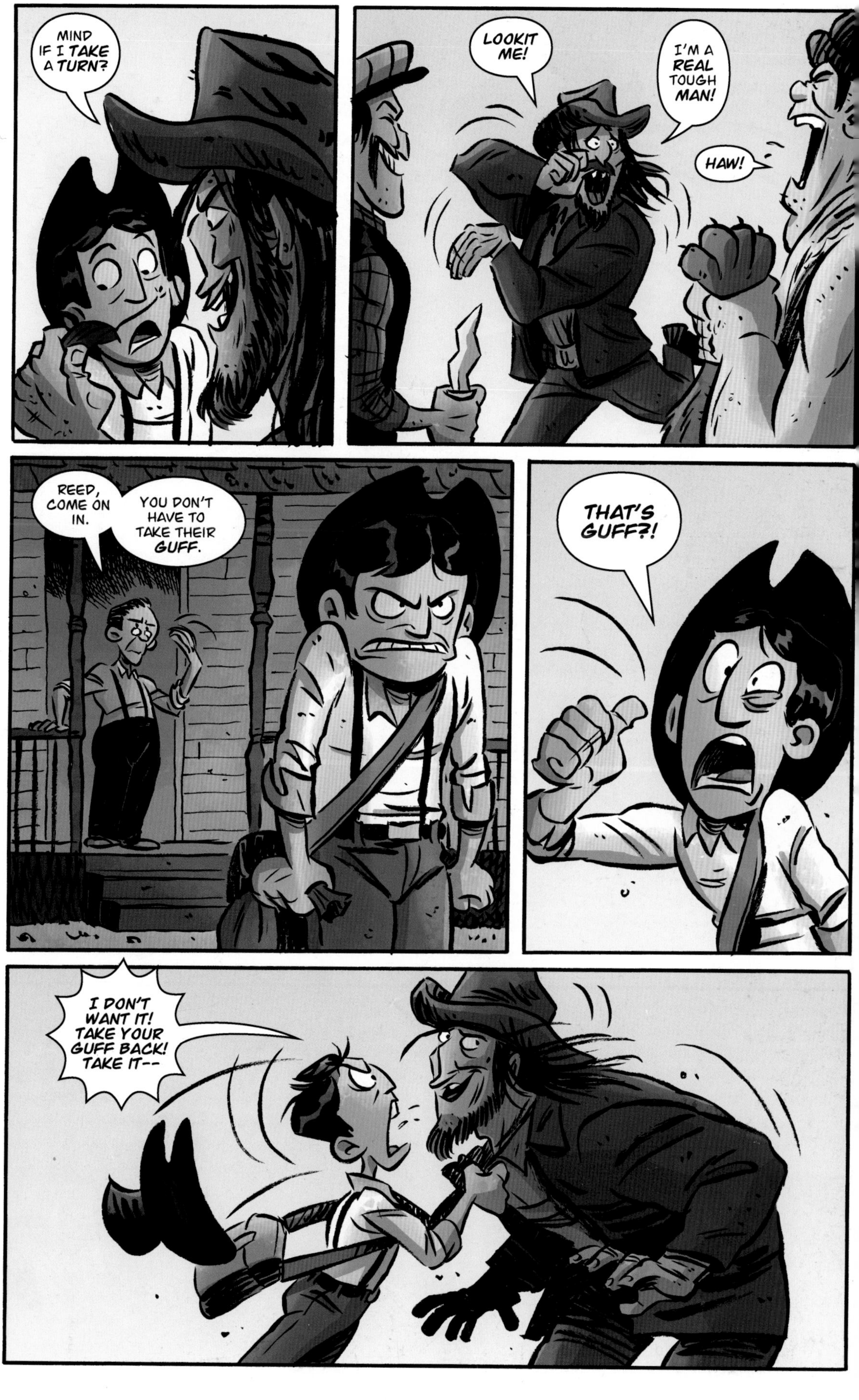

MIND IF I TAKE A TURN?
LOOKIT ME!
I'M A REAL TOUGH MAN!
HAW!
REED, COME ON IN.
YOU DON'T HAVE TO TAKE THEIR GUFF.
THAT'S GUFF?!
I DON'T WANT IT! TAKE YOUR GUFF BACK! TAKE IT--

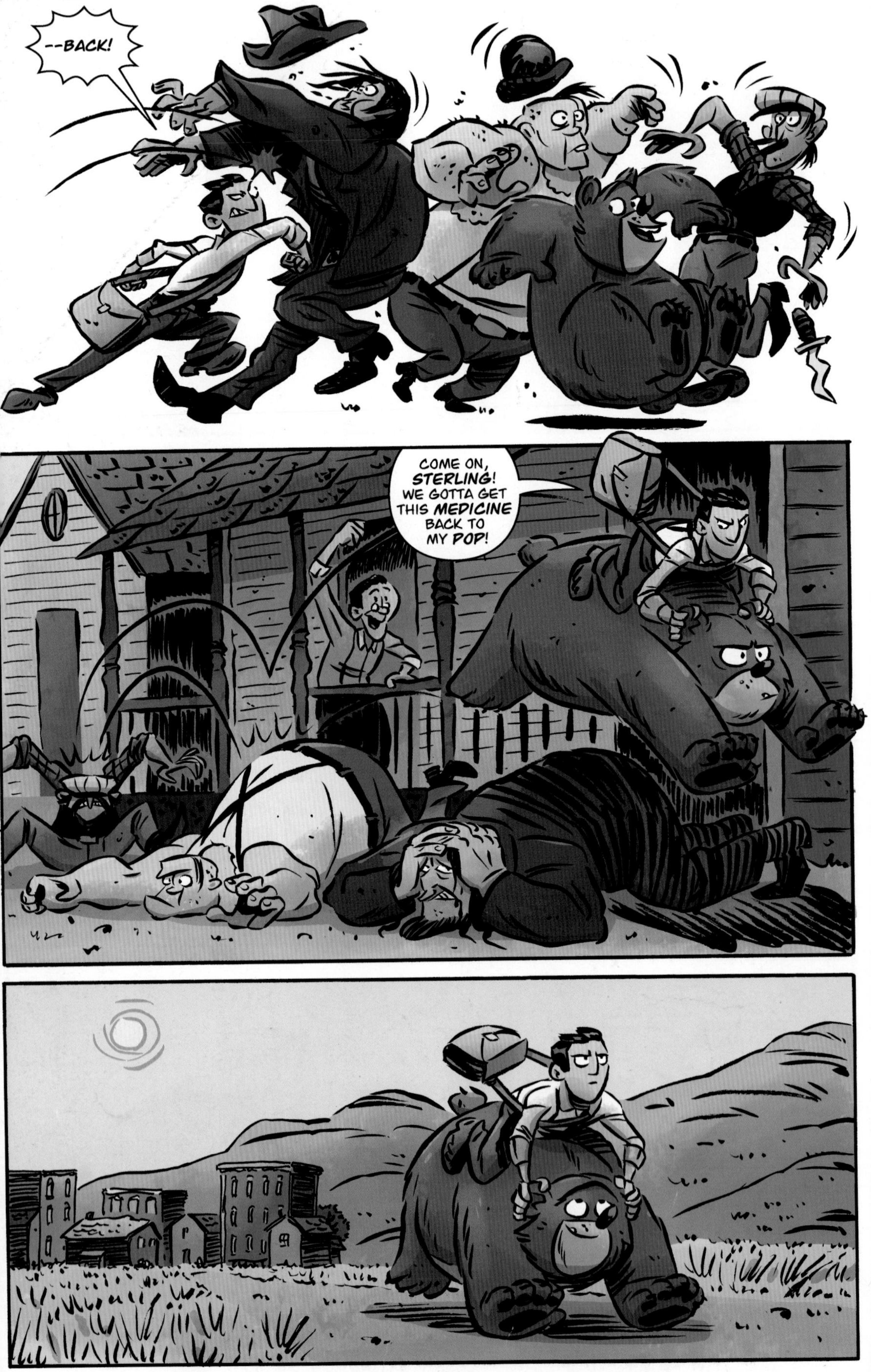
--BACK!
COME ON, STERLING! WE GOTTA GET THIS MEDICINE BACK TO MY POP!

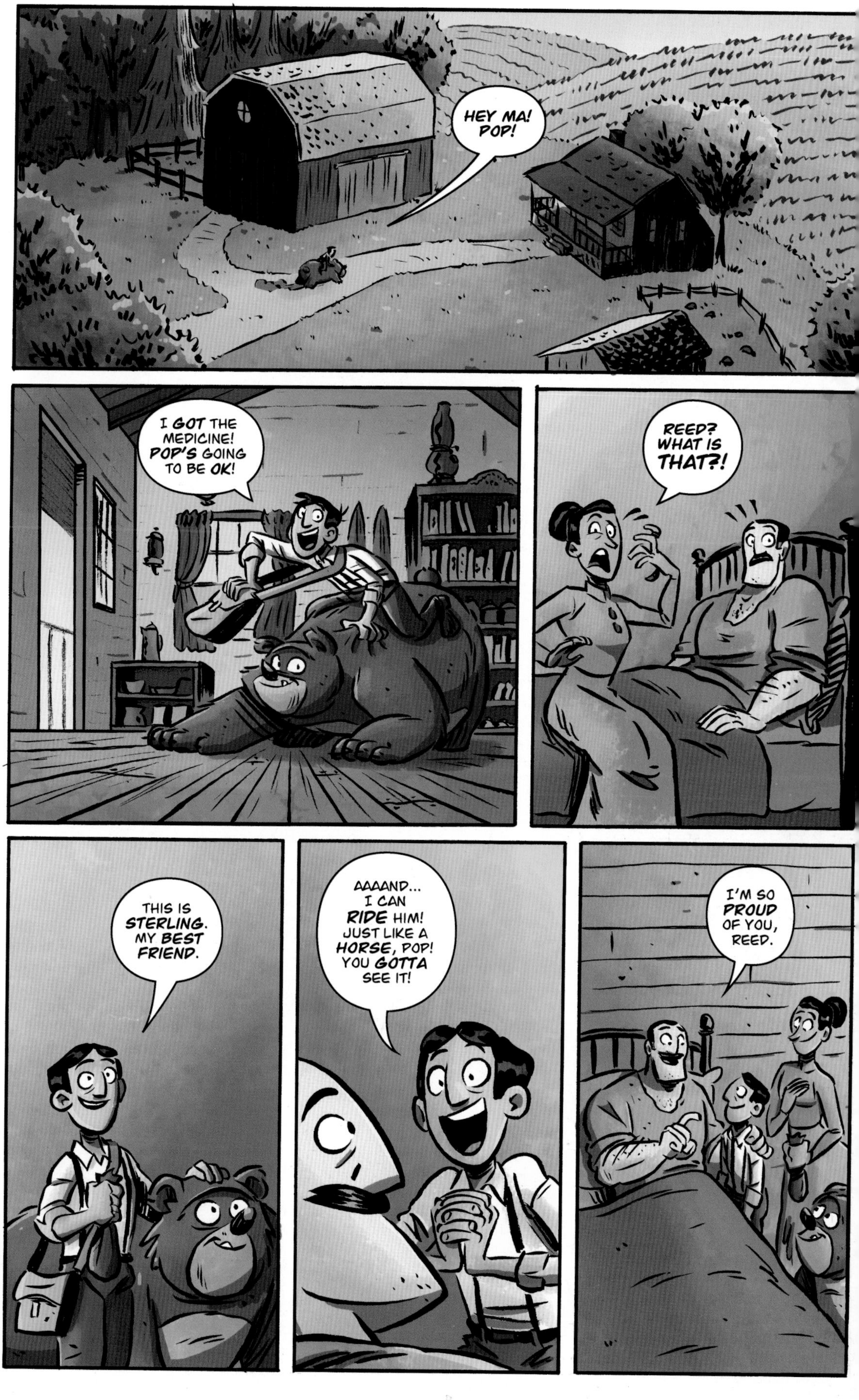
HEY MA! POP!
I GOT THE MEDICINE! POP'S GOING TO BE OK!
REED? WHAT IS THAT?!
THIS IS STERLING. MY BEST FRIEND.
AAAAND... I CAN RIDE HIM! JUST LIKE A HORSE, POP! YOU GOTTA SEE IT!
I'M SO PROUD OF YOU, REED.

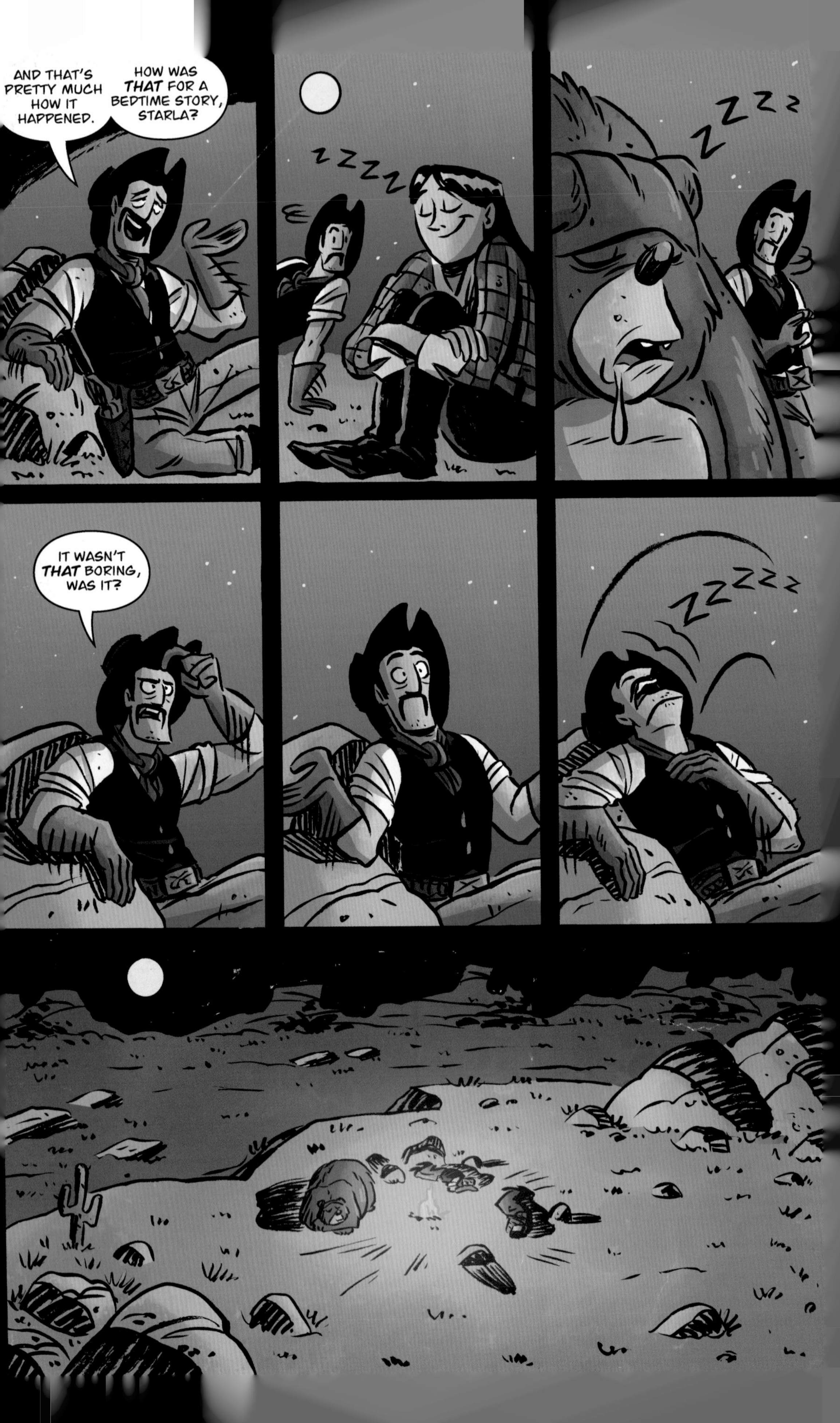
AND THAT'S PRETTY MUCH HOW IT HAPPENED.
HOW WAS *THAT* FOR A BEDTIME STORY, STARLA?
ZZZZZ
ZZZZ
IT WASN'T *THAT* BORING, WAS IT?
ZZZZZZ

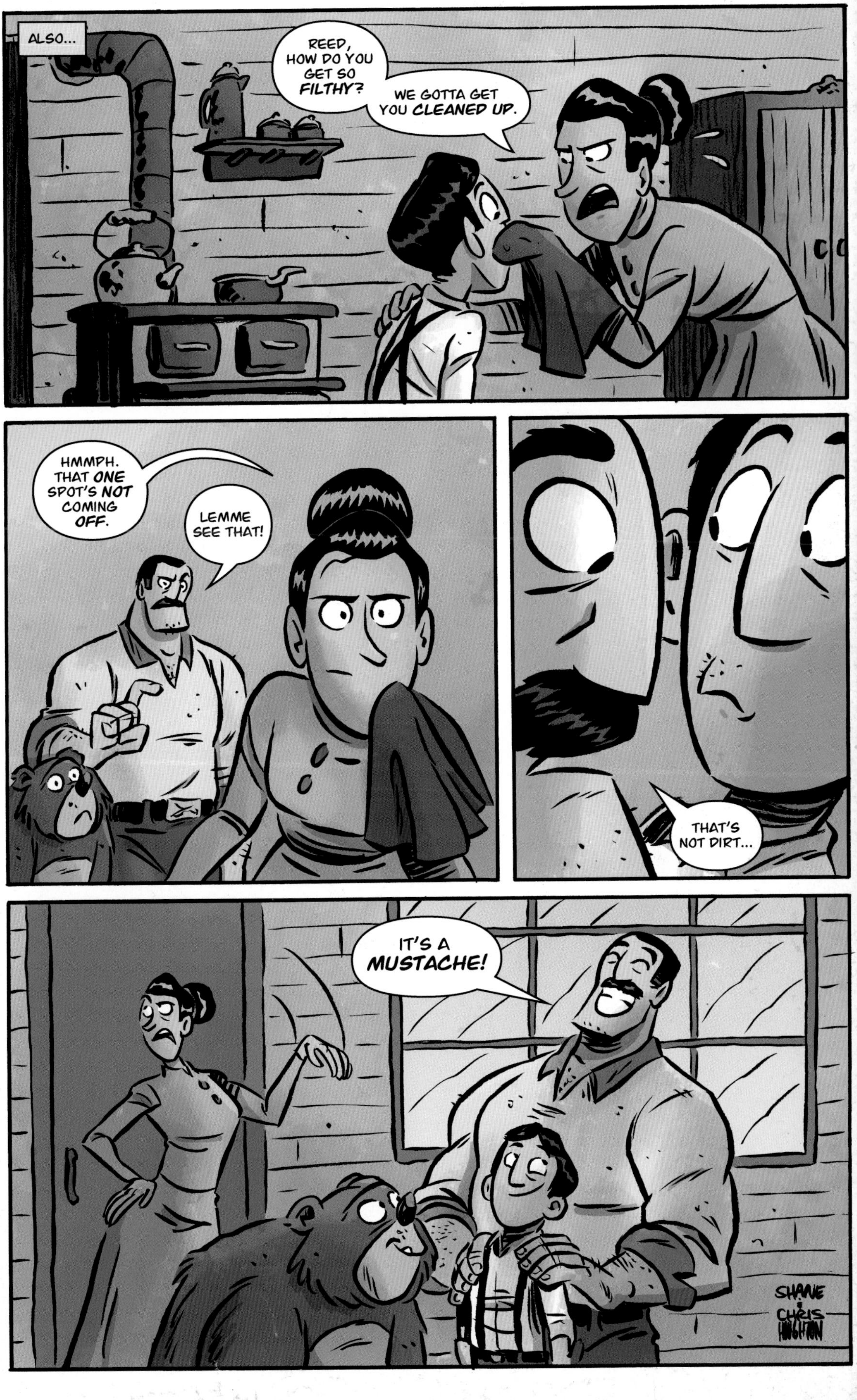
ALSO...
REED, HOW DO YOU GET SO FILTHY?
WE GOTTA GET YOU CLEANED UP.
HMMPH. THAT ONE SPOT'S NOT COMING OFF.
LEMME SEE THAT!
THAT'S NOT DIRT...
IT'S A MUSTACHE!
SHANE & CHRIS HOUGHTON

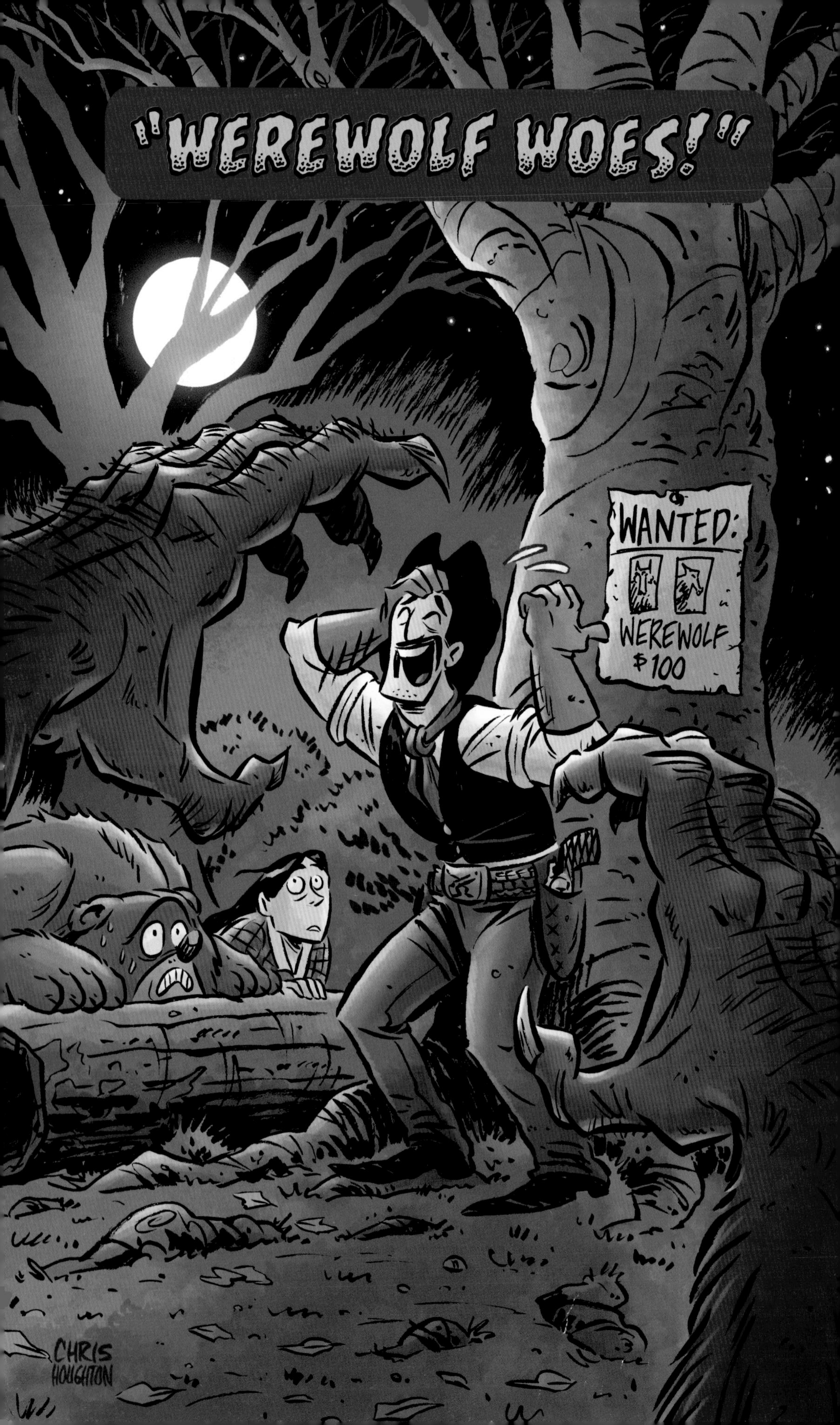
"WEREWOLF WOES!"
WANTED:
WEREWOLF
$100
CHRIS
HOUGHTON

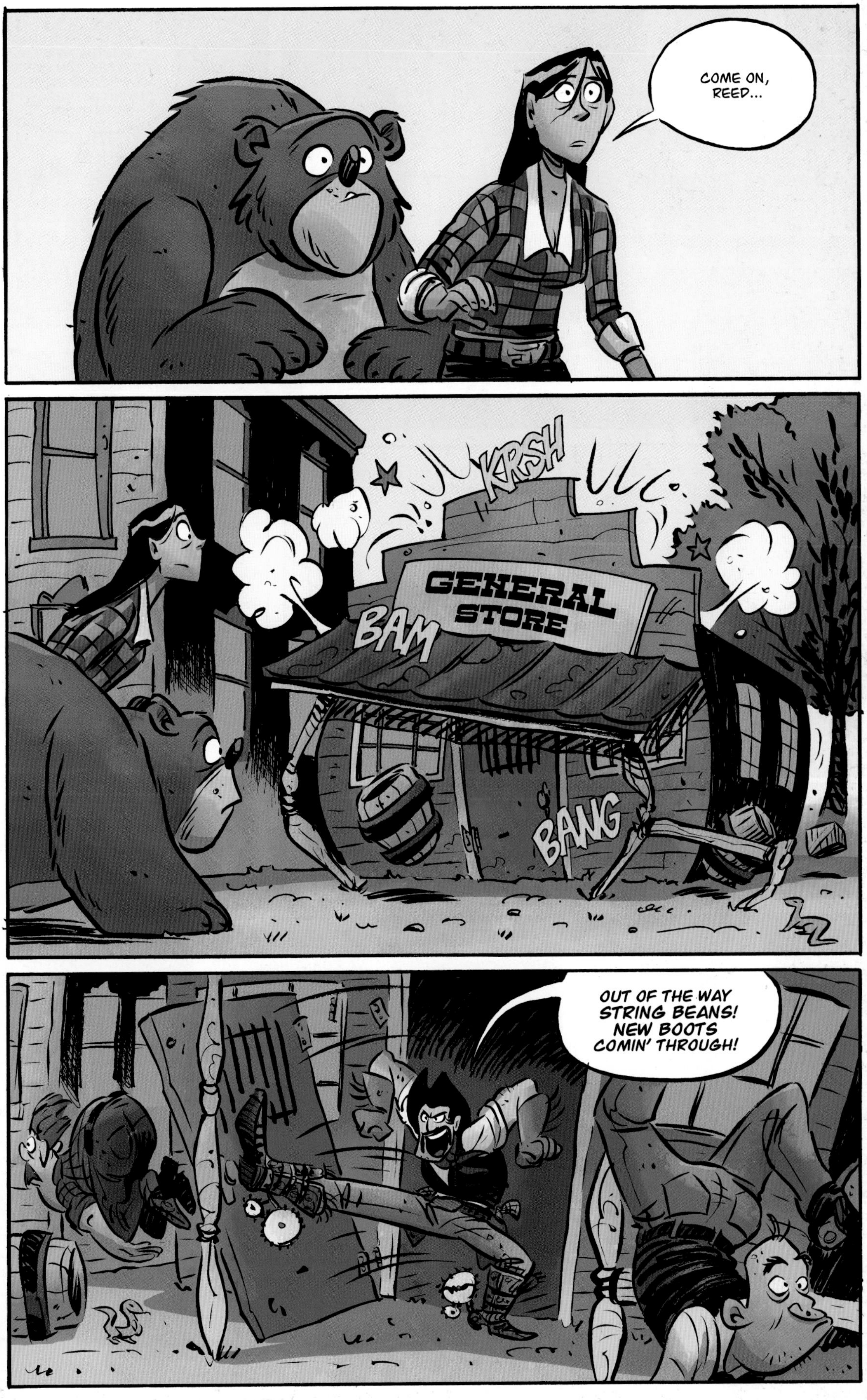
COME ON, REED...
KRSH
GENERAL STORE
BAM
BANG
OUT OF THE WAY STRING BEANS! NEW BOOTS COMIN' THROUGH!

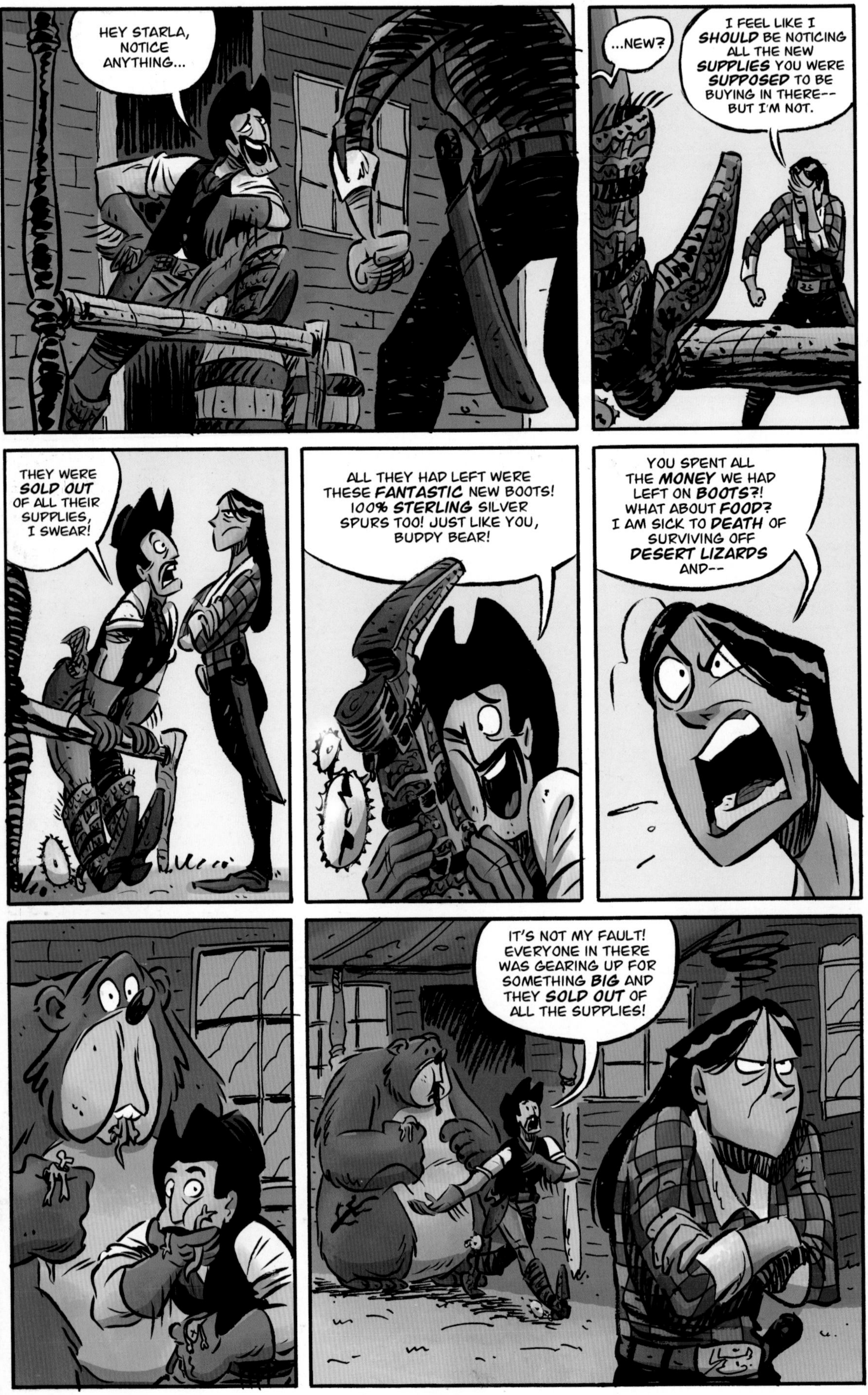
HEY STARLA, NOTICE ANYTHING...
...NEW?
I FEEL LIKE I SHOULD BE NOTICING ALL THE NEW SUPPLIES YOU WERE SUPPOSED TO BE BUYING IN THERE-- BUT I'M NOT.
THEY WERE SOLD OUT OF ALL THEIR SUPPLIES, I SWEAR!
ALL THEY HAD LEFT WERE THESE FANTASTIC NEW BOOTS! 100% STERLING SILVER SPURS TOO! JUST LIKE YOU, BUDDY BEAR!
YOU SPENT ALL THE MONEY WE HAD LEFT ON BOOTS?! WHAT ABOUT FOOD? I AM SICK TO DEATH OF SURVIVING OFF DESERT LIZARDS AND--
IT'S NOT MY FAULT! EVERYONE IN THERE WAS GEARING UP FOR SOMETHING BIG AND THEY SOLD OUT OF ALL THE SUPPLIES!

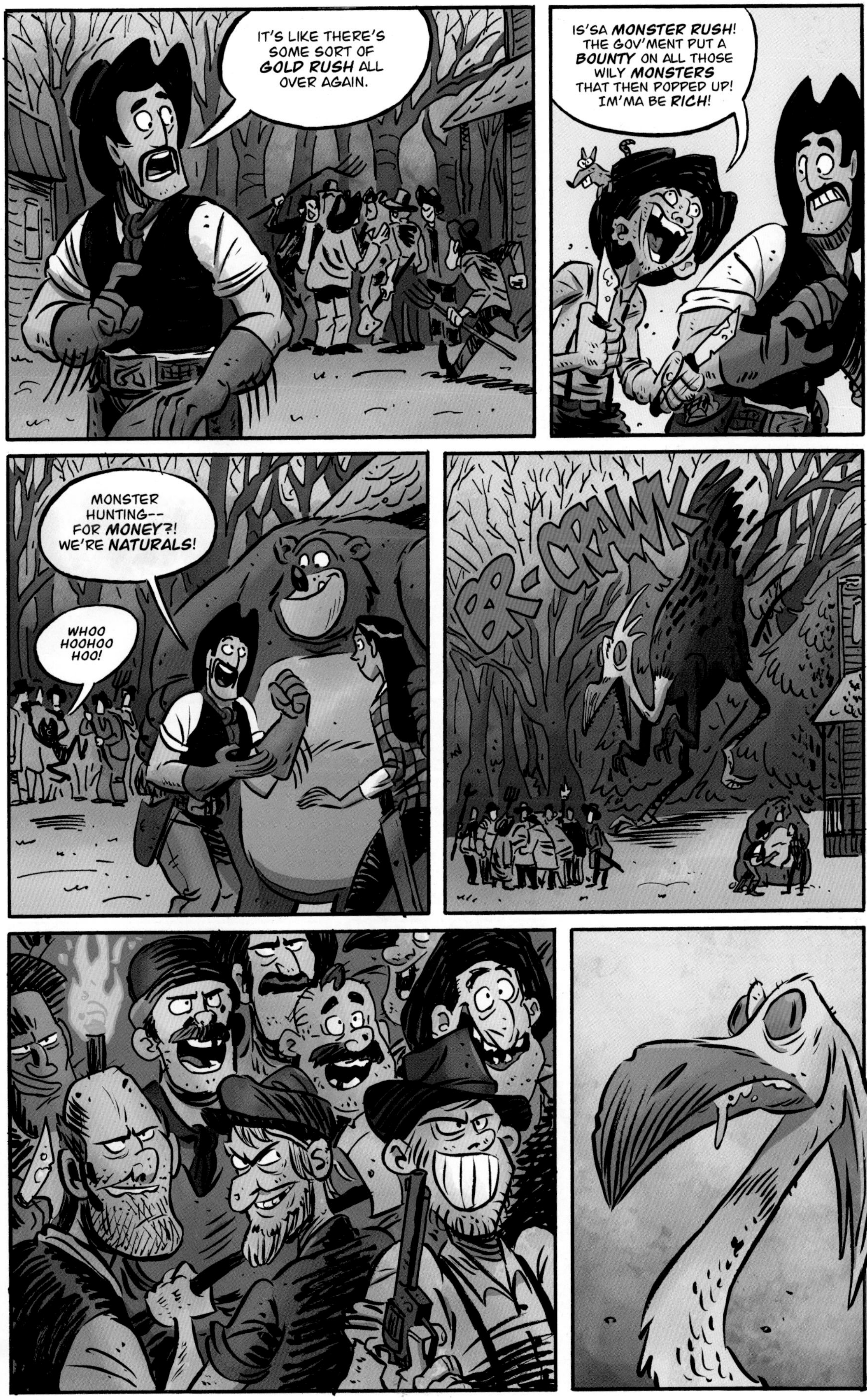
IT'S LIKE THERE'S SOME SORT OF GOLD RUSH ALL OVER AGAIN.
IS'SA MONSTER RUSH! THE GOV'MENT PUT A BOUNTY ON ALL THOSE WILY MONSTERS THAT THEN POPPED UP! IM'MA BE RICH!
MONSTER HUNTING-- FOR MONEY?! WE'RE NATURALS!
WHOO HOOHOO HOO!
B-CRAWK

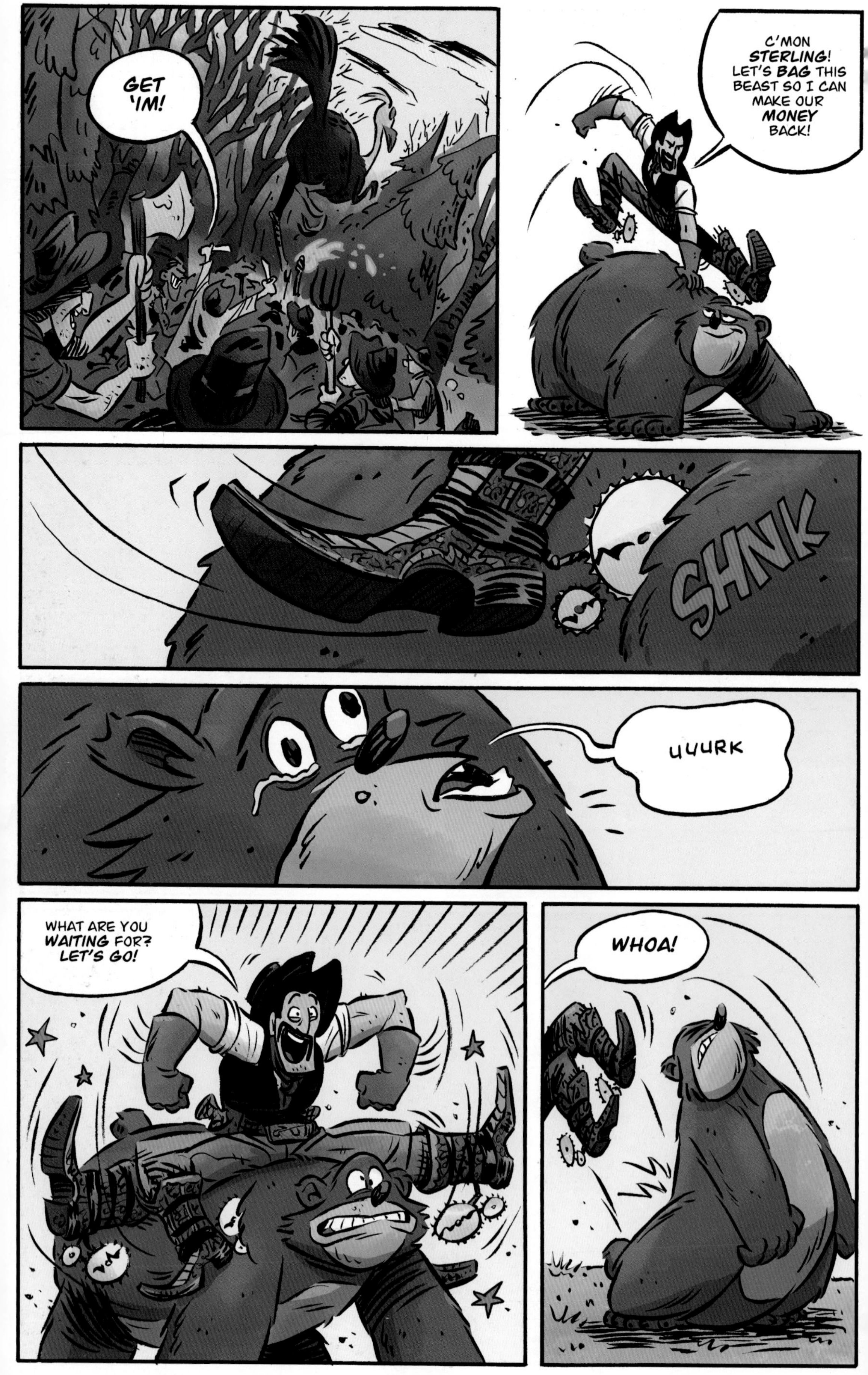
GET 'IM!
C'MON STERLING! LET'S BAG THIS BEAST SO I CAN MAKE OUR MONEY BACK!
SHNK
UUURK
WHAT ARE YOU WAITING FOR? LET'S GO!
WHOA!

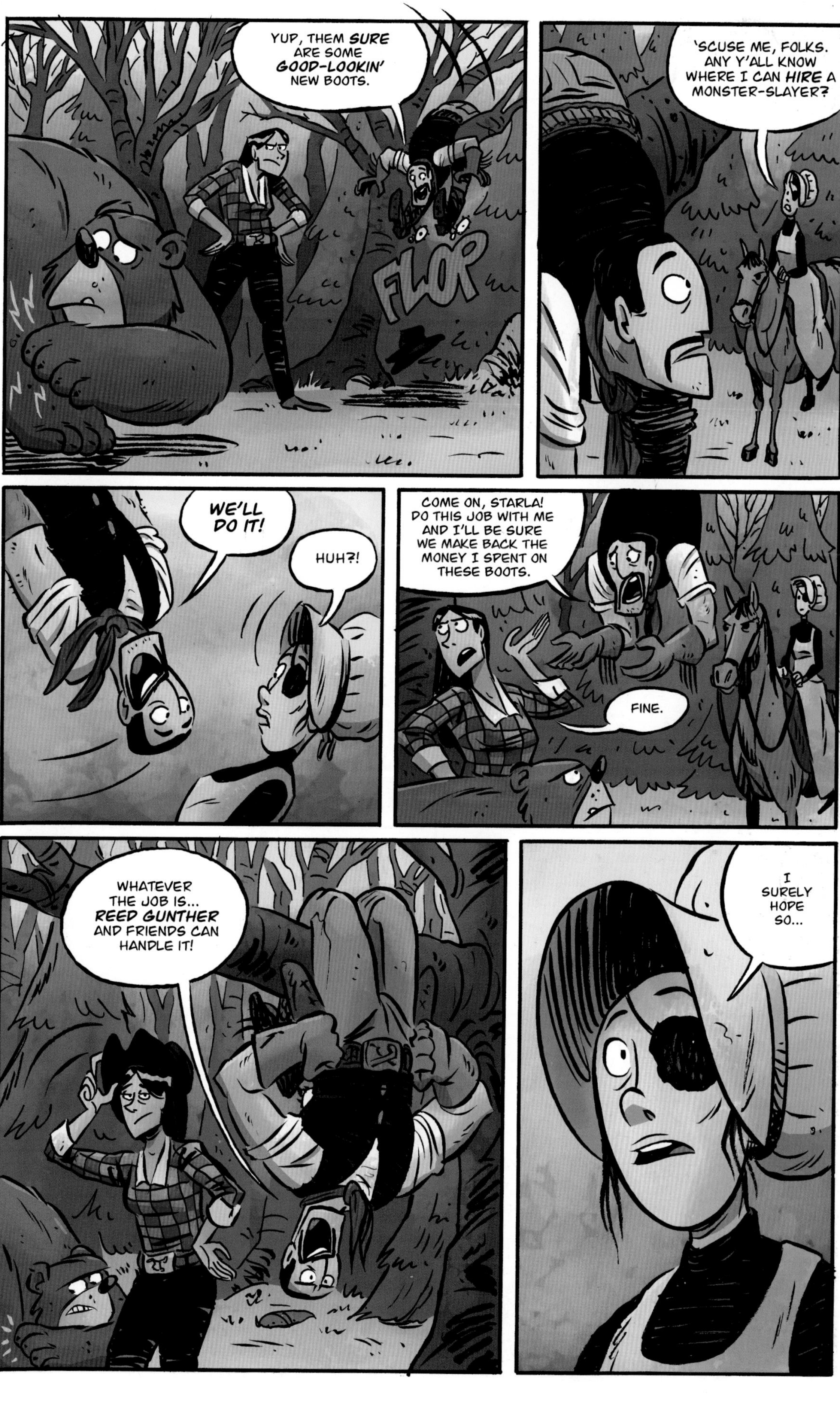
YUP, THEM SURE ARE SOME GOOD-LOOKIN' NEW BOOTS.
FLOP
'SCUSE ME, FOLKS. ANY Y'ALL KNOW WHERE I CAN HIRE A MONSTER-SLAYER?
WE'LL DO IT!
HUH?!
COME ON, STARLA! DO THIS JOB WITH ME AND I'LL BE SURE WE MAKE BACK THE MONEY I SPENT ON THESE BOOTS.
FINE.
WHATEVER THE JOB IS... REED GUNTHER AND FRIENDS CAN HANDLE IT!
I SURELY HOPE SO...

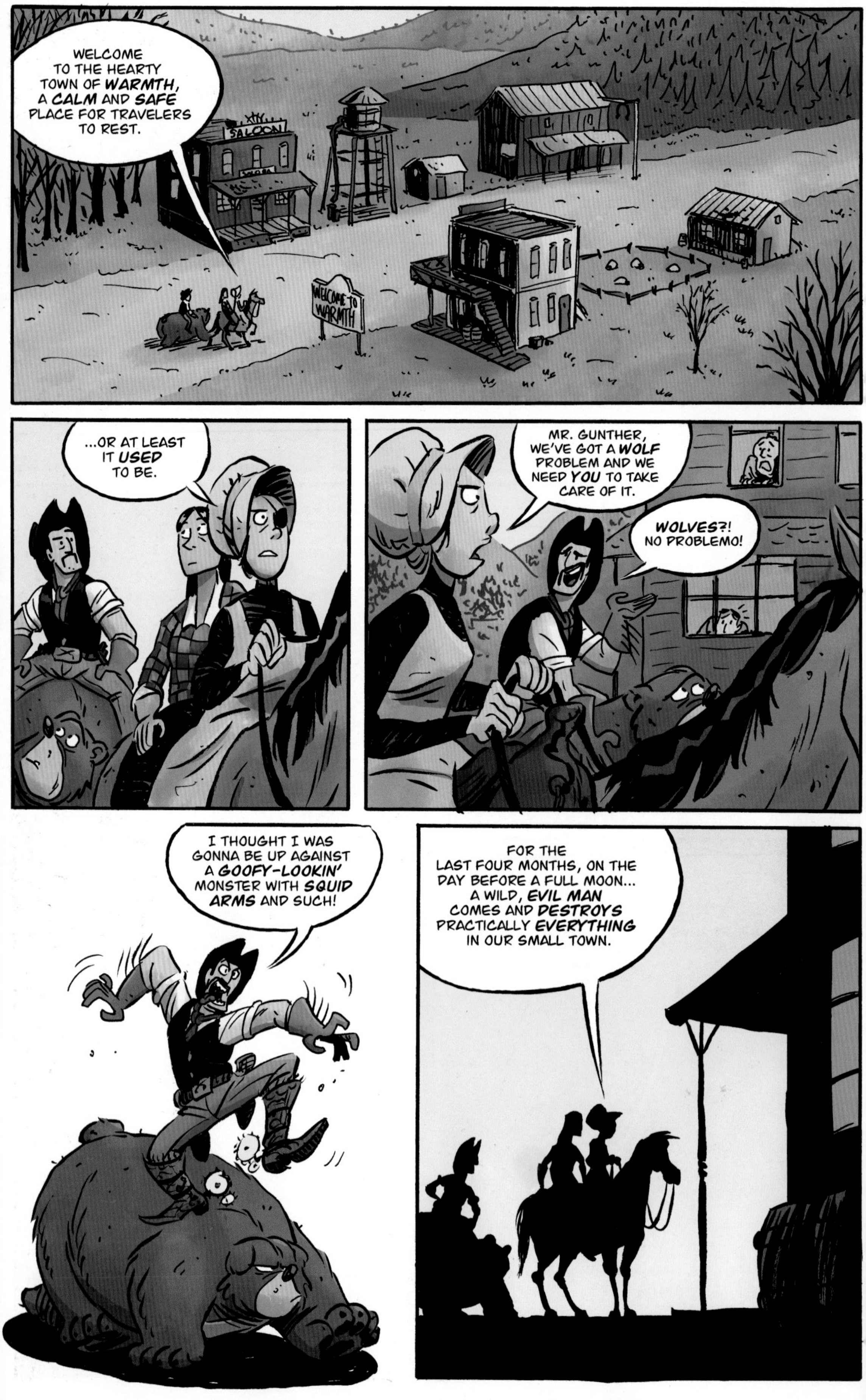
WELCOME TO THE HEARTY TOWN OF WARMTH, A CALM AND SAFE PLACE FOR TRAVELERS TO REST.
SALOON
WELCOME TO WARMTH
...OR AT LEAST IT USED TO BE.
MR. GUNTHER, WE'VE GOT A WOLF PROBLEM AND WE NEED YOU TO TAKE CARE OF IT.
WOLVES?! NO PROBLEMO!
I THOUGHT I WAS GONNA BE UP AGAINST A GOOFY-LOOKIN' MONSTER WITH SQUID ARMS AND SUCH!
FOR THE LAST FOUR MONTHS, ON THE DAY BEFORE A FULL MOON... A WILD, EVIL MAN COMES AND DESTROYS PRACTICALLY EVERYTHING IN OUR SMALL TOWN.

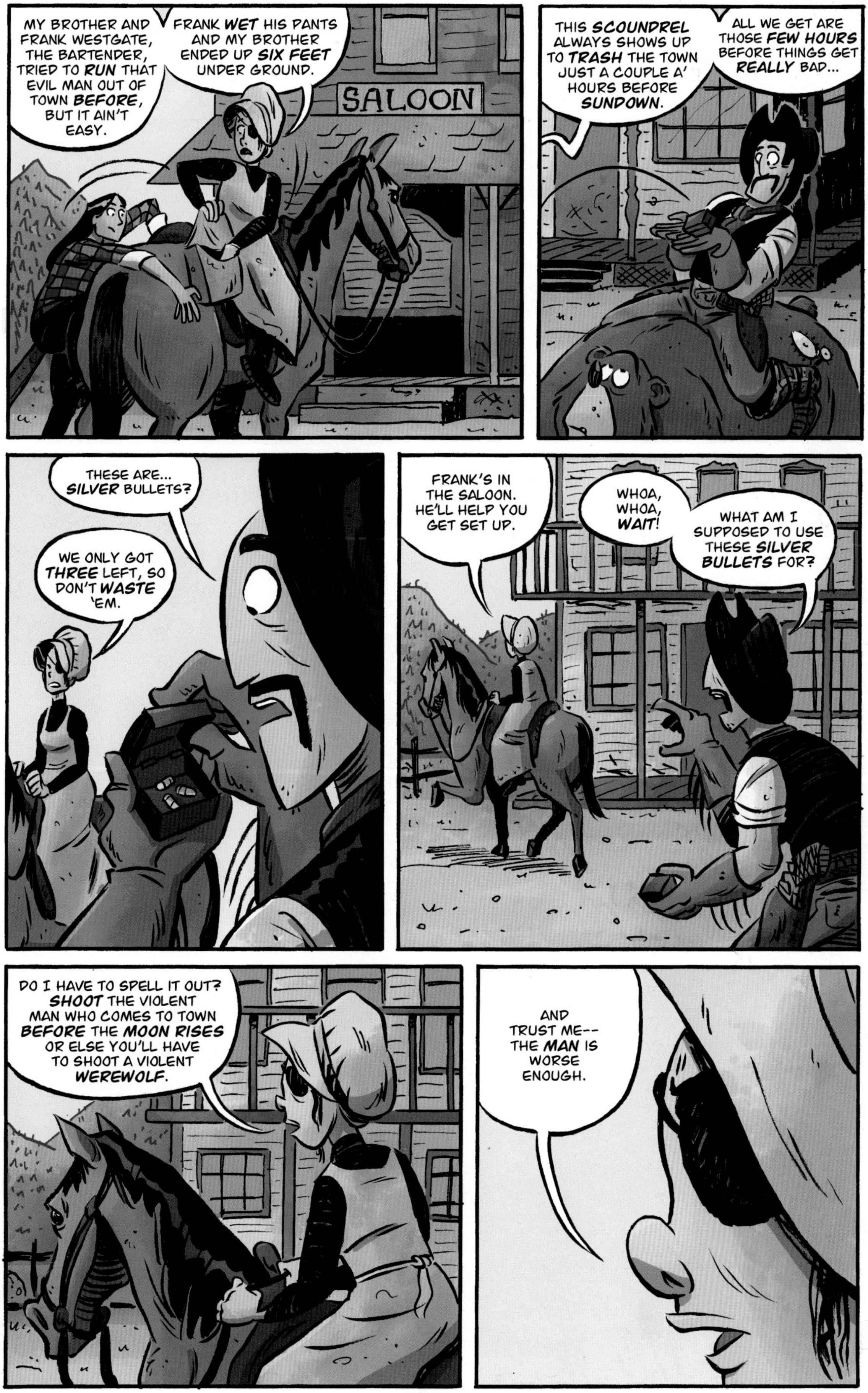

MY BROTHER AND FRANK WESTGATE, THE BARTENDER, TRIED TO RUN THAT EVIL MAN OUT OF TOWN BEFORE, BUT IT AIN'T EASY.
FRANK WET HIS PANTS AND MY BROTHER ENDED UP SIX FEET UNDER GROUND.
SALOON
THIS SCOUNDREL ALWAYS SHOWS UP TO TRASH THE TOWN JUST A COUPLE A' HOURS BEFORE SUNDOWN.
ALL WE GET ARE THOSE FEW HOURS BEFORE THINGS GET REALLY BAD...
THESE ARE... SILVER BULLETS?
WE ONLY GOT THREE LEFT, SO DON'T WASTE 'EM.
FRANK'S IN THE SALOON. HE'LL HELP YOU GET SET UP.
WHOA, WHOA, WAIT!
WHAT AM I SUPPOSED TO USE THESE SILVER BULLETS FOR?
DO I HAVE TO SPELL IT OUT? SHOOT THE VIOLENT MAN WHO COMES TO TOWN BEFORE THE MOON RISES OR ELSE YOU'LL HAVE TO SHOOT A VIOLENT WEREWOLF.
AND TRUST ME-- THE MAN IS WORSE ENOUGH.

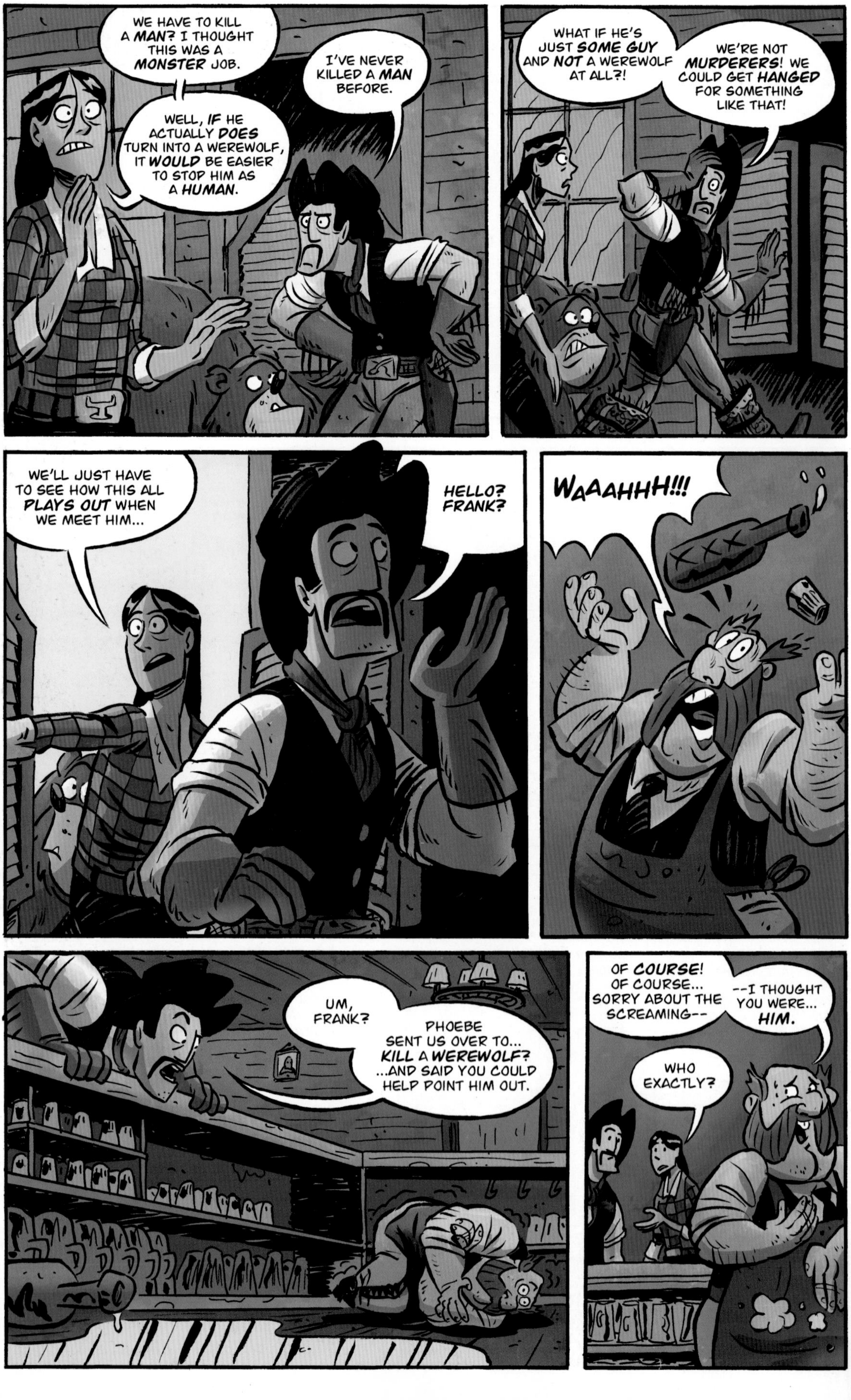
WE HAVE TO KILL A MAN? I THOUGHT THIS WAS A MONSTER JOB.
WELL, IF HE ACTUALLY DOES TURN INTO A WEREWOLF, IT WOULD BE EASIER TO STOP HIM AS A HUMAN.
I'VE NEVER KILLED A MAN BEFORE.
WHAT IF HE'S JUST SOME GUY AND NOT A WEREWOLF AT ALL?!
WE'RE NOT MURDERERS! WE COULD GET HANGED FOR SOMETHING LIKE THAT!
WE'LL JUST HAVE TO SEE HOW THIS ALL PLAYS OUT WHEN WE MEET HIM...
HELLO? FRANK?
WAAAHHH!!!
UM, FRANK?
PHOEBE SENT US OVER TO... KILL A WEREWOLF? ...AND SAID YOU COULD HELP POINT HIM OUT.
OF COURSE! OF COURSE... SORRY ABOUT THE SCREAMING--
--I THOUGHT YOU WERE... HIM.
WHO EXACTLY?

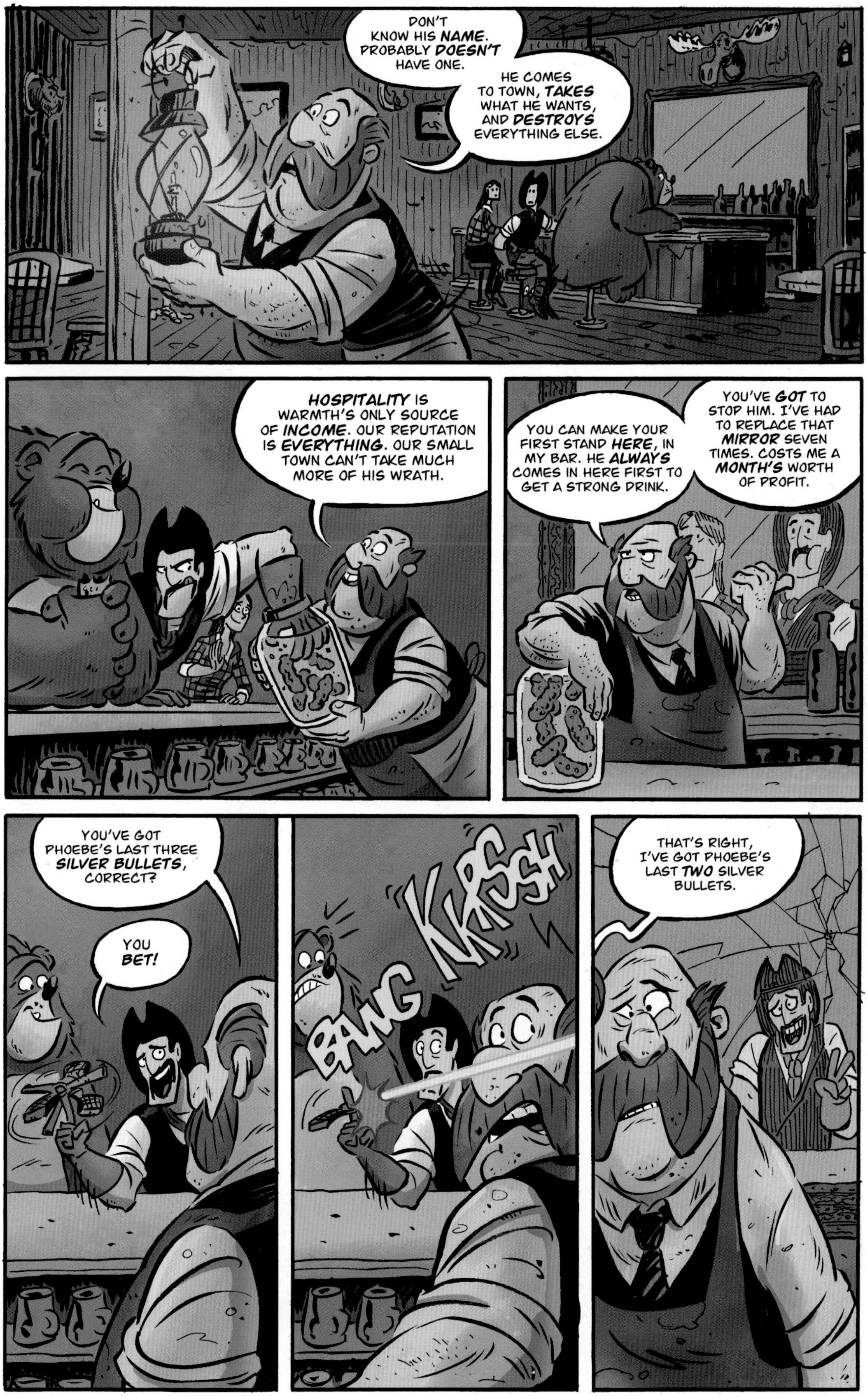
DON'T KNOW HIS NAME. PROBABLY DOESN'T HAVE ONE.
HE COMES TO TOWN, TAKES WHAT HE WANTS, AND DESTROYS EVERYTHING ELSE.
HOSPITALITY IS WARMTH'S ONLY SOURCE OF INCOME. OUR REPUTATION IS EVERYTHING. OUR SMALL TOWN CAN'T TAKE MUCH MORE OF HIS WRATH.
YOU CAN MAKE YOUR FIRST STAND HERE, IN MY BAR. HE ALWAYS COMES IN HERE FIRST TO GET A STRONG DRINK.
YOU'VE GOT TO STOP HIM. I'VE HAD TO REPLACE THAT MIRROR SEVEN TIMES. COSTS ME A MONTH'S WORTH OF PROFIT.
YOU'VE GOT PHOEBE'S LAST THREE SILVER BULLETS, CORRECT?
YOU BET!
KKRSSH
BANG
THAT'S RIGHT, I'VE GOT PHOEBE'S LAST TWO SILVER BULLETS.

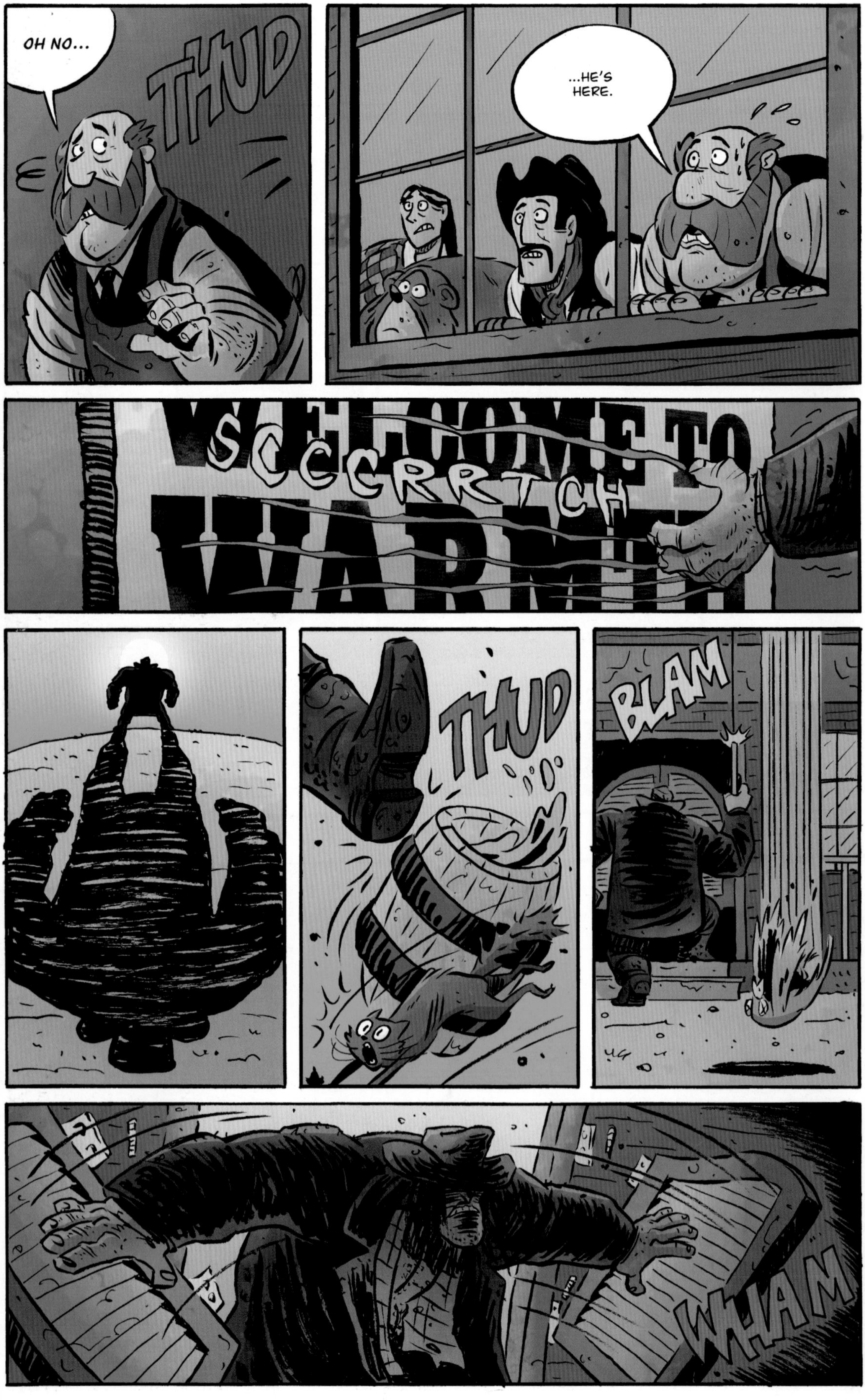

OH NO...
THUD
...HE'S HERE.
SCCRRTCH
THUD
BLAM
WHAM

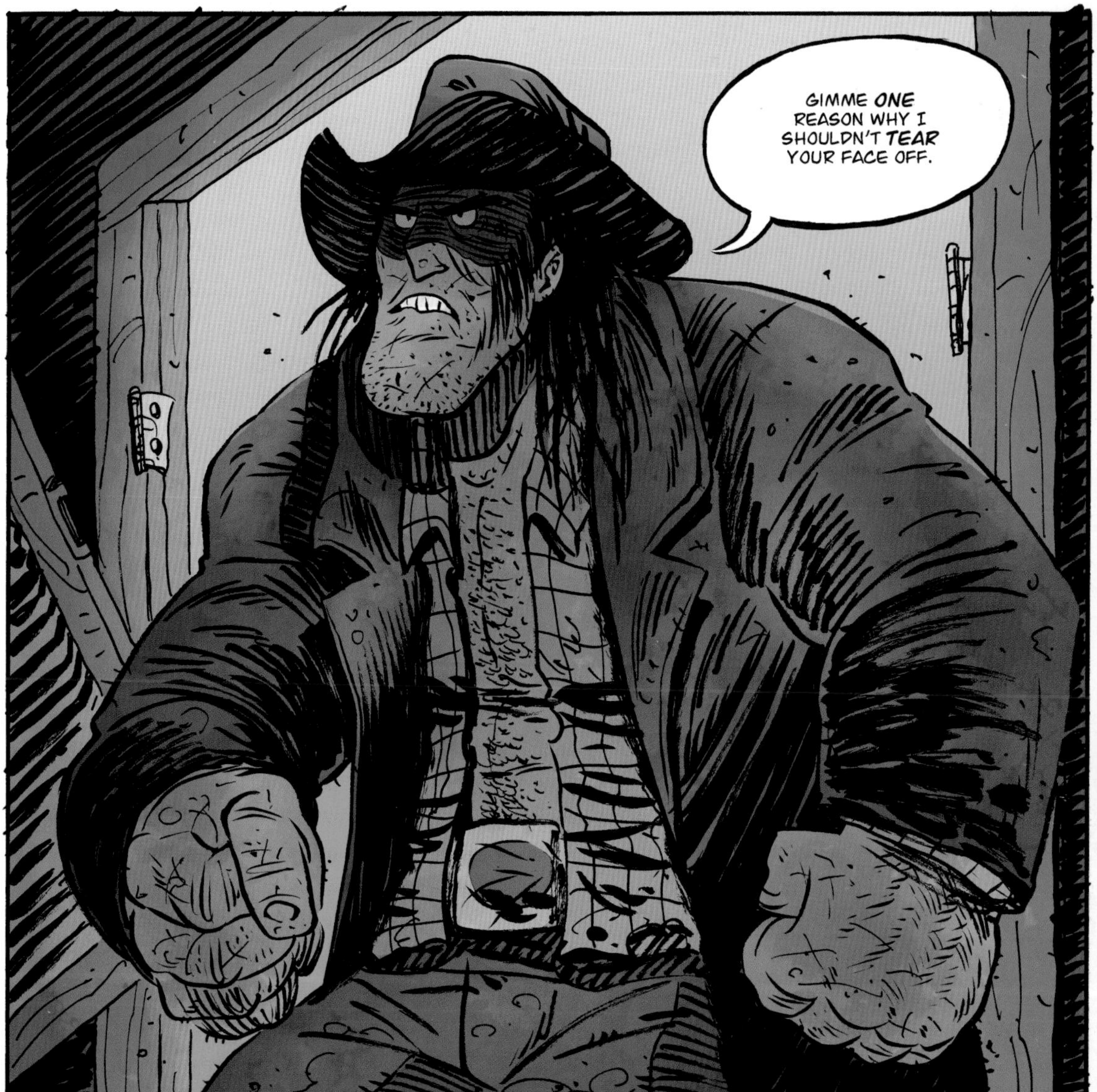
GIMME ONE REASON WHY I SHOULDN'T TEAR YOUR FACE OFF.

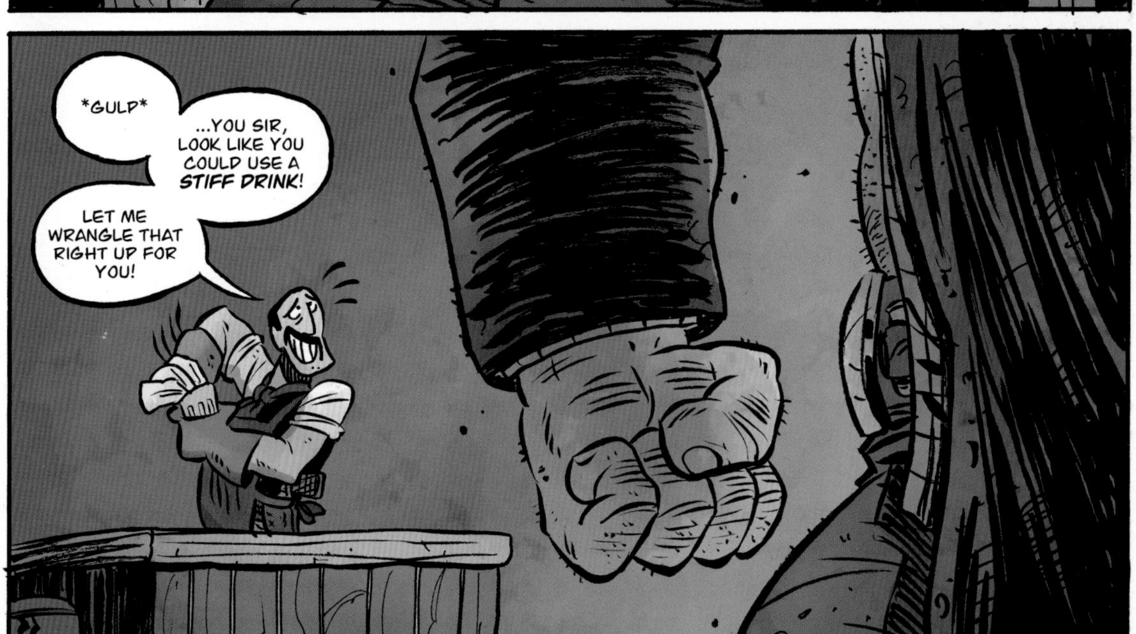
GULP
...YOU SIR, LOOK LIKE YOU COULD USE A STIFF DRINK!
LET ME WRANGLE THAT RIGHT UP FOR YOU!

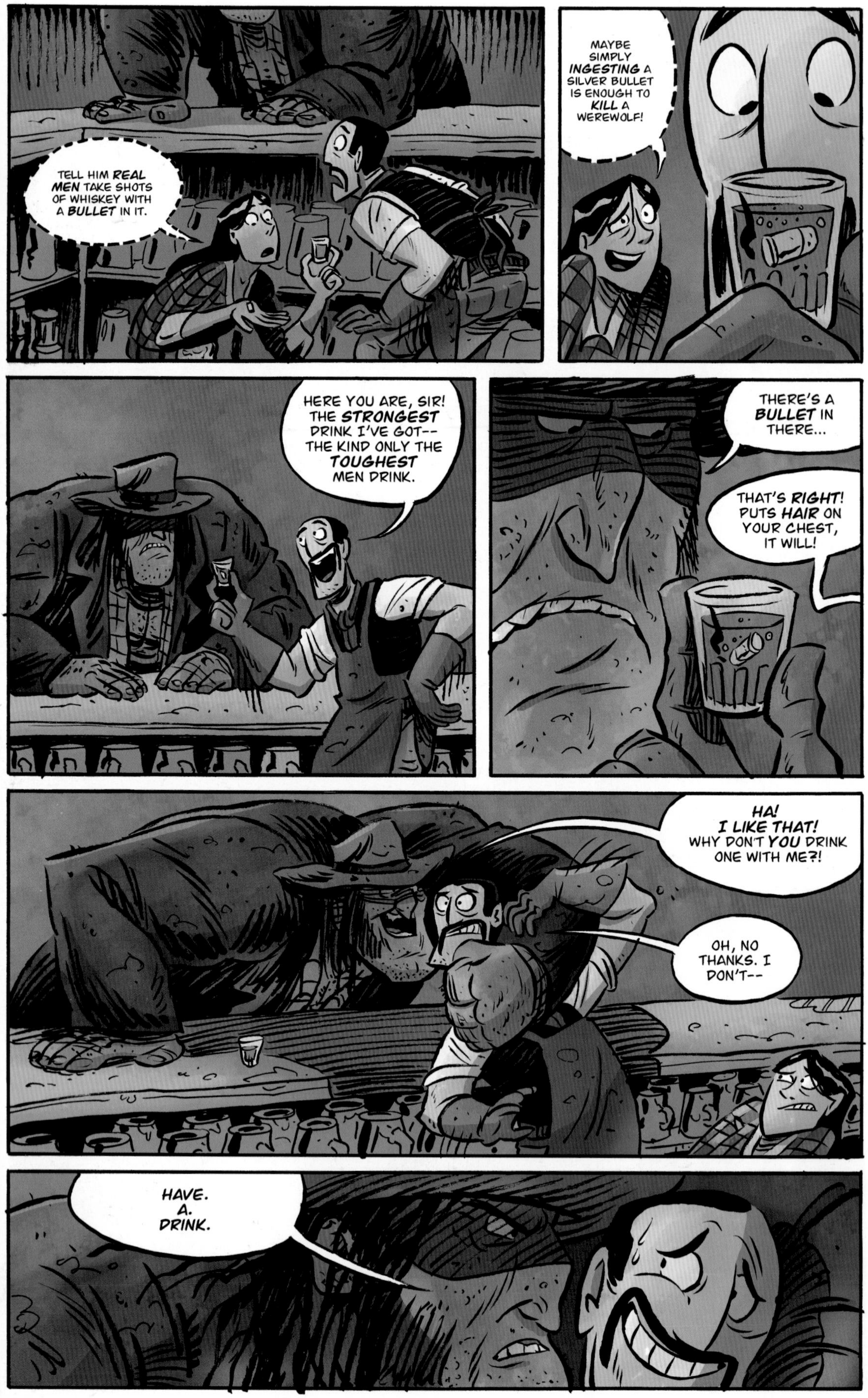
TELL HIM REAL MEN TAKE SHOTS OF WHISKEY WITH A BULLET IN IT.
MAYBE SIMPLY INGESTING A SILVER BULLET IS ENOUGH TO KILL A WEREWOLF!
HERE YOU ARE, SIR! THE STRONGEST DRINK I'VE GOT-- THE KIND ONLY THE TOUGHEST MEN DRINK.
THERE'S A BULLET IN THERE...
THAT'S RIGHT! PUTS HAIR ON YOUR CHEST, IT WILL!
HA! I LIKE THAT! WHY DON'T YOU DRINK ONE WITH ME?!
OH, NO THANKS. I DON'T--
HAVE. A. DRINK.

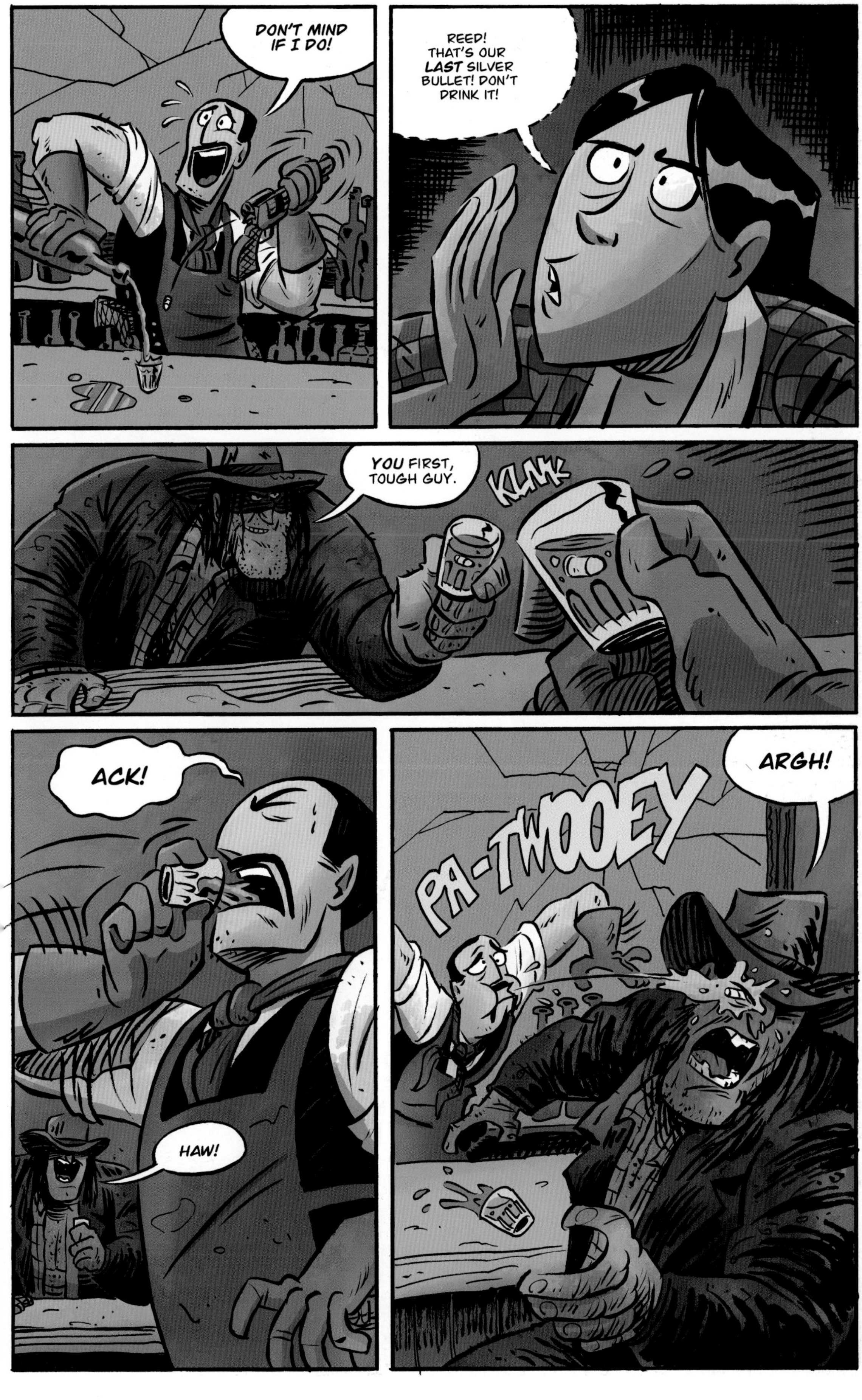
DON'T MIND IF I DO!
REED! THAT'S OUR LAST SILVER BULLET! DON'T DRINK IT!
YOU FIRST, TOUGH GUY.
KLINK
ACK!
HAW!
PA-TWOOEY
ARGH!

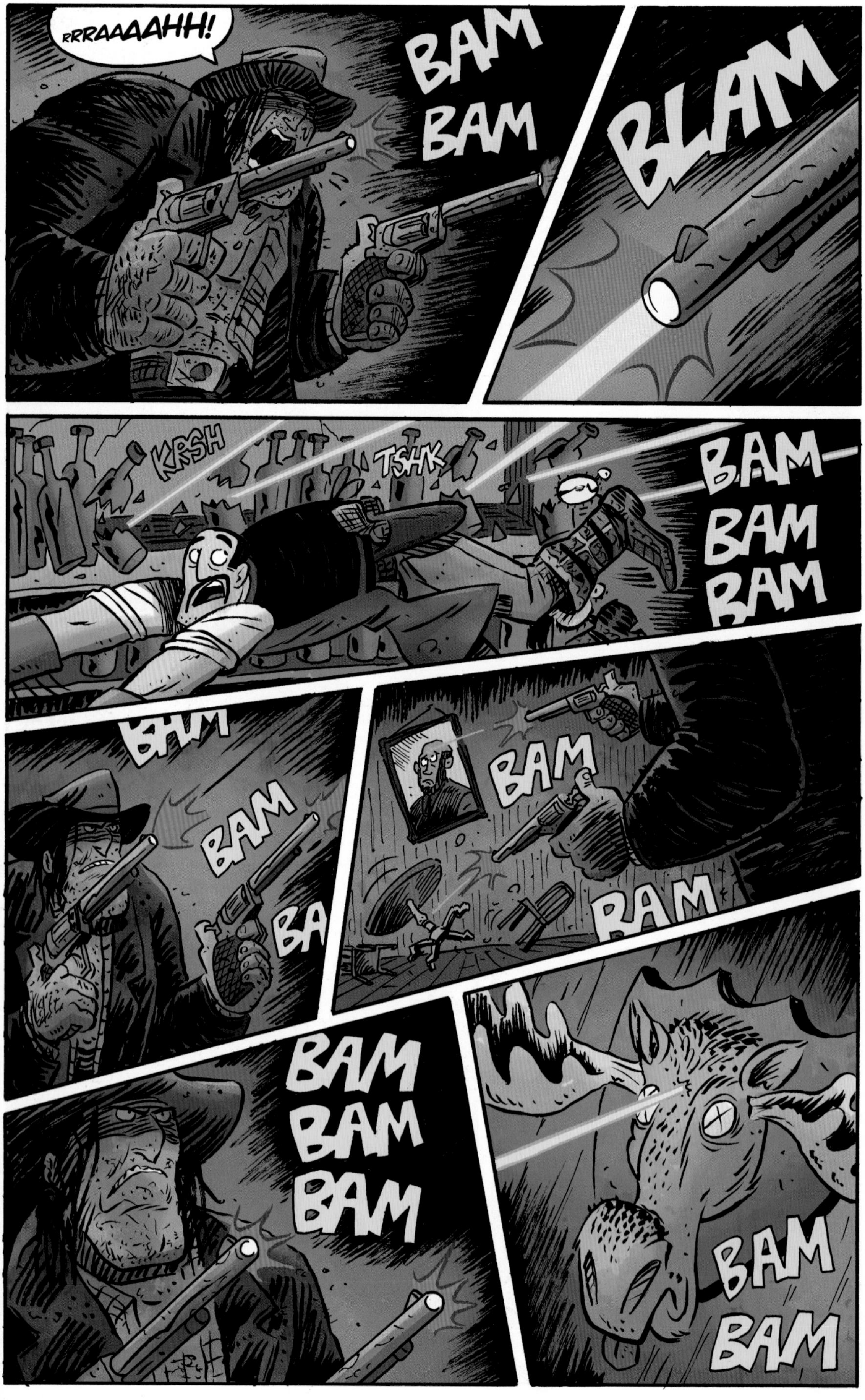
rRRAAAAHH!
BAM
BAM
BLAM
KRSH
TSHK
BAM
BAM
BAM
BAM
BAM
BA
BAM
BAM
BAM
BAM
BAM
BAM
BAM

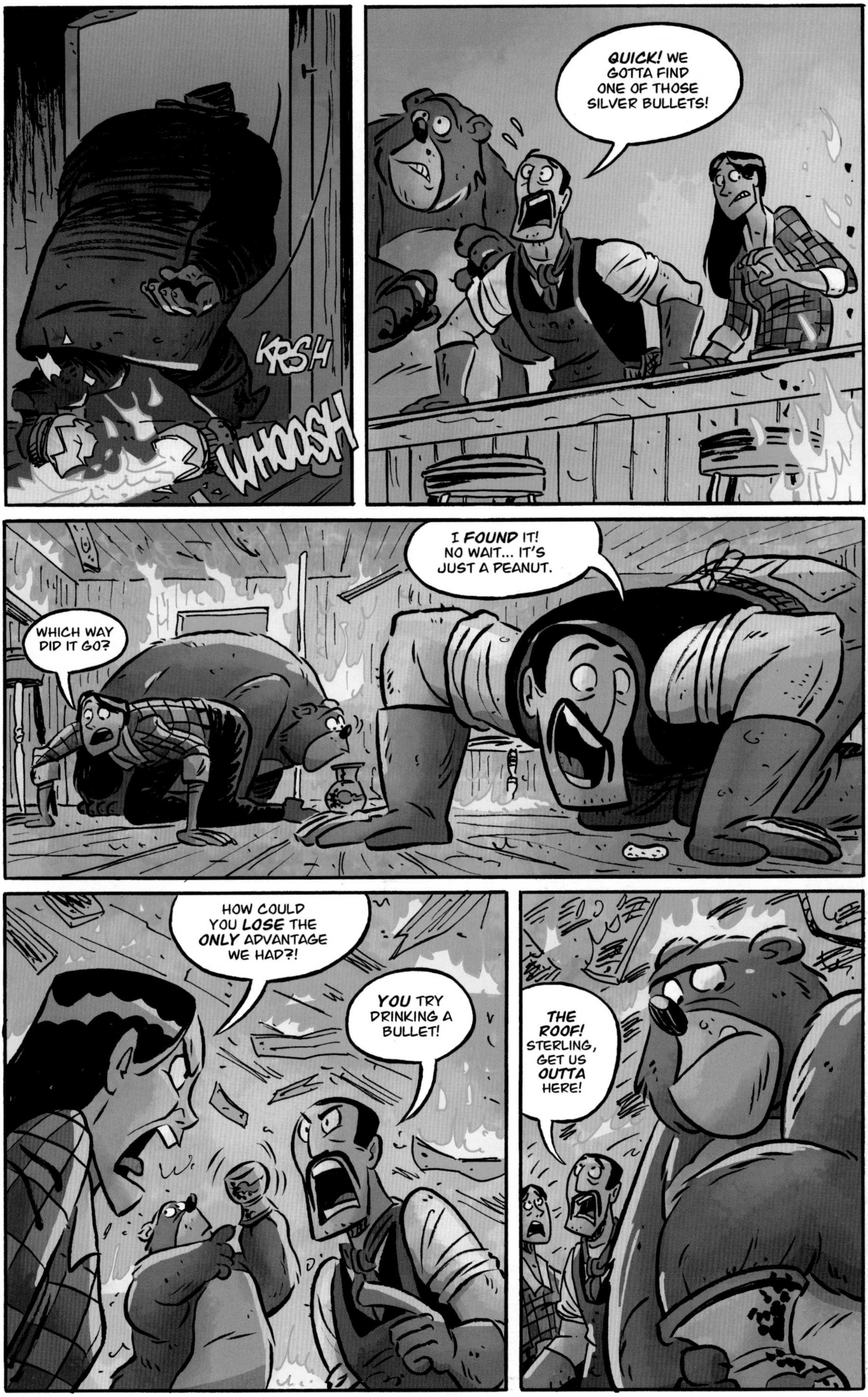
KRSH
WHOOSH
QUICK! WE GOTTA FIND ONE OF THOSE SILVER BULLETS!
I FOUND IT! NO WAIT... IT'S JUST A PEANUT.
WHICH WAY DID IT GO?
HOW COULD YOU LOSE THE ONLY ADVANTAGE WE HAD?!
YOU TRY DRINKING A BULLET!
THE ROOF! STERLING, GET US OUTTA HERE!

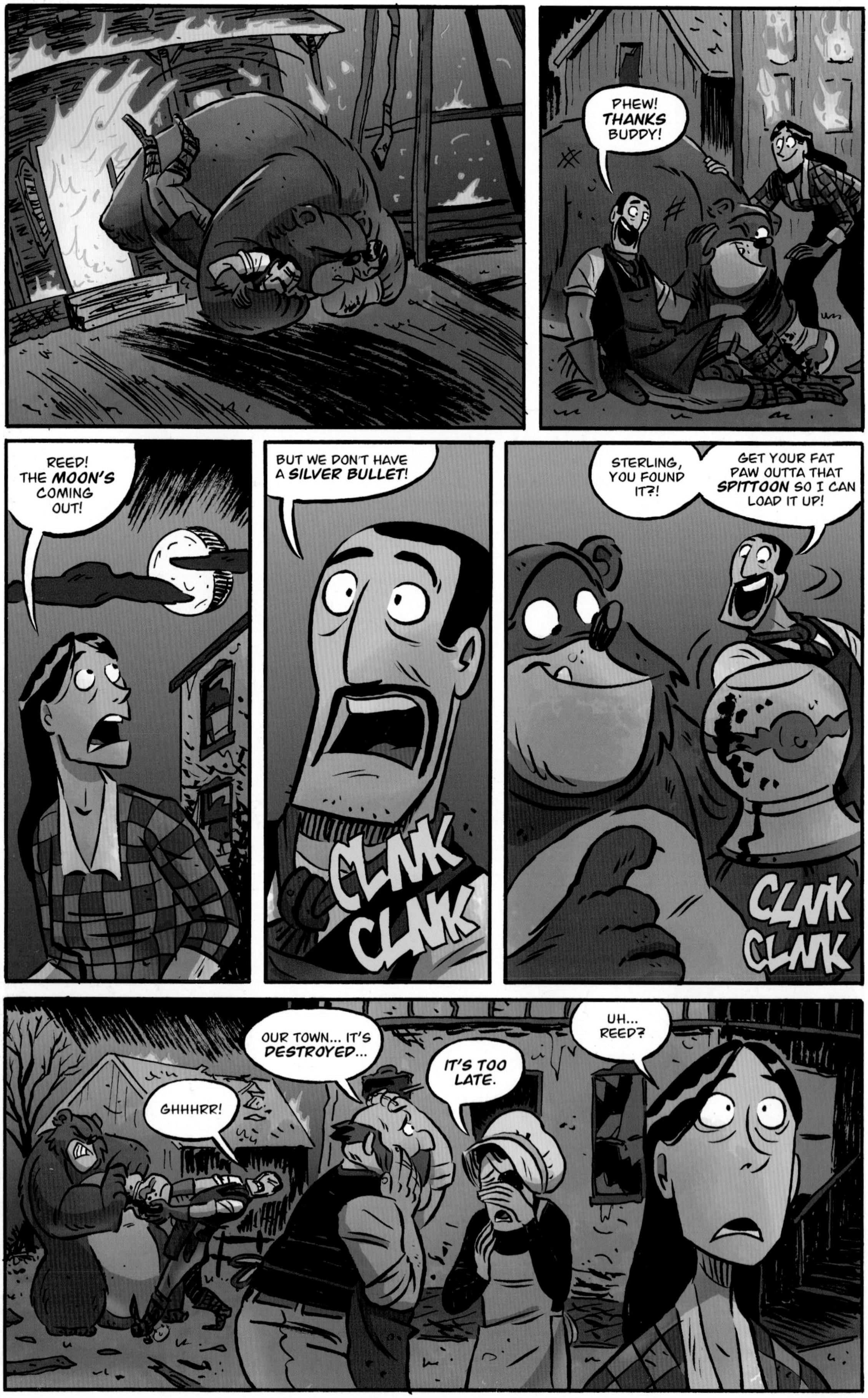
PHEW! THANKS BUDDY!
REED! THE MOON'S COMING OUT!
BUT WE DON'T HAVE A SILVER BULLET!
CLNK CLNK
STERLING, YOU FOUND IT?!
GET YOUR FAT PAW OUTTA THAT SPITTOON SO I CAN LOAD IT UP!
CLNK CLNK
GHHHRR!
OUR TOWN... IT'S DESTROYED...
IT'S TOO LATE.
UH... REED?

AAaAAWHOOooo!
REALLY GONNA NEED THAT SILVER BULLET...
WOAH!

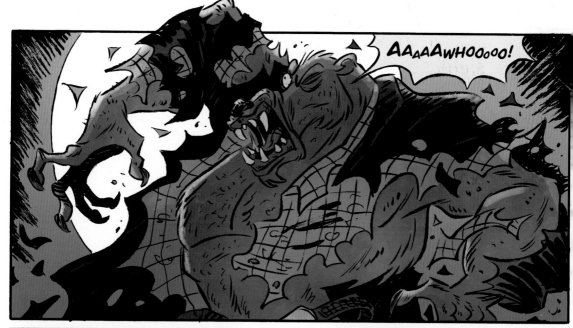

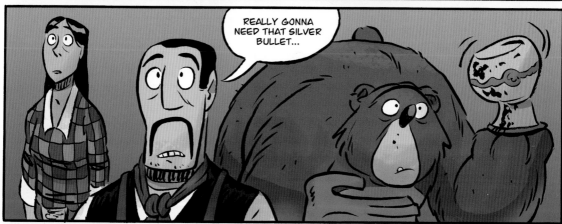

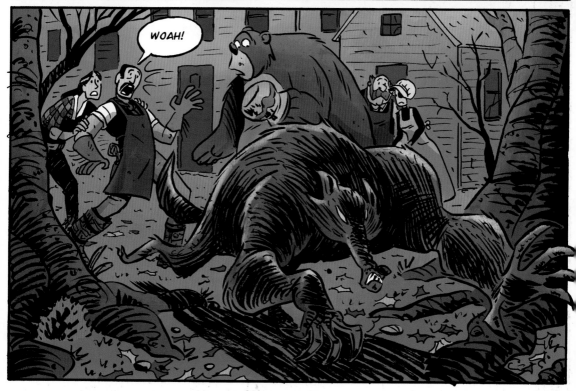

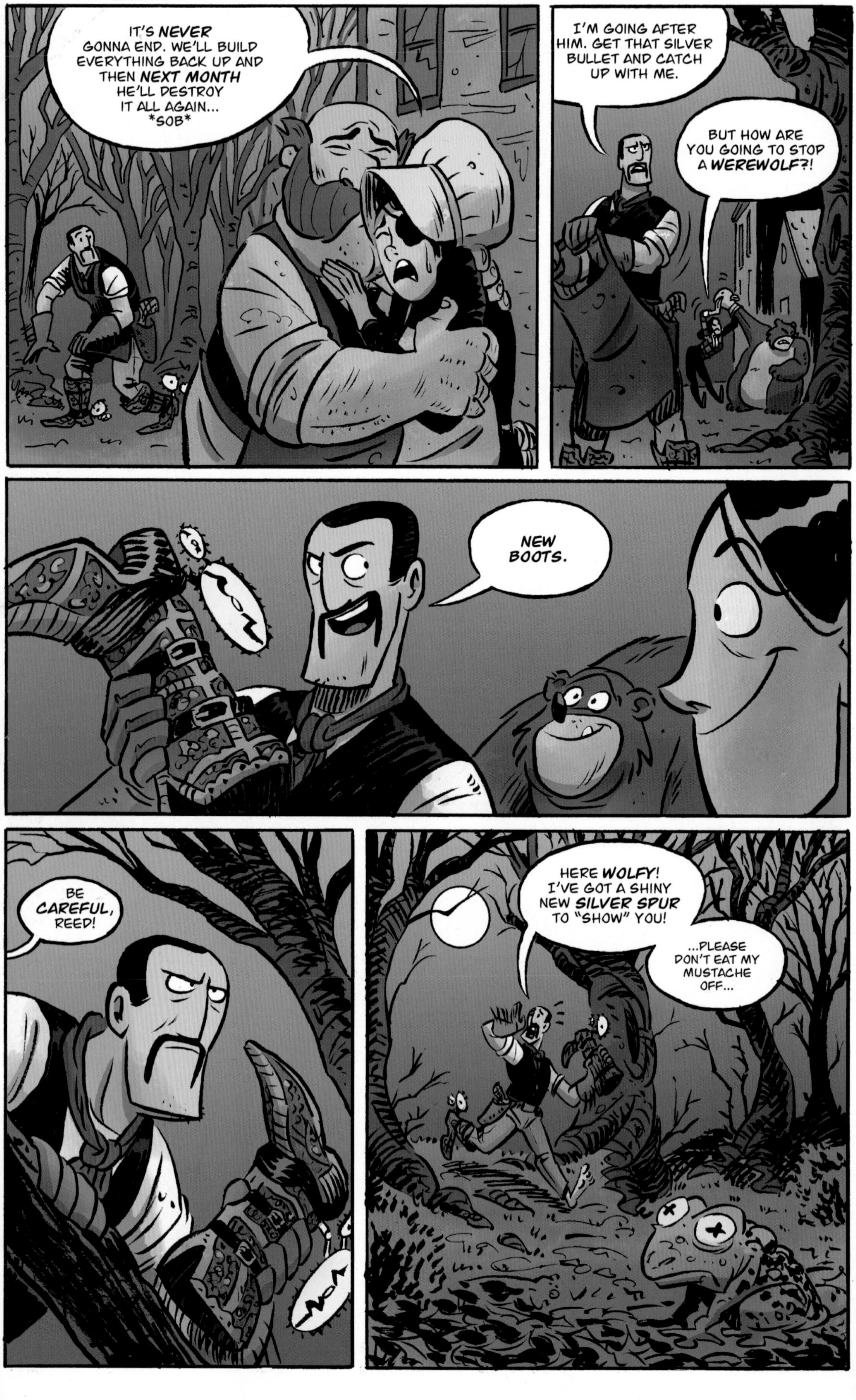

IT'S NEVER GONNA END. WE'LL BUILD EVERYTHING BACK UP AND THEN NEXT MONTH HE'LL DESTROY IT ALL AGAIN... *SOB*
I'M GOING AFTER HIM. GET THAT SILVER BULLET AND CATCH UP WITH ME.
BUT HOW ARE YOU GOING TO STOP A WEREWOLF?!
NEW BOOTS.
BE CAREFUL, REED!
HERE WOLFY! I'VE GOT A SHINY NEW SILVER SPUR TO "SHOW" YOU!
...PLEASE DON'T EAT MY MUSTACHE OFF...

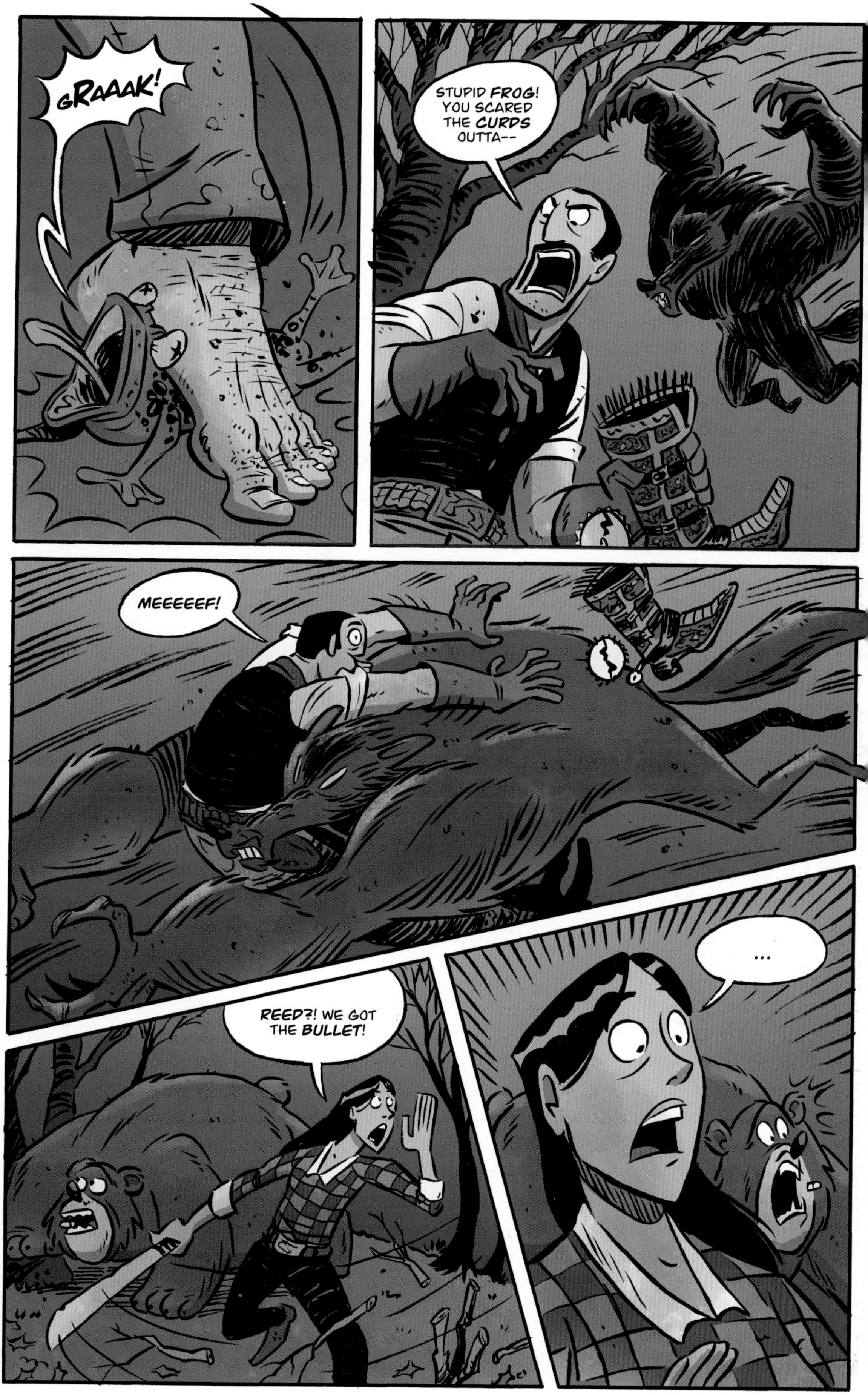
gRAAAK!
STUPID FROG! YOU SCARED THE CURDS OUTTA--
MEEEEEF!
REED?! WE GOT THE BULLET!
...

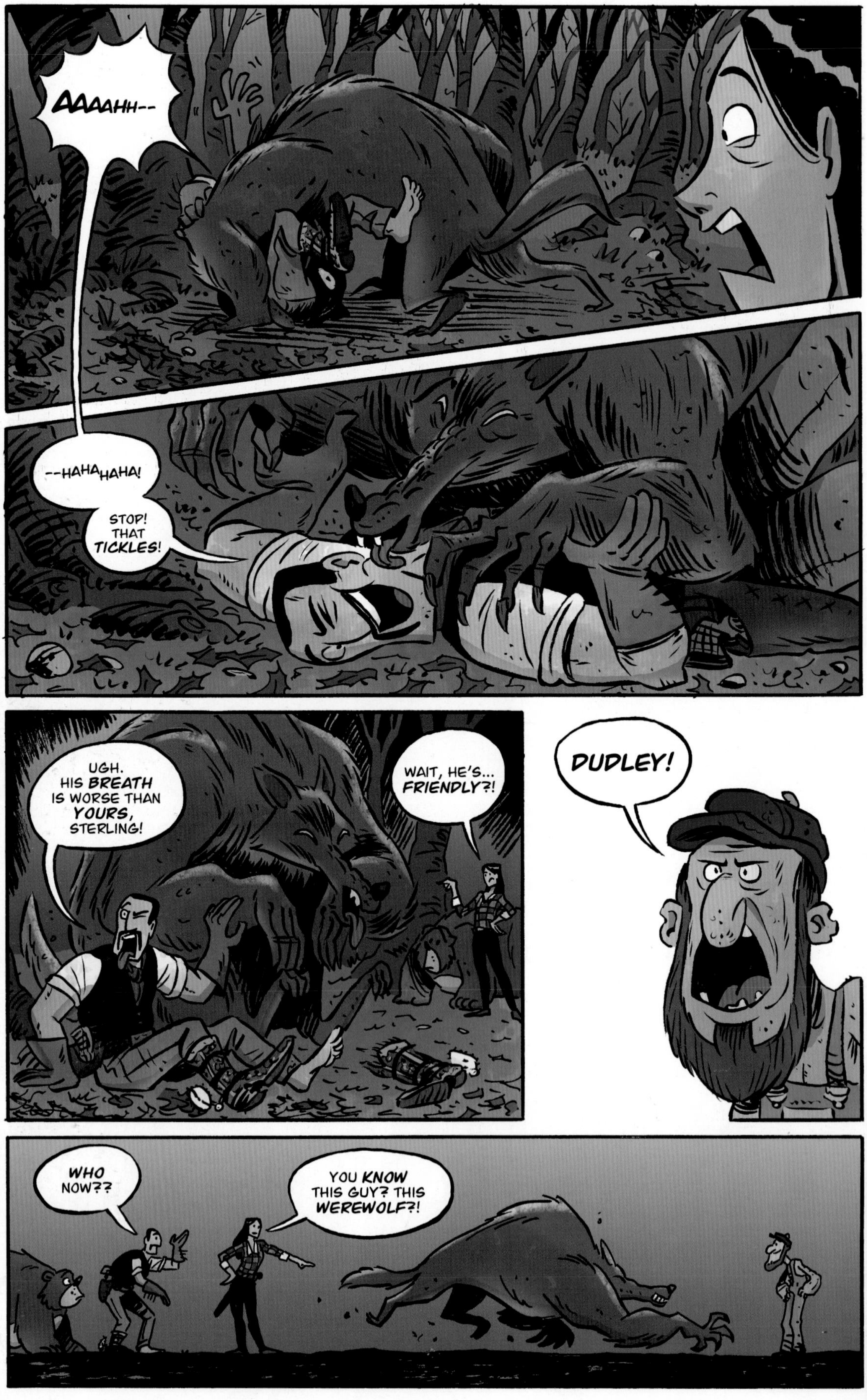

AAAAHH--
--HAHAHAHA!
STOP! THAT TICKLES!
UGH. HIS BREATH IS WORSE THAN YOURS, STERLING!
WAIT, HE'S... FRIENDLY?!
DUDLEY!
WHO NOW??
YOU KNOW THIS GUY? THIS WEREWOLF?!

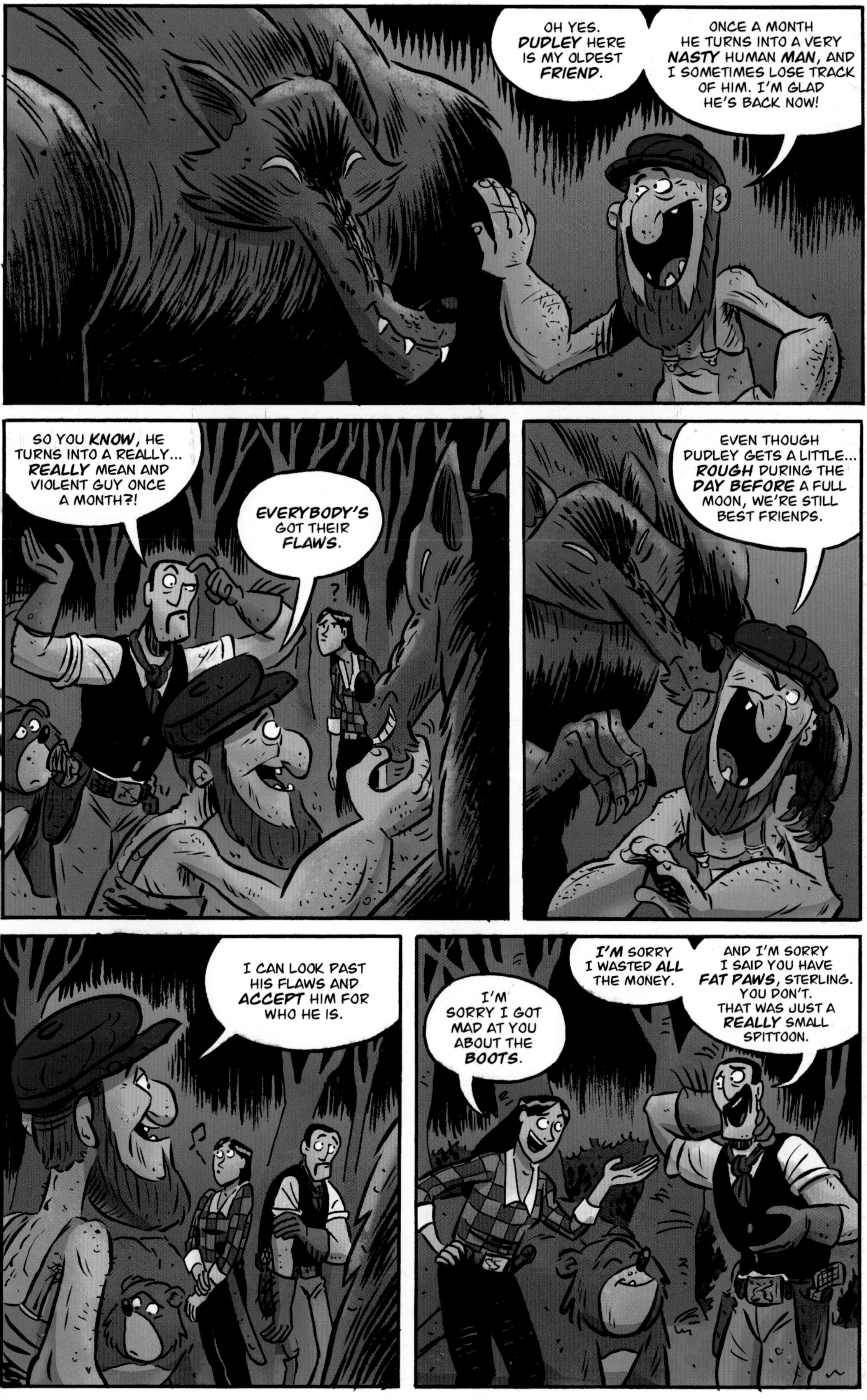
OH YES. DUDLEY HERE IS MY OLDEST FRIEND.
ONCE A MONTH HE TURNS INTO A VERY NASTY HUMAN MAN, AND I SOMETIMES LOSE TRACK OF HIM. I'M GLAD HE'S BACK NOW!
SO YOU KNOW, HE TURNS INTO A REALLY... REALLY MEAN AND VIOLENT GUY ONCE A MONTH?!
EVERYBODY'S GOT THEIR FLAWS.
?
EVEN THOUGH DUDLEY GETS A LITTLE... ROUGH DURING THE DAY BEFORE A FULL MOON, WE'RE STILL BEST FRIENDS.
I CAN LOOK PAST HIS FLAWS AND ACCEPT HIM FOR WHO HE IS.
I'M SORRY I GOT MAD AT YOU ABOUT THE BOOTS.
I'M SORRY I WASTED ALL THE MONEY.
AND I'M SORRY I SAID YOU HAVE FAT PAWS, STERLING. YOU DON'T. THAT WAS JUST A REALLY SMALL SPITTOON.

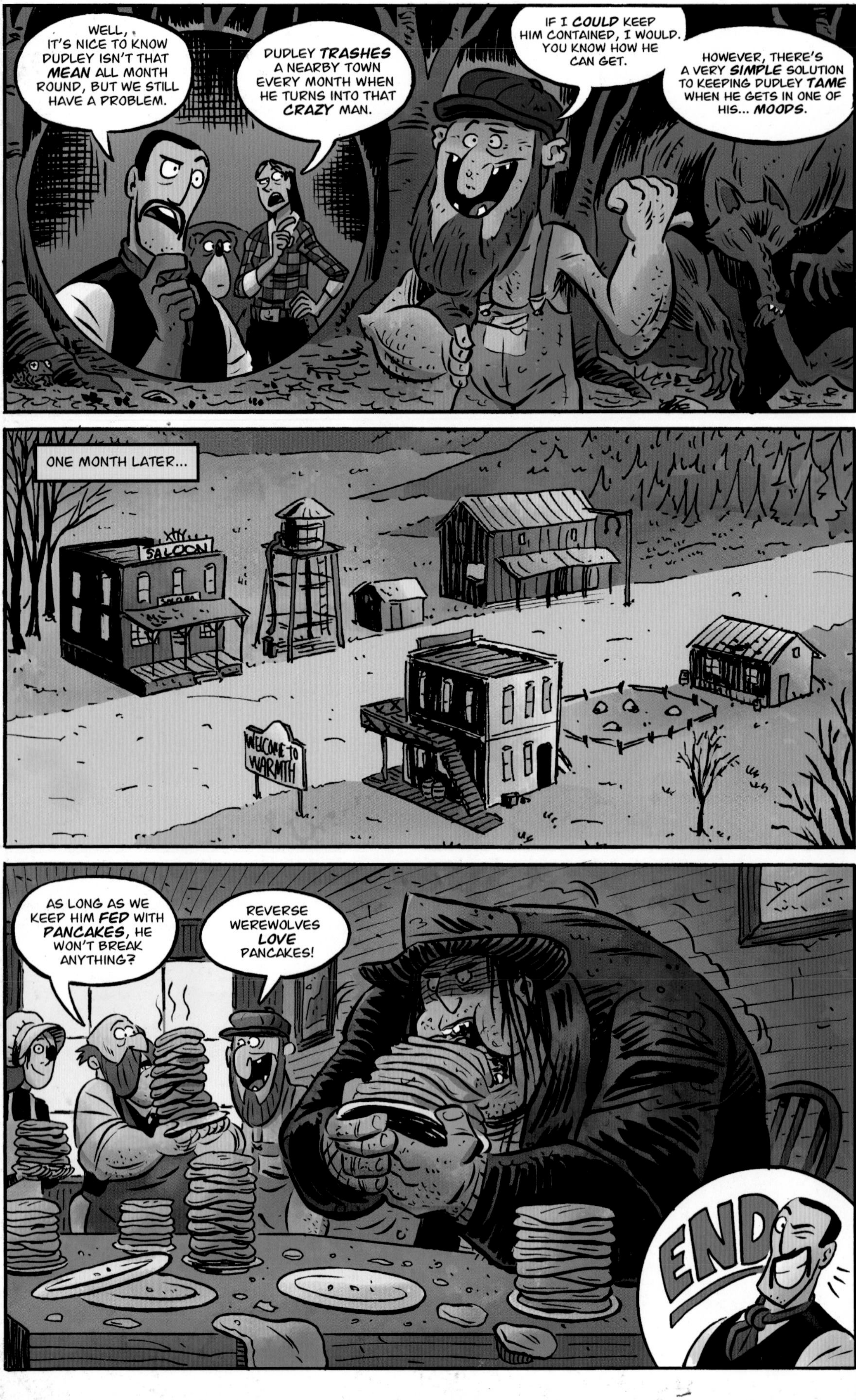
WELL, IT'S NICE TO KNOW DUDLEY ISN'T THAT MEAN ALL MONTH ROUND, BUT WE STILL HAVE A PROBLEM.
DUDLEY TRASHES A NEARBY TOWN EVERY MONTH WHEN HE TURNS INTO THAT CRAZY MAN.
IF I COULD KEEP HIM CONTAINED, I WOULD. YOU KNOW HOW HE CAN GET.
HOWEVER, THERE'S A VERY SIMPLE SOLUTION TO KEEPING DUDLEY TAME WHEN HE GETS IN ONE OF HIS... MOODS.
ONE MONTH LATER...
SALOON
WELCOME TO WARMTH
AS LONG AS WE KEEP HIM FED WITH PANCAKES, HE WON'T BREAK ANYTHING?
REVERSE WEREWOLVES LOVE PANCAKES!
END

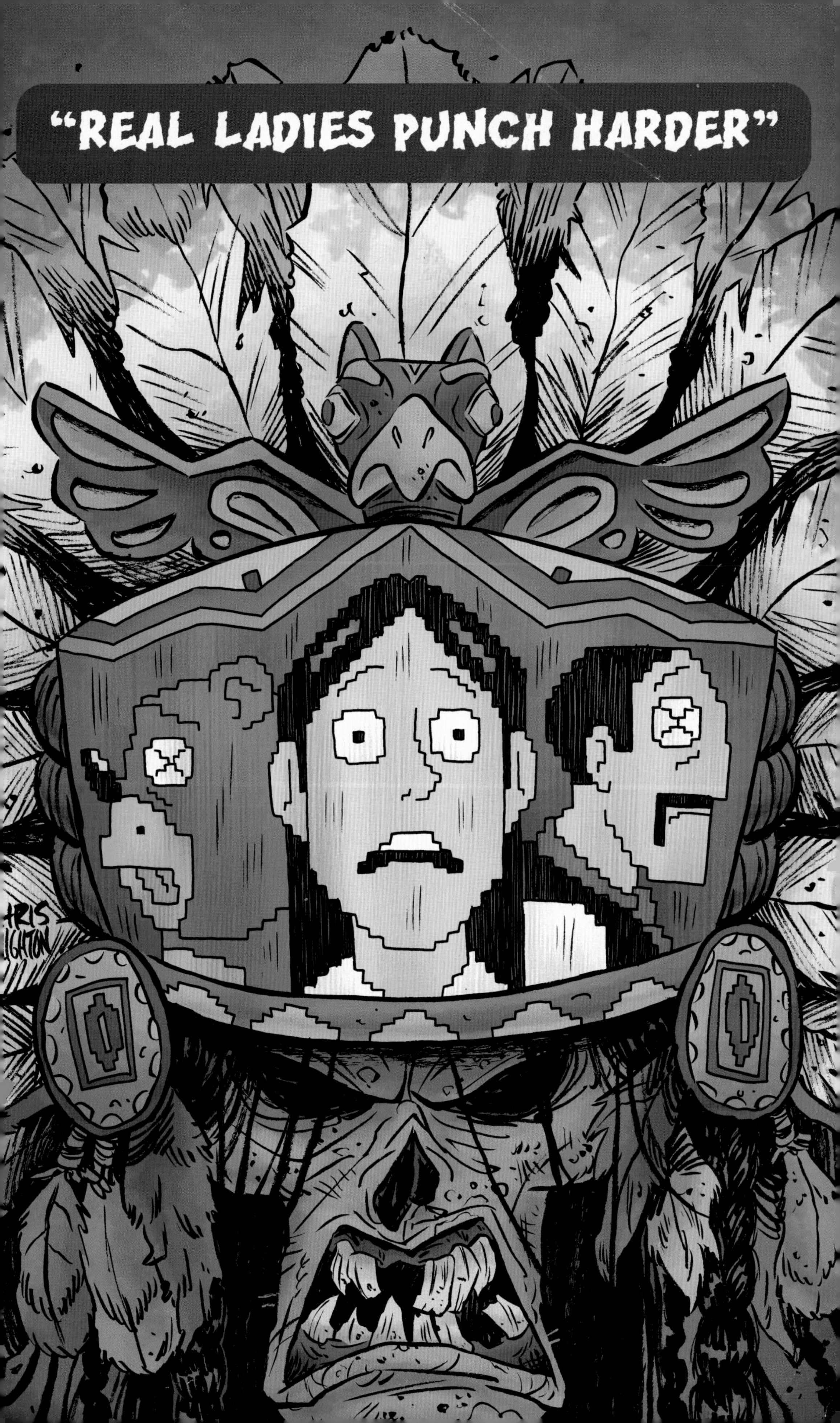
"REAL LADIES PUNCH HARDER"

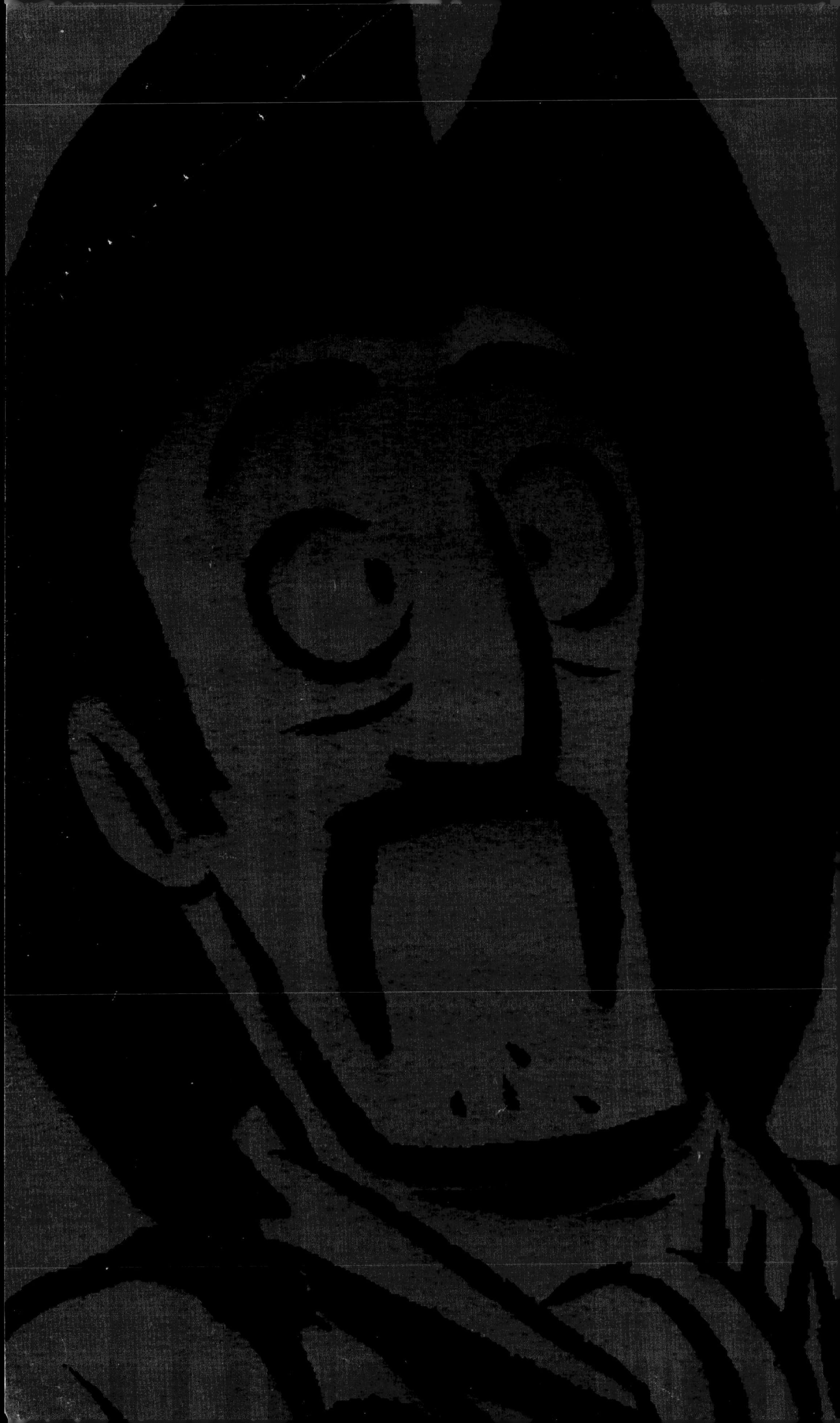

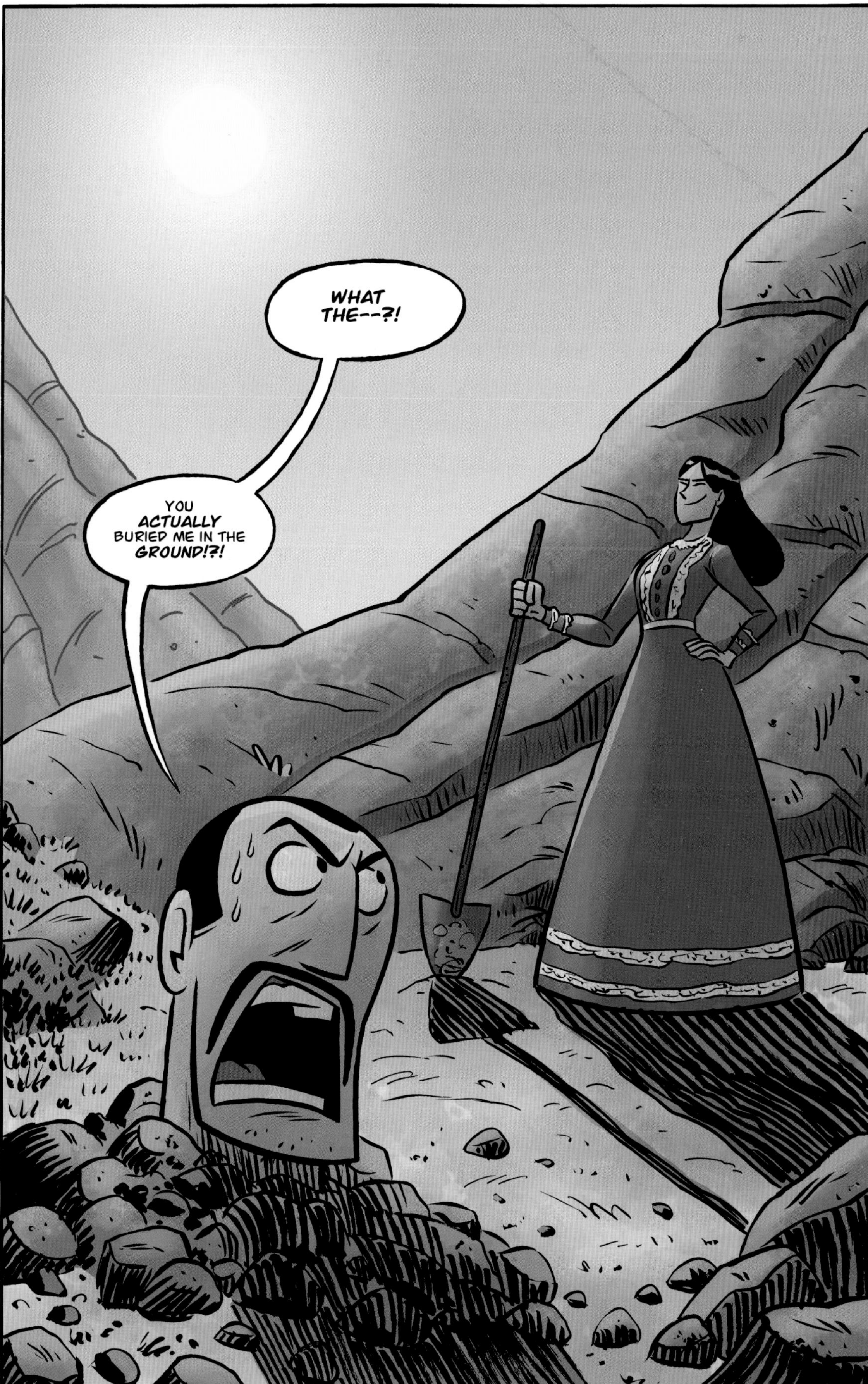
WHAT THE--?!
YOU ACTUALLY BURIED ME IN THE GROUND!?!

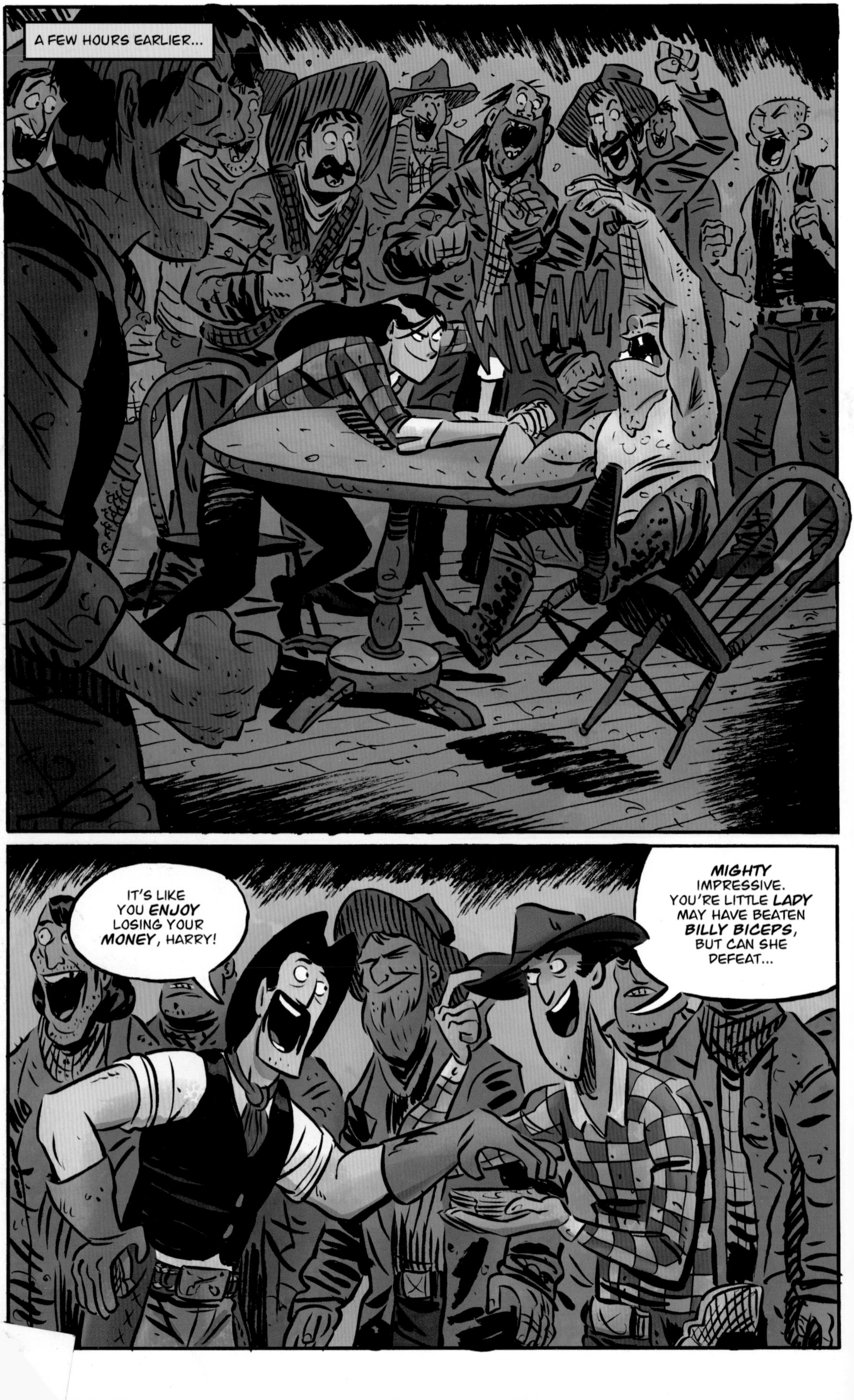
A FEW HOURS EARLIER...
WHAM
IT'S LIKE YOU ENJOY LOSING YOUR MONEY, HARRY!
MIGHTY IMPRESSIVE. YOU'RE LITTLE LADY MAY HAVE BEATEN BILLY BICEPS, BUT CAN SHE DEFEAT...

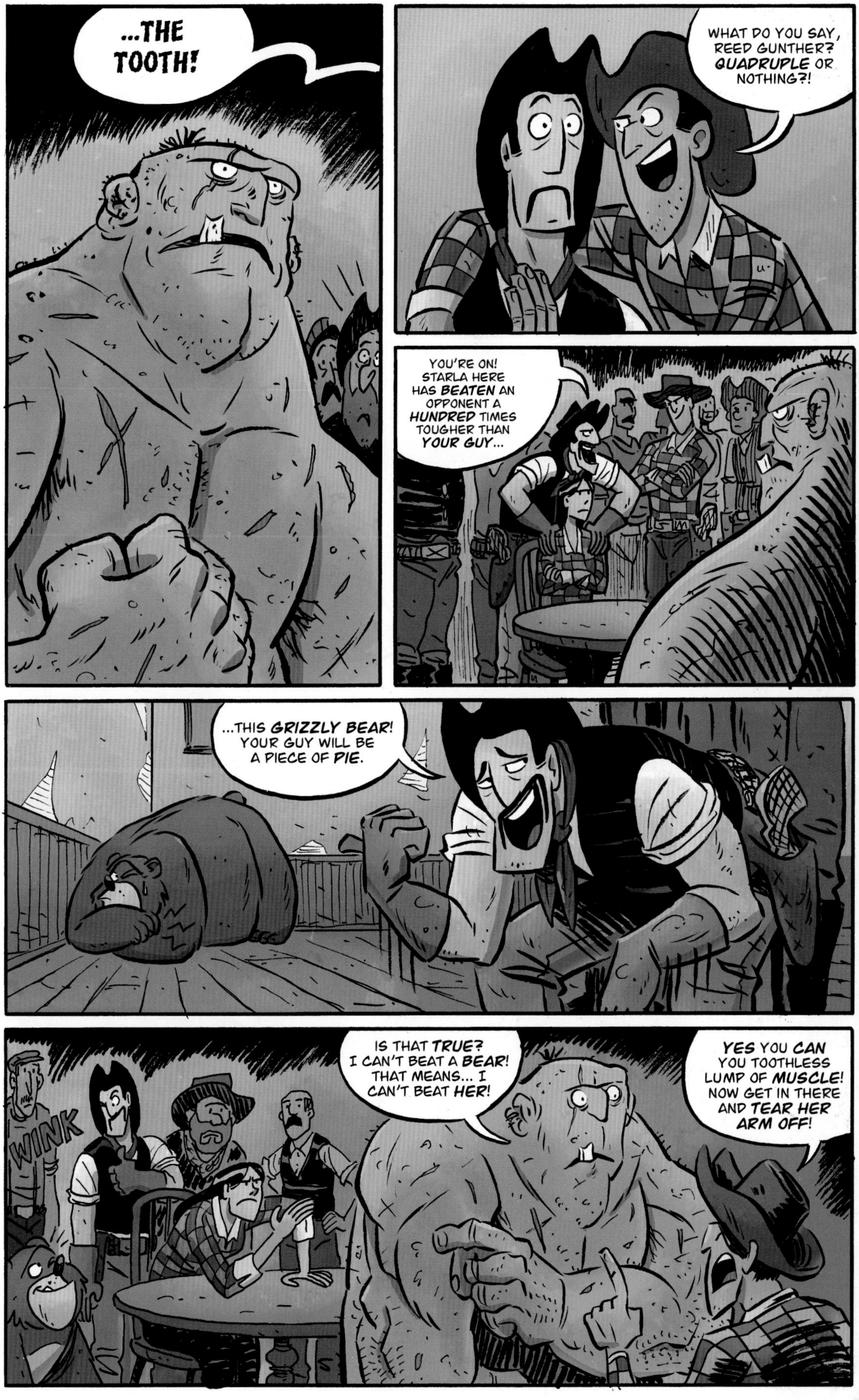
...THE TOOTH!
WHAT DO YOU SAY, REED GUNTHER? QUADRUPLE OR NOTHING?!
YOU'RE ON! STARLA HERE HAS BEATEN AN OPPONENT A HUNDRED TIMES TOUGHER THAN YOUR GUY...
...THIS GRIZZLY BEAR! YOUR GUY WILL BE A PIECE OF PIE.
WINK
IS THAT TRUE? I CAN'T BEAT A BEAR! THAT MEANS... I CAN'T BEAT HER!
YES YOU CAN YOU TOOTHLESS LUMP OF MUSCLE! NOW GET IN THERE AND TEAR HER ARM OFF!

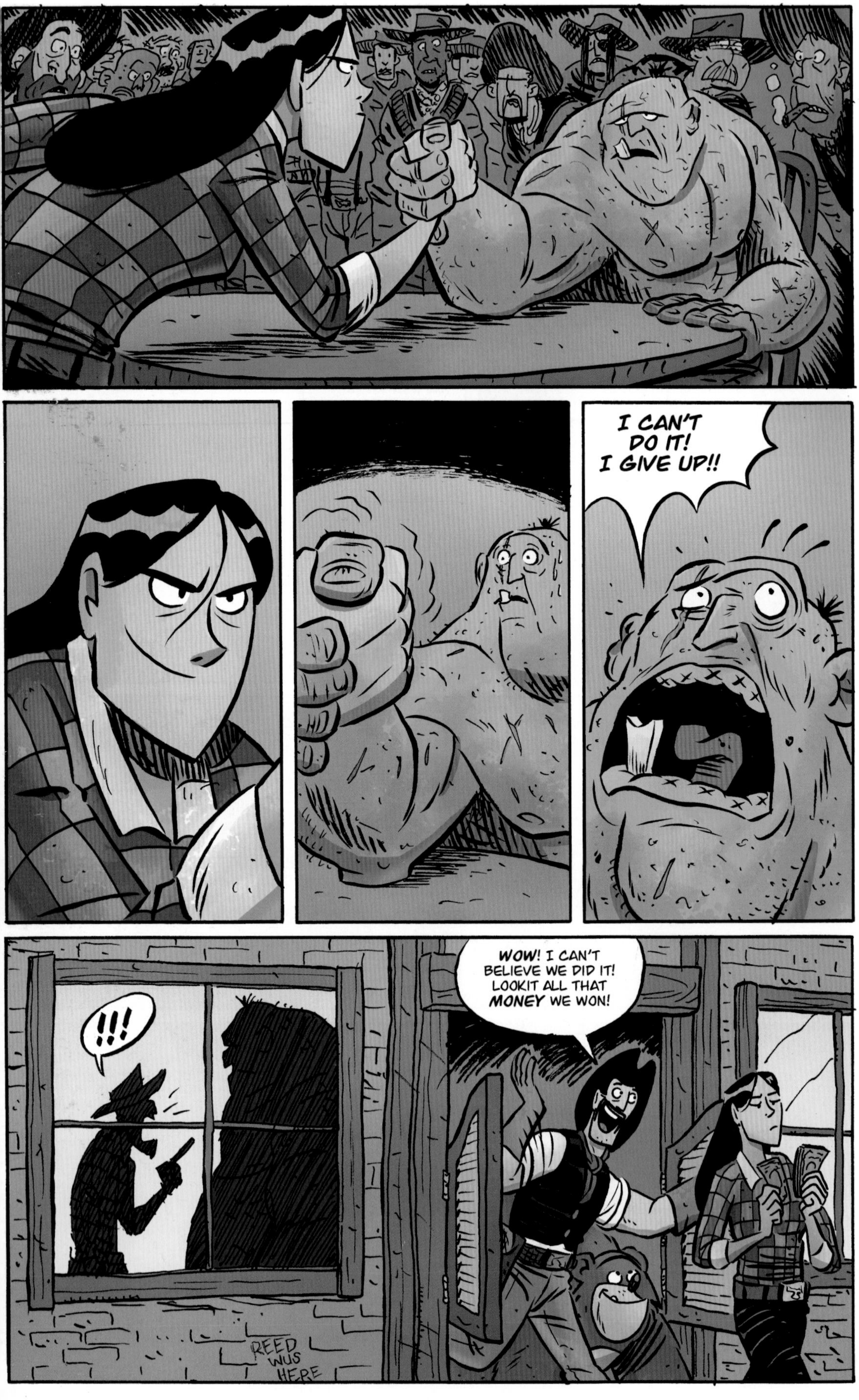
I CAN'T DO IT! I GIVE UP!!
!!!
WOW! I CAN'T BELIEVE WE DID IT! LOOKIT ALL THAT MONEY WE WON!
REED WUS HERE

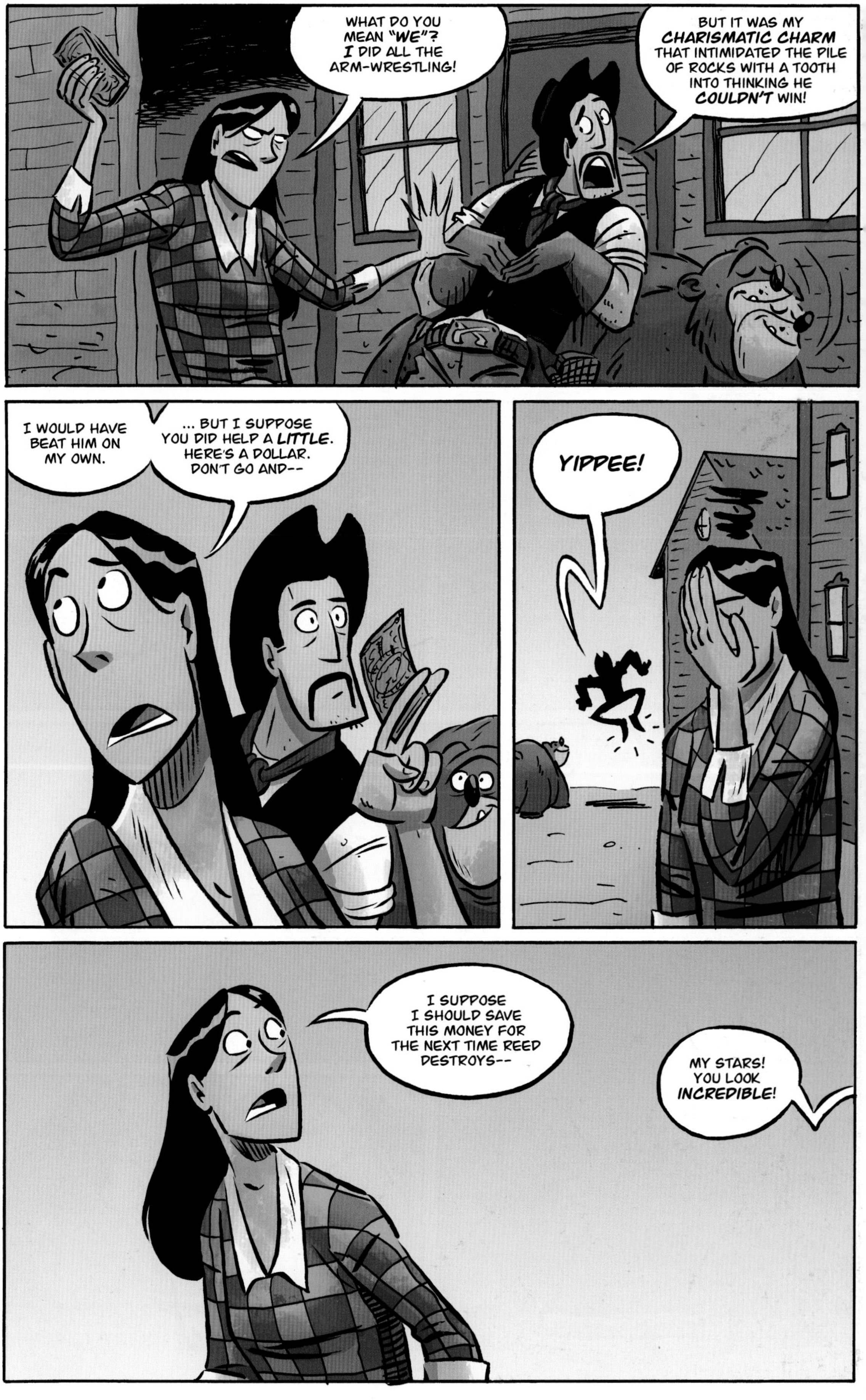
WHAT DO YOU MEAN "WE"? I DID ALL THE ARM-WRESTLING!
BUT IT WAS MY CHARISMATIC CHARM THAT INTIMIDATED THE PILE OF ROCKS WITH A TOOTH INTO THINKING HE COULDN'T WIN!
I WOULD HAVE BEAT HIM ON MY OWN.
... BUT I SUPPOSE YOU DID HELP A LITTLE. HERE'S A DOLLAR. DON'T GO AND--
YIPPEE!
I SUPPOSE I SHOULD SAVE THIS MONEY FOR THE NEXT TIME REED DESTROYS--
MY STARS! YOU LOOK INCREDIBLE!

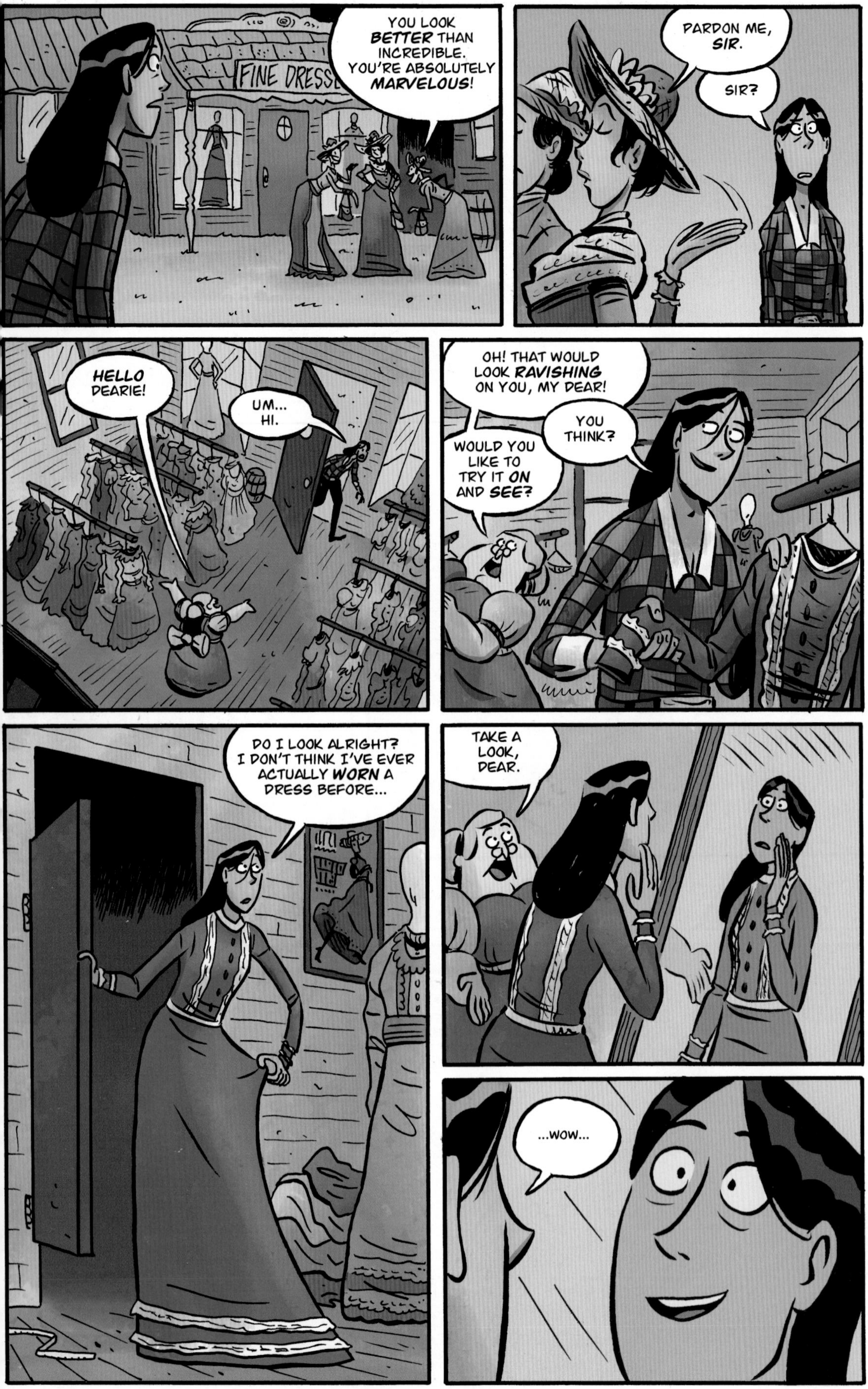
FINE DRESSES
YOU LOOK BETTER THAN INCREDIBLE. YOU'RE ABSOLUTELY MARVELOUS!
PARDON ME, SIR.
SIR?
HELLO DEARIE!
UM... HI.
OH! THAT WOULD LOOK RAVISHING ON YOU, MY DEAR!
YOU THINK?
WOULD YOU LIKE TO TRY IT ON AND SEE?
DO I LOOK ALRIGHT? I DON'T THINK I'VE EVER ACTUALLY WORN A DRESS BEFORE...
TAKE A LOOK, DEAR.
...WOW...

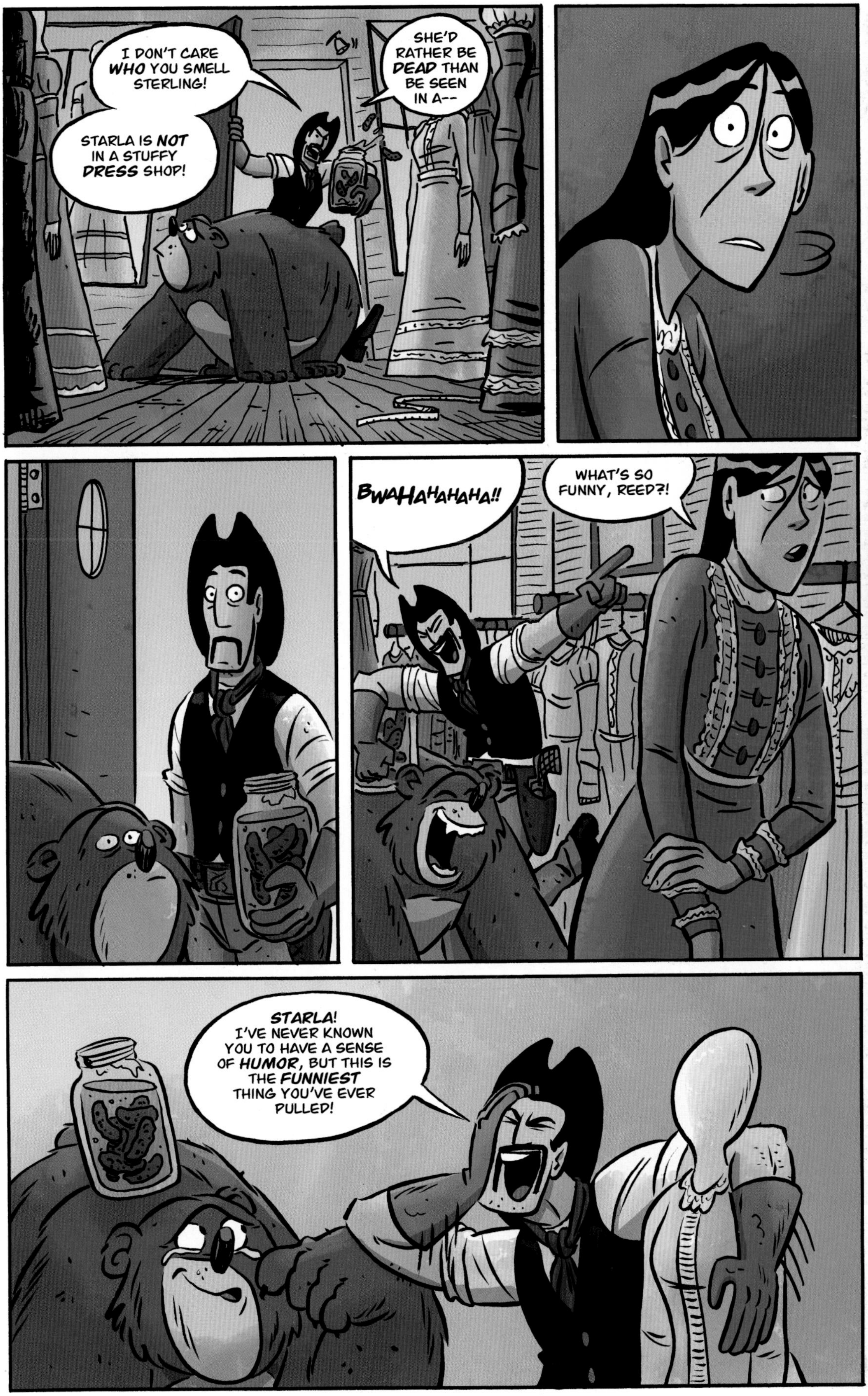
I DON'T CARE WHO YOU SMELL STERLING!
STARLA IS NOT IN A STUFFY DRESS SHOP!
SHE'D RATHER BE DEAD THAN BE SEEN IN A--
BWAHAHAHAHA!!
WHAT'S SO FUNNY, REED?!
STARLA! I'VE NEVER KNOWN YOU TO HAVE A SENSE OF HUMOR, BUT THIS IS THE FUNNIEST THING YOU'VE EVER PULLED!

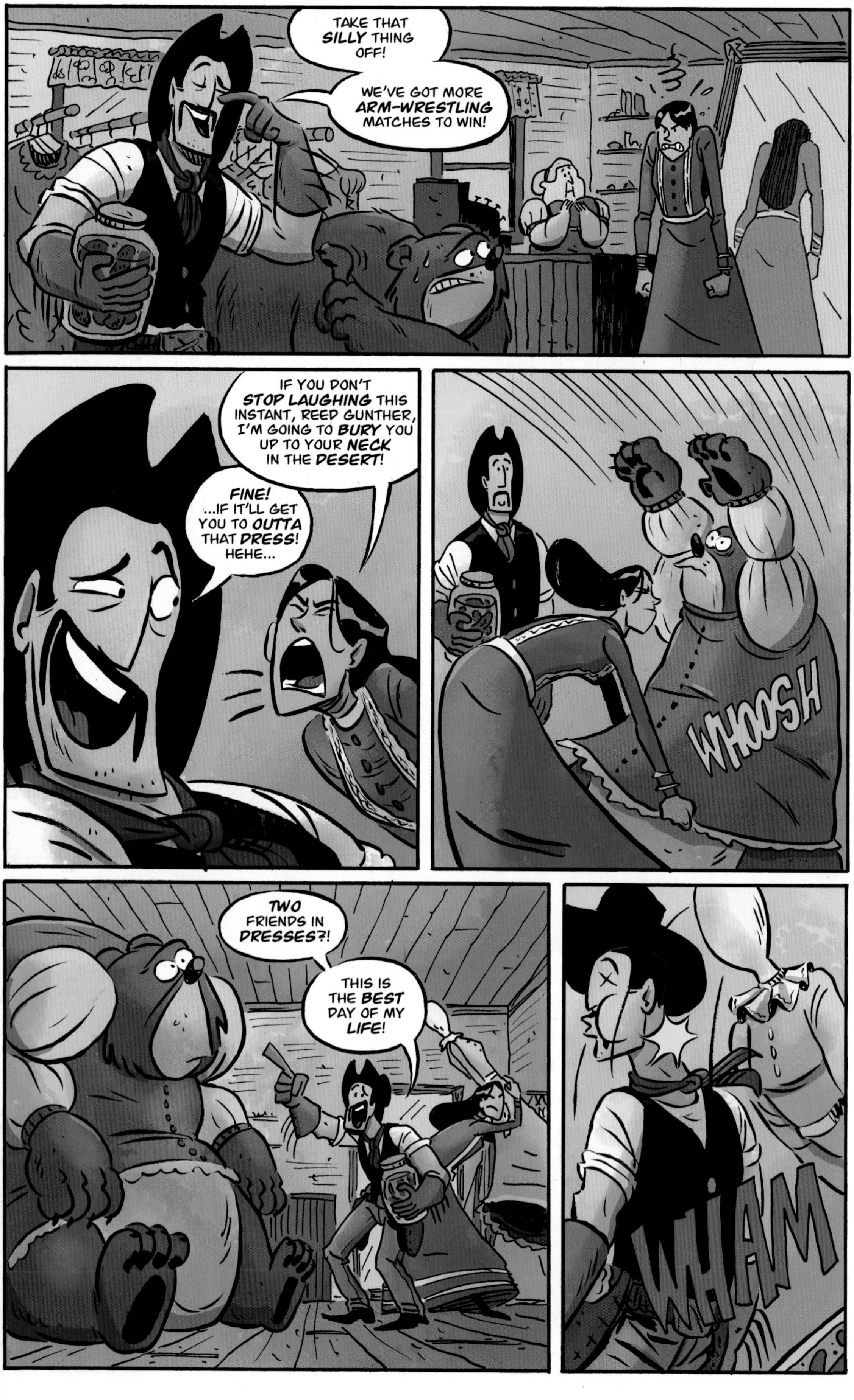
TAKE THAT SILLY THING OFF!
WE'VE GOT MORE ARM-WRESTLING MATCHES TO WIN!
IF YOU DON'T STOP LAUGHING THIS INSTANT, REED GUNTHER, I'M GOING TO BURY YOU UP TO YOUR NECK IN THE DESERT!
FINE! ...IF IT'LL GET YOU TO OUTTA THAT DRESS! HEHE...
WHOOSH
TWO FRIENDS IN DRESSES?!
THIS IS THE BEST DAY OF MY LIFE!
WHAM

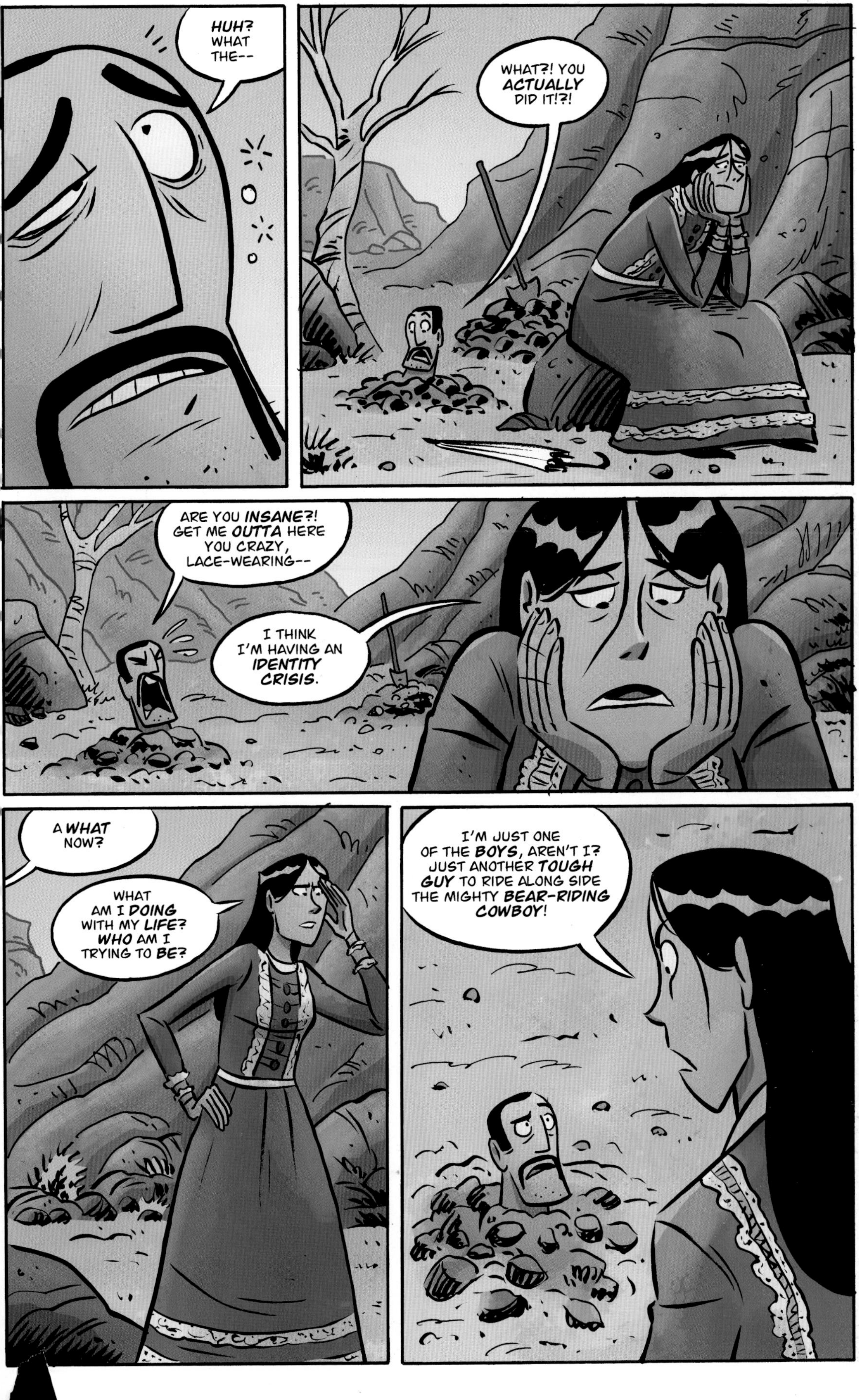
HUH? WHAT THE--
WHAT?! YOU ACTUALLY DID IT!?!
ARE YOU INSANE?! GET ME OUTTA HERE YOU CRAZY, LACE-WEARING--
I THINK I'M HAVING AN IDENTITY CRISIS.
A WHAT NOW?
WHAT AM I DOING WITH MY LIFE? WHO AM I TRYING TO BE?
I'M JUST ONE OF THE BOYS, AREN'T I? JUST ANOTHER TOUGH GUY TO RIDE ALONG SIDE THE MIGHTY BEAR-RIDING COWBOY!

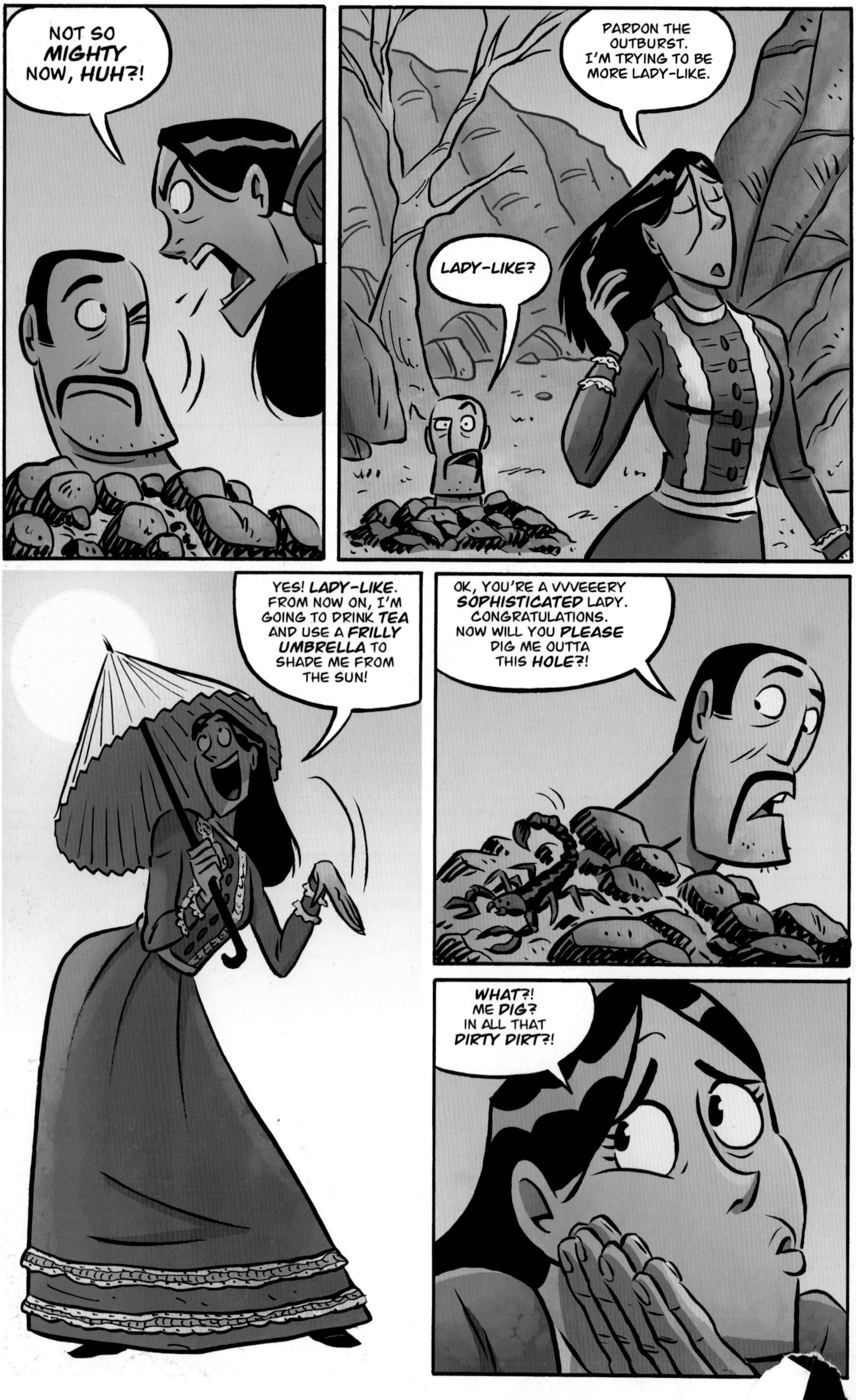
NOT SO MIGHTY NOW, HUH?!
PARDON THE OUTBURST. I'M TRYING TO BE MORE LADY-LIKE.
LADY-LIKE?
YES! LADY-LIKE. FROM NOW ON, I'M GOING TO DRINK TEA AND USE A FRILLY UMBRELLA TO SHADE ME FROM THE SUN!
OK, YOU'RE A VVVEEERY SOPHISTICATED LADY. CONGRATULATIONS. NOW WILL YOU PLEASE DIG ME OUTTA THIS HOLE?!
WHAT?! ME DIG? IN ALL THAT DIRTY DIRT?!

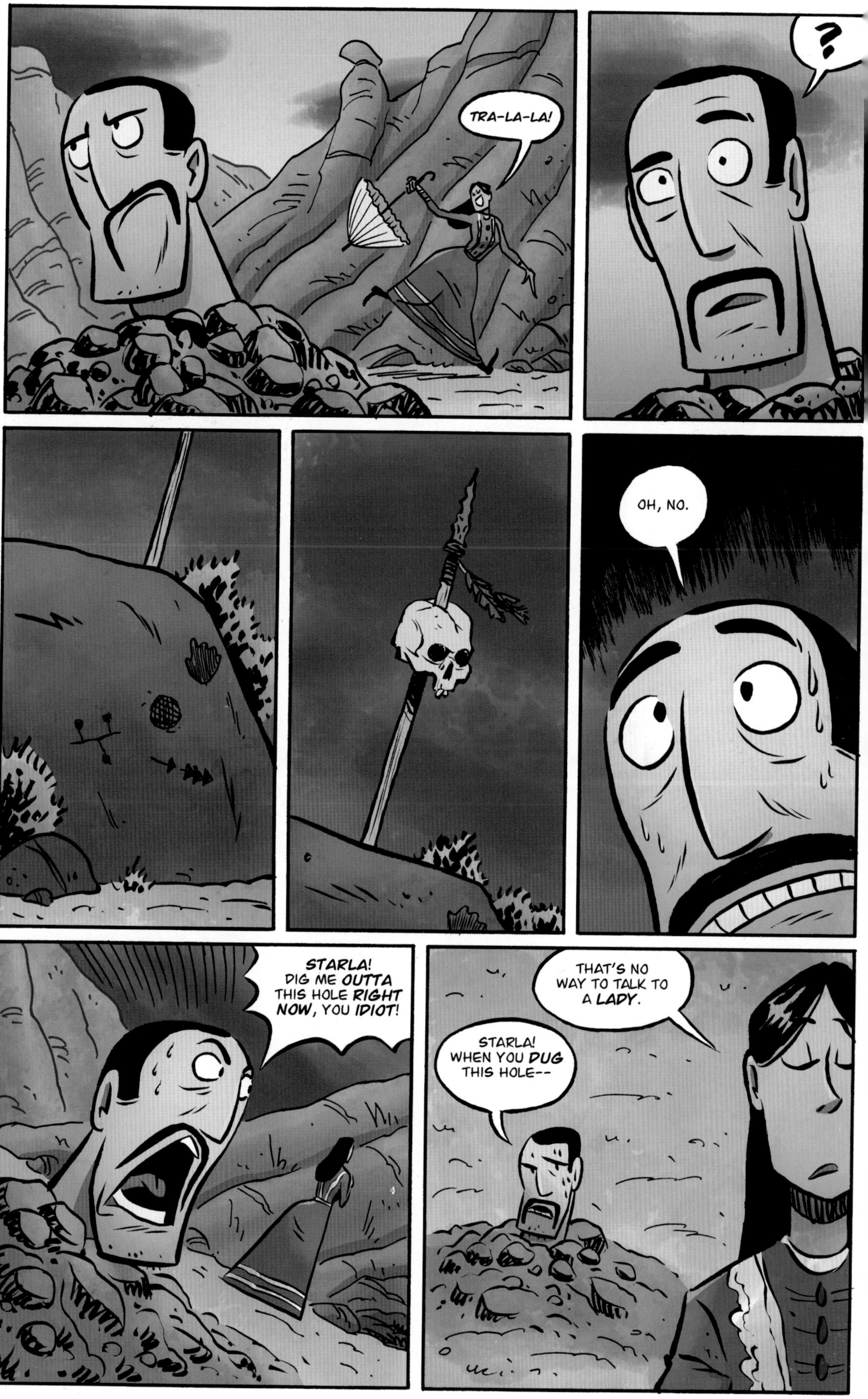
TRA-LA-LA!
?
OH, NO.
STARLA! DIG ME OUTTA THIS HOLE RIGHT NOW, YOU IDIOT!
THAT'S NO WAY TO TALK TO A LADY.
STARLA! WHEN YOU DUG THIS HOLE--

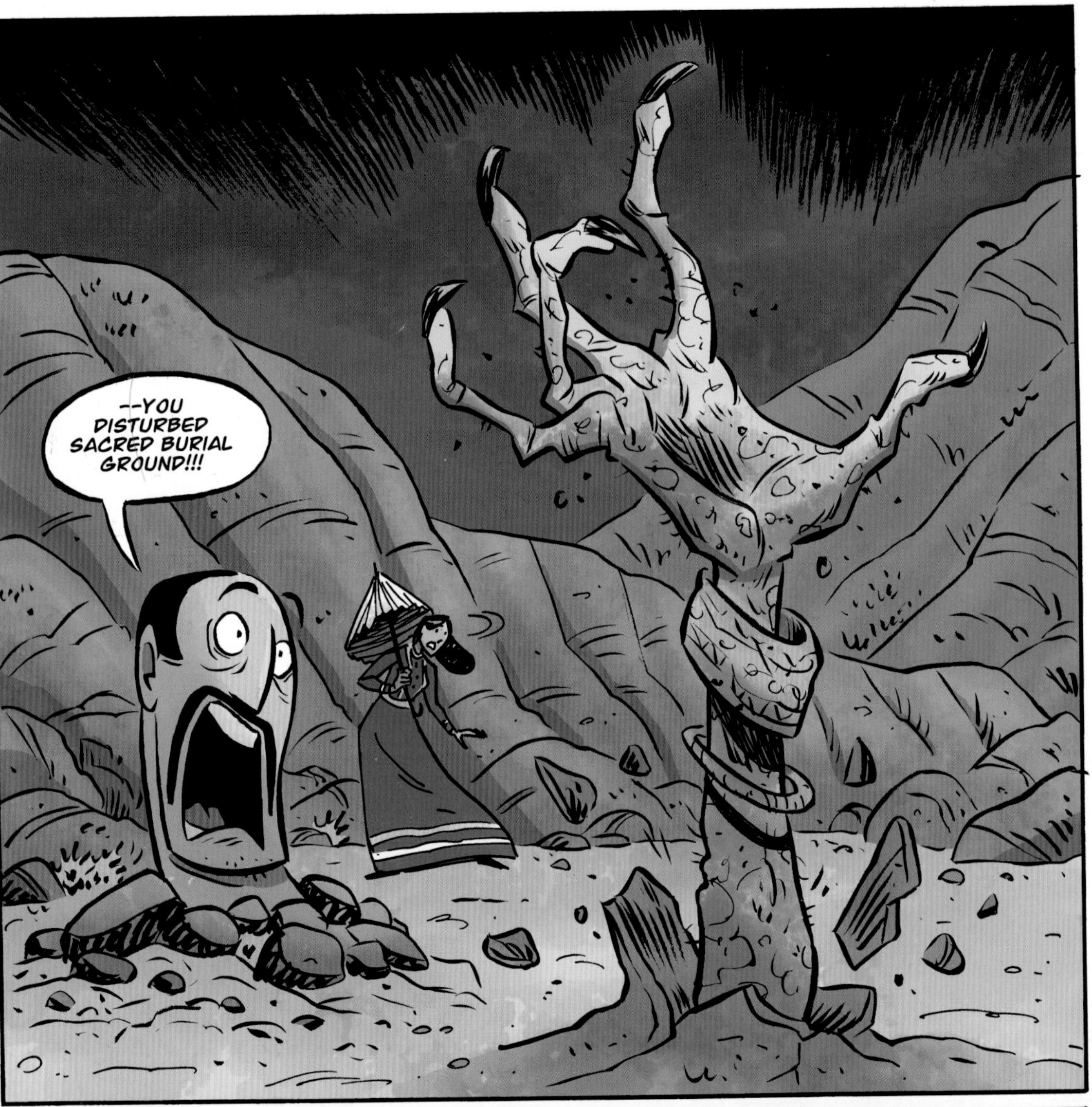
--YOU DISTURBED SACRED BURIAL GROUND!!!

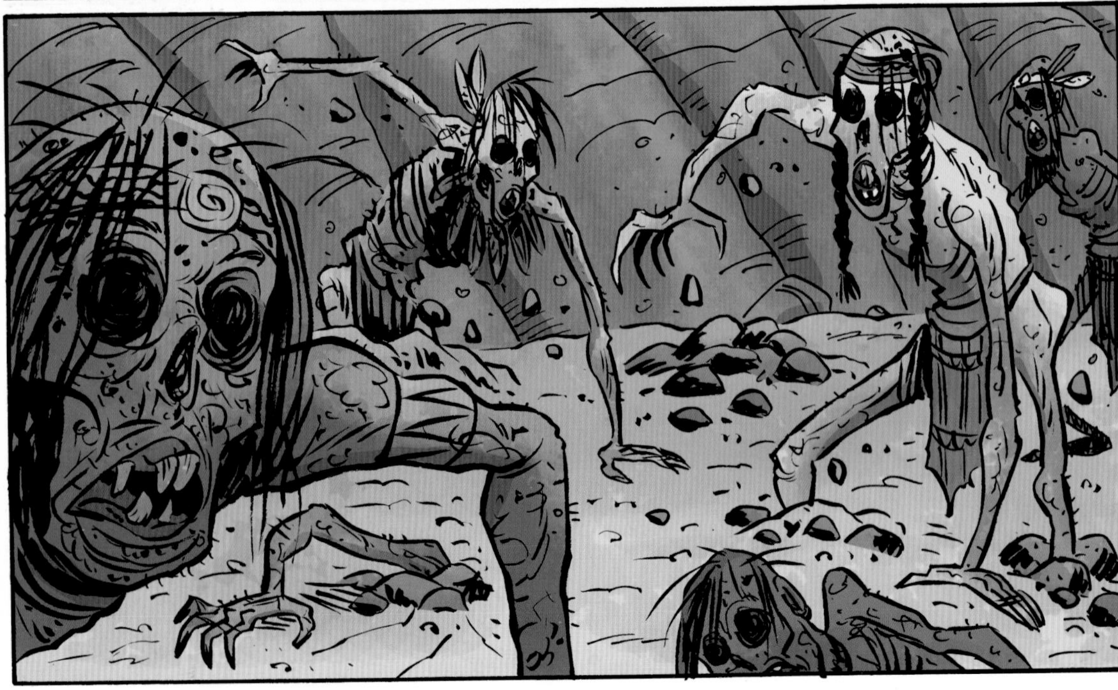

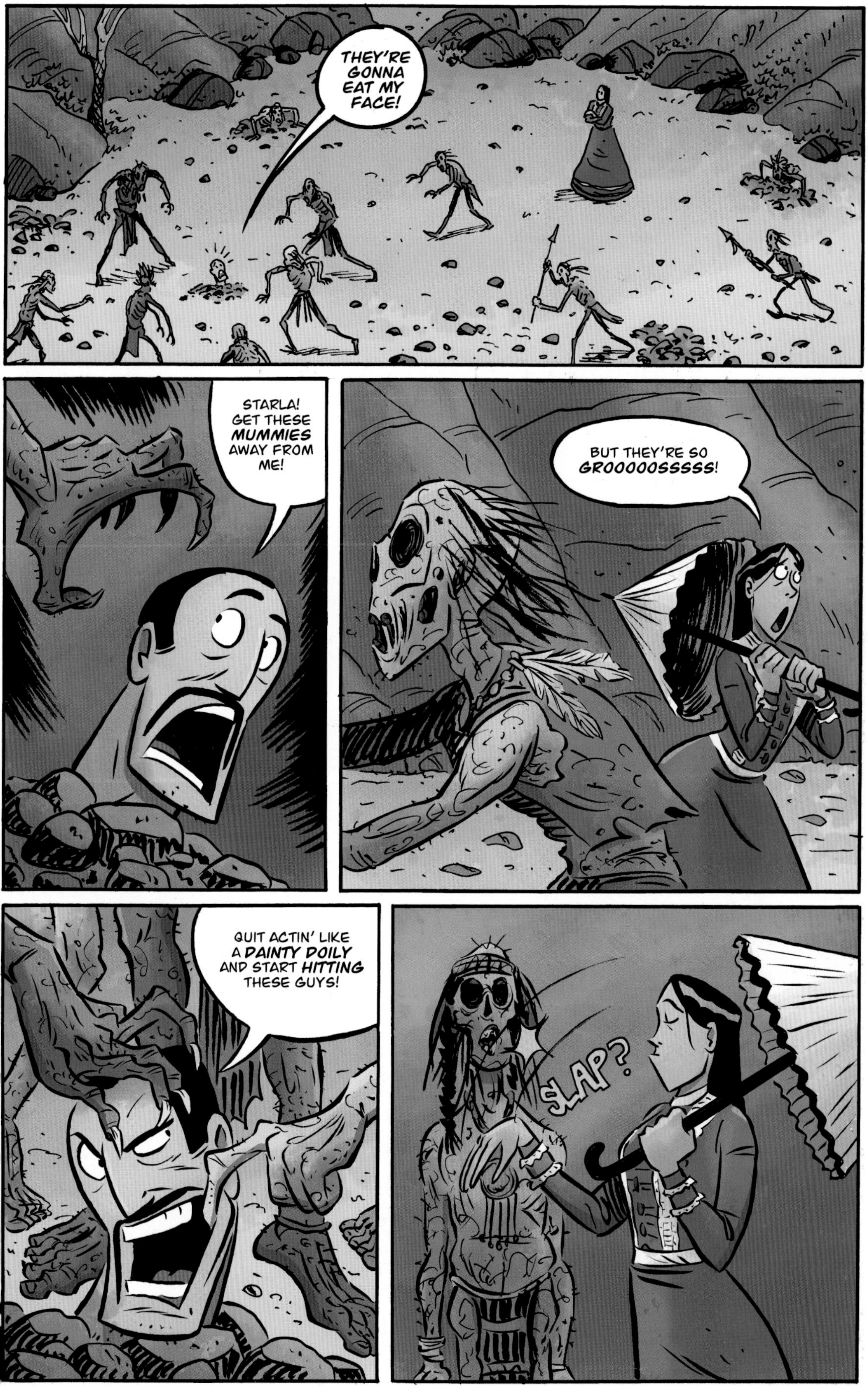
THEY'RE GONNA EAT MY FACE!
STARLA! GET THESE MUMMIES AWAY FROM ME!
BUT THEY'RE SO GROOOOOSSSSS!
QUIT ACTIN' LIKE A DAINTY DOILY AND START HITTING THESE GUYS!
SLAP?

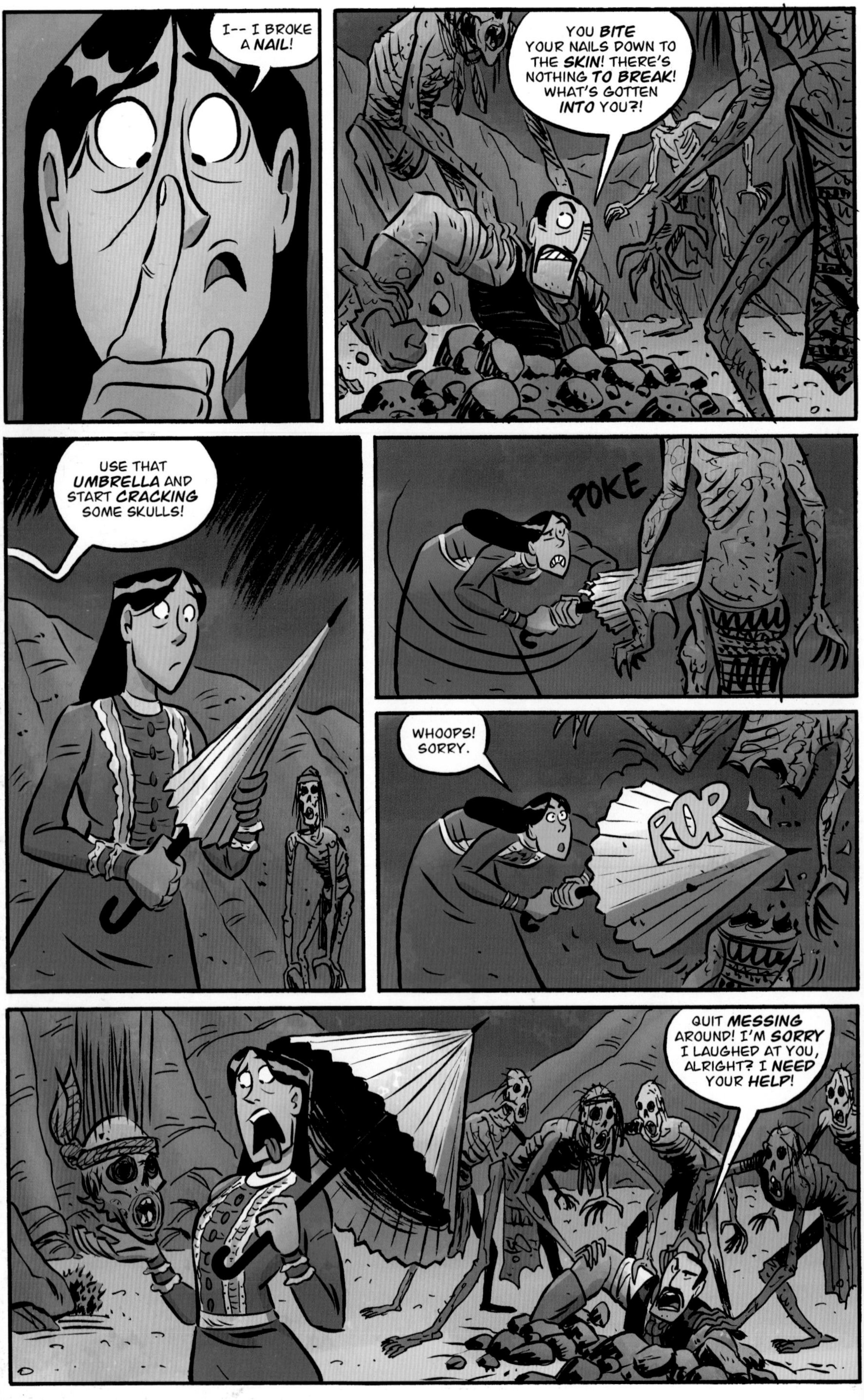
I-- I BROKE A NAIL!
YOU BITE YOUR NAILS DOWN TO THE SKIN! THERE'S NOTHING TO BREAK! WHAT'S GOTTEN INTO YOU?!
USE THAT UMBRELLA AND START CRACKING SOME SKULLS!
POKE
WHOOPS! SORRY.
POP
QUIT MESSING AROUND! I'M SORRY I LAUGHED AT YOU, ALRIGHT? I NEED YOUR HELP!

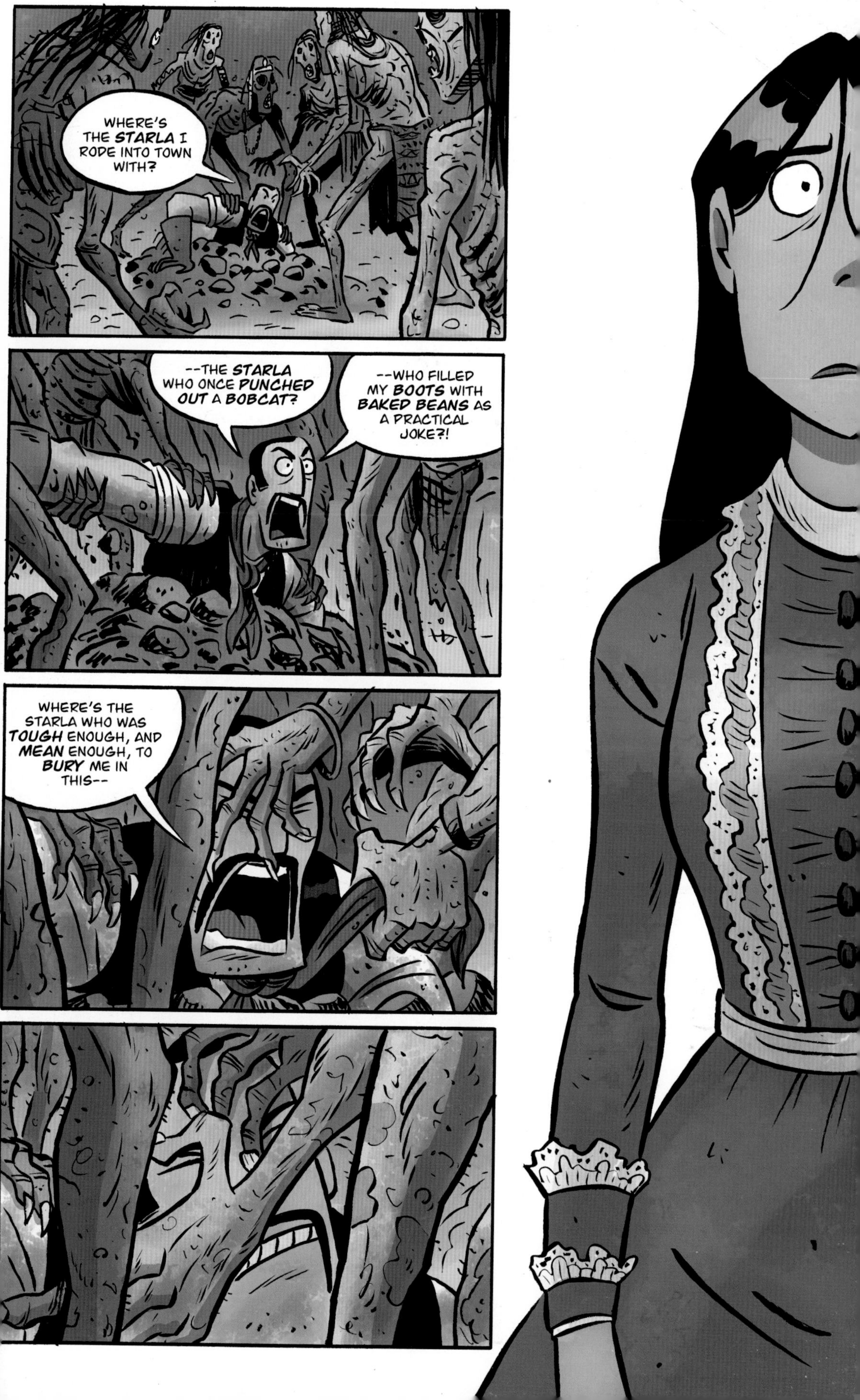
WHERE'S THE STARLA I RODE INTO TOWN WITH?
--THE STARLA WHO ONCE PUNCHED OUT A BOBCAT?
--WHO FILLED MY BOOTS WITH BAKED BEANS AS A PRACTICAL JOKE?!
WHERE'S THE STARLA WHO WAS TOUGH ENOUGH, AND MEAN ENOUGH, TO BURY ME IN THIS--

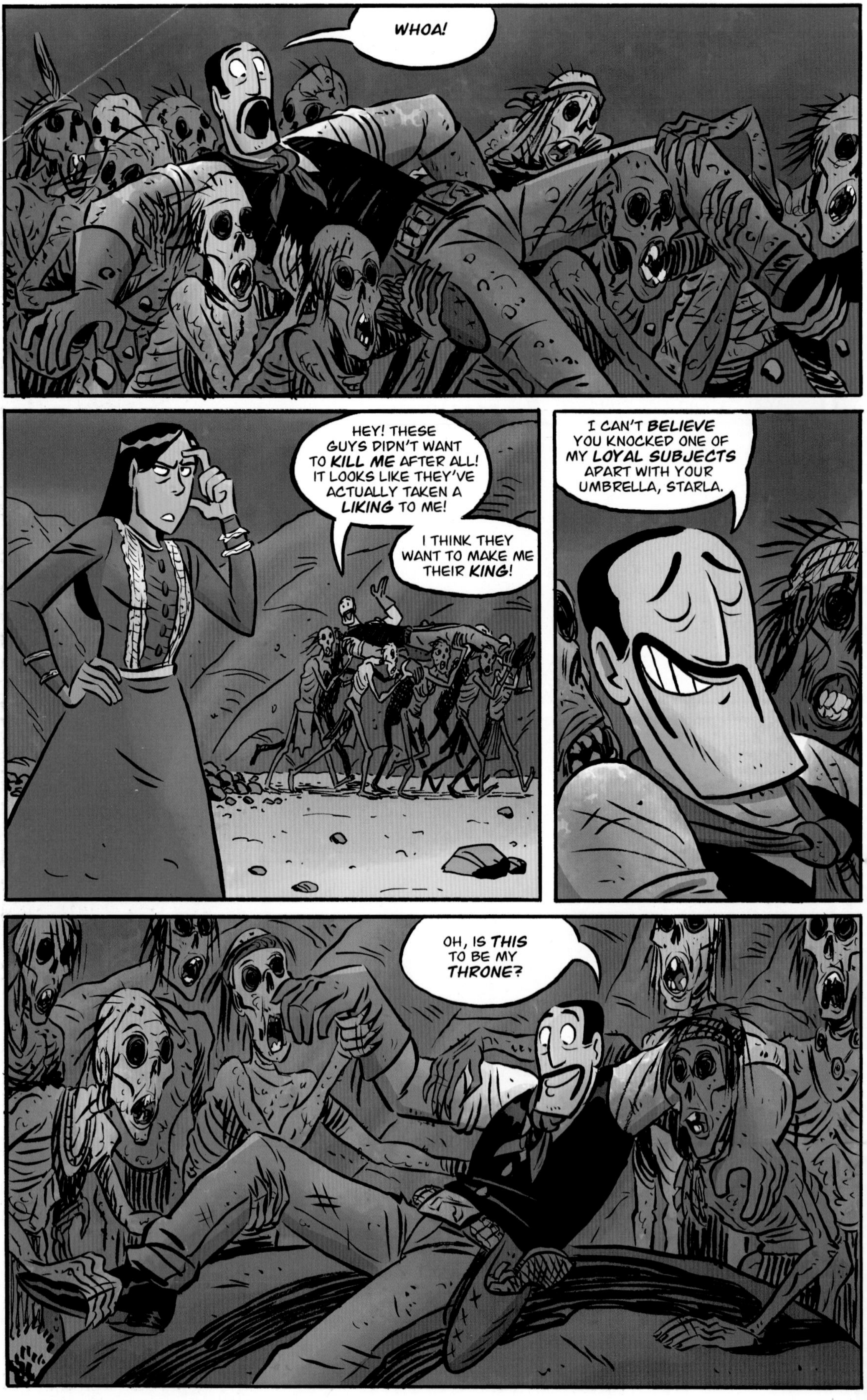
WHOA!
HEY! THESE GUYS DIDN'T WANT TO KILL ME AFTER ALL! IT LOOKS LIKE THEY'VE ACTUALLY TAKEN A LIKING TO ME!
I THINK THEY WANT TO MAKE ME THEIR KING!
I CAN'T BELIEVE YOU KNOCKED ONE OF MY LOYAL SUBJECTS APART WITH YOUR UMBRELLA, STARLA.
OH, IS THIS TO BE MY THRONE?

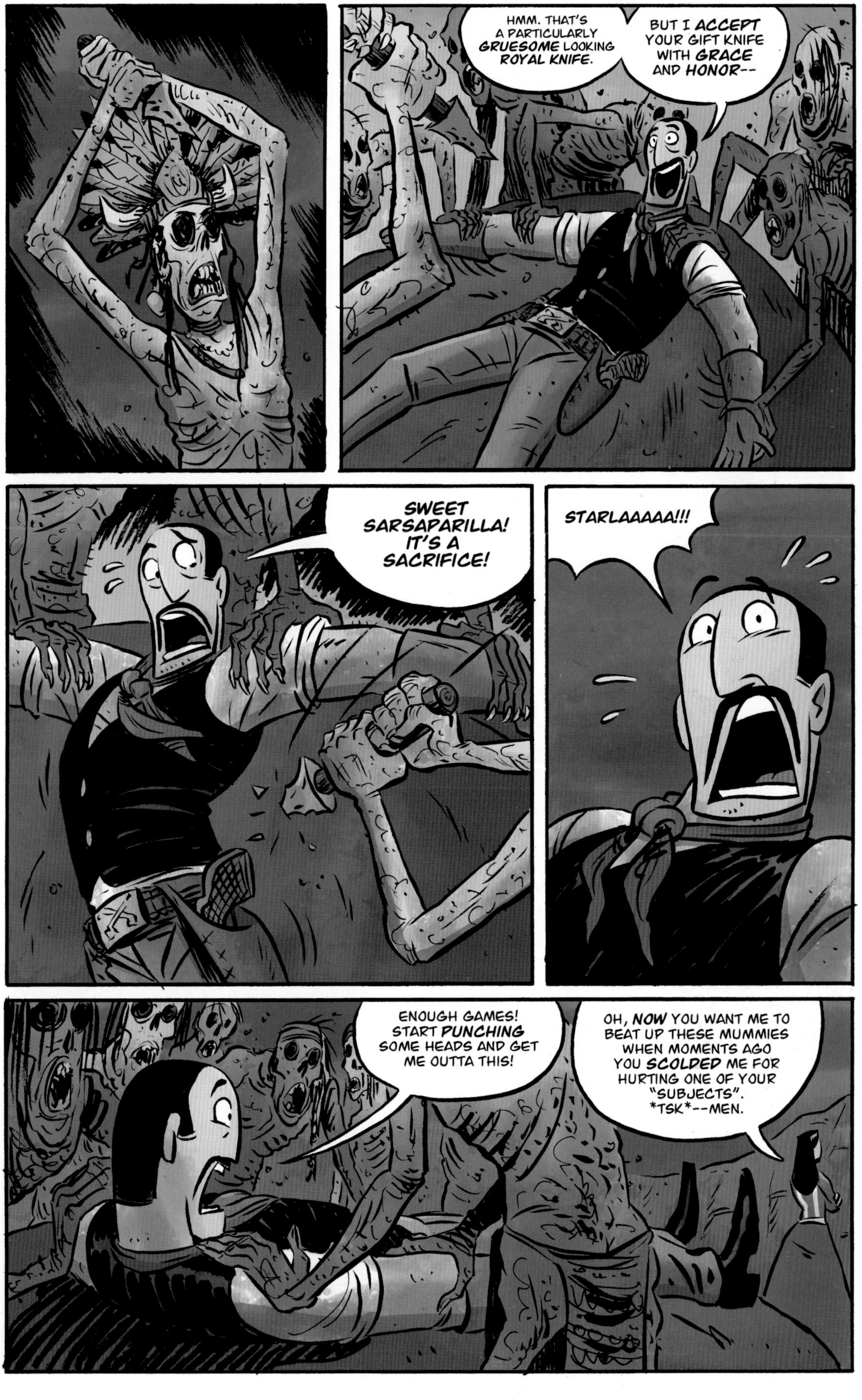
HMM. THAT'S A PARTICULARLY GRUESOME LOOKING ROYAL KNIFE.
BUT I ACCEPT YOUR GIFT KNIFE WITH GRACE AND HONOR--
SWEET SARSAPARILLA! IT'S A SACRIFICE!
STARLAAAAA!!!
ENOUGH GAMES! START PUNCHING SOME HEADS AND GET ME OUTTA THIS!
OH, NOW YOU WANT ME TO BEAT UP THESE MUMMIES WHEN MOMENTS AGO YOU SCOLDED ME FOR HURTING ONE OF YOUR "SUBJECTS". *TSK*--MEN.

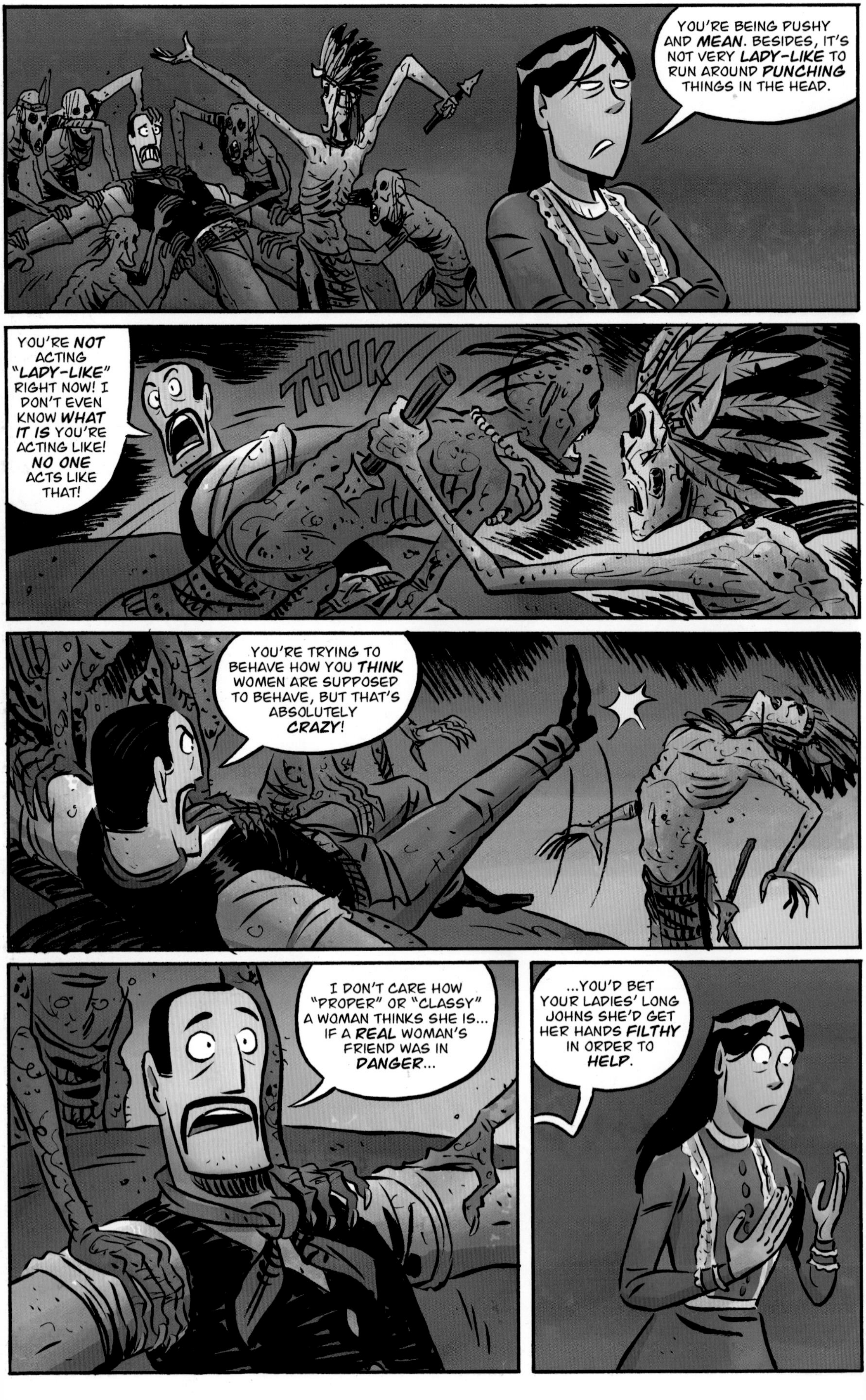
YOU'RE BEING PUSHY AND MEAN. BESIDES, IT'S NOT VERY LADY-LIKE TO RUN AROUND PUNCHING THINGS IN THE HEAD.
YOU'RE NOT ACTING "LADY-LIKE" RIGHT NOW! I DON'T EVEN KNOW WHAT IT IS YOU'RE ACTING LIKE! NO ONE ACTS LIKE THAT!
THUK
YOU'RE TRYING TO BEHAVE HOW YOU THINK WOMEN ARE SUPPOSED TO BEHAVE, BUT THAT'S ABSOLUTELY CRAZY!
I DON'T CARE HOW "PROPER" OR "CLASSY" A WOMAN THINKS SHE IS... IF A REAL WOMAN'S FRIEND WAS IN DANGER...
...YOU'D BET YOUR LADIES' LONG JOHNS SHE'D GET HER HANDS FILTHY IN ORDER TO HELP.

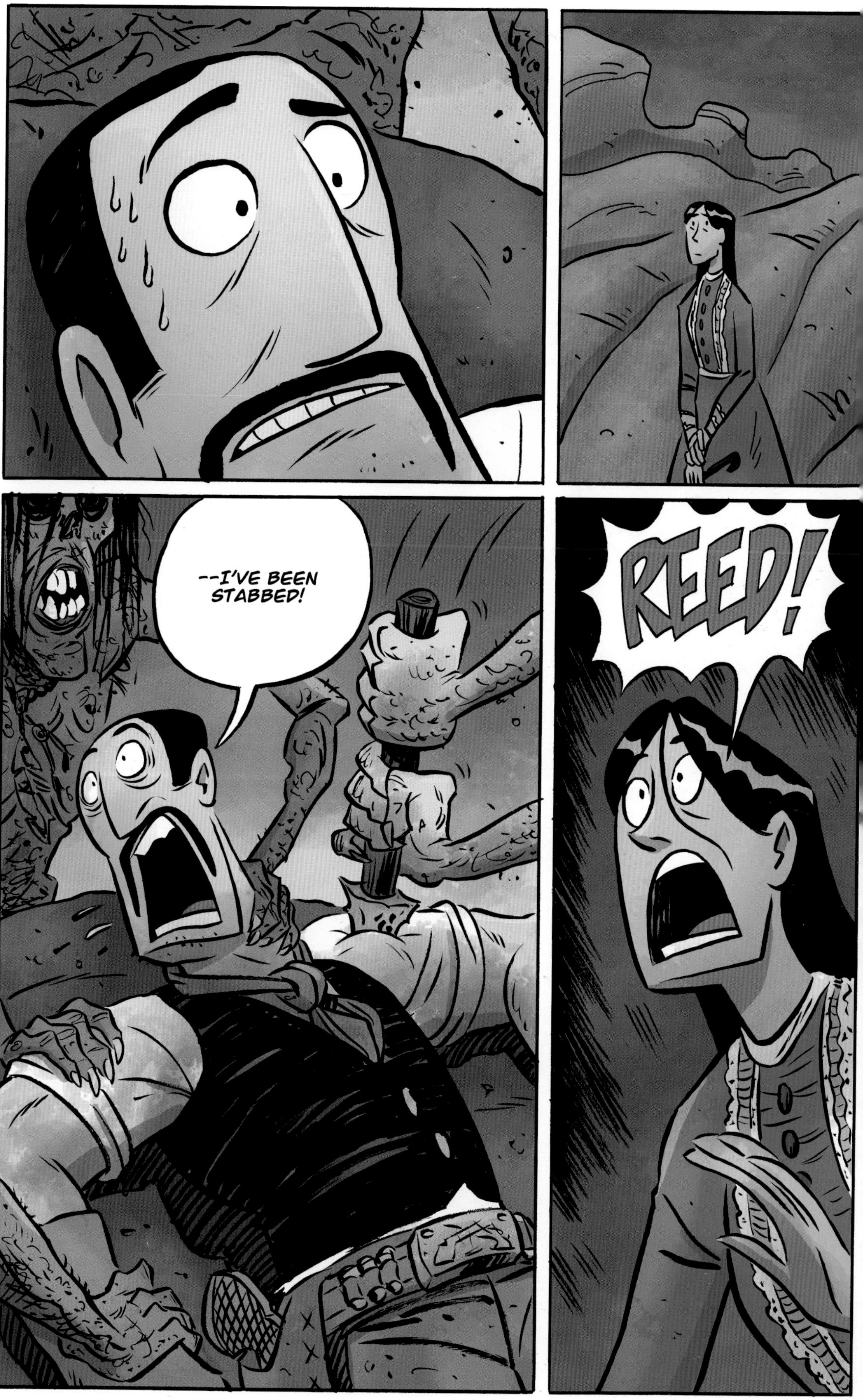
--I'VE BEEN STABBED!
REED!

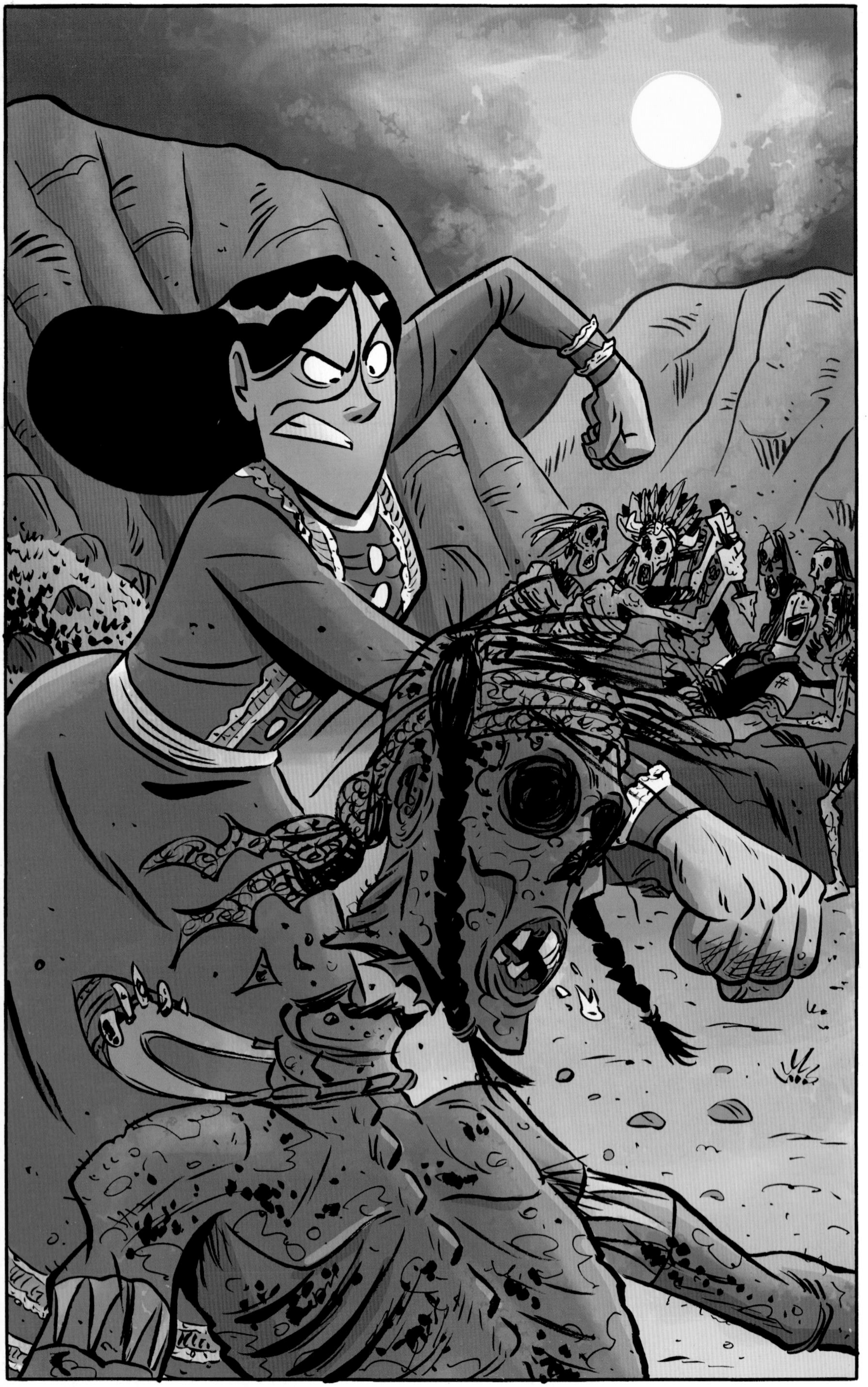

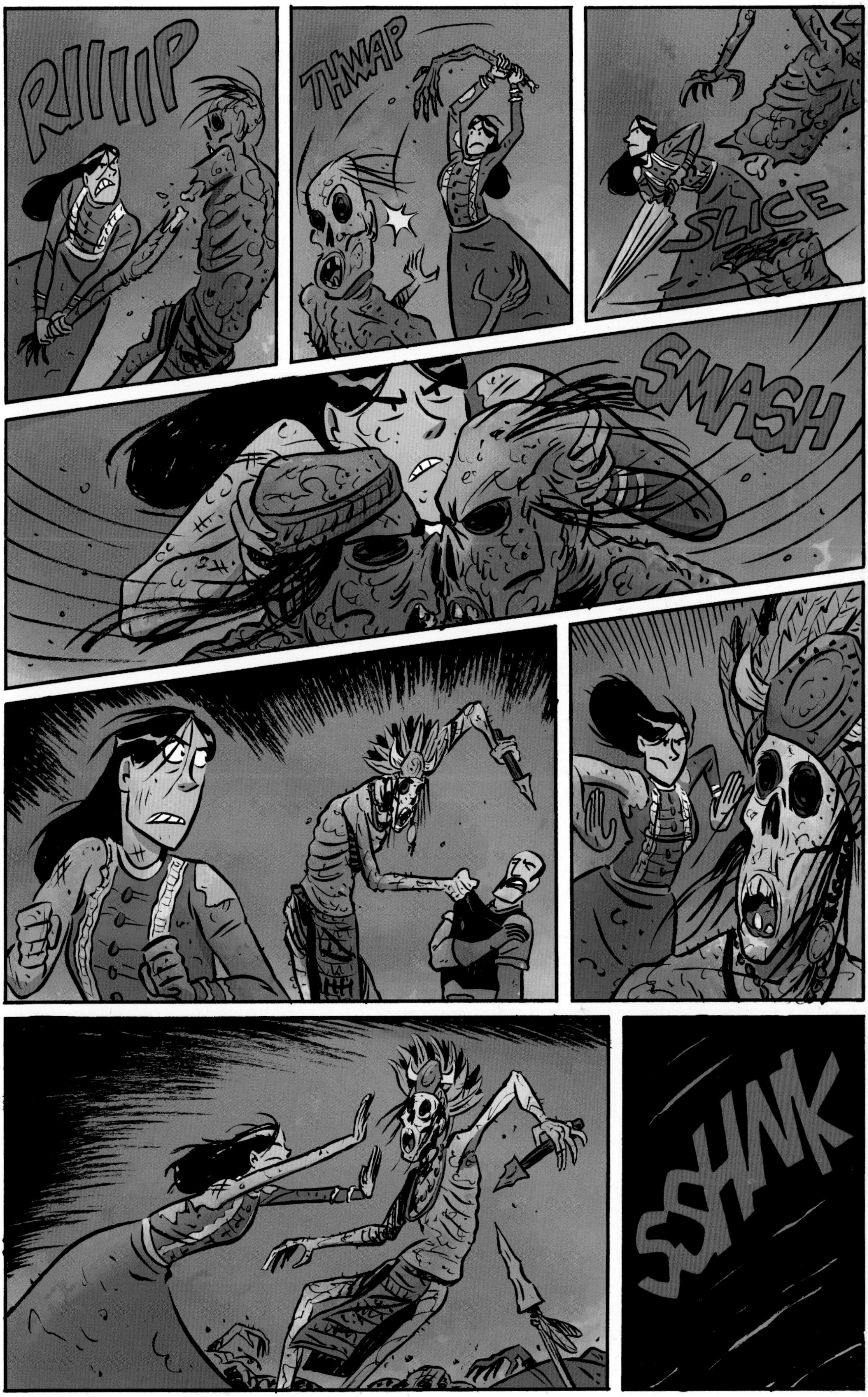
RIIIIP
THWAP
SLICE
SMASH
SHHNK

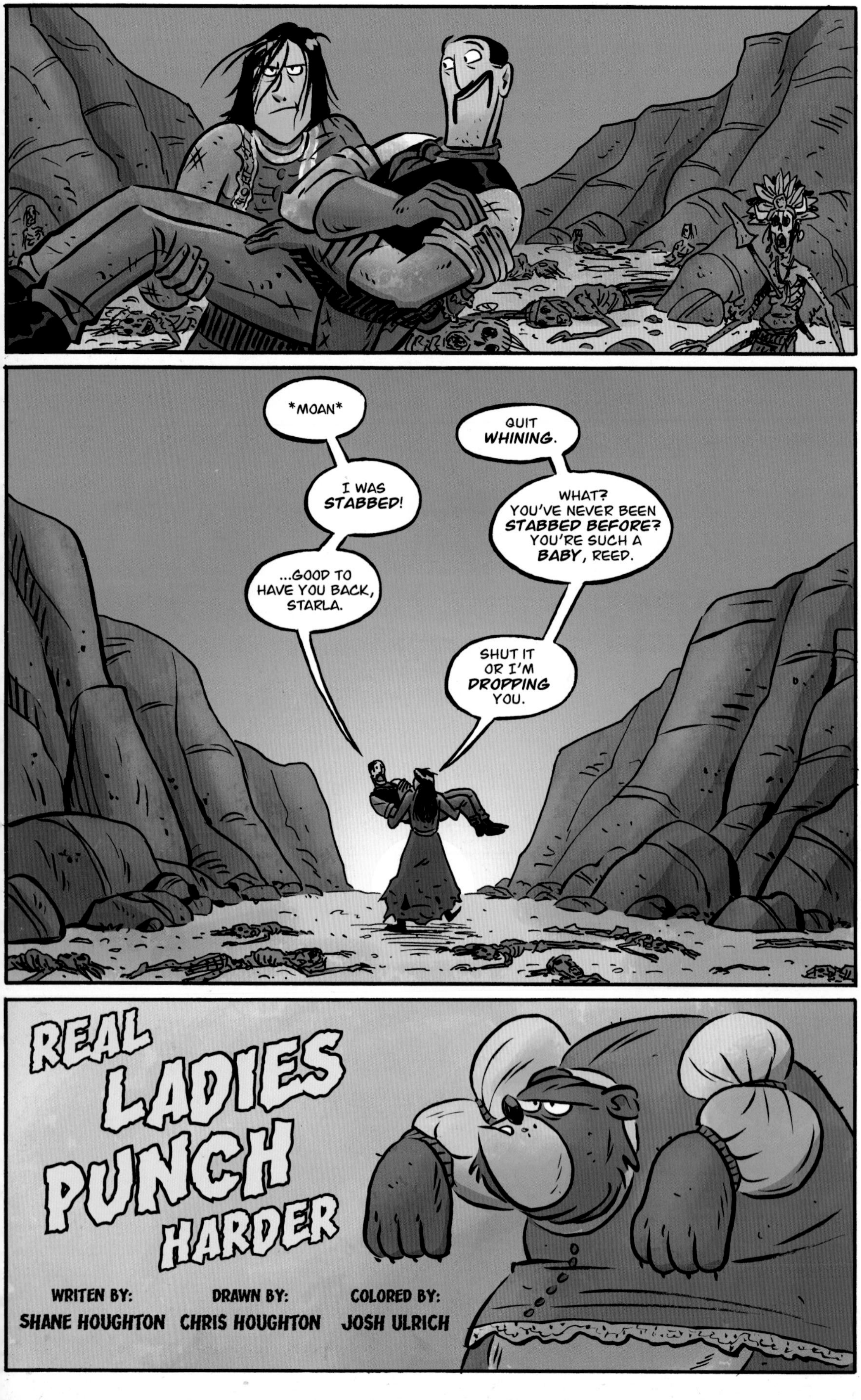
MOAN
I WAS STABBED!
...GOOD TO HAVE YOU BACK, STARLA.
QUIT WHINING.
WHAT? YOU'VE NEVER BEEN STABBED BEFORE? YOU'RE SUCH A BABY, REED.
SHUT IT OR I'M DROPPING YOU.
REAL LADIES PUNCH HARDER
WRITEN BY: SHANE HOUGHTON
DRAWN BY: CHRIS HOUGHTON
COLORED BY: JOSH ULRICH

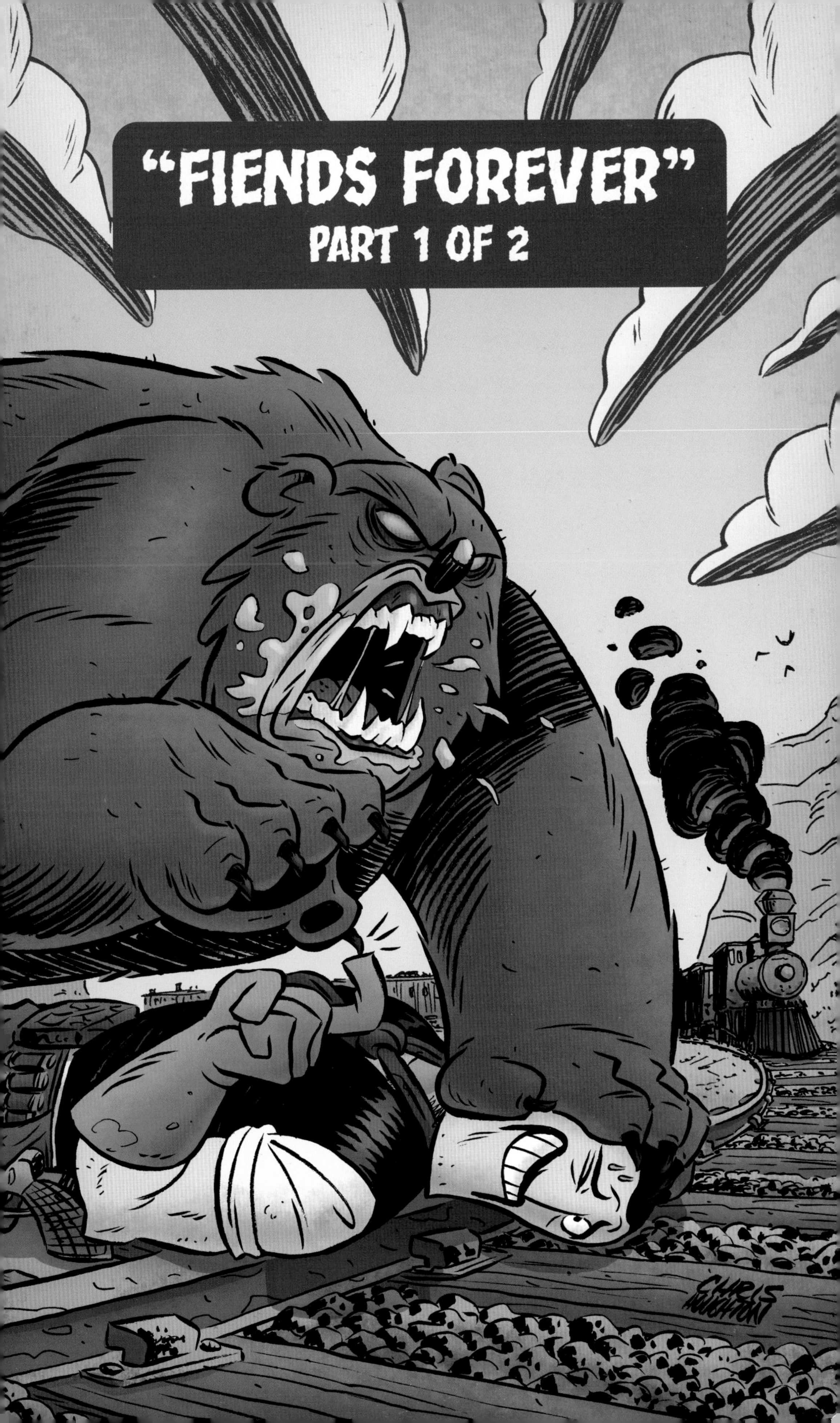

"FIENDS FOREVER"
PART 1 OF 2
CHRIS HOUGHTON

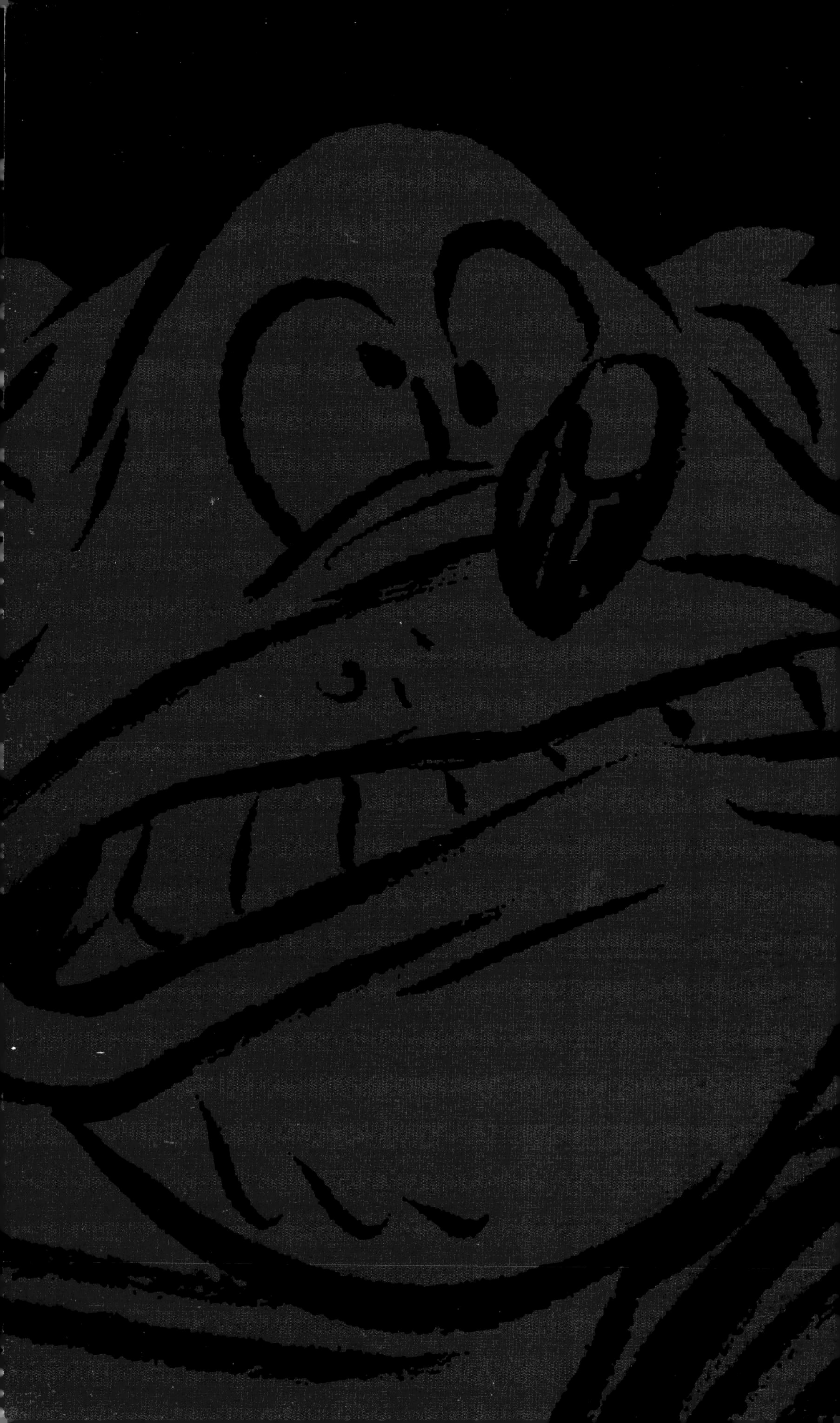

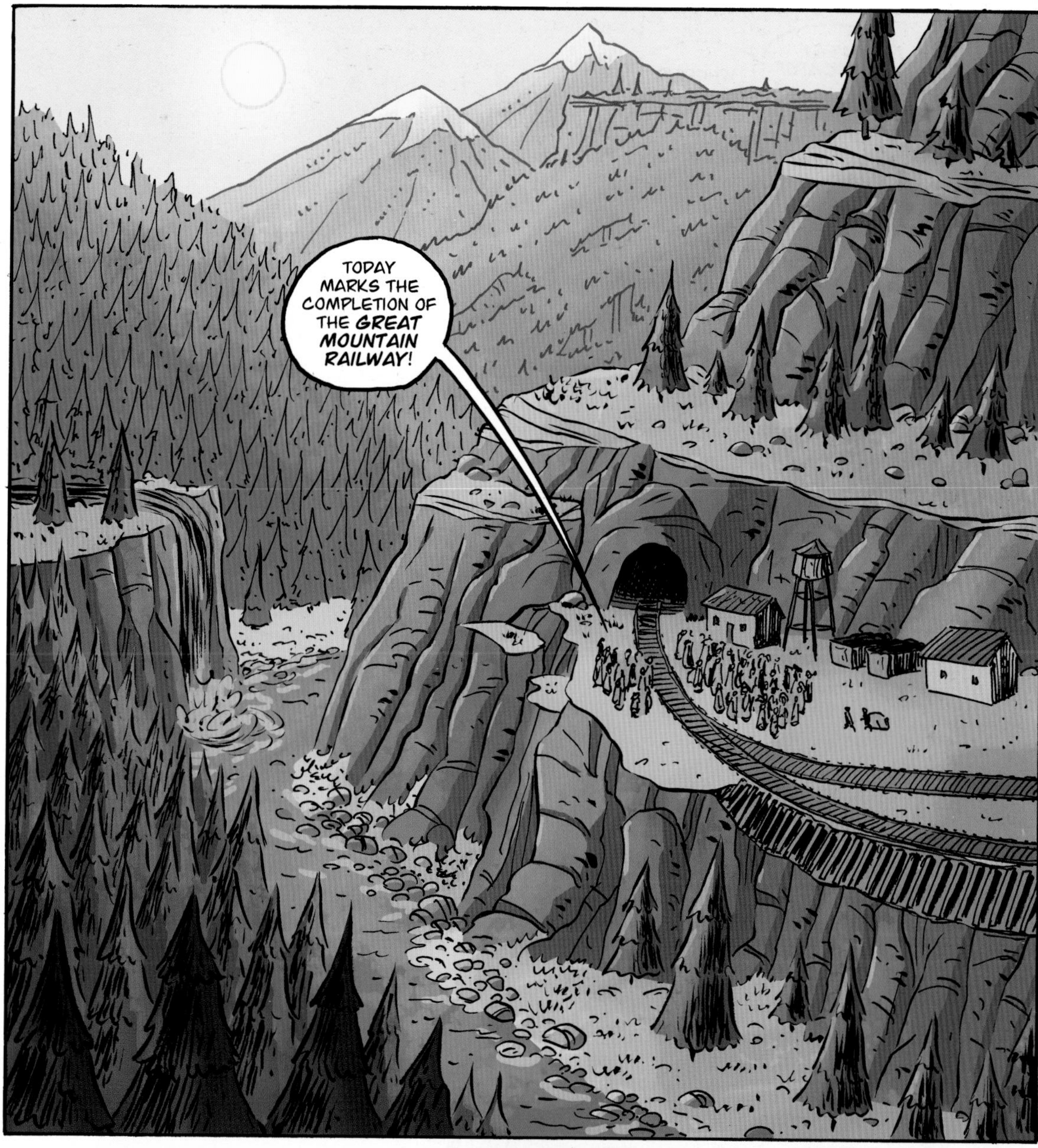
TODAY MARKS THE COMPLETION OF THE GREAT MOUNTAIN RAILWAY!

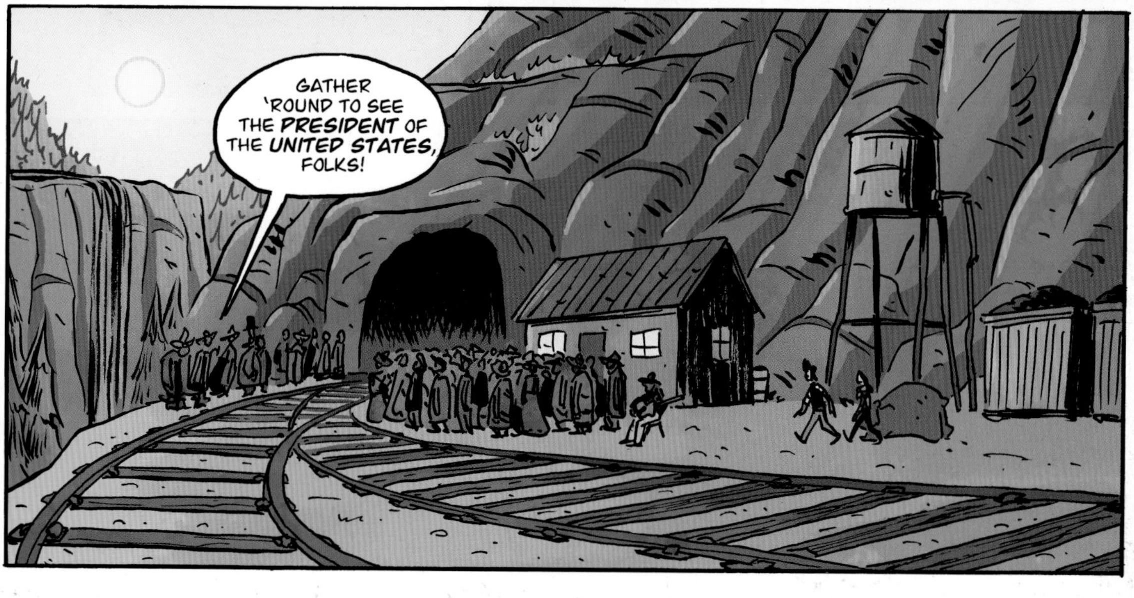
GATHER 'ROUND TO SEE THE PRESIDENT OF THE UNITED STATES, FOLKS!

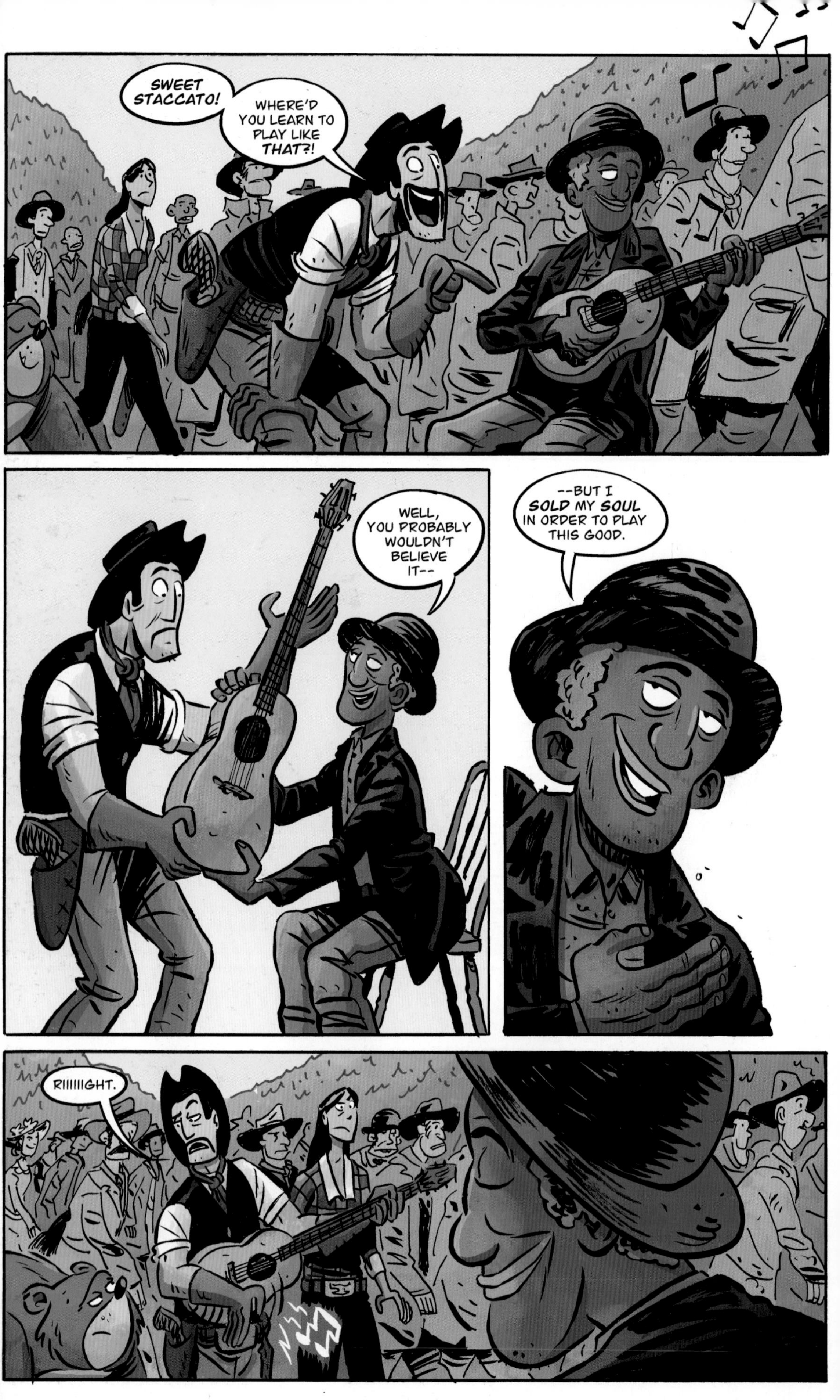
SWEET STACCATO!
WHERE'D YOU LEARN TO PLAY LIKE THAT?!
WELL, YOU PROBABLY WOULDN'T BELIEVE IT--
--BUT I SOLD MY SOUL IN ORDER TO PLAY THIS GOOD.
RIIIIIGHT.

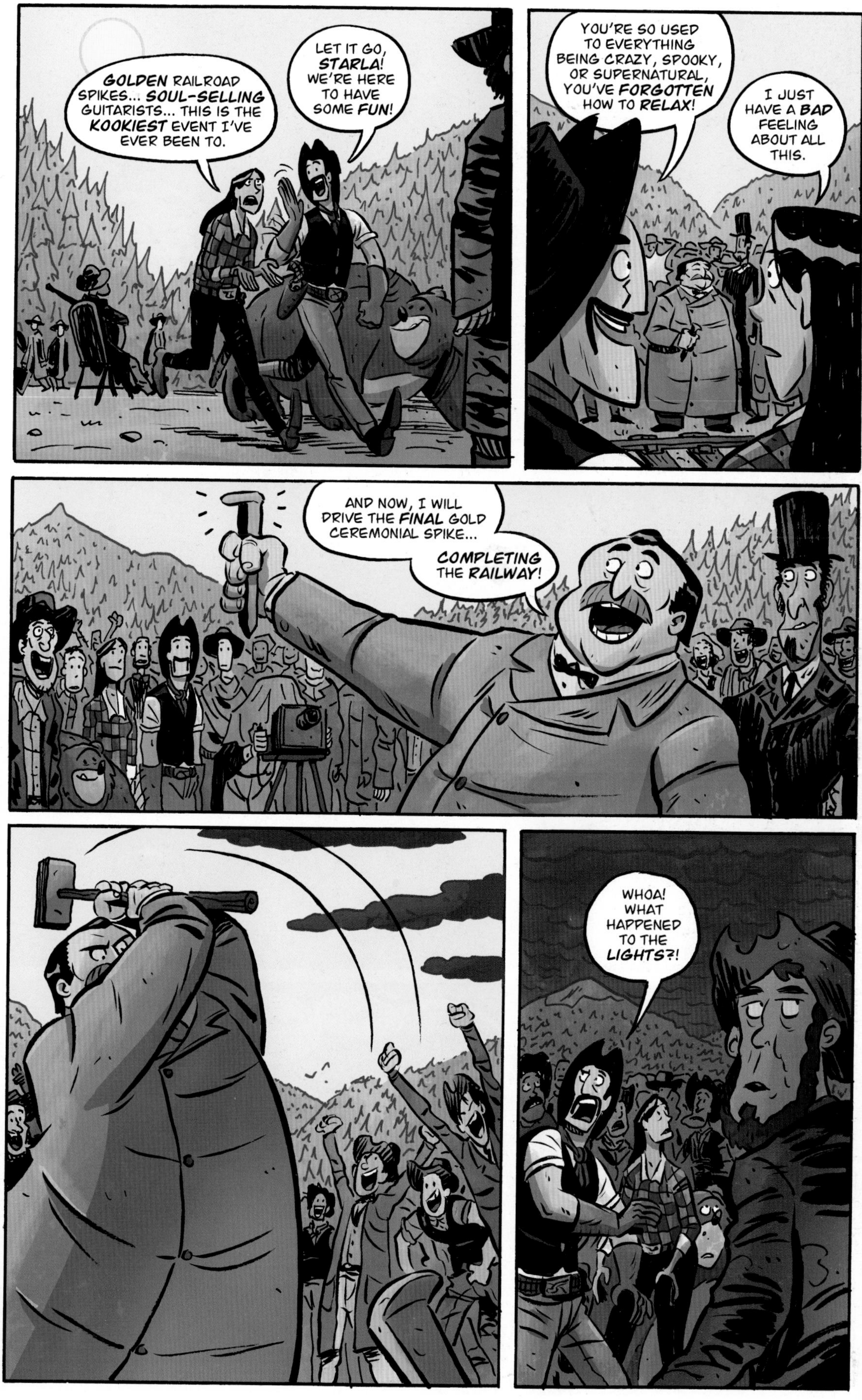
GOLDEN RAILROAD SPIKES... SOUL-SELLING GUITARISTS... THIS IS THE KOOKIEST EVENT I'VE EVER BEEN TO.
LET IT GO, STARLA! WE'RE HERE TO HAVE SOME FUN!
YOU'RE SO USED TO EVERYTHING BEING CRAZY, SPOOKY, OR SUPERNATURAL, YOU'VE FORGOTTEN HOW TO RELAX!
I JUST HAVE A BAD FEELING ABOUT ALL THIS.
AND NOW, I WILL DRIVE THE FINAL GOLD CEREMONIAL SPIKE...
COMPLETING THE RAILWAY!
WHOA! WHAT HAPPENED TO THE LIGHTS?!

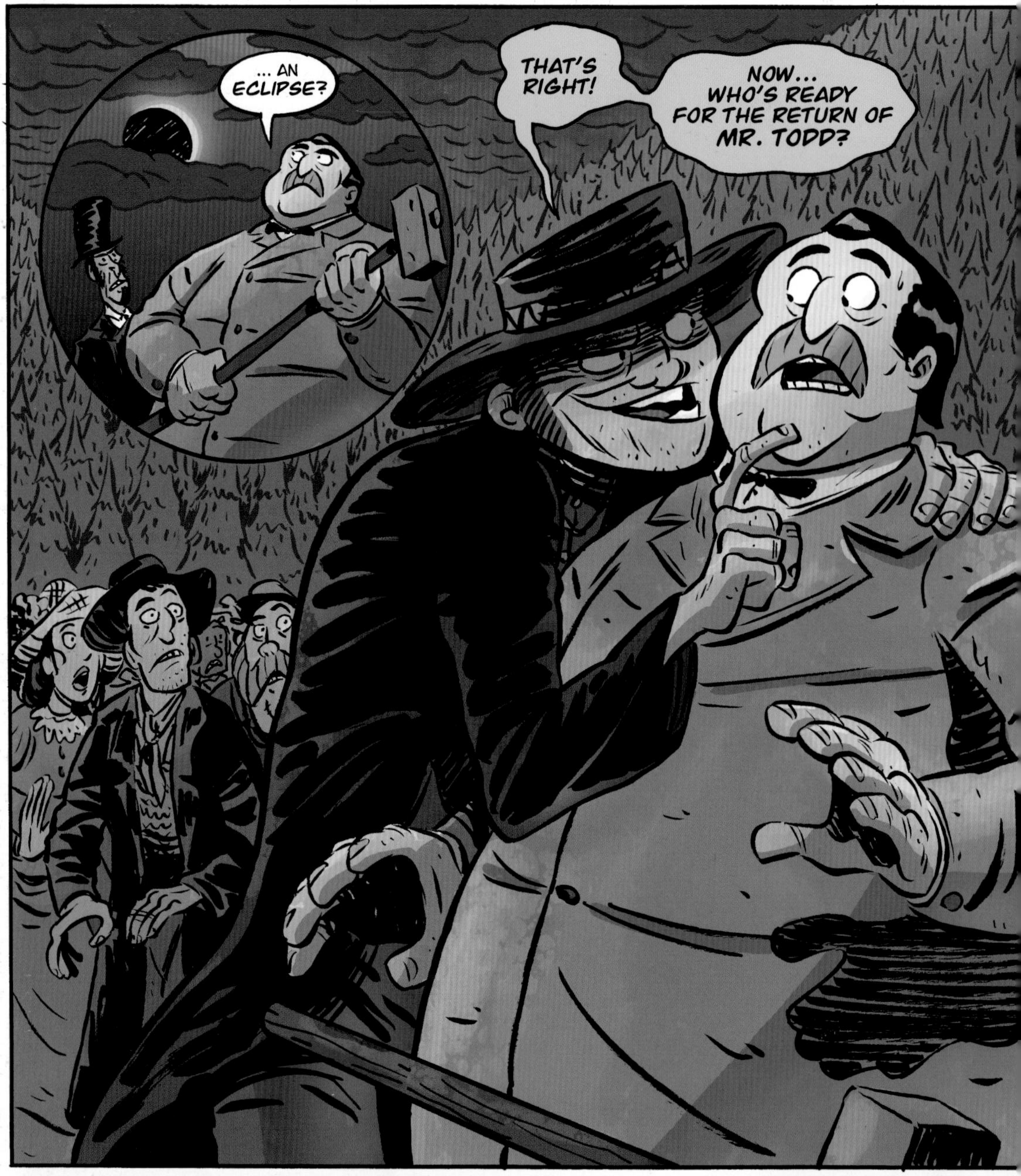
... AN ECLIPSE?
THAT'S RIGHT!
NOW... WHO'S READY FOR THE RETURN OF MR. TODD?

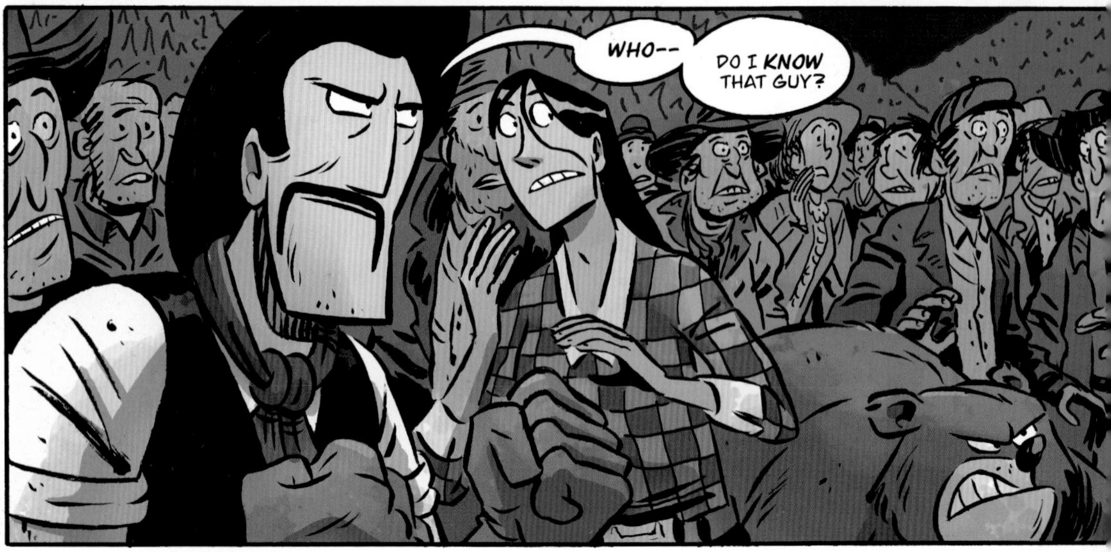
WHO--
DO I KNOW THAT GUY?

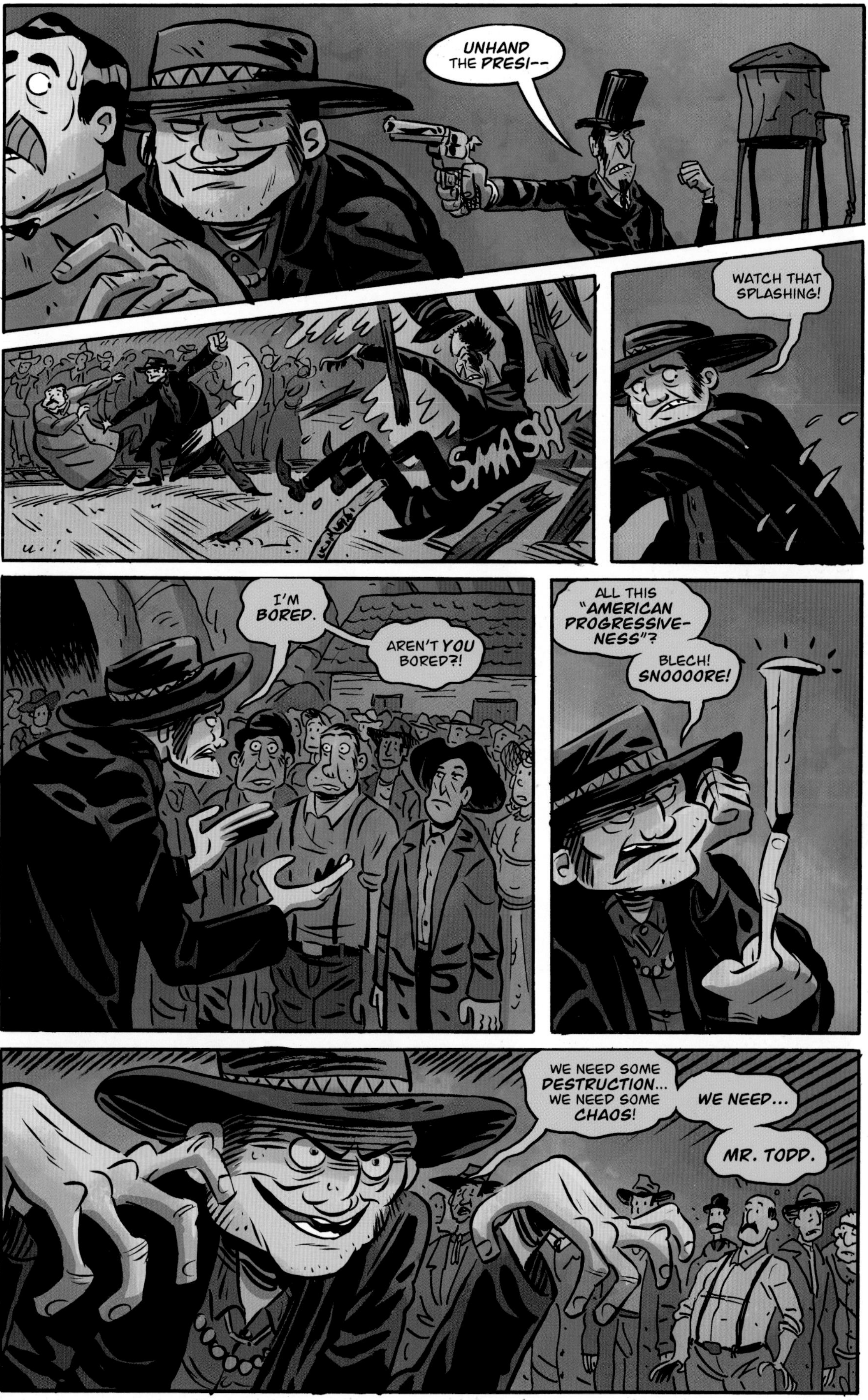
UNHAND THE PRESI--
SMASH
WATCH THAT SPLASHING!
I'M BORED.
AREN'T YOU BORED?!
ALL THIS "AMERICAN PROGRESSIVENESS"?
BLECH! SNOOOORE!
WE NEED SOME DESTRUCTION... WE NEED SOME CHAOS!
WE NEED...
MR. TODD.

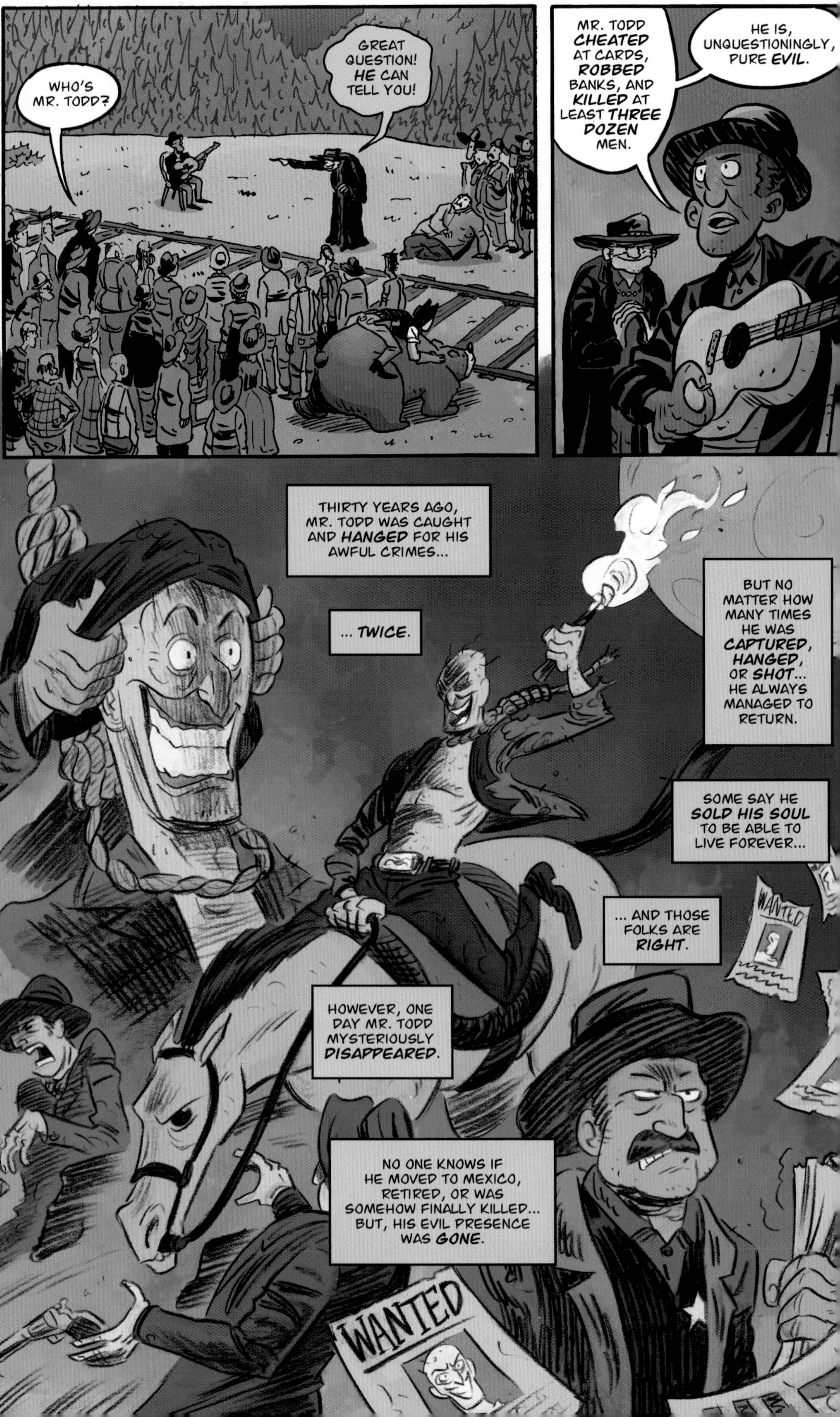
WHO'S MR. TODD?
GREAT QUESTION! HE CAN TELL YOU!
MR. TODD CHEATED AT CARDS, ROBBED BANKS, AND KILLED AT LEAST THREE DOZEN MEN.
HE IS, UNQUESTIONINGLY, PURE EVIL.
THIRTY YEARS AGO, MR. TODD WAS CAUGHT AND HANGED FOR HIS AWFUL CRIMES...
... TWICE.
BUT NO MATTER HOW MANY TIMES HE WAS CAPTURED, HANGED, OR SHOT... HE ALWAYS MANAGED TO RETURN.
SOME SAY HE SOLD HIS SOUL TO BE ABLE TO LIVE FOREVER...
... AND THOSE FOLKS ARE RIGHT.
WANTED
HOWEVER, ONE DAY MR. TODD MYSTERIOUSLY DISAPPEARED.
NO ONE KNOWS IF HE MOVED TO MEXICO, RETIRED, OR WAS SOMEHOW FINALLY KILLED... BUT, HIS EVIL PRESENCE WAS GONE.
WANTED

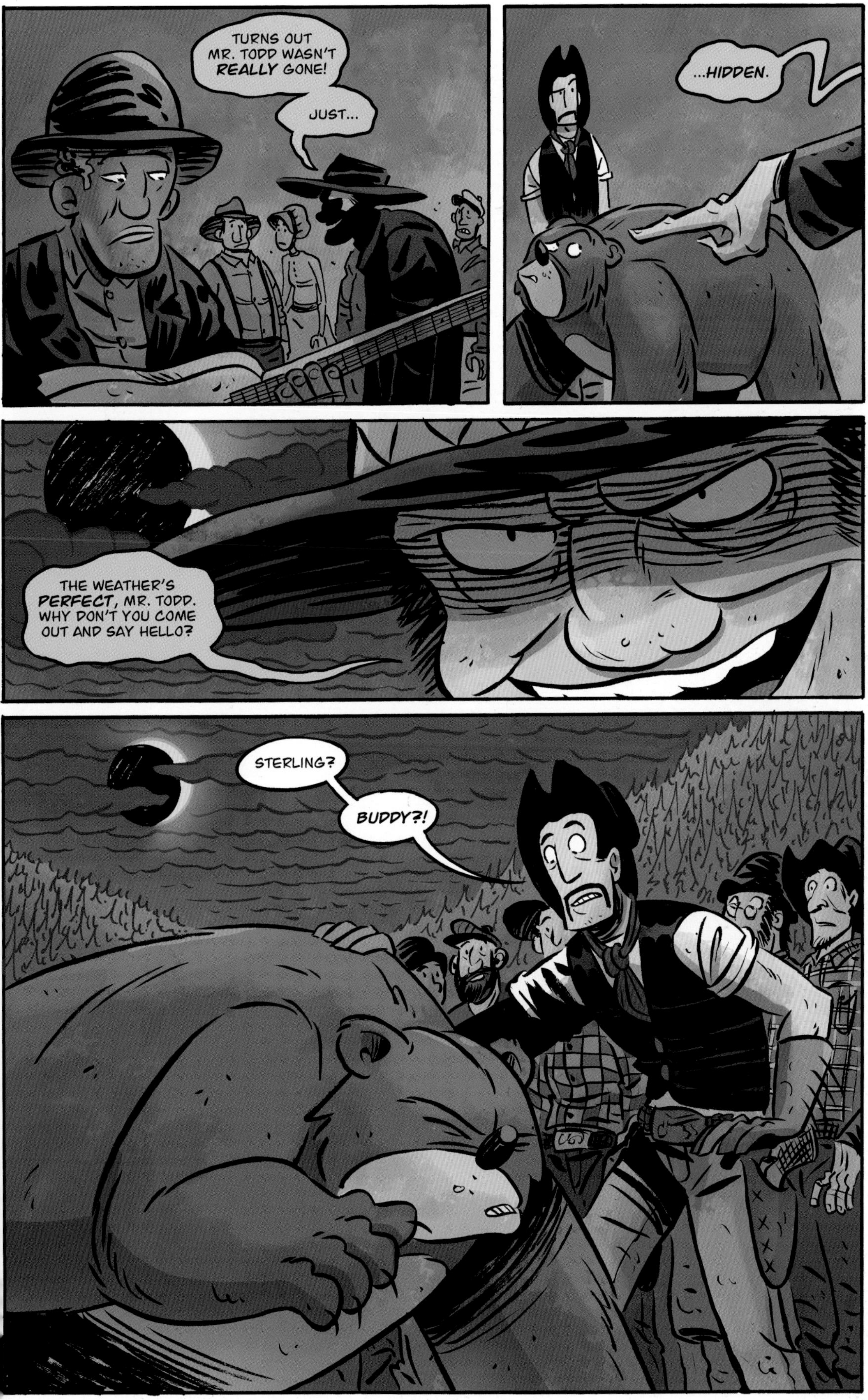
TURNS OUT MR. TODD WASN'T REALLY GONE!
JUST...
...HIDDEN.
THE WEATHER'S PERFECT, MR. TODD. WHY DON'T YOU COME OUT AND SAY HELLO?
STERLING?
BUDDY?!

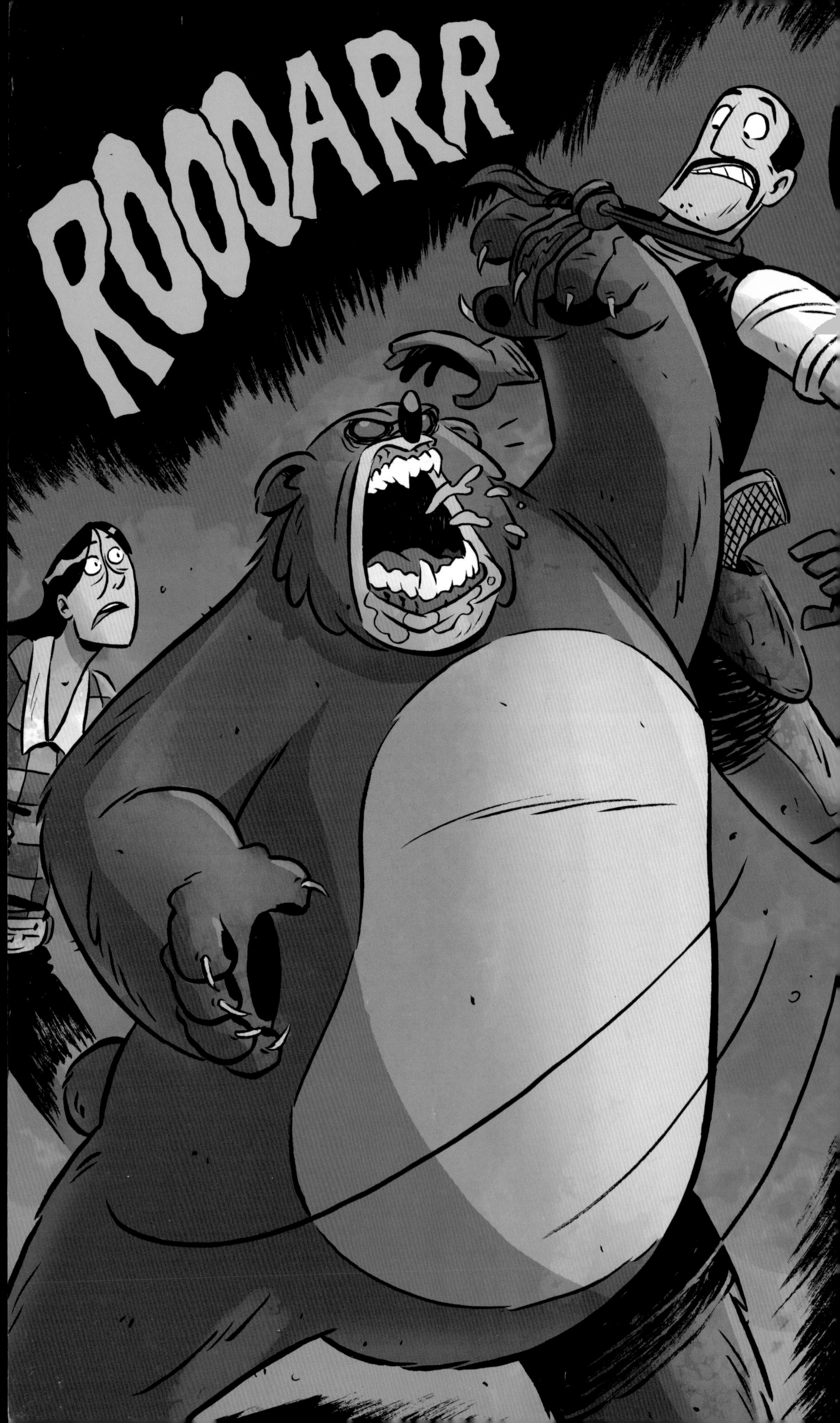
ROOOARR

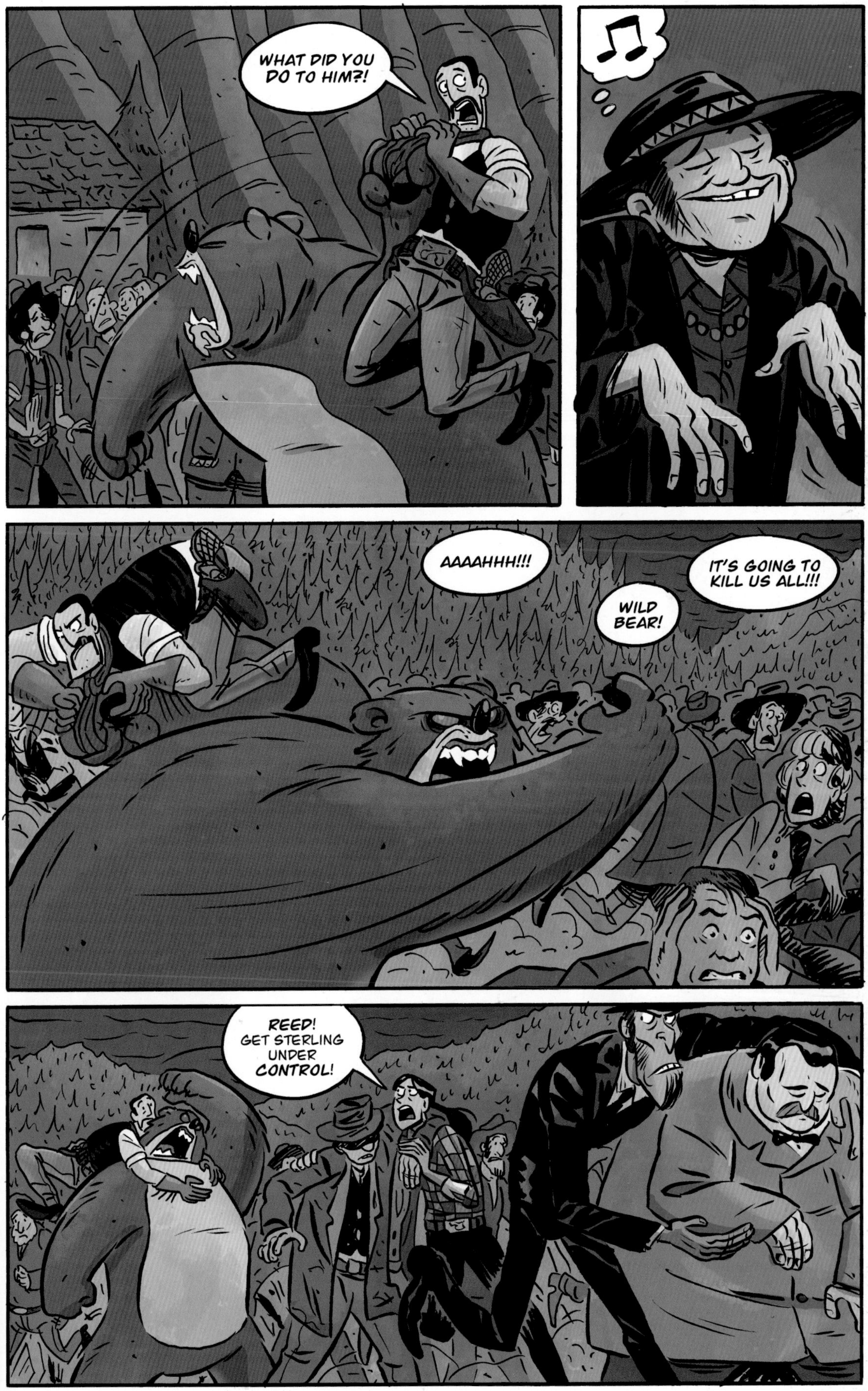
WHAT DID YOU DO TO HIM?!
♫
AAAAHHH!!!
IT'S GOING TO KILL US ALL!!!
WILD BEAR!
REED! GET STERLING UNDER CONTROL!

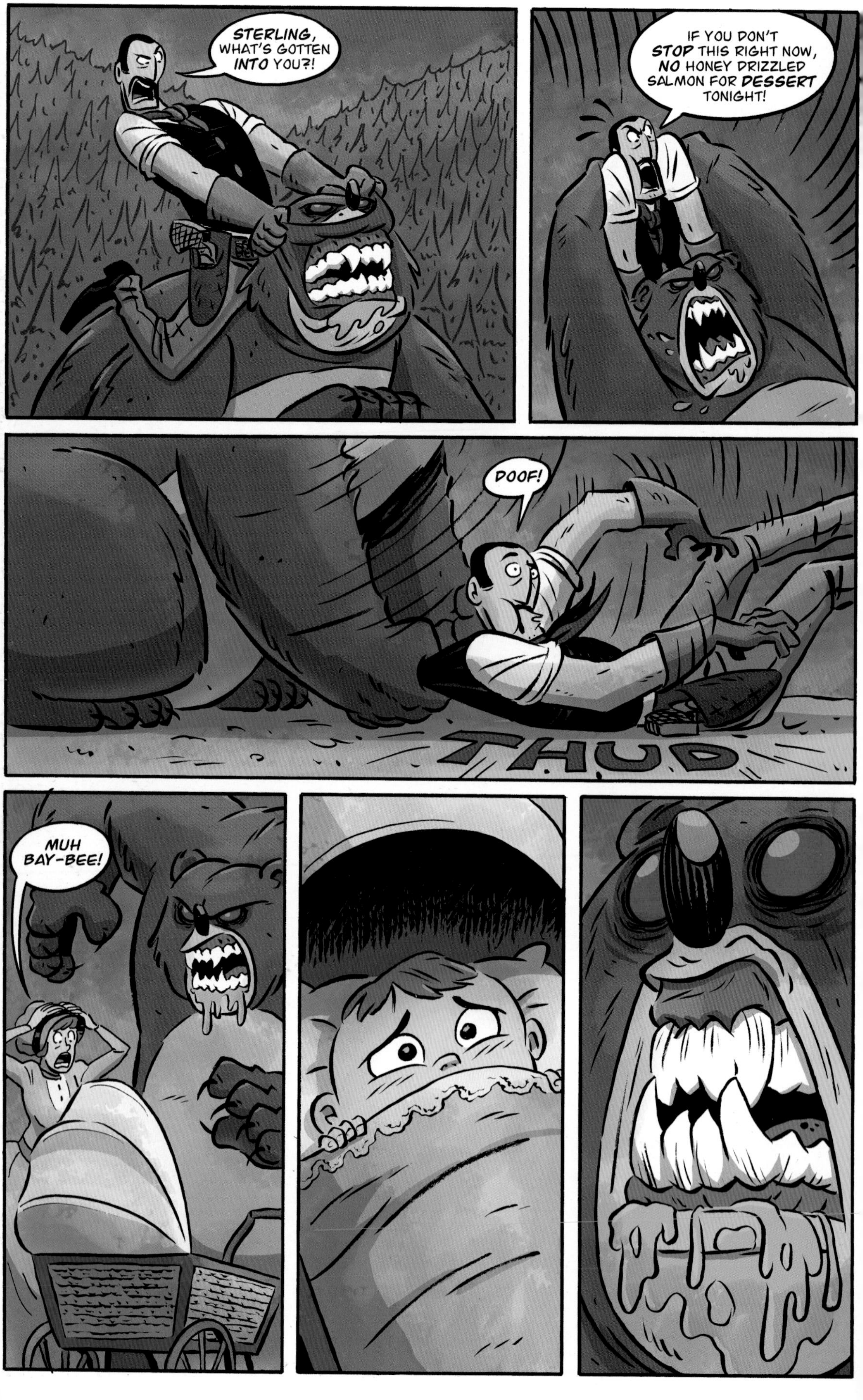
STERLING, WHAT'S GOTTEN INTO YOU?!
IF YOU DON'T STOP THIS RIGHT NOW, NO HONEY DRIZZLED SALMON FOR DESSERT TONIGHT!
DOOF!
THUD
MUH BAY-BEE!

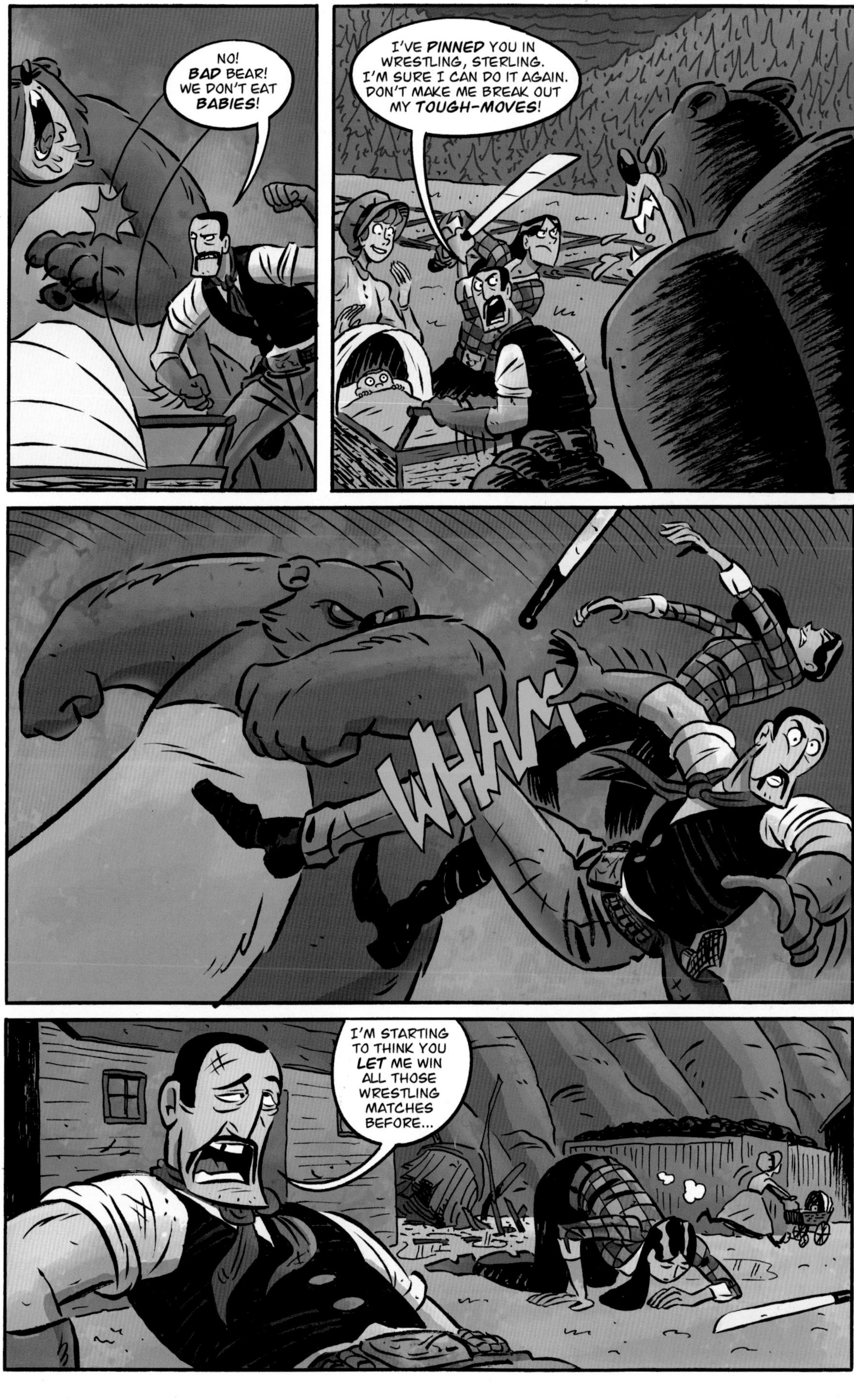
NO! BAD BEAR! WE DON'T EAT BABIES!
I'VE PINNED YOU IN WRESTLING, STERLING. I'M SURE I CAN DO IT AGAIN. DON'T MAKE ME BREAK OUT MY TOUGH-MOVES!
WHAM
I'M STARTING TO THINK YOU LET ME WIN ALL THOSE WRESTLING MATCHES BEFORE...

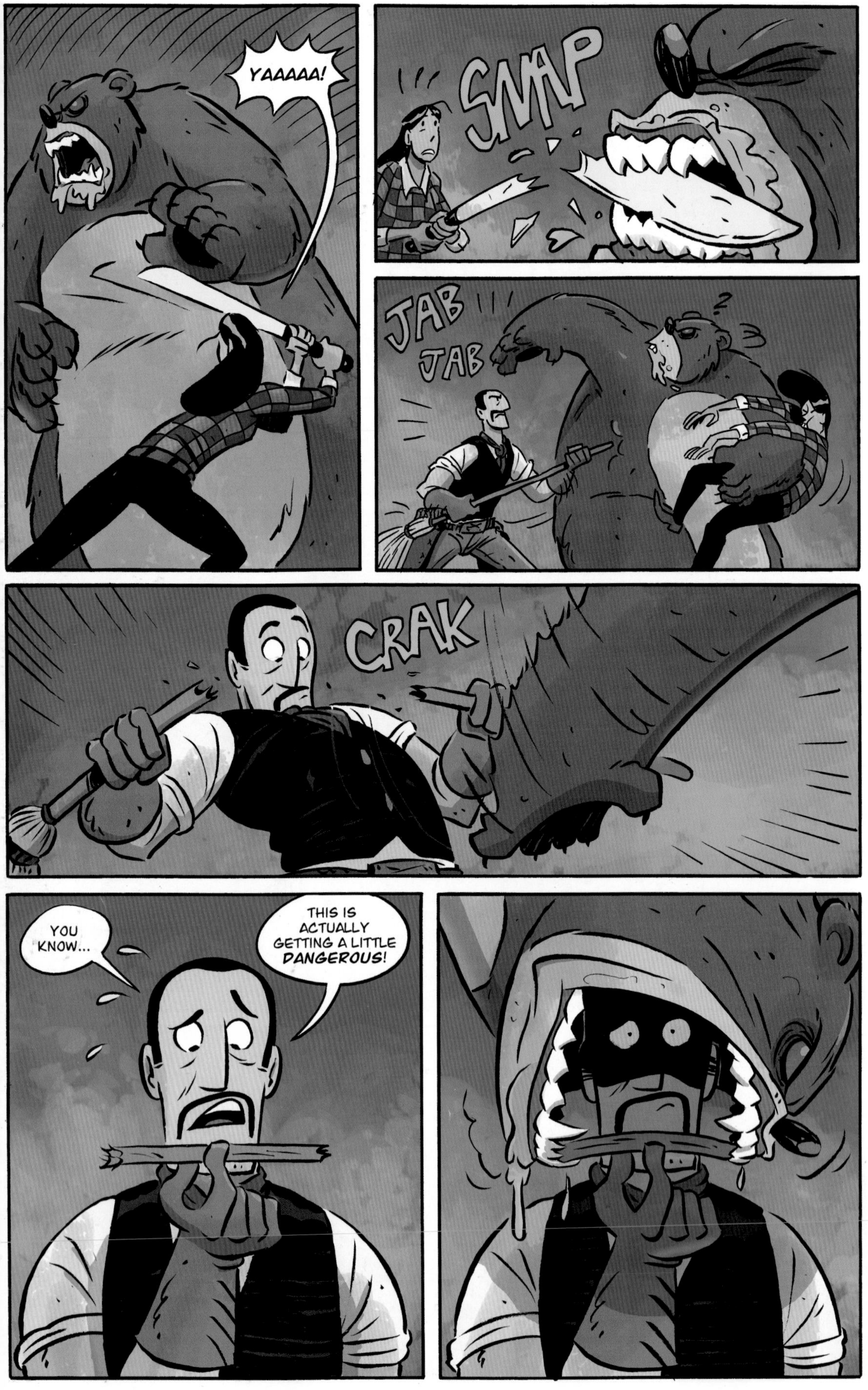
YAAAAA!
SNAP
JAB
JAB
CRAK
YOU KNOW...
THIS IS ACTUALLY GETTING A LITTLE DANGEROUS!

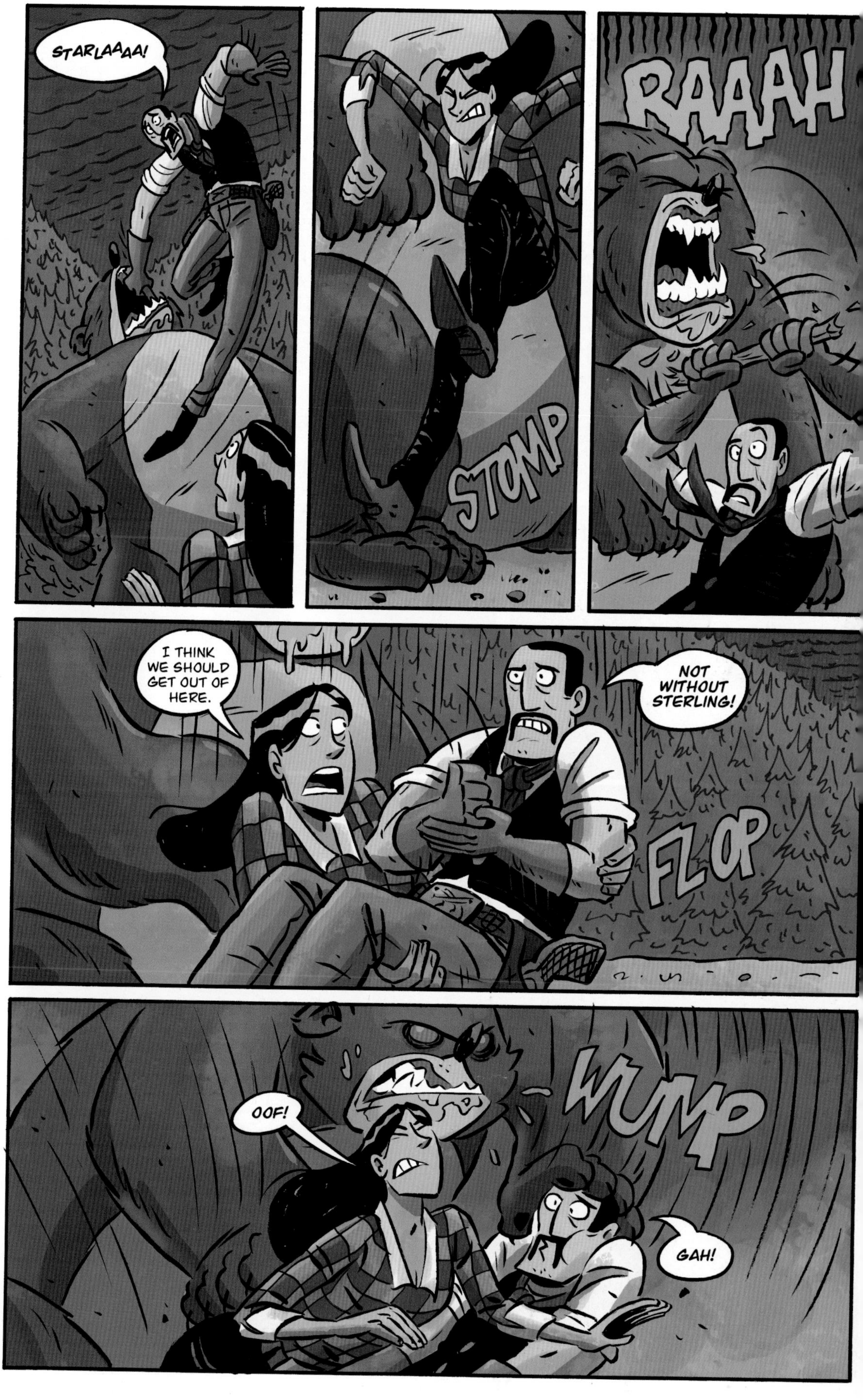
STARLAAAA!
STOMP
RAAAH
I THINK WE SHOULD GET OUT OF HERE.
NOT WITHOUT STERLING!
FLOP
WUMP
OOF!
GAH!

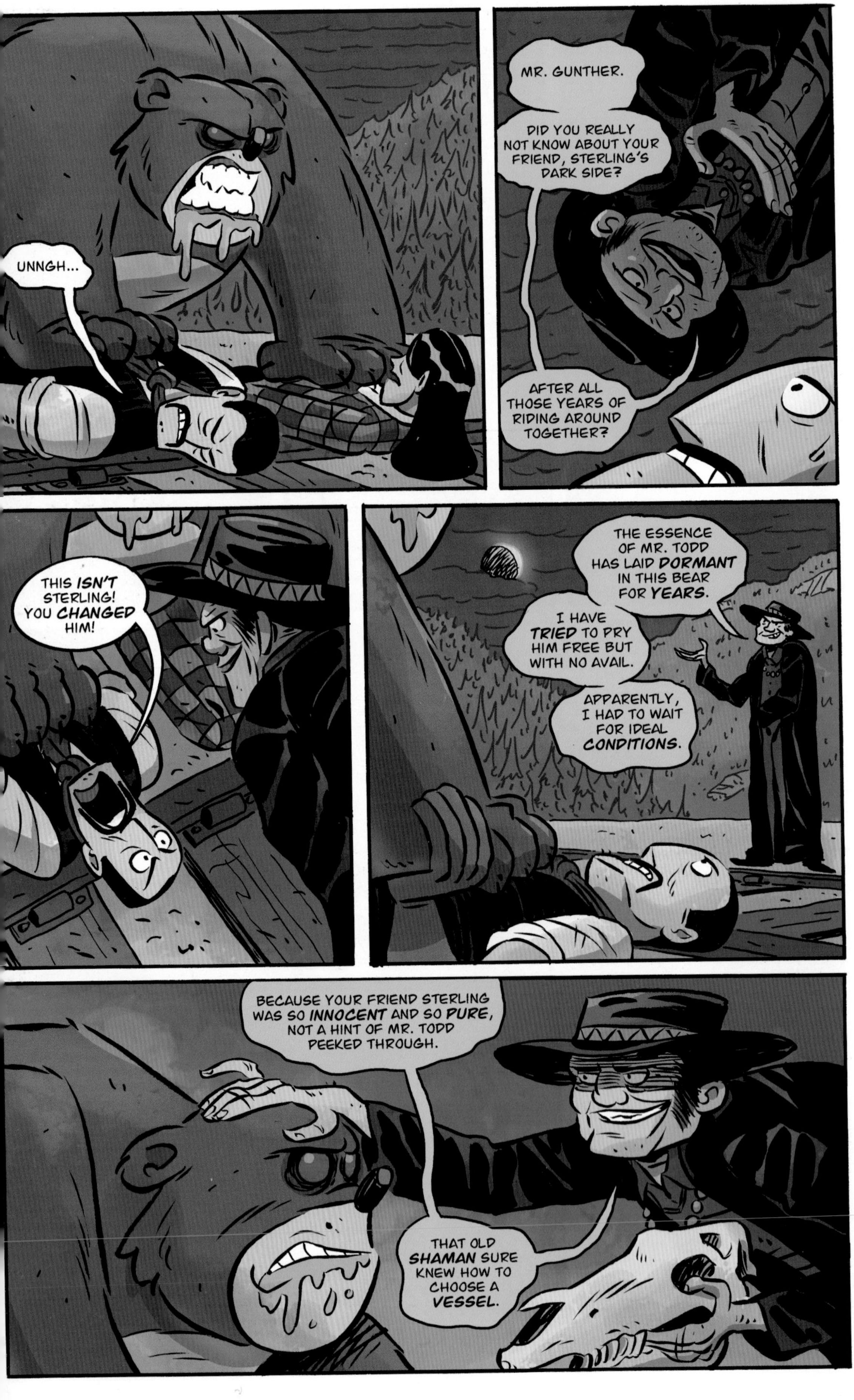
UNNGH...
MR. GUNTHER.
DID YOU REALLY NOT KNOW ABOUT YOUR FRIEND, STERLING'S DARK SIDE?
AFTER ALL THOSE YEARS OF RIDING AROUND TOGETHER?
THIS ISN'T STERLING! YOU CHANGED HIM!
THE ESSENCE OF MR. TODD HAS LAID DORMANT IN THIS BEAR FOR YEARS.
I HAVE TRIED TO PRY HIM FREE BUT WITH NO AVAIL.
APPARENTLY, I HAD TO WAIT FOR IDEAL CONDITIONS.
BECAUSE YOUR FRIEND STERLING WAS SO INNOCENT AND SO PURE, NOT A HINT OF MR. TODD PEEKED THROUGH.
THAT OLD SHAMAN SURE KNEW HOW TO CHOOSE A VESSEL.

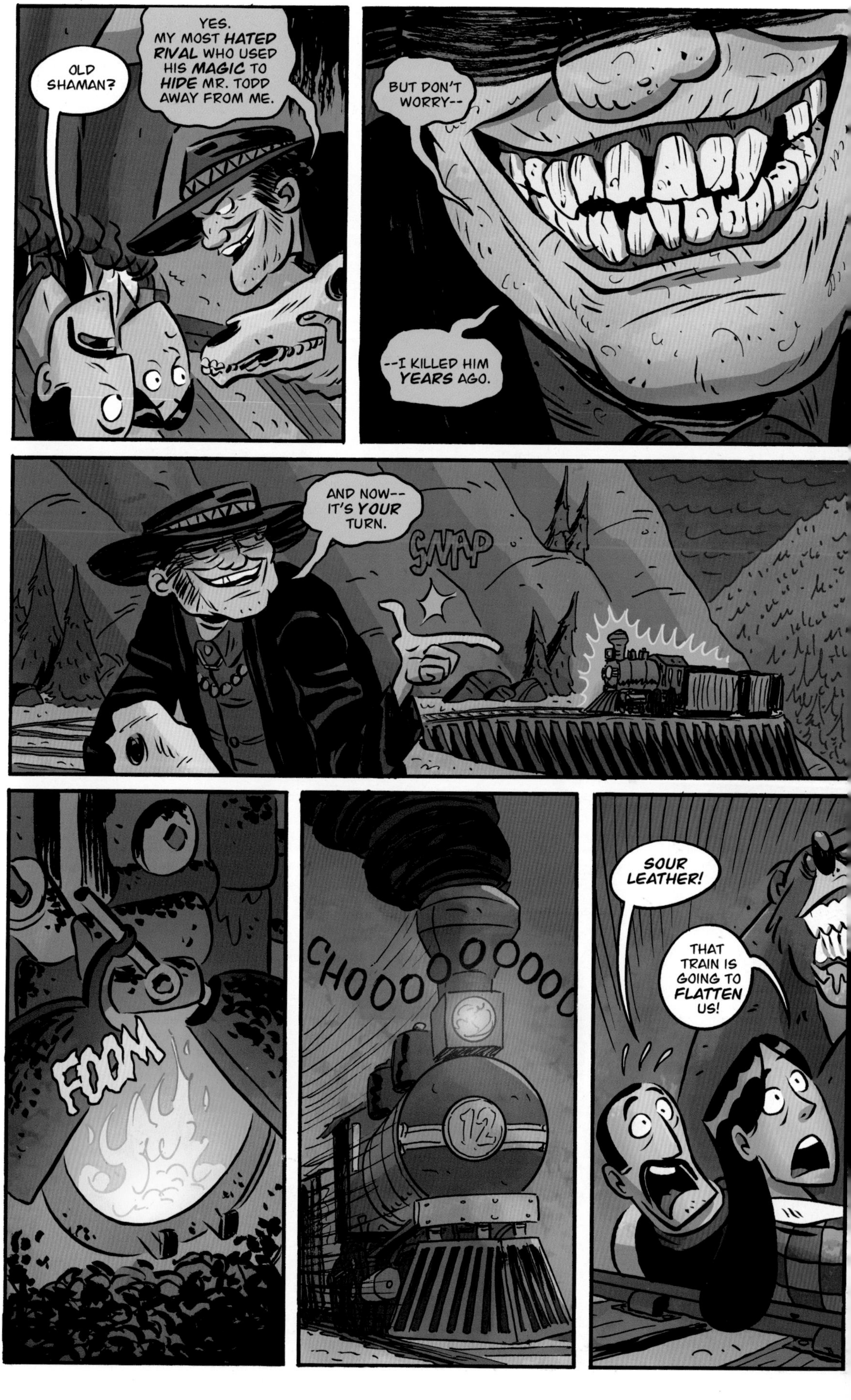
OLD SHAMAN?
YES. MY MOST HATED RIVAL WHO USED HIS MAGIC TO HIDE MR. TODD AWAY FROM ME.
BUT DON'T WORRY--
--I KILLED HIM YEARS AGO.
AND NOW-- IT'S YOUR TURN.
SNAP
FOOM
CHOOOOOOOOOO
SOUR LEATHER!
THAT TRAIN IS GOING TO FLATTEN US!
12

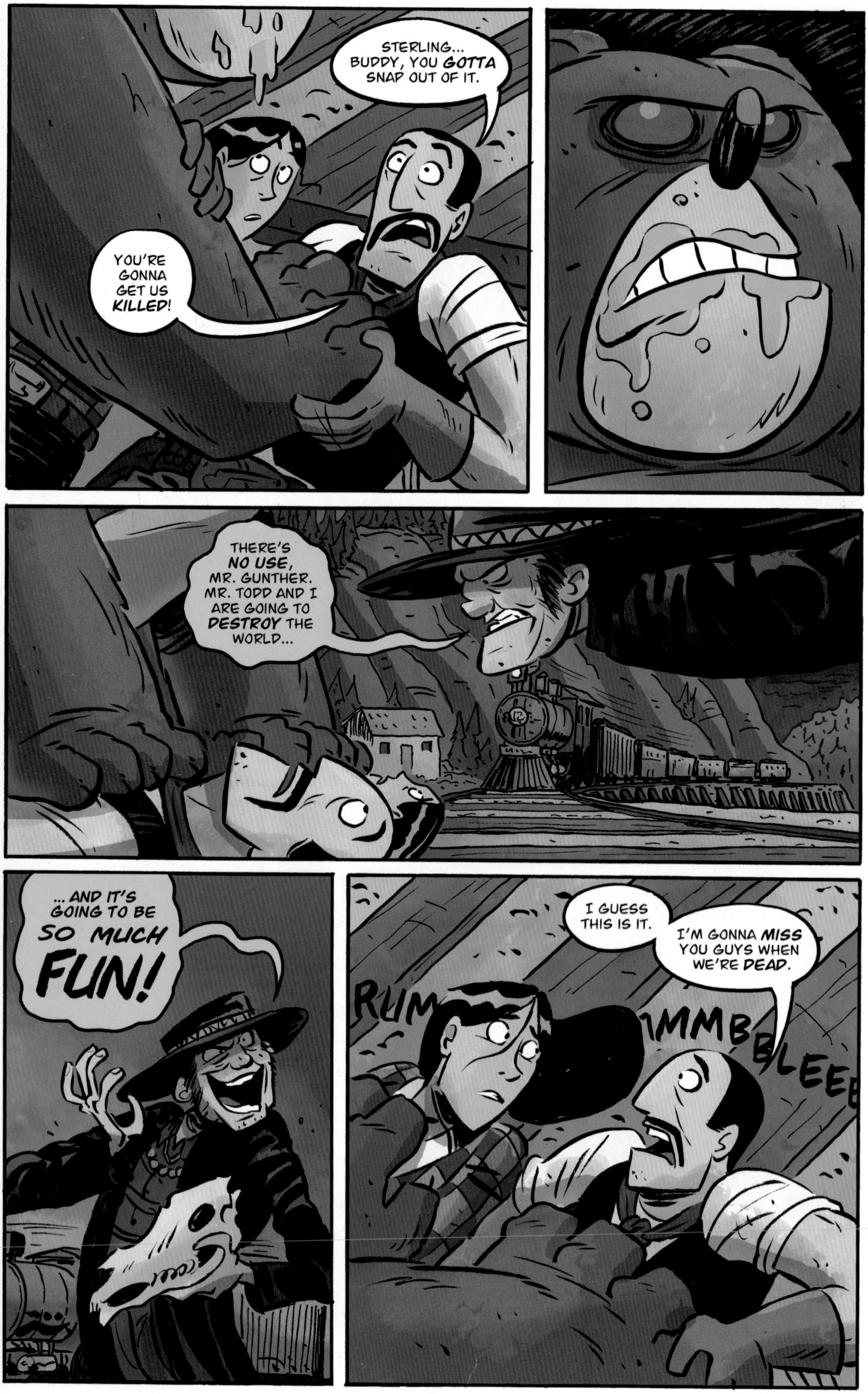
STERLING... BUDDY, YOU GOTTA SNAP OUT OF IT.
YOU'RE GONNA GET US KILLED!
THERE'S NO USE, MR. GUNTHER. MR. TODD AND I ARE GOING TO DESTROY THE WORLD...
... AND IT'S GOING TO BE SO MUCH FUN!
I GUESS THIS IS IT.
I'M GONNA MISS YOU GUYS WHEN WE'RE DEAD.
RUM
MMBBLEEE

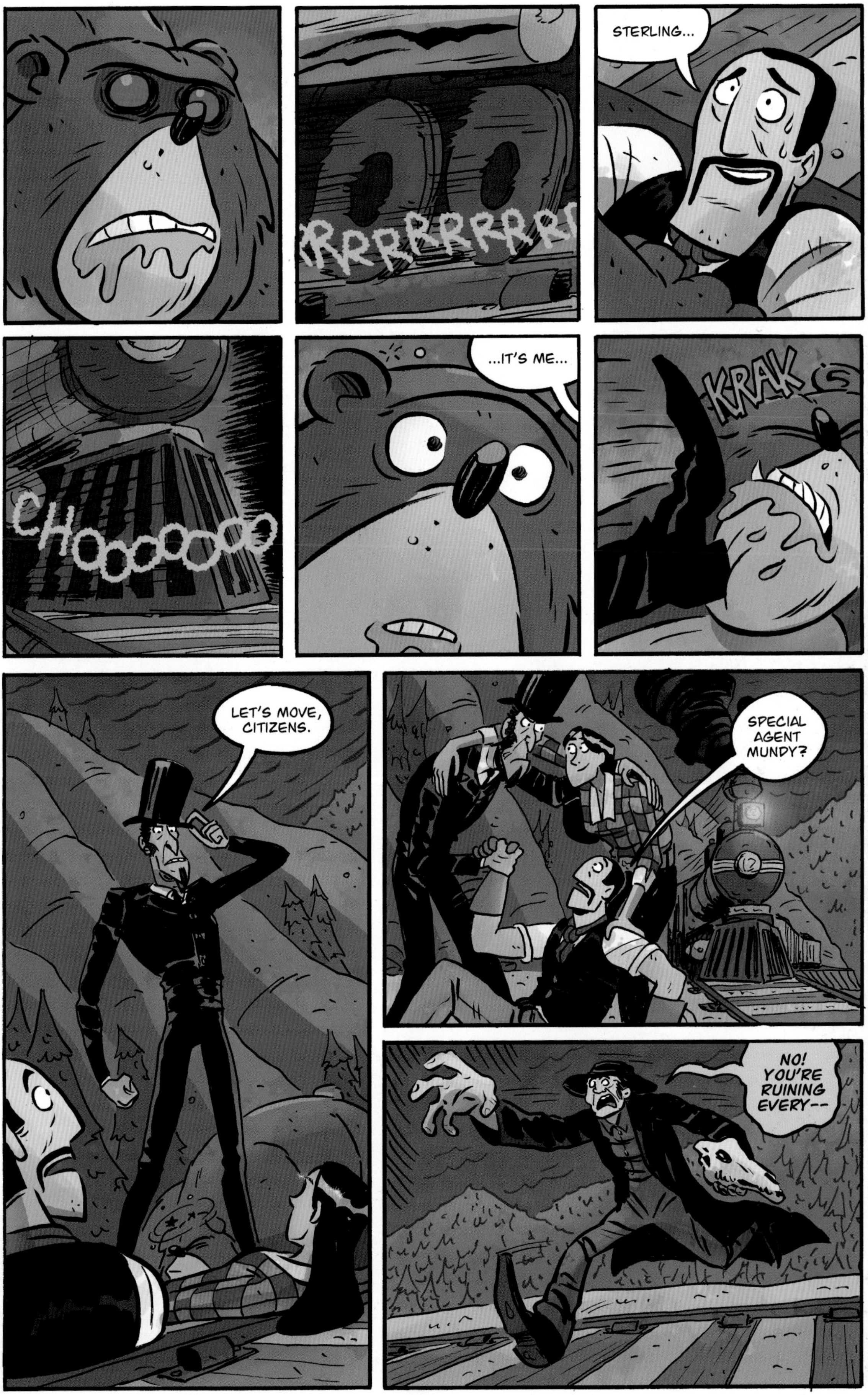
RRRRRRRRR
STERLING...
CHOOOOOOOO
...IT'S ME...
KRAK
LET'S MOVE, CITIZENS.
SPECIAL AGENT MUNDY?
NO! YOU'RE RUINING EVERY--

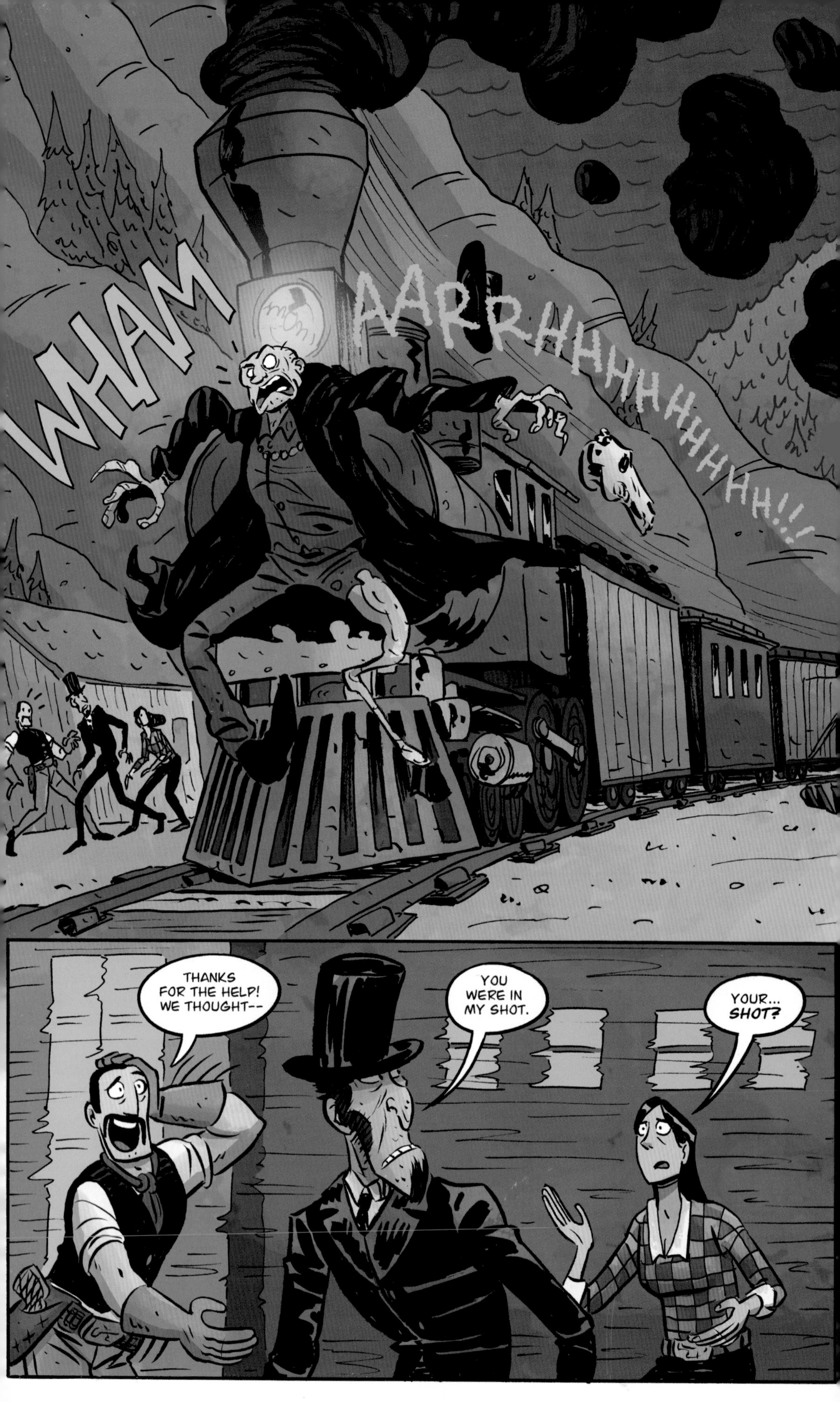
WHAM
AARRHHHHHHHHHH!!!
THANKS FOR THE HELP! WE THOUGHT--
YOU WERE IN MY SHOT.
YOUR... SHOT?

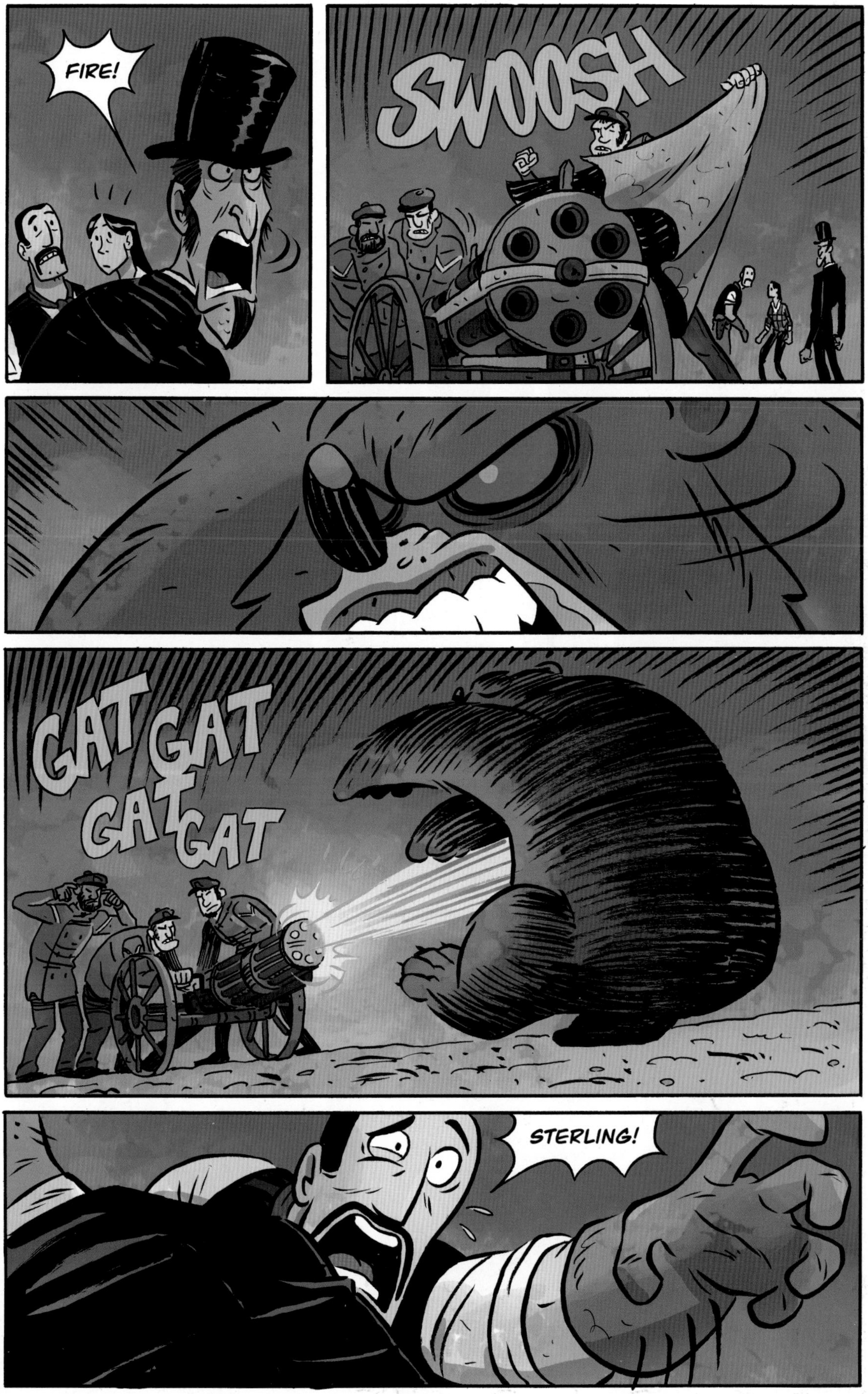
FIRE!
SWOOSH
GAT GAT
GAT GAT
STERLING!

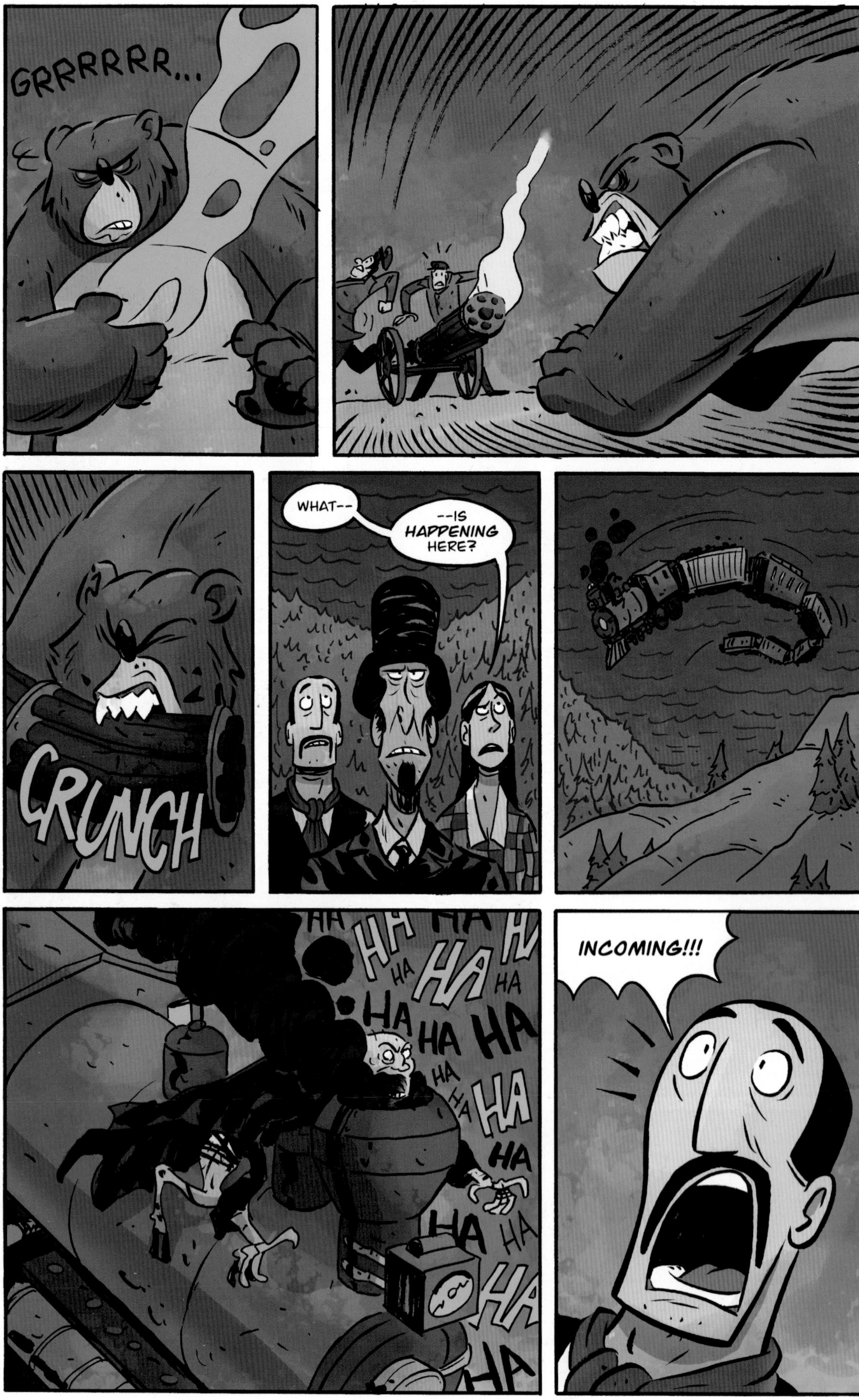
GRRRRRR...
CRUNCH
WHAT--
--IS HAPPENING HERE?
HA HA HA HA HA HA HA HA HA HA HA HA HA HA HA HA HA HA HA HA HA
INCOMING!!!

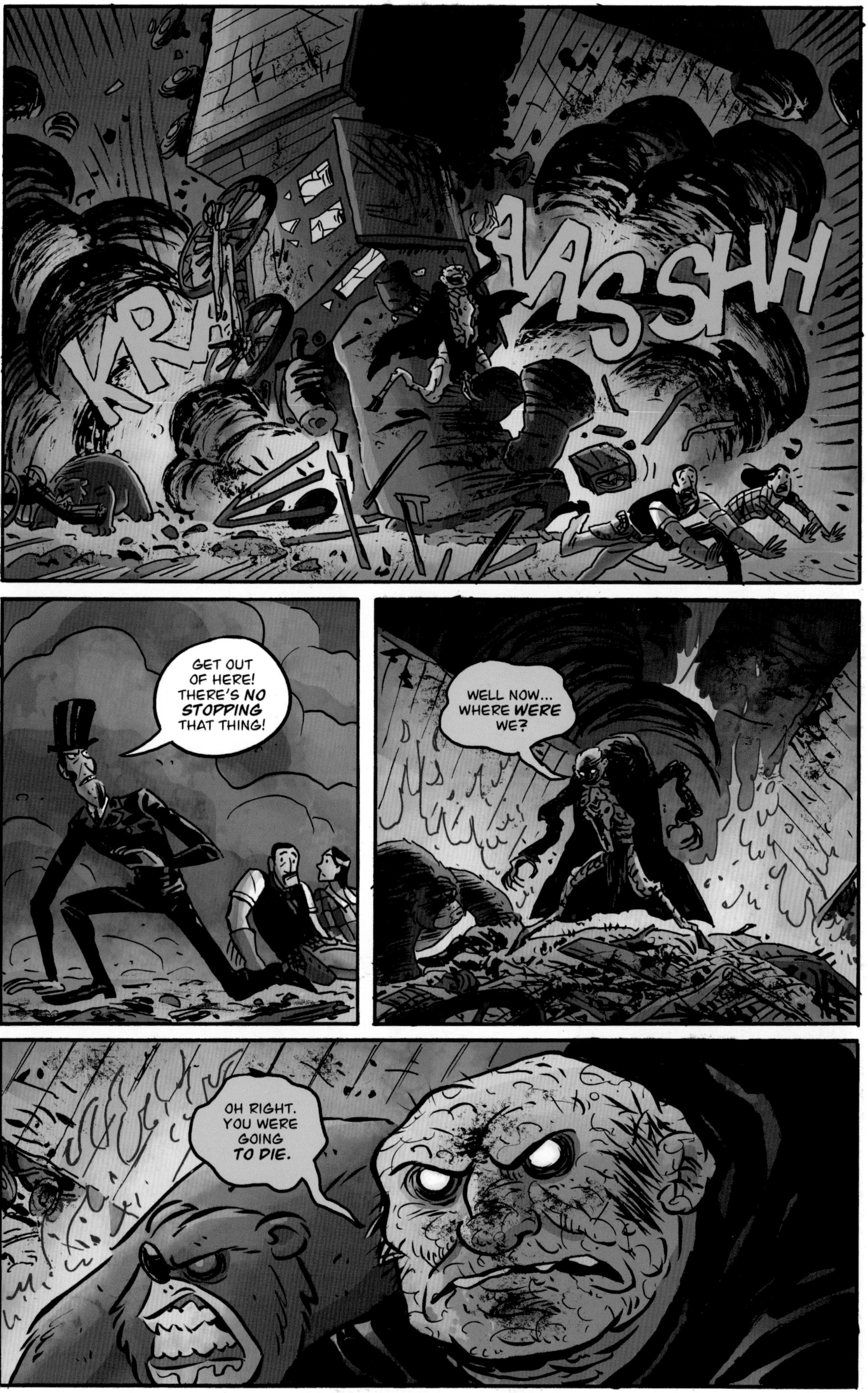
KRASSHH
GET OUT OF HERE! THERE'S NO STOPPING THAT THING!
WELL NOW... WHERE WERE WE?
OH RIGHT. YOU WERE GOING TO DIE.

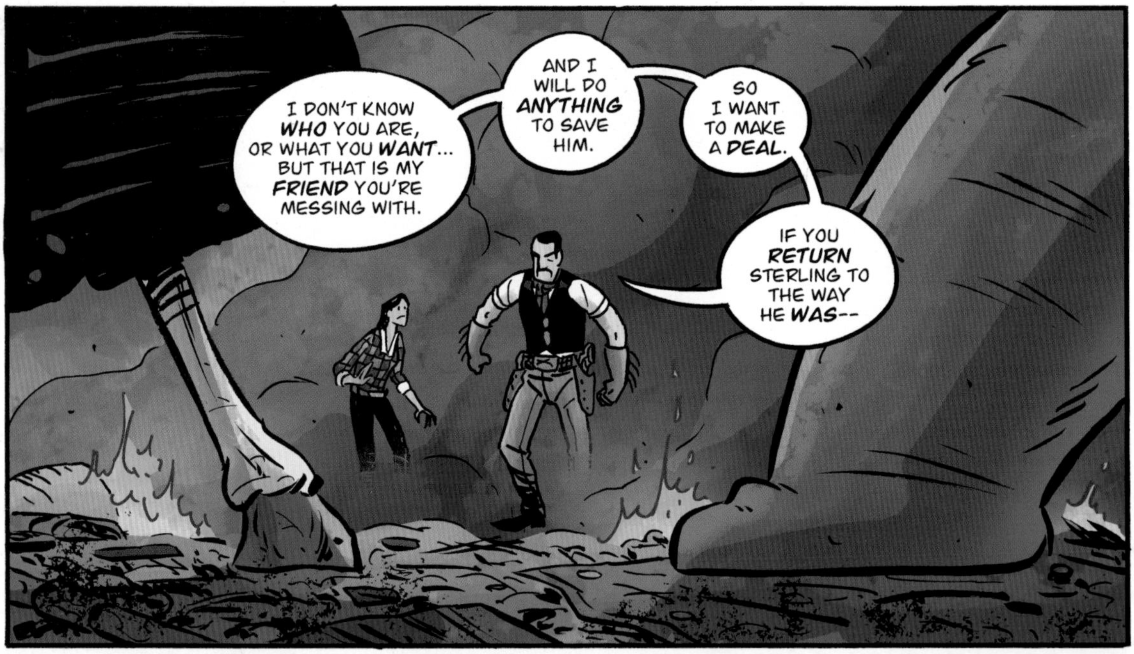
I DON'T KNOW WHO YOU ARE, OR WHAT YOU WANT... BUT THAT IS MY FRIEND YOU'RE MESSING WITH.
AND I WILL DO ANYTHING TO SAVE HIM.
SO I WANT TO MAKE A DEAL.
IF YOU RETURN STERLING TO THE WAY HE WAS--

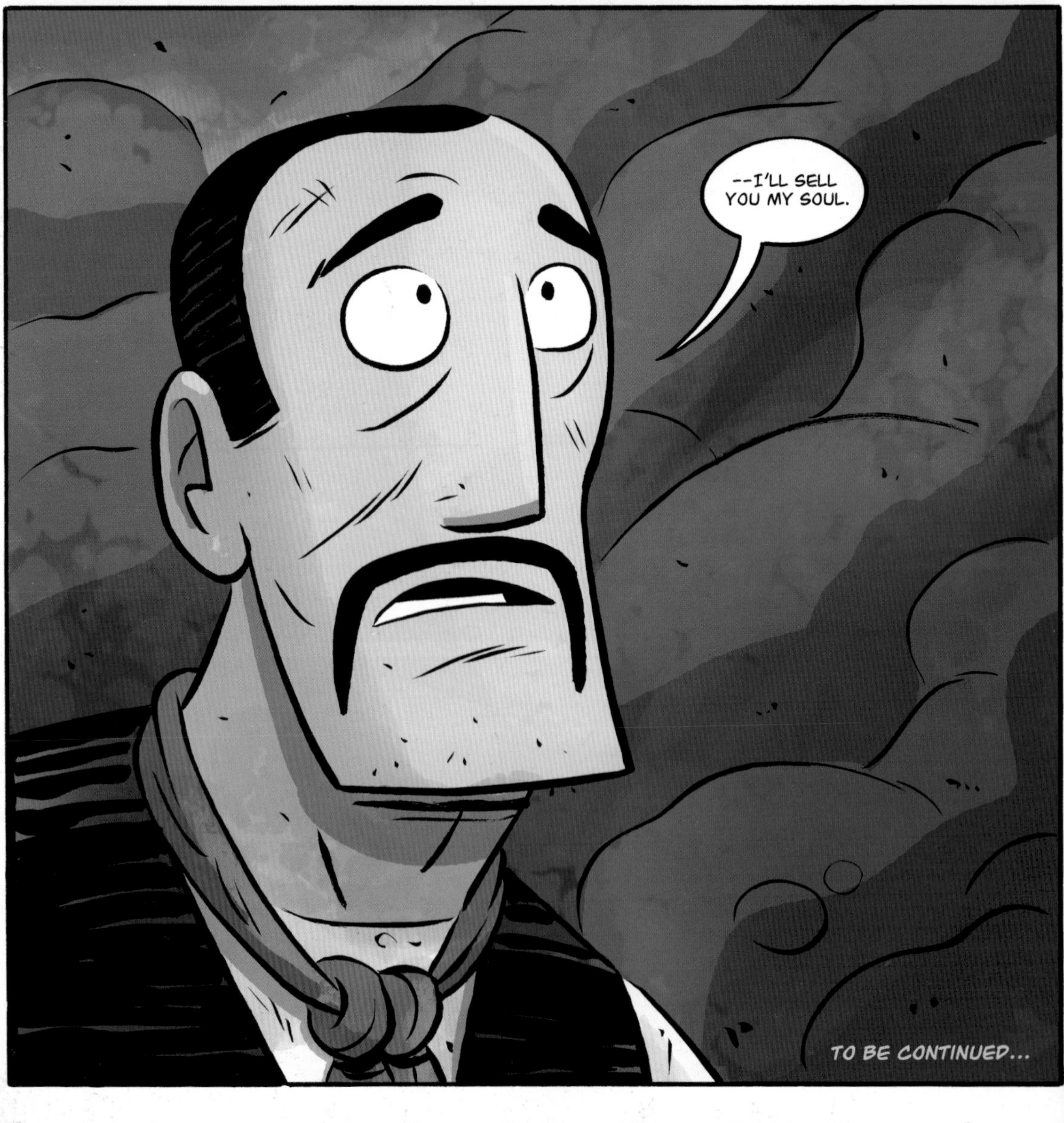
--I'LL SELL YOU MY SOUL.
TO BE CONTINUED...

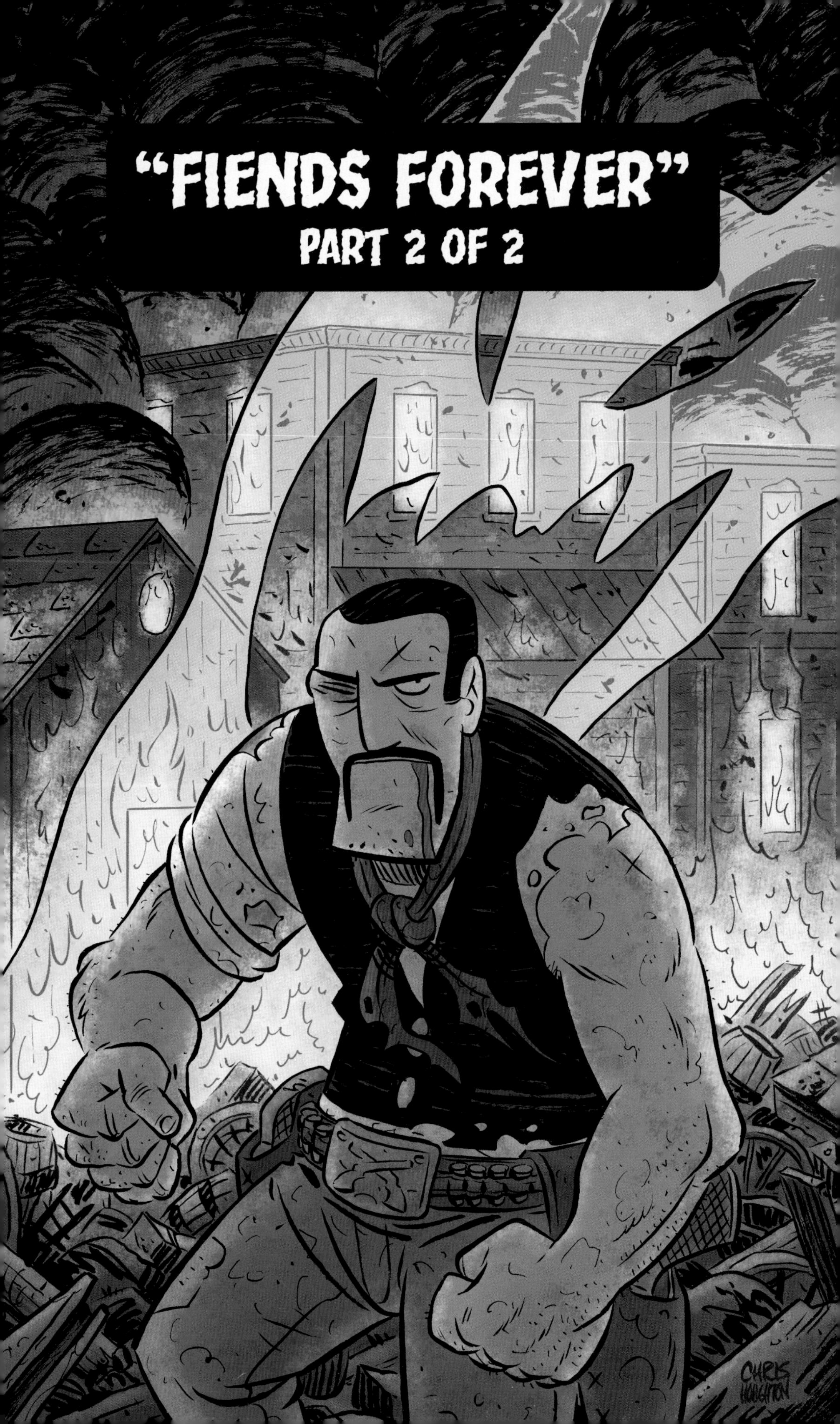
"FIENDS FOREVER"
PART 2 OF 2
CHRIS HOUGHTON

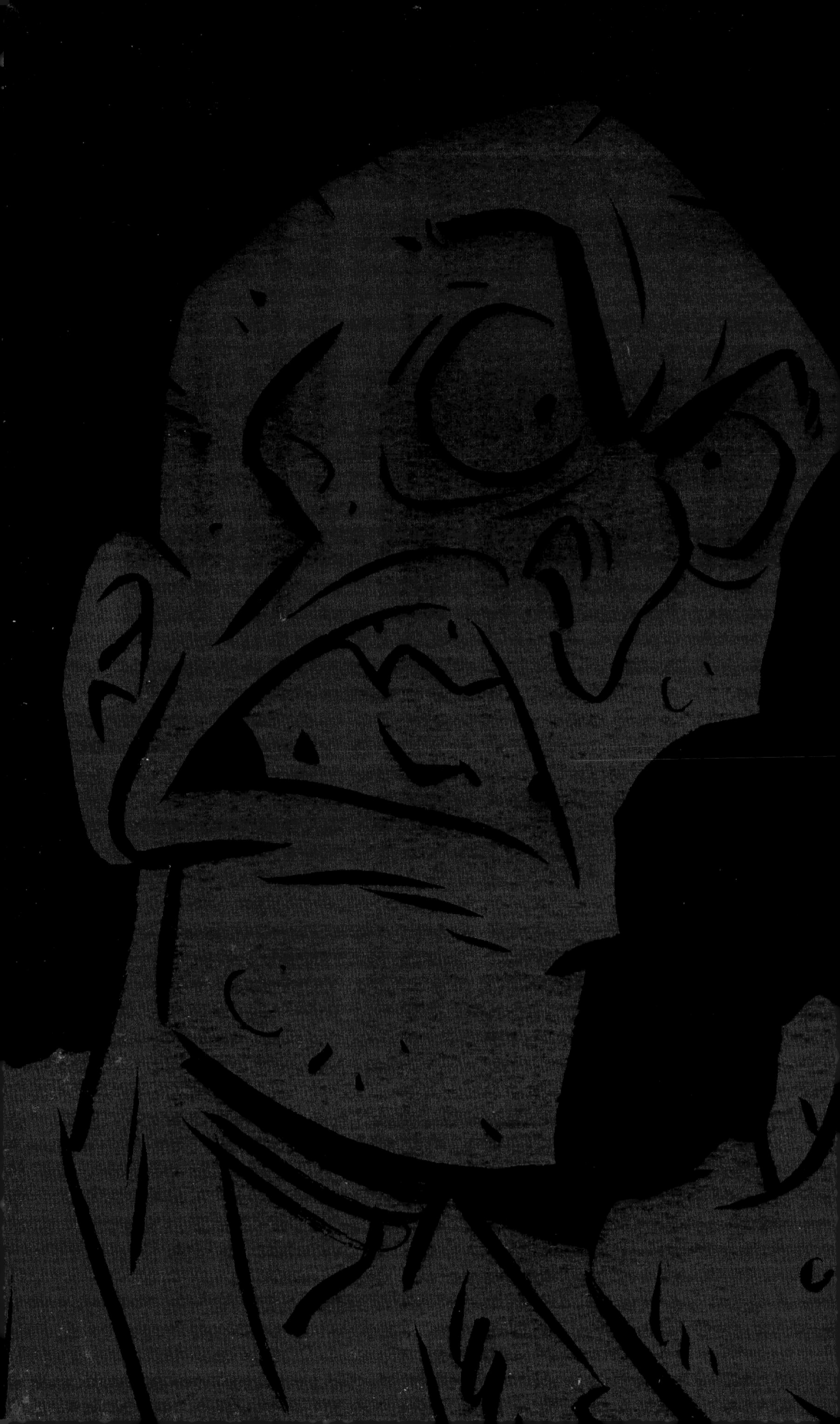

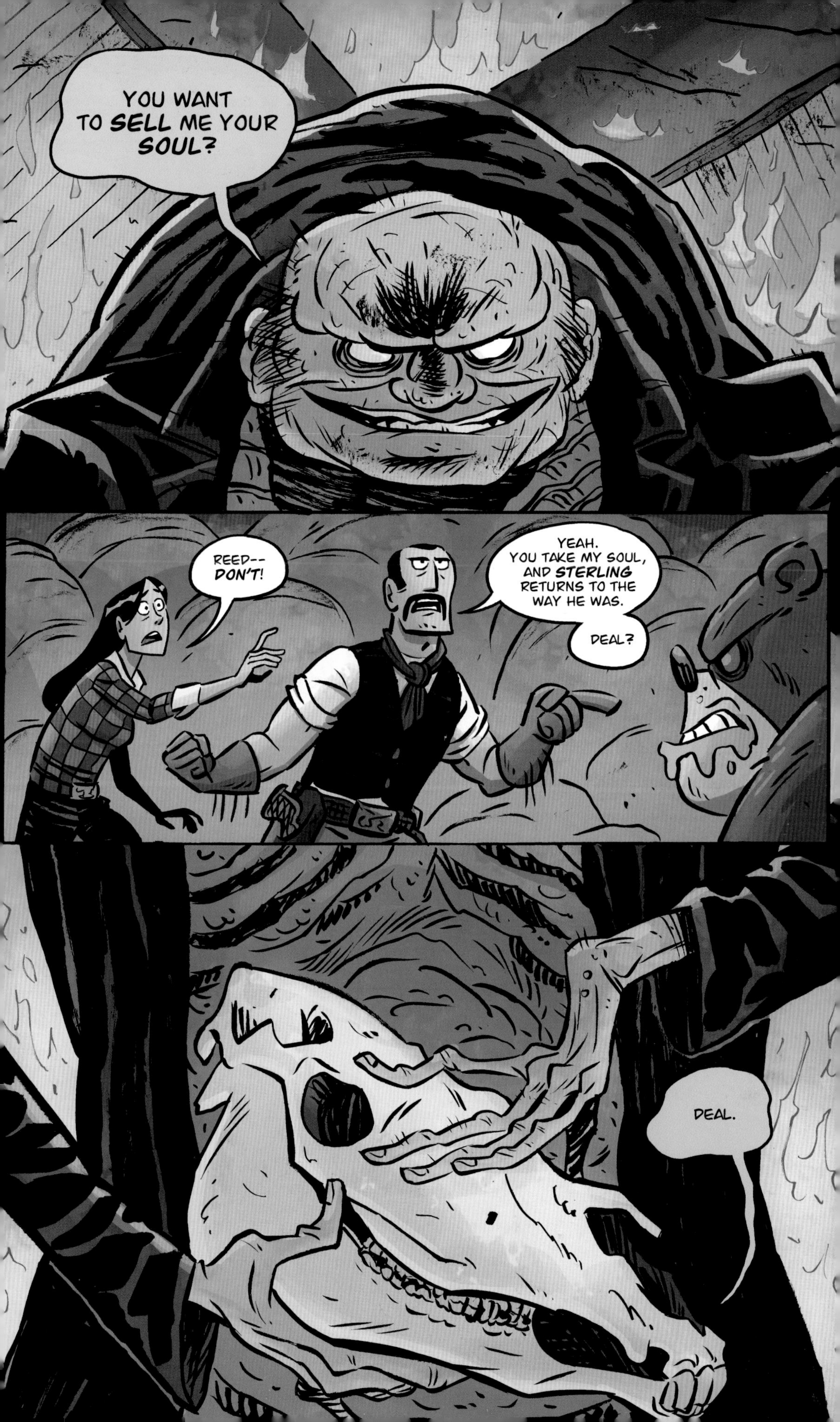

YOU WANT TO **SELL** ME YOUR **SOUL?**
REED-- **DON'T!**
YEAH. YOU TAKE MY SOUL, AND **STERLING** RETURNS TO THE WAY HE WAS.
DEAL?
DEAL.

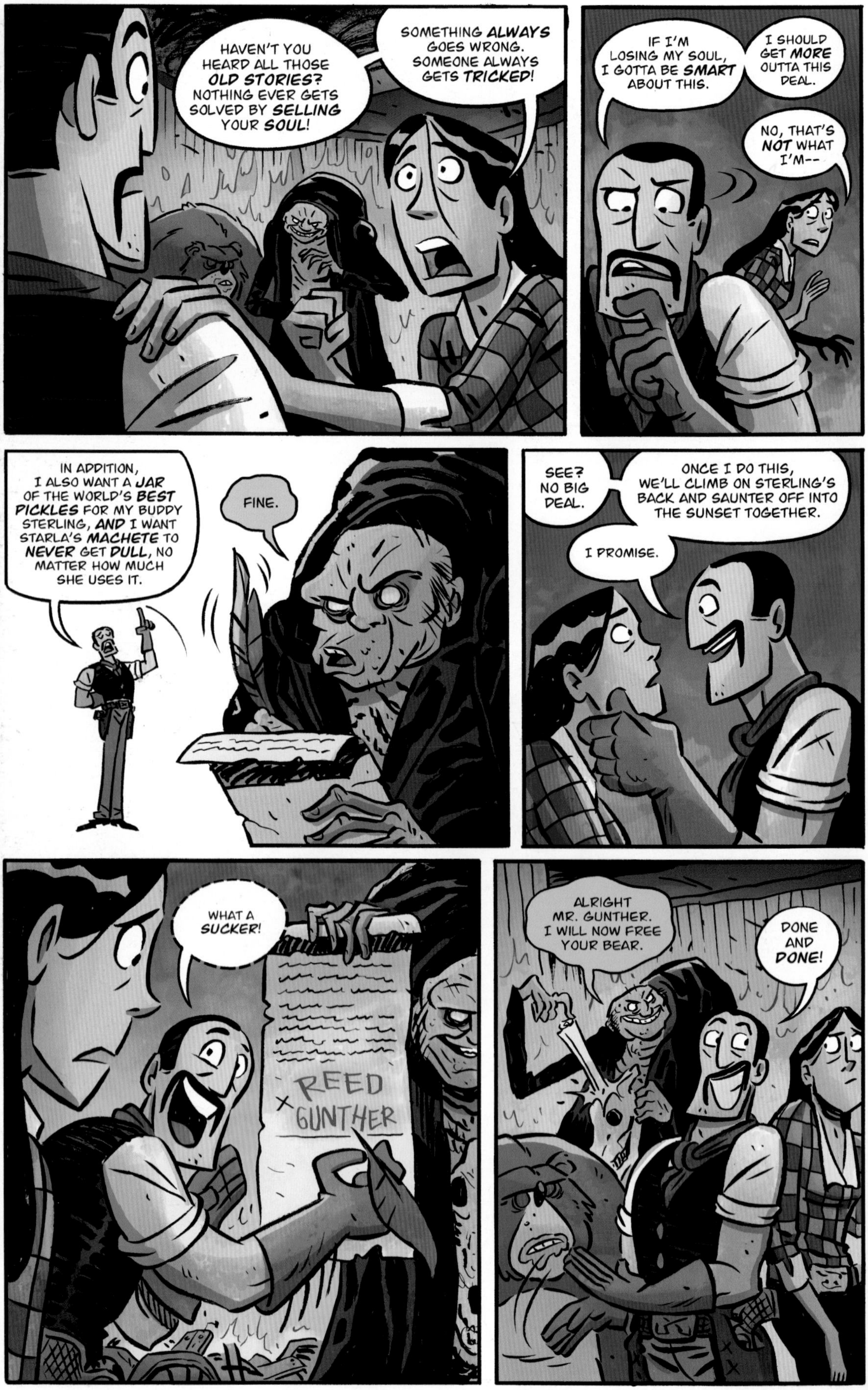
HAVEN'T YOU HEARD ALL THOSE OLD STORIES? NOTHING EVER GETS SOLVED BY SELLING YOUR SOUL!
SOMETHING ALWAYS GOES WRONG. SOMEONE ALWAYS GETS TRICKED!
IF I'M LOSING MY SOUL, I GOTTA BE SMART ABOUT THIS.
I SHOULD GET MORE OUTTA THIS DEAL.
NO, THAT'S NOT WHAT I'M--
IN ADDITION, I ALSO WANT A JAR OF THE WORLD'S BEST PICKLES FOR MY BUDDY STERLING, AND I WANT STARLA'S MACHETE TO NEVER GET DULL, NO MATTER HOW MUCH SHE USES IT.
FINE.
SEE? NO BIG DEAL.
ONCE I DO THIS, WE'LL CLIMB ON STERLING'S BACK AND SAUNTER OFF INTO THE SUNSET TOGETHER.
I PROMISE.
WHAT A SUCKER!
REED GUNTHER
ALRIGHT MR. GUNTHER. I WILL NOW FREE YOUR BEAR.
DONE AND DONE!

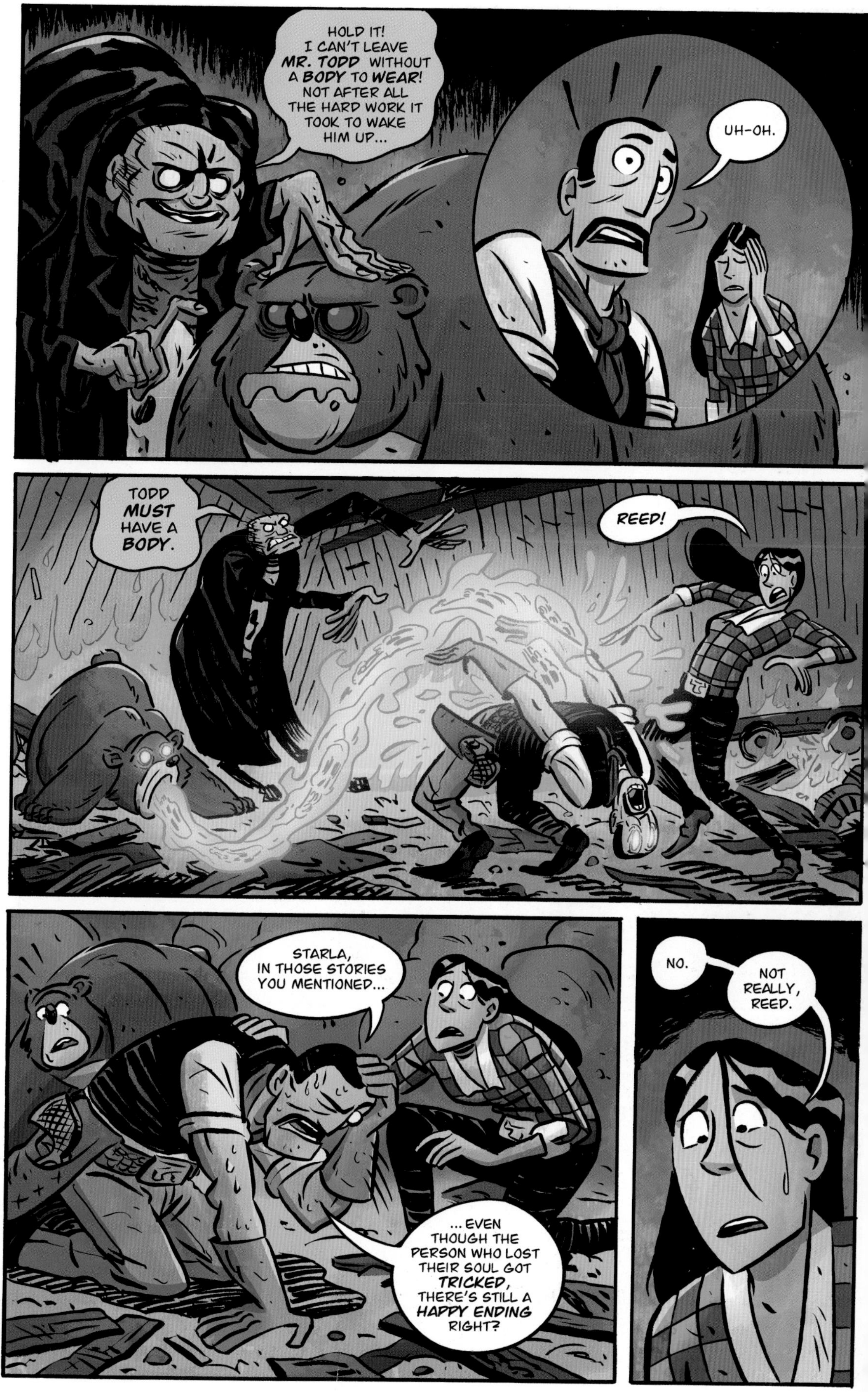
HOLD IT! I CAN'T LEAVE MR. TODD WITHOUT A BODY TO WEAR! NOT AFTER ALL THE HARD WORK IT TOOK TO WAKE HIM UP...
UH-OH.
TODD MUST HAVE A BODY.
REED!
STARLA, IN THOSE STORIES YOU MENTIONED...
...EVEN THOUGH THE PERSON WHO LOST THEIR SOUL GOT TRICKED, THERE'S STILL A HAPPY ENDING RIGHT?
NO.
NOT REALLY, REED.

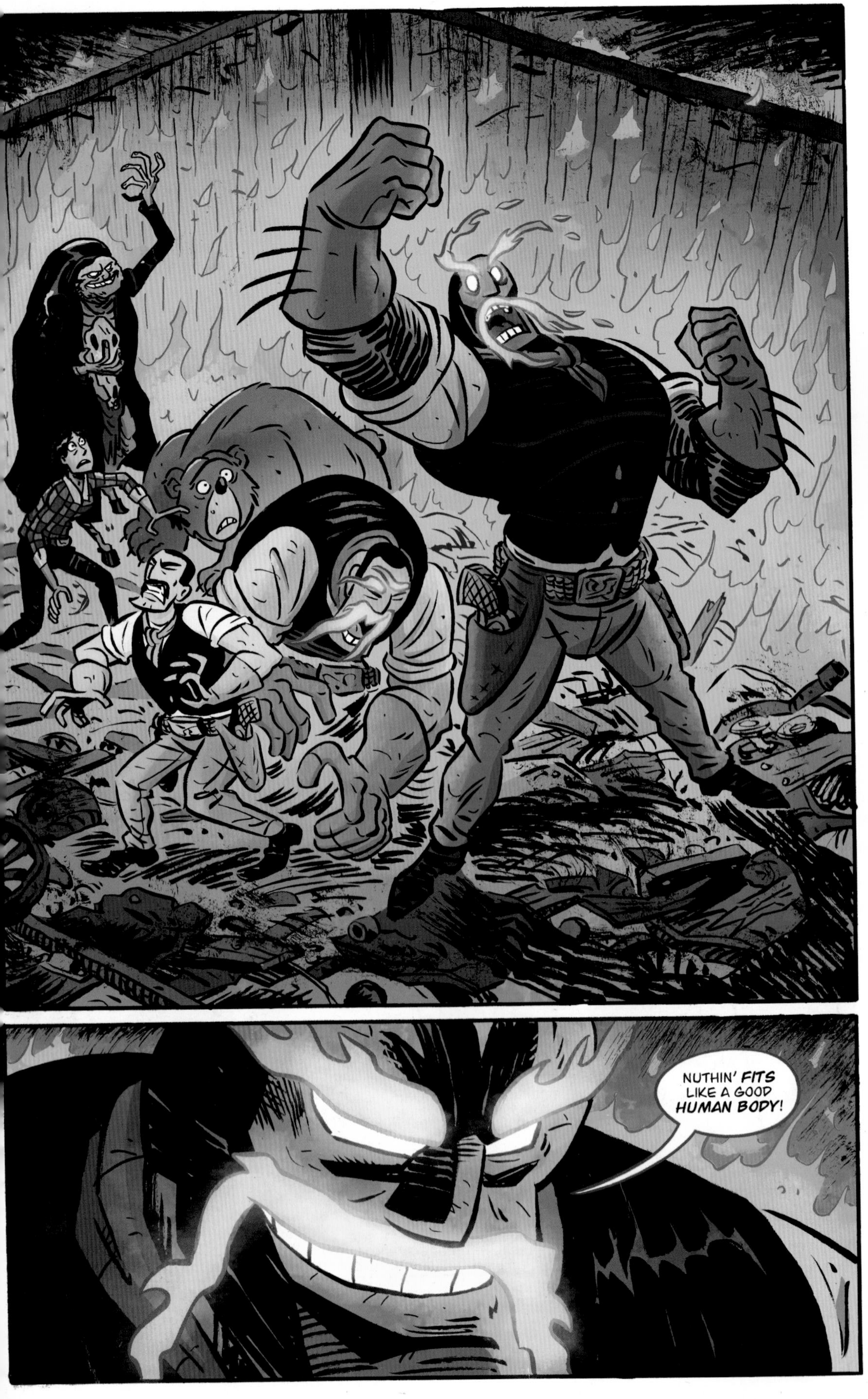
NUTHIN' **FITS** LIKE A GOOD **HUMAN BODY**!

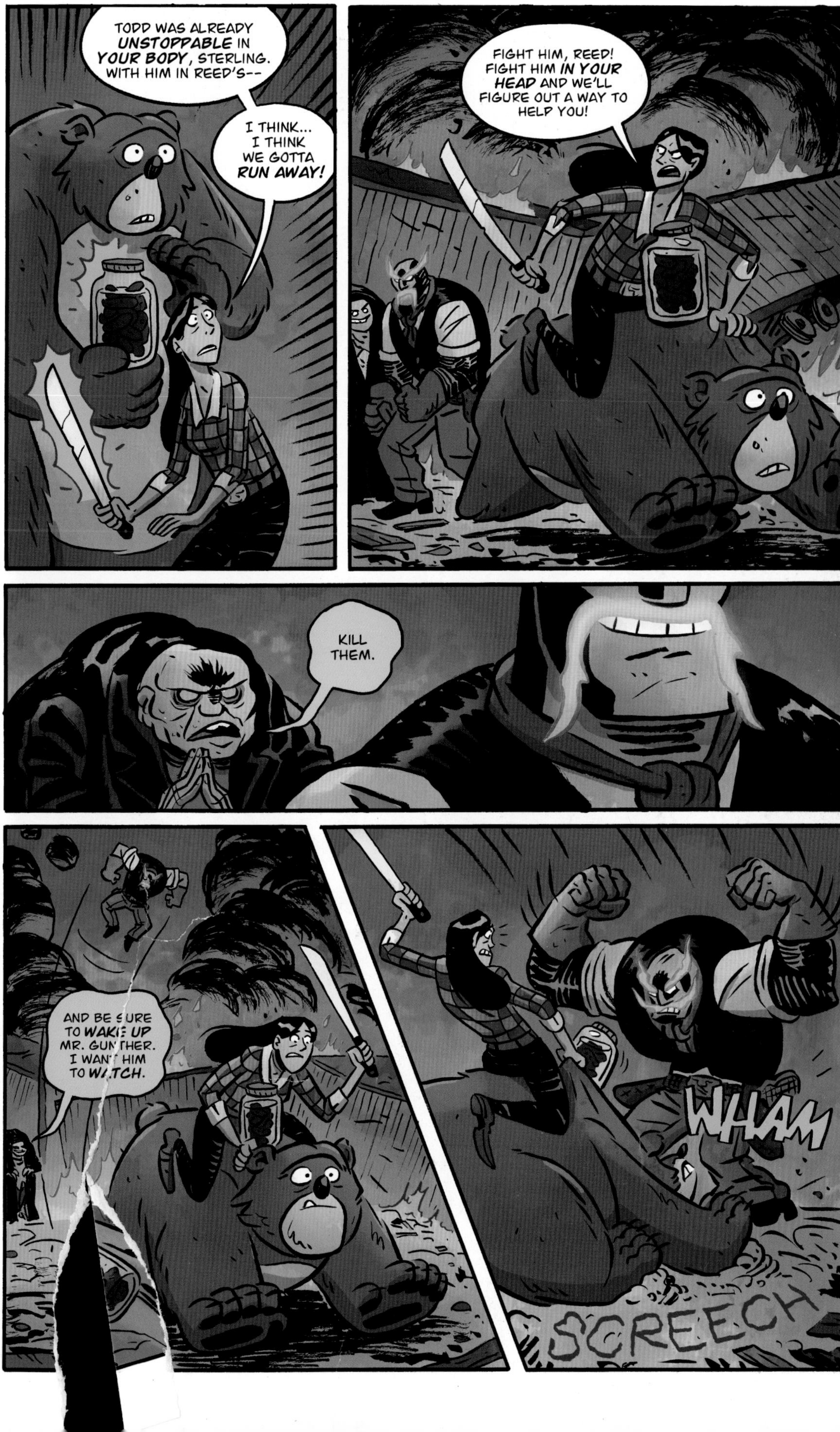

TODD WAS ALREADY UNSTOPPABLE IN YOUR BODY, STERLING. WITH HIM IN REED'S--
I THINK... I THINK WE GOTTA RUN AWAY!
FIGHT HIM, REED! FIGHT HIM IN YOUR HEAD AND WE'LL FIGURE OUT A WAY TO HELP YOU!
KILL THEM.
AND BE SURE TO WAKE UP MR. GUNTHER. I WANT HIM TO WATCH.
WHAM
SCREECH

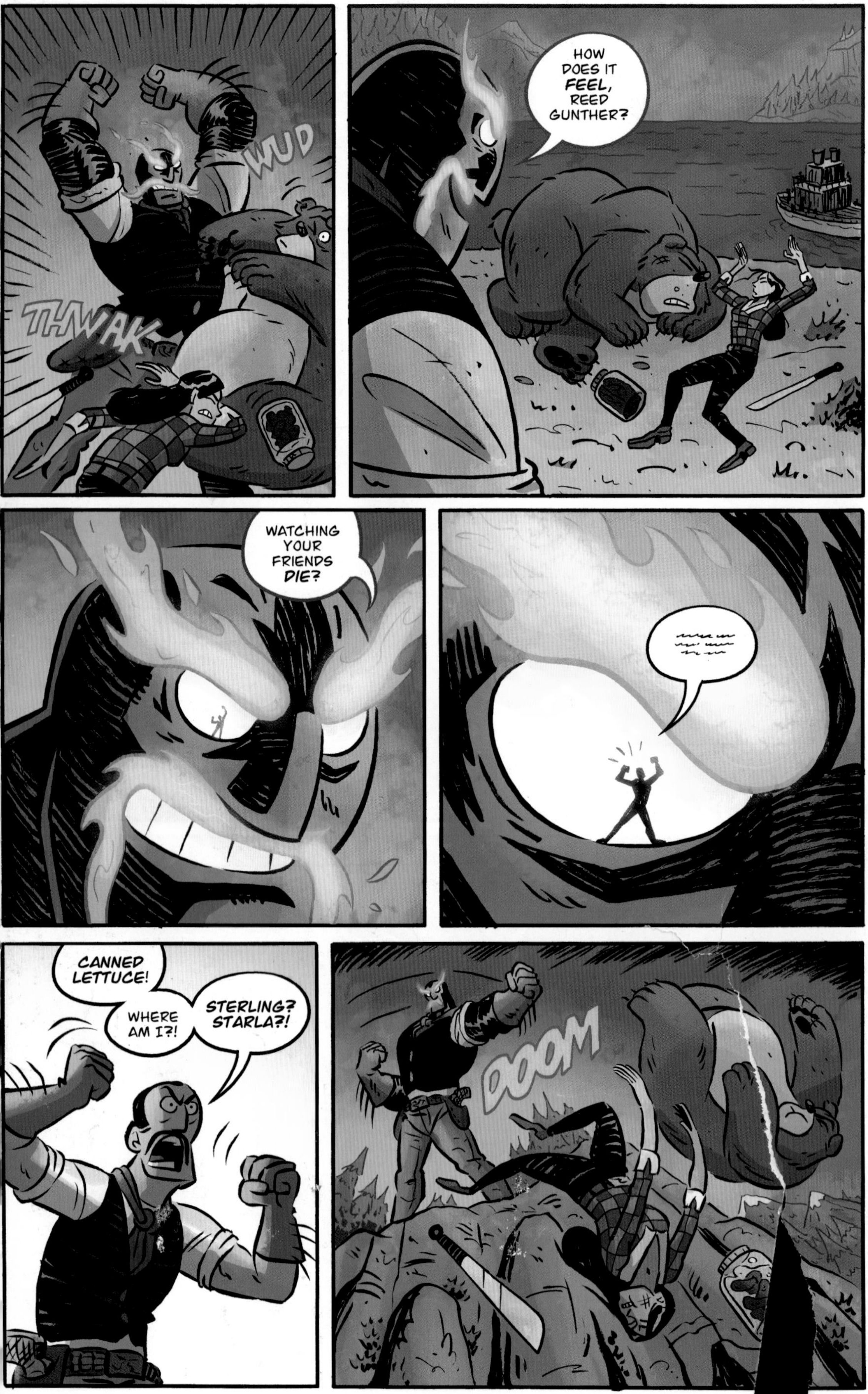
WUD
THWAK
HOW DOES IT FEEL, REED GUNTHER?
WATCHING YOUR FRIENDS DIE?
CANNED LETTUCE!
WHERE AM I?!
STERLING? STARLA?!
DOOM

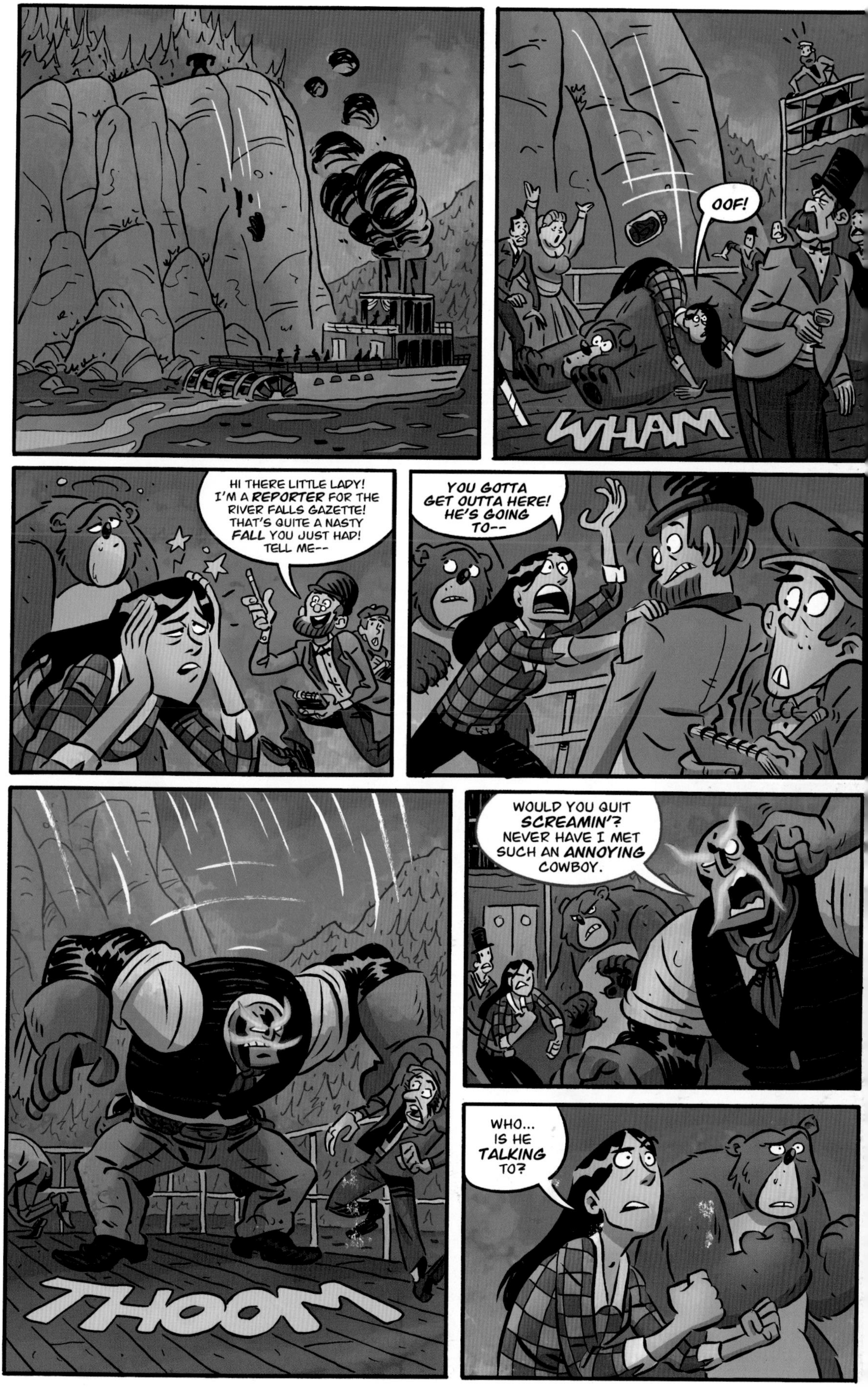
OOF!
WHAM
HI THERE LITTLE LADY! I'M A REPORTER FOR THE RIVER FALLS GAZETTE! THAT'S QUITE A NASTY FALL YOU JUST HAD! TELL ME--
YOU GOTTA GET OUTTA HERE! HE'S GOING TO--
THOOM
WOULD YOU QUIT SCREAMIN'? NEVER HAVE I MET SUCH AN ANNOYING COWBOY.
WHO... IS HE TALKING TO?

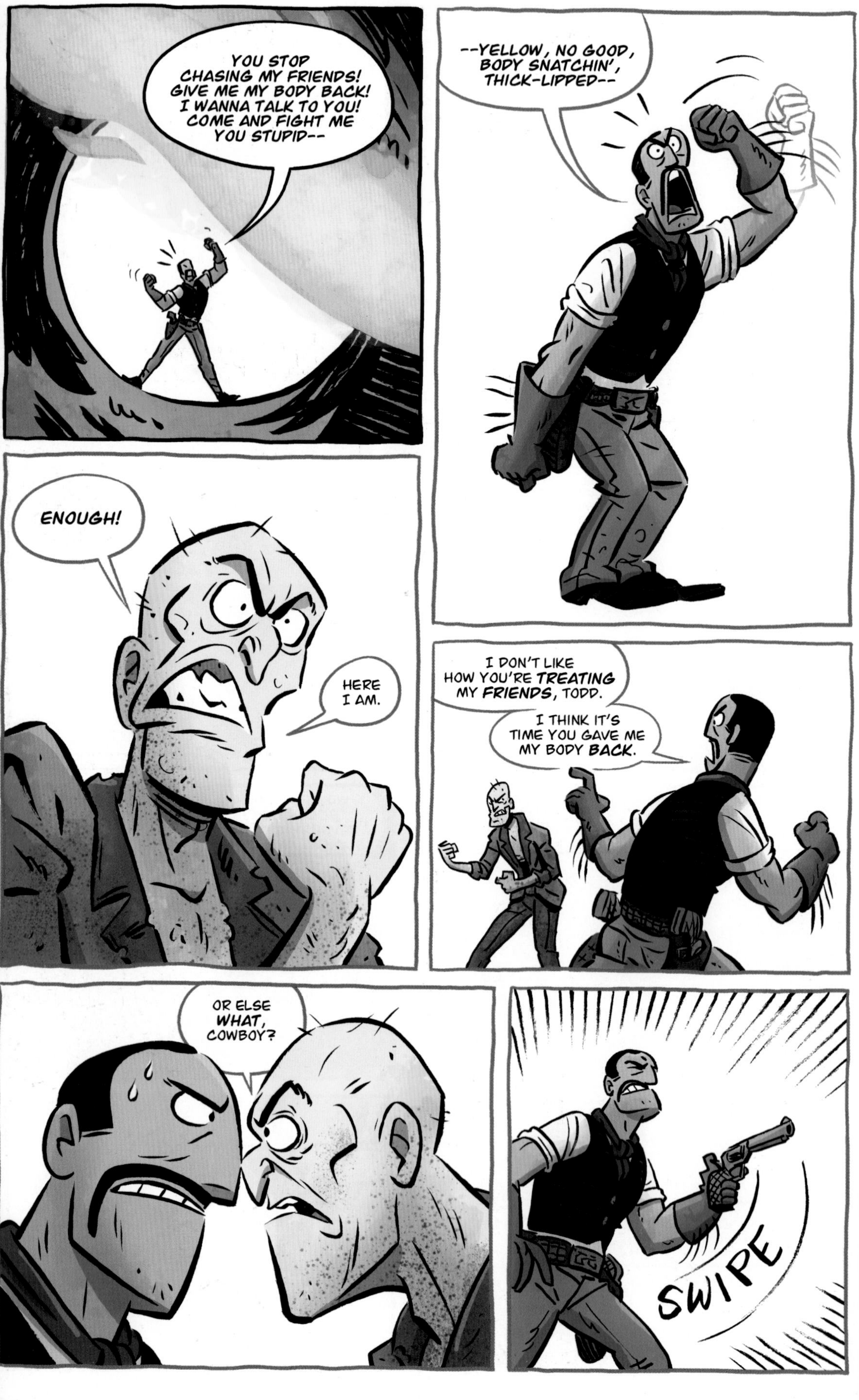
YOU STOP CHASING MY FRIENDS! GIVE ME MY BODY BACK! I WANNA TALK TO YOU! COME AND FIGHT ME YOU STUPID--
--YELLOW, NO GOOD, BODY SNATCHIN', THICK-LIPPED--
ENOUGH!
HERE I AM.
I DON'T LIKE HOW YOU'RE TREATING MY FRIENDS, TODD.
I THINK IT'S TIME YOU GAVE ME MY BODY BACK.
OR ELSE WHAT, COWBOY?
SWIPE

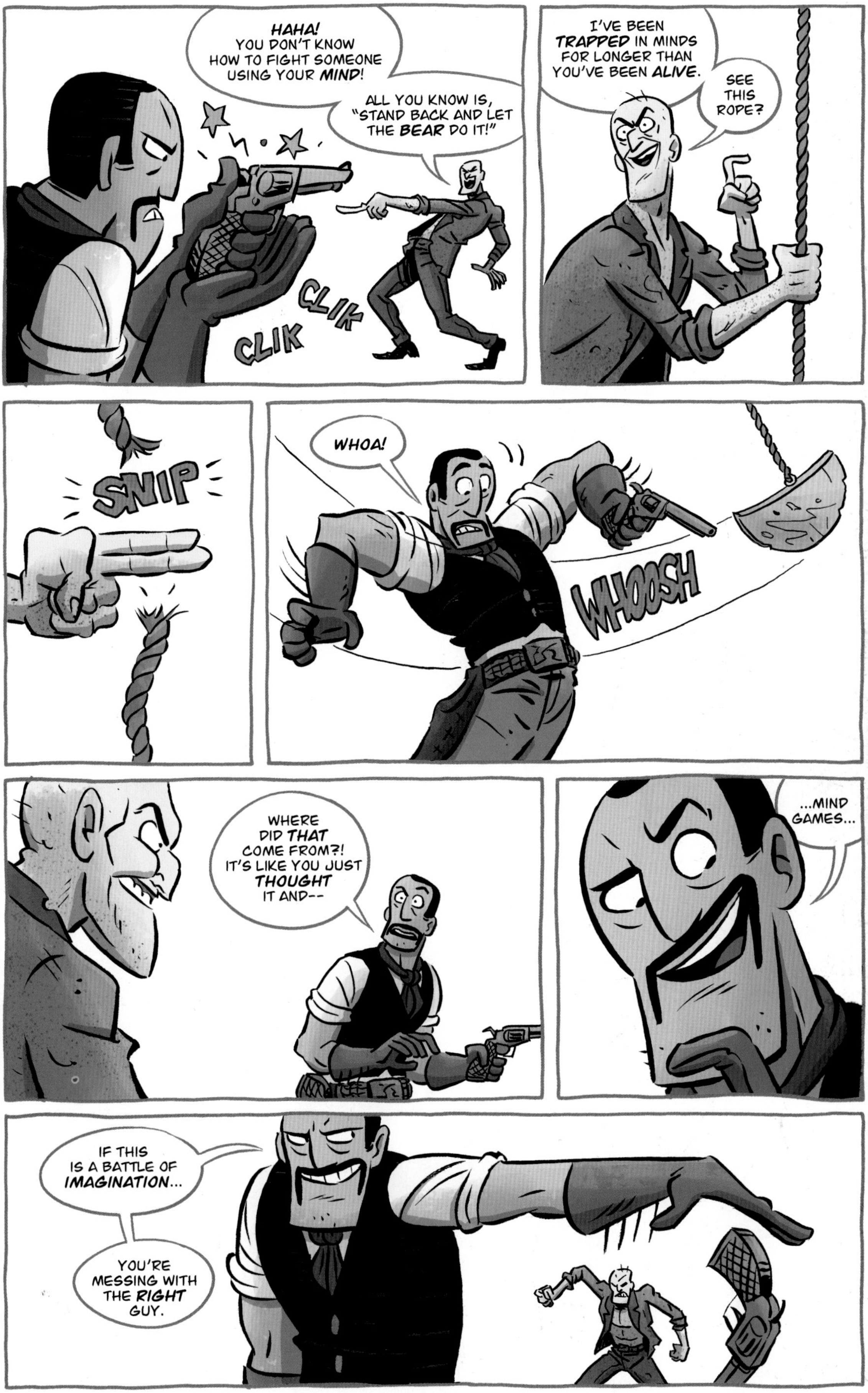
HAHA! YOU DON'T KNOW HOW TO FIGHT SOMEONE USING YOUR MIND!
ALL YOU KNOW IS, "STAND BACK AND LET THE BEAR DO IT!"
CLIK
CLIK
I'VE BEEN TRAPPED IN MINDS FOR LONGER THAN YOU'VE BEEN ALIVE.
SEE THIS ROPE?
SNIP
WHOA!
WHOOSH
WHERE DID THAT COME FROM?! IT'S LIKE YOU JUST THOUGHT IT AND--
...MIND GAMES...
IF THIS IS A BATTLE OF IMAGINATION...
YOU'RE MESSING WITH THE RIGHT GUY.

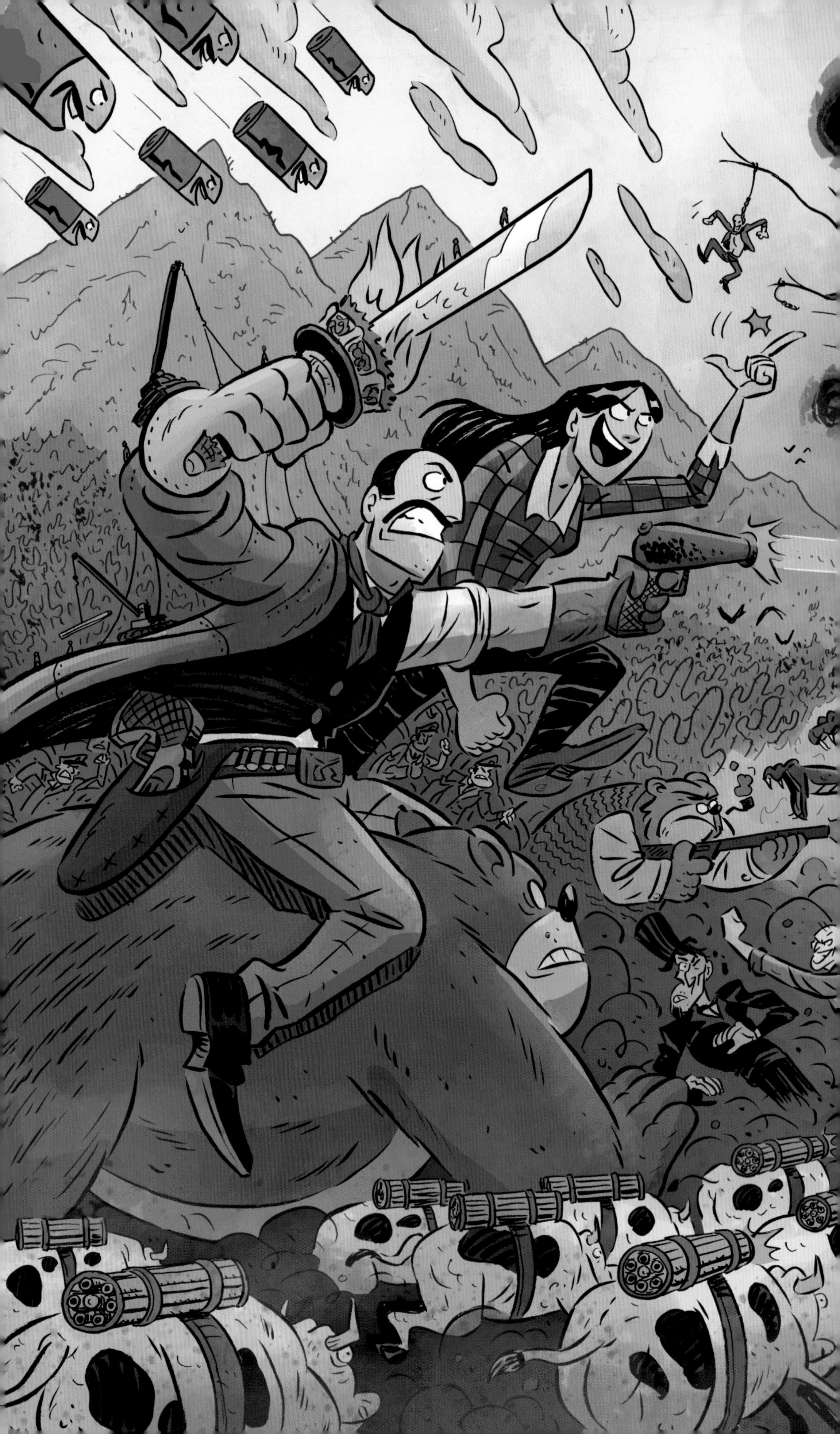

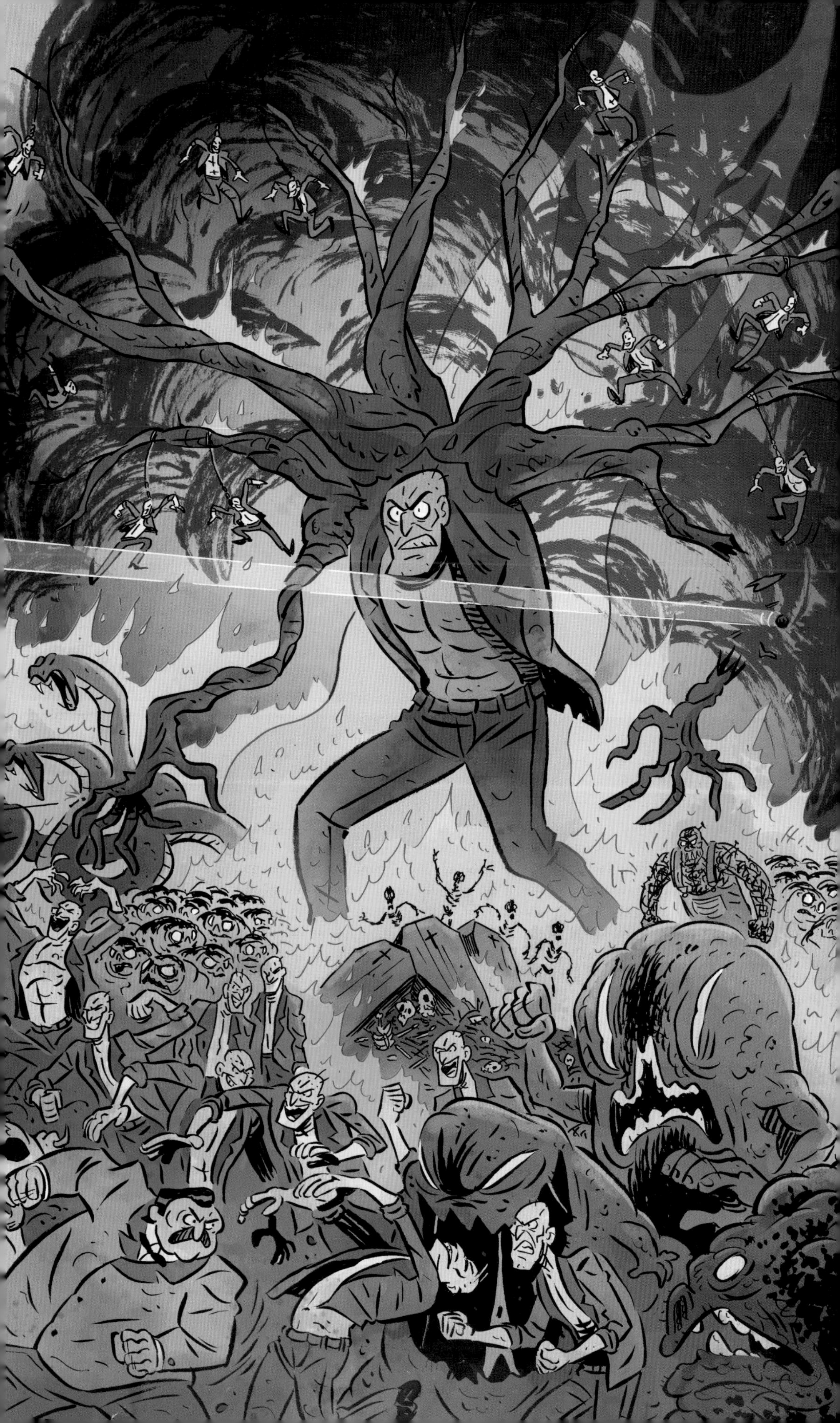

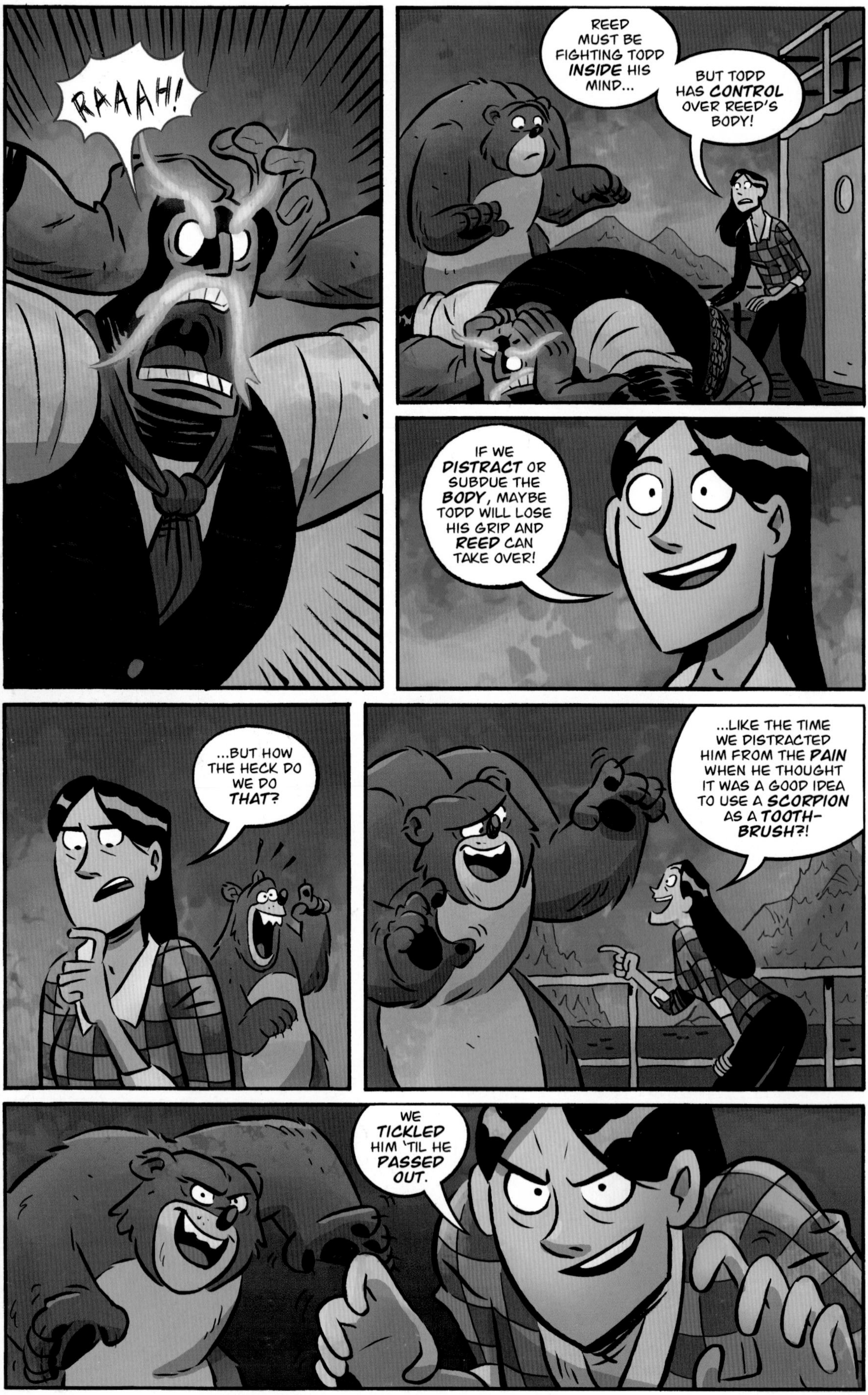
RAAAH!
REED MUST BE FIGHTING TODD INSIDE HIS MIND...
BUT TODD HAS CONTROL OVER REED'S BODY!
IF WE DISTRACT OR SUBDUE THE BODY, MAYBE TODD WILL LOSE HIS GRIP AND REED CAN TAKE OVER!
...BUT HOW THE HECK DO WE DO THAT?
...LIKE THE TIME WE DISTRACTED HIM FROM THE PAIN WHEN HE THOUGHT IT WAS A GOOD IDEA TO USE A SCORPION AS A TOOTH-BRUSH?!
WE TICKLED HIM 'TIL HE PASSED OUT.

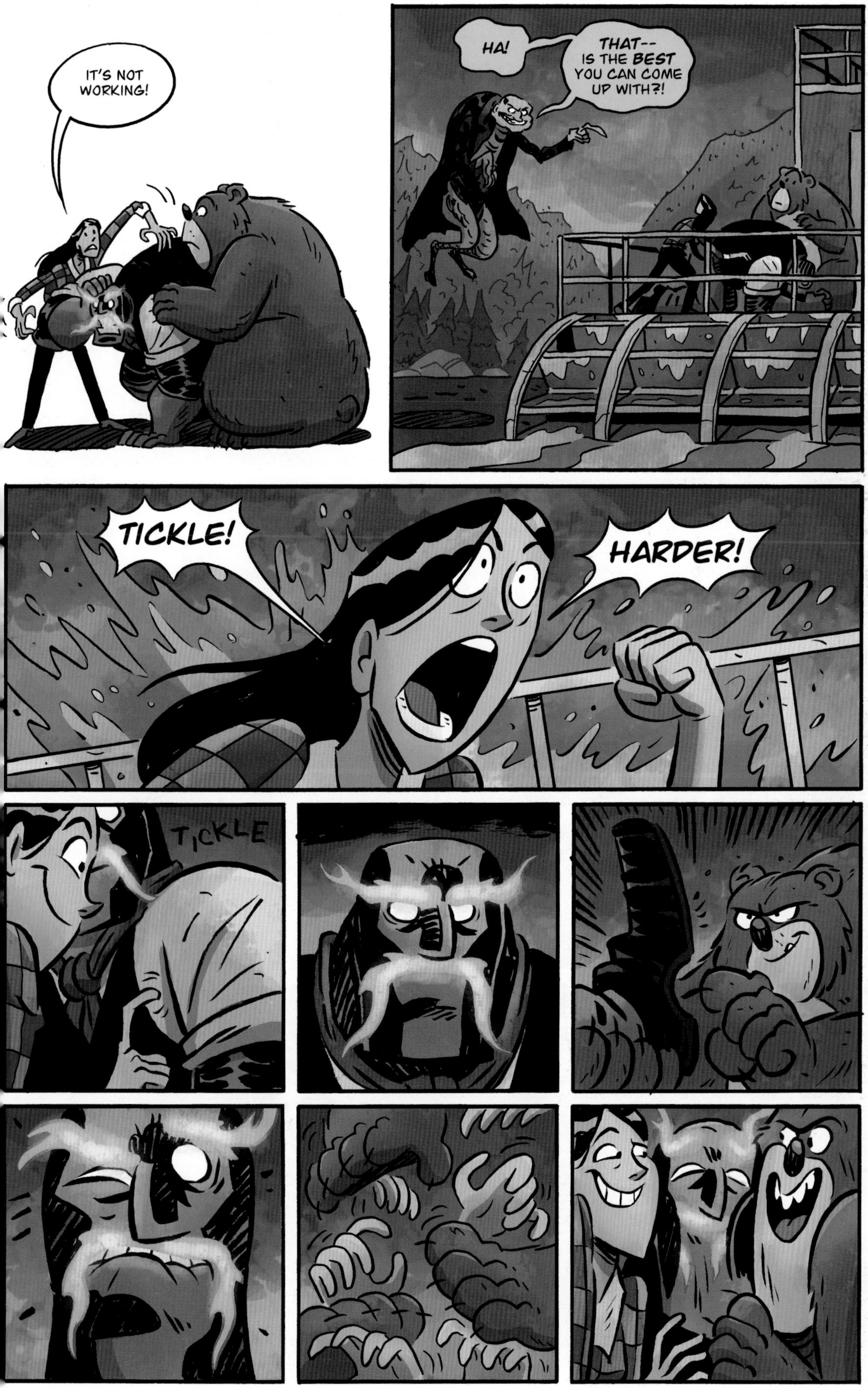
IT'S NOT WORKING!
HA!
THAT-- IS THE BEST YOU CAN COME UP WITH?!
TICKLE!
HARDER!
TICKLE

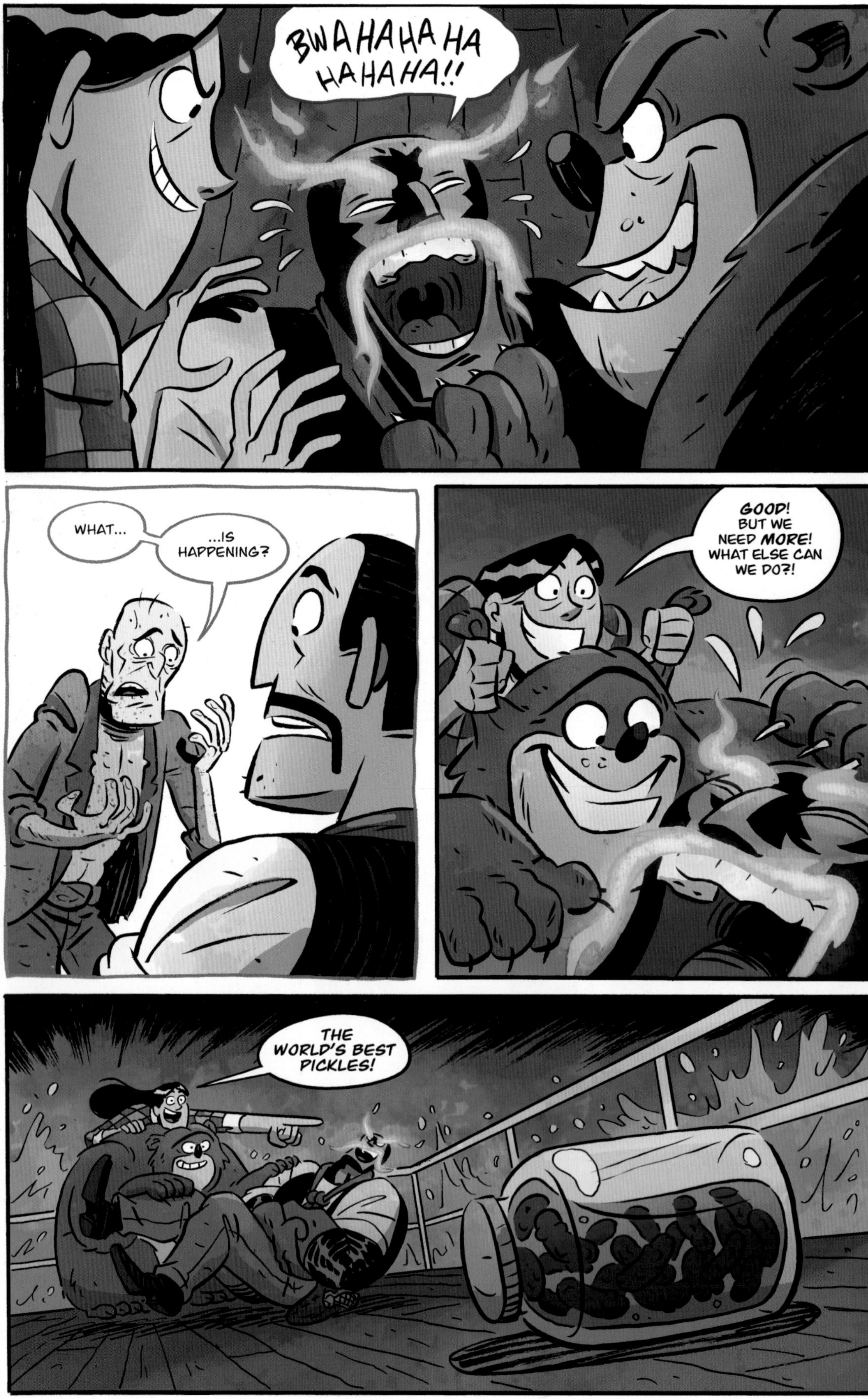
BWAHAHAHA HAHAHA!!
WHAT...
...IS HAPPENING?
GOOD! BUT WE NEED MORE! WHAT ELSE CAN WE DO?!
THE WORLD'S BEST PICKLES!

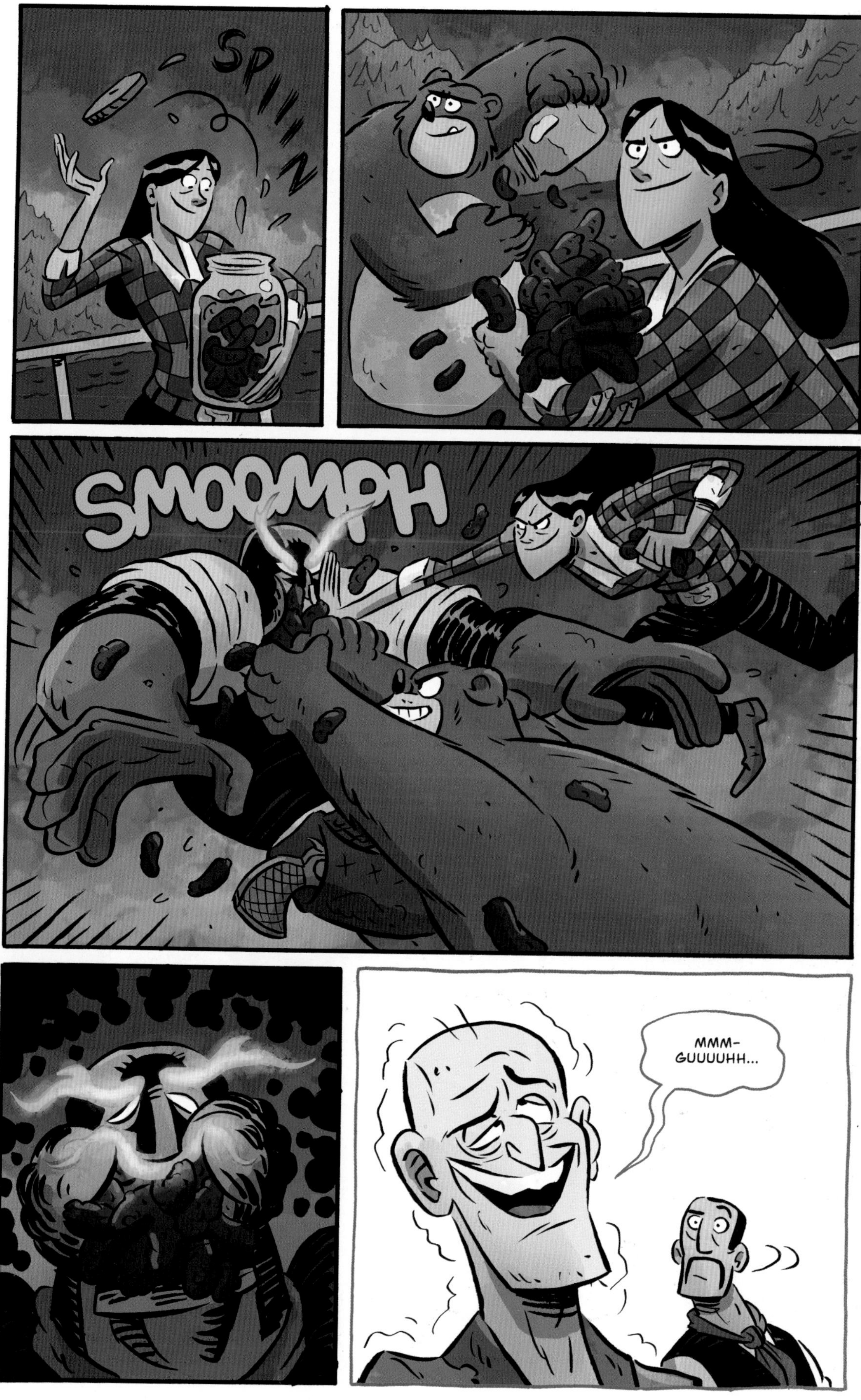
SP
IN
SMOOMPH
MMM-
GUUUUHH...

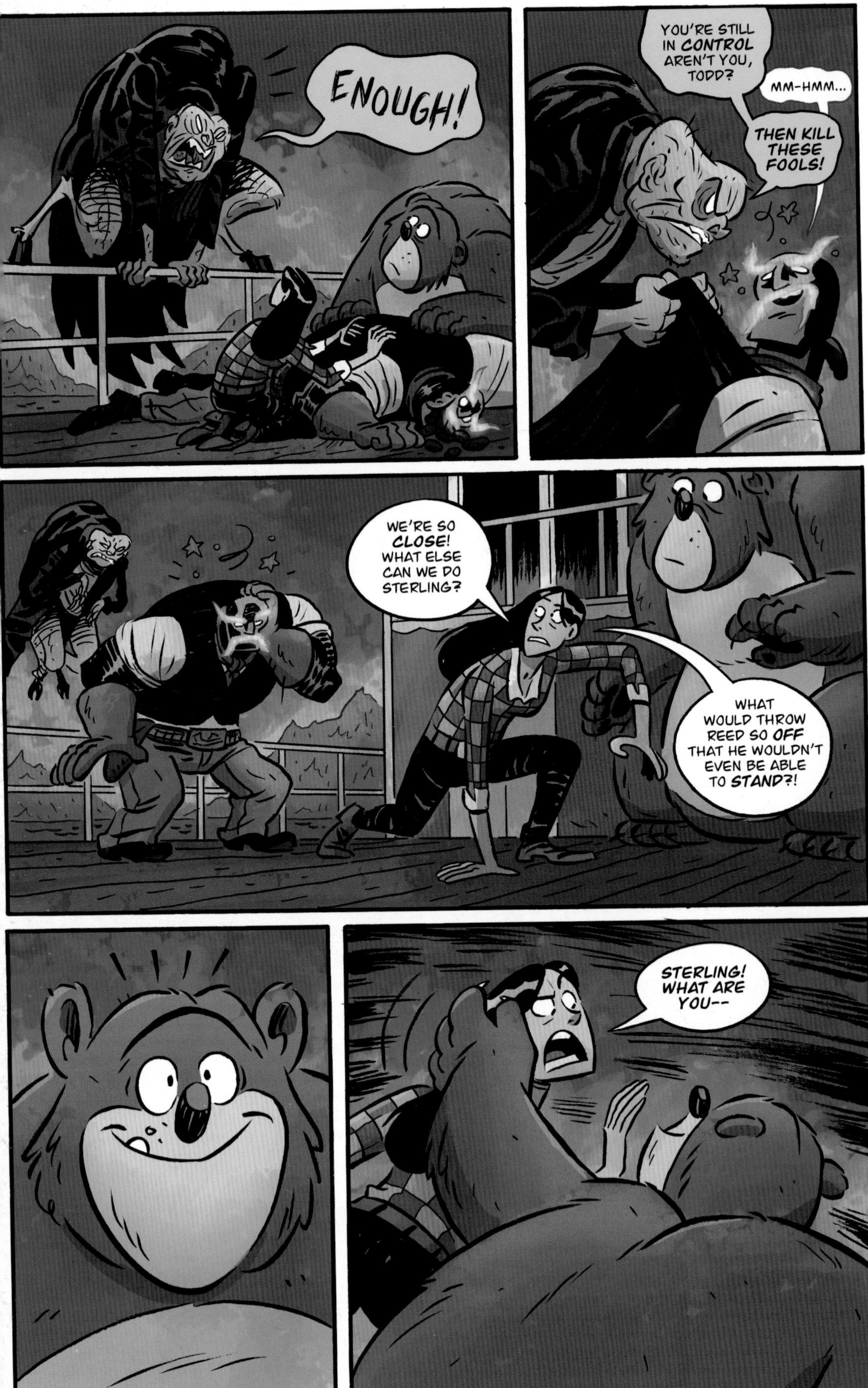
ENOUGH!
YOU'RE STILL IN CONTROL AREN'T YOU, TODD?
MM-HMM...
THEN KILL THESE FOOLS!
WE'RE SO CLOSE! WHAT ELSE CAN WE DO STERLING?
WHAT WOULD THROW REED SO OFF THAT HE WOULDN'T EVEN BE ABLE TO STAND?!
STERLING! WHAT ARE YOU--

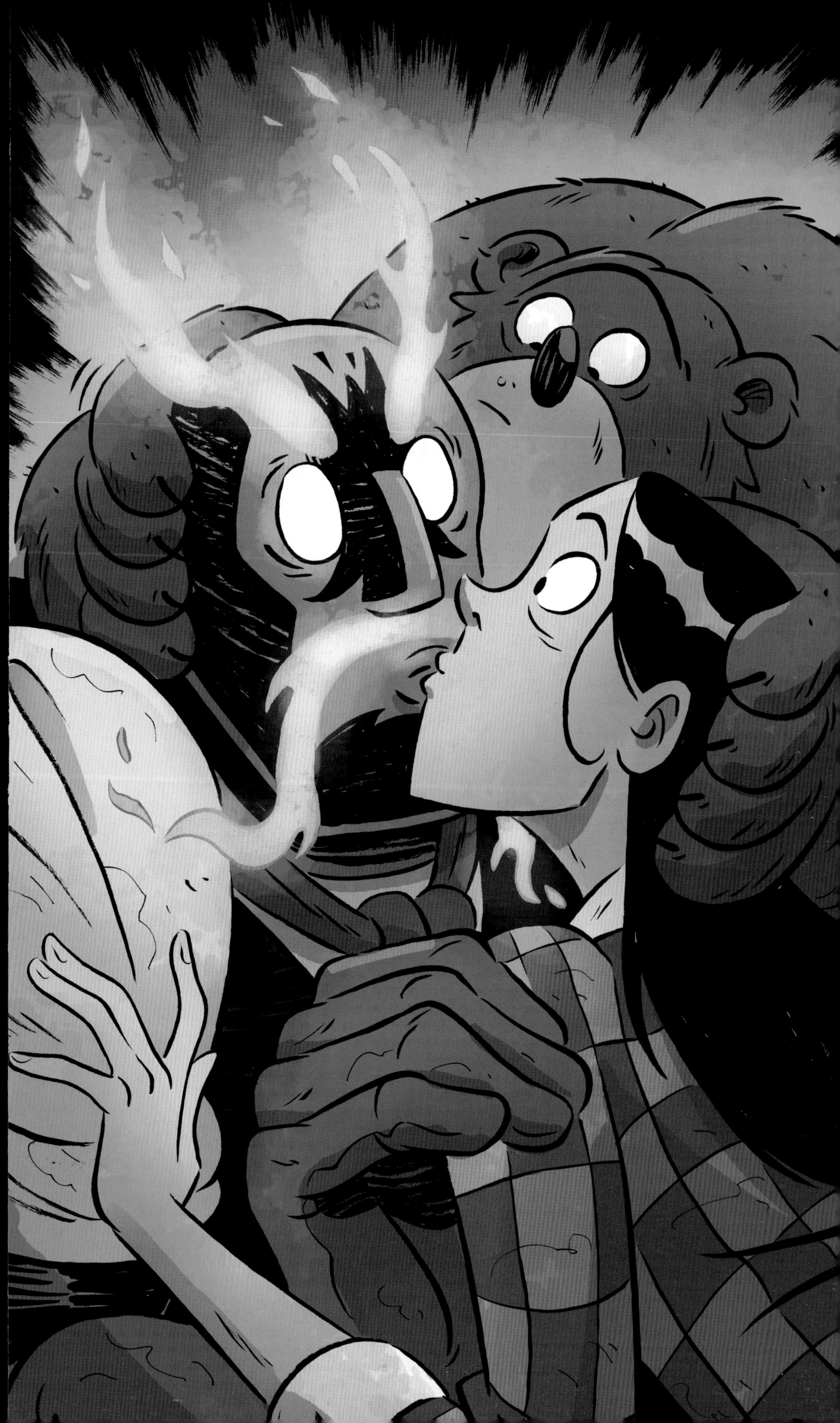

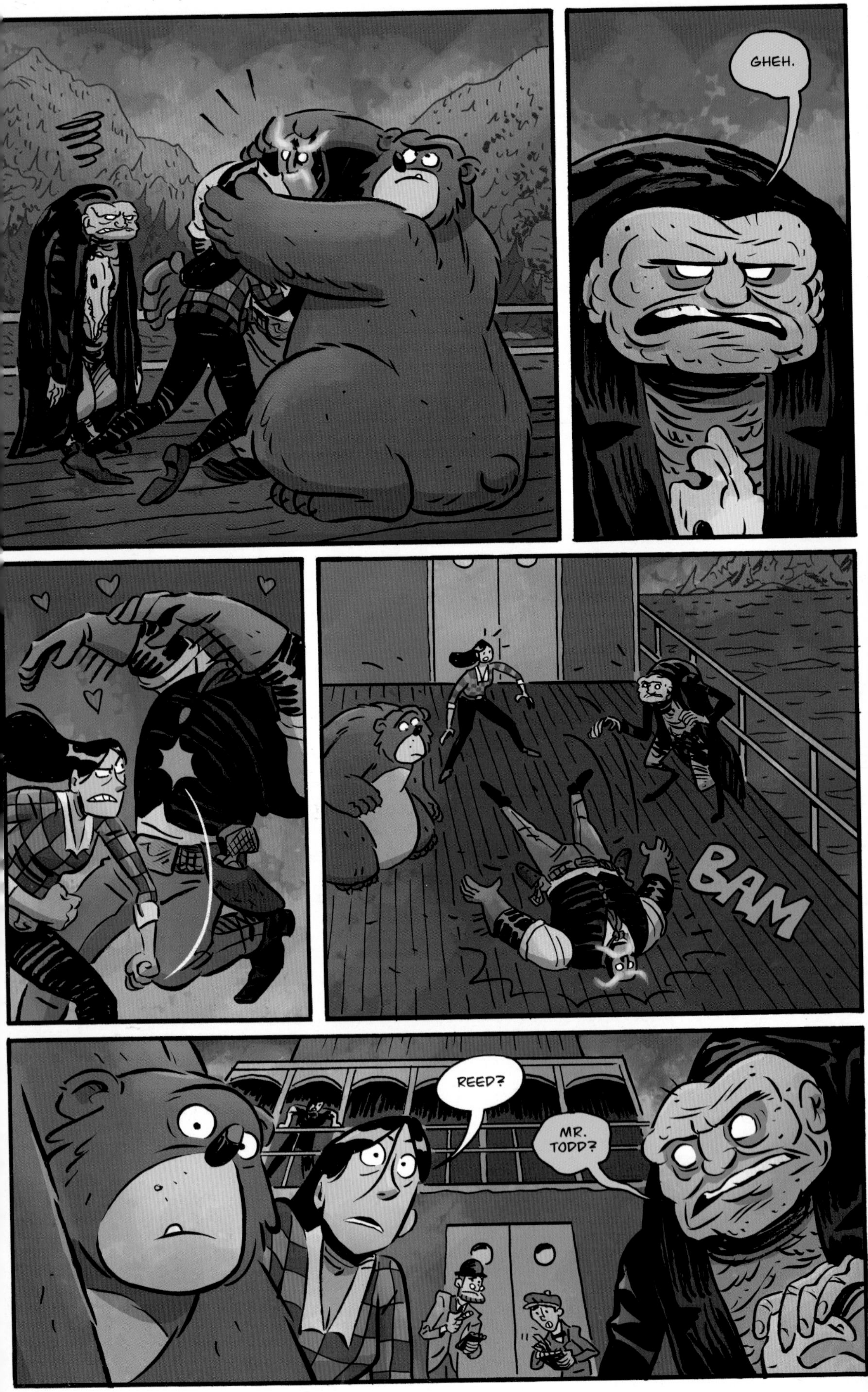
GHEH.
BAM
REED?
MR. TODD?

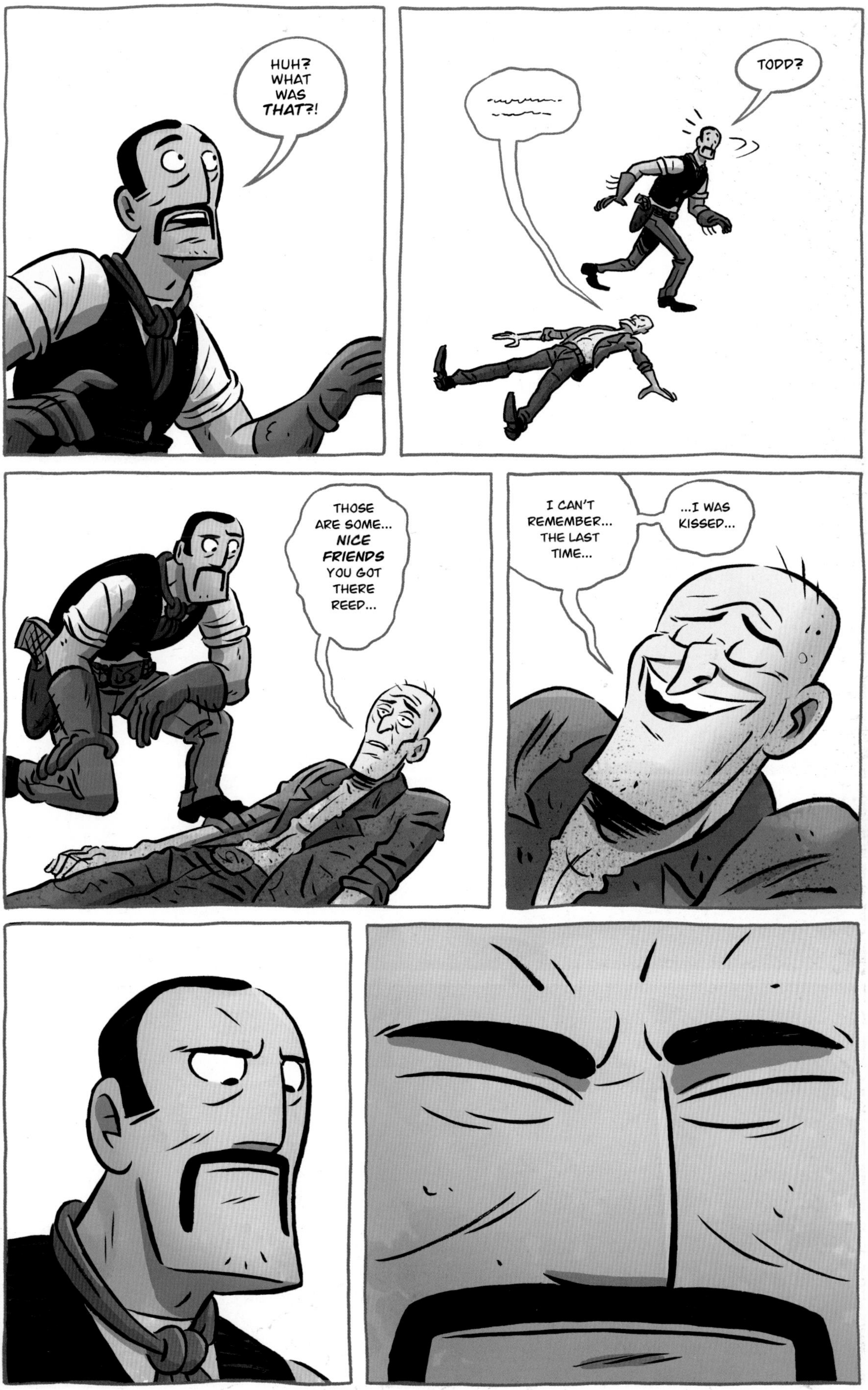
HUH? WHAT WAS THAT?!
TODD?
THOSE ARE SOME... NICE FRIENDS YOU GOT THERE REED...
I CAN'T REMEMBER... THE LAST TIME...
...I WAS KISSED...

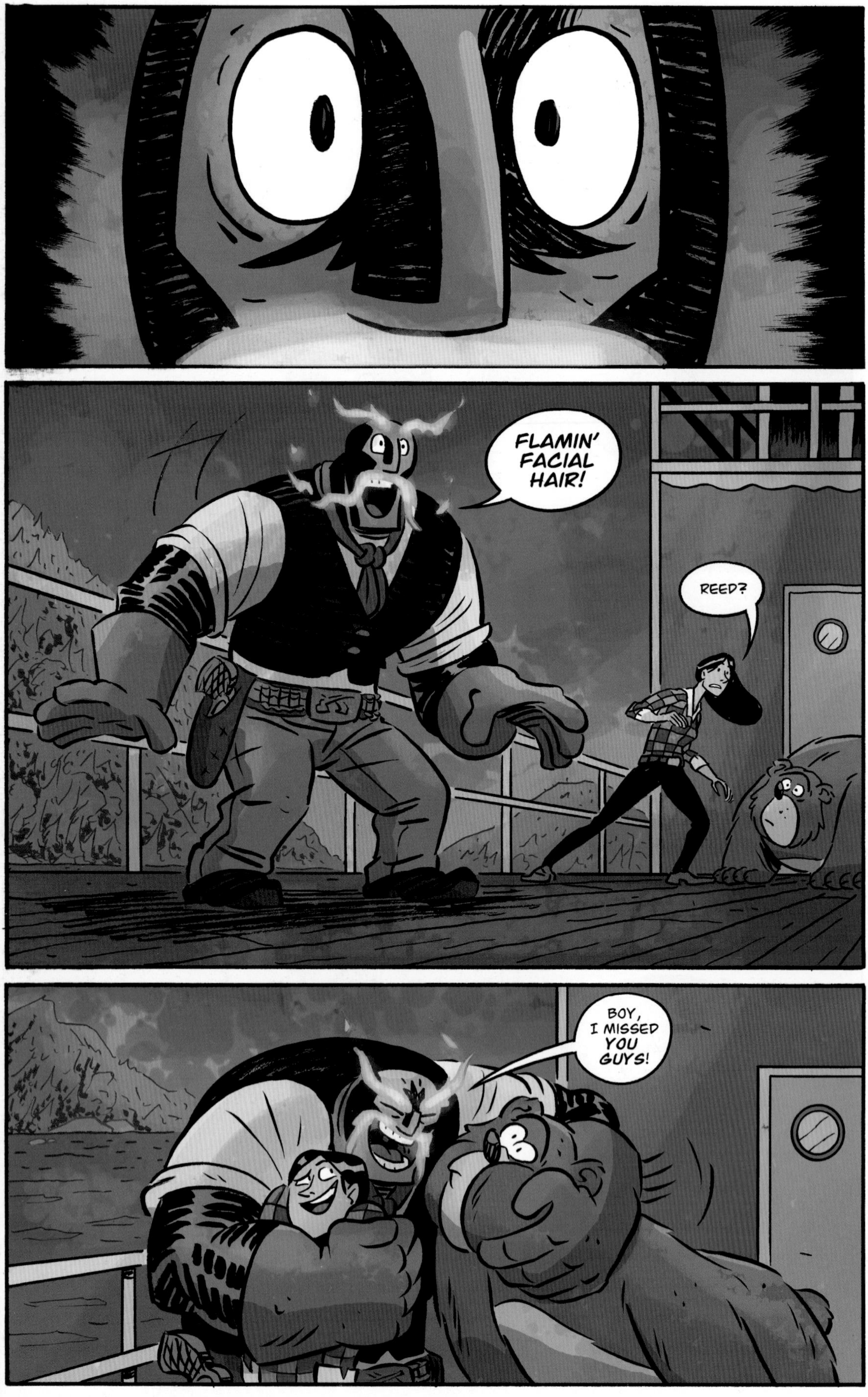
FLAMIN' FACIAL HAIR!
REED?
BOY, I MISSED YOU GUYS!

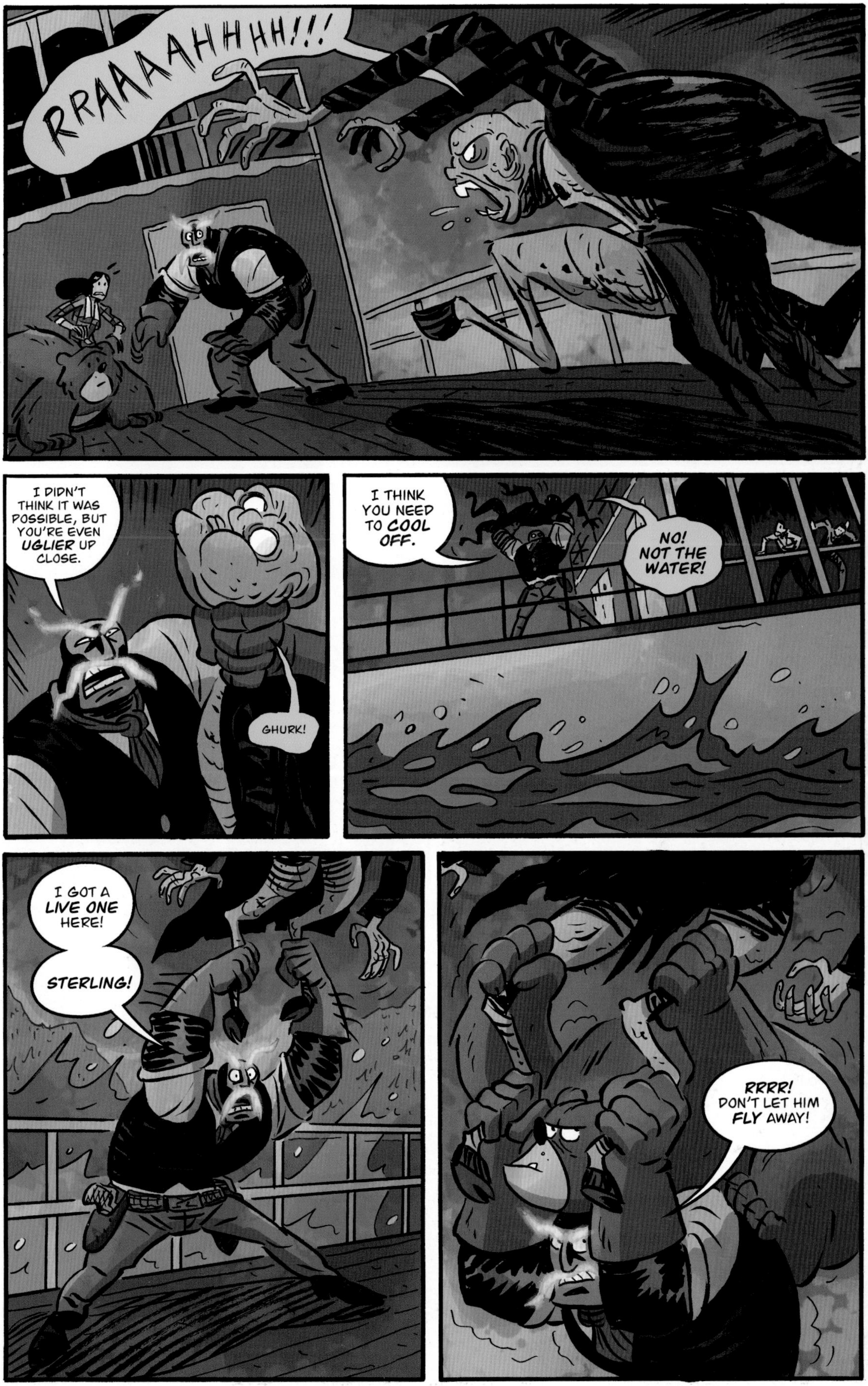
RRAAAAHHHHH!!!
I DIDN'T THINK IT WAS POSSIBLE, BUT YOU'RE EVEN UGLIER UP CLOSE.
GHURK!
I THINK YOU NEED TO COOL OFF.
NO! NOT THE WATER!
I GOT A LIVE ONE HERE!
STERLING!
RRRR! DON'T LET HIM FLY AWAY!

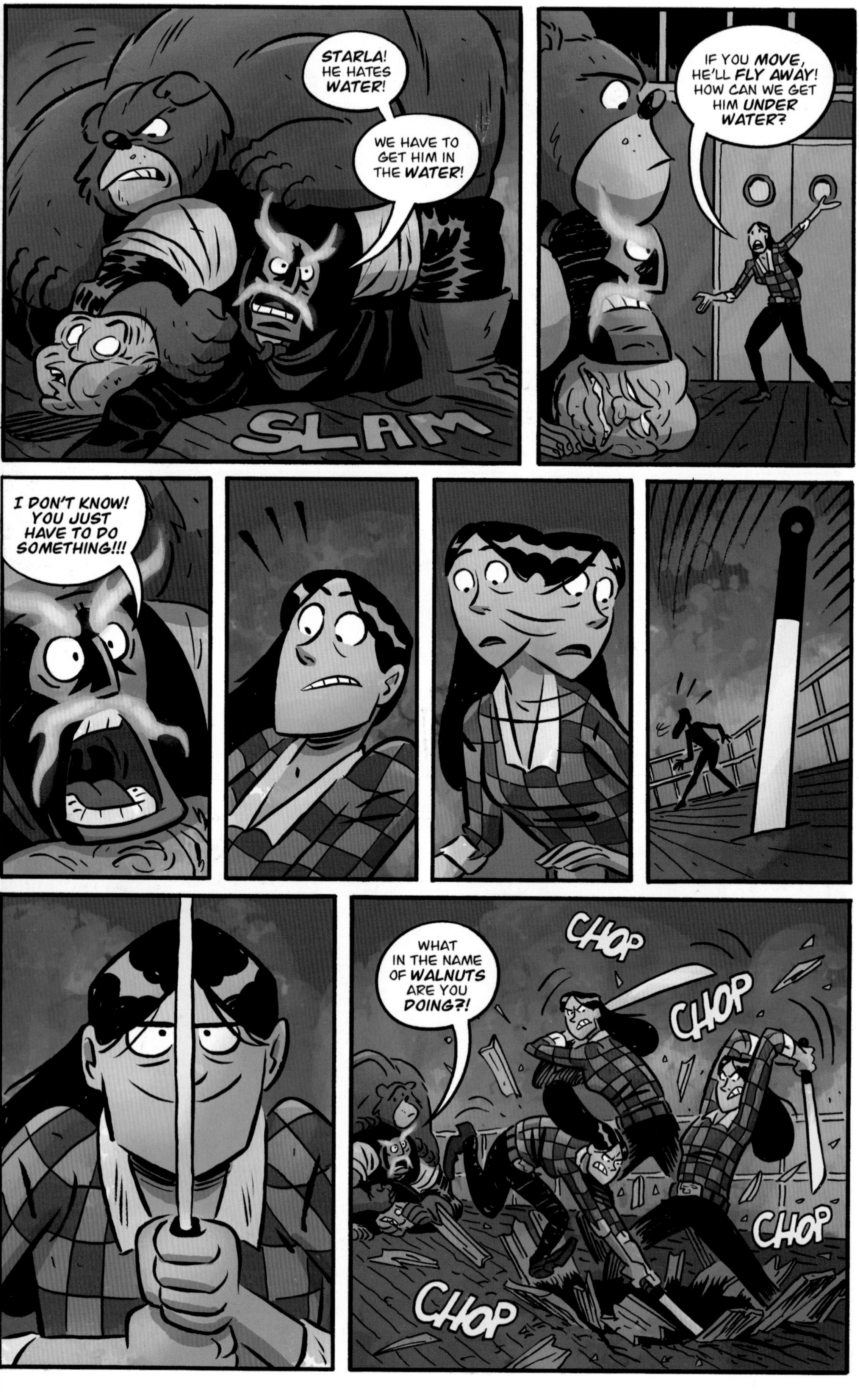
STARLA! HE HATES WATER!
WE HAVE TO GET HIM IN THE WATER!
SLAM
IF YOU MOVE, HE'LL FLY AWAY! HOW CAN WE GET HIM UNDER WATER?
I DON'T KNOW! YOU JUST HAVE TO DO SOMETHING!!!
WHAT IN THE NAME OF WALNUTS ARE YOU DOING?!
CHOP
CHOP
CHOP
CHOP

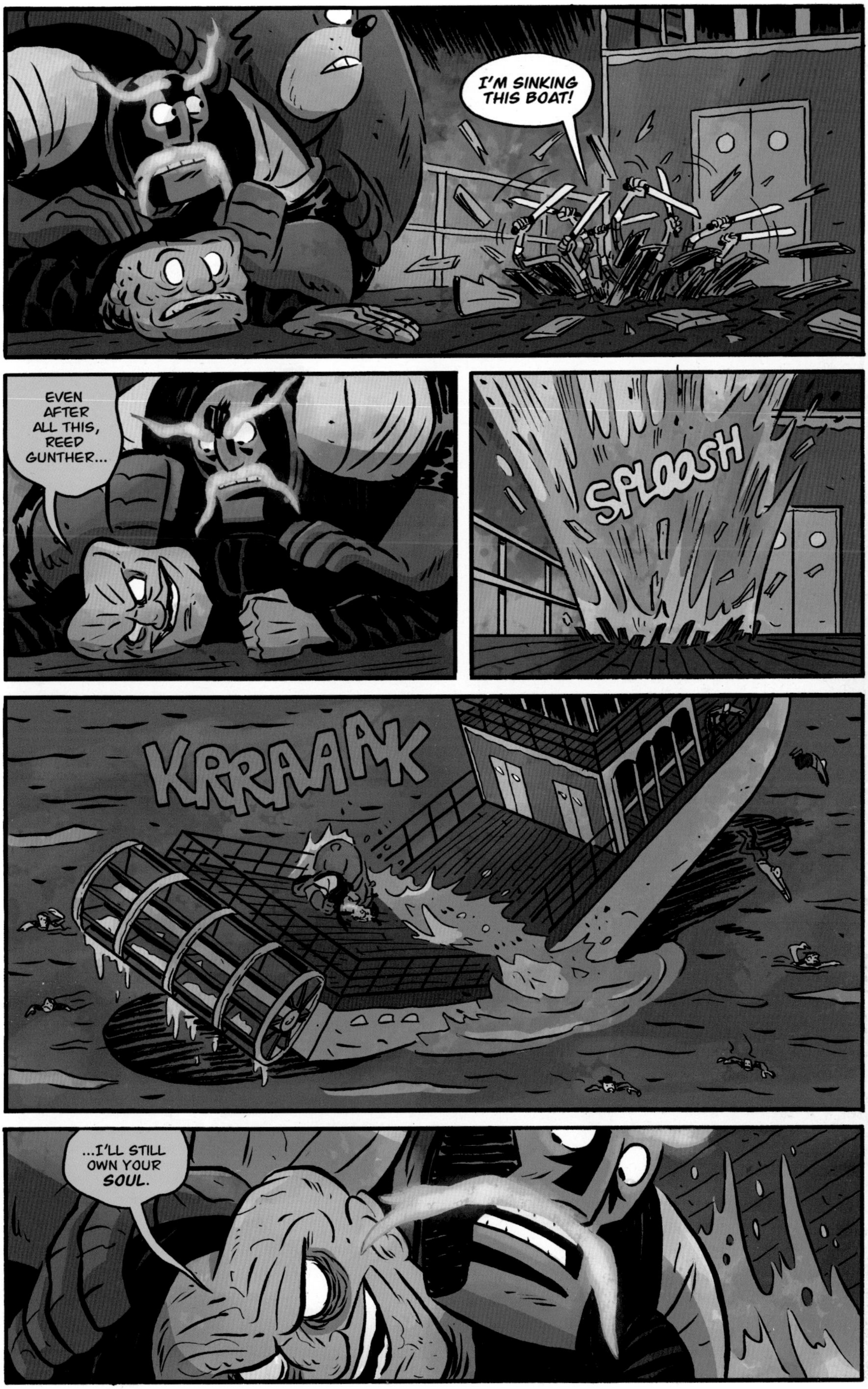
I'M SINKING THIS BOAT!
EVEN AFTER ALL THIS, REED GUNTHER...
SPLOOSH
KRRAAAK
...I'LL STILL OWN YOUR SOUL.

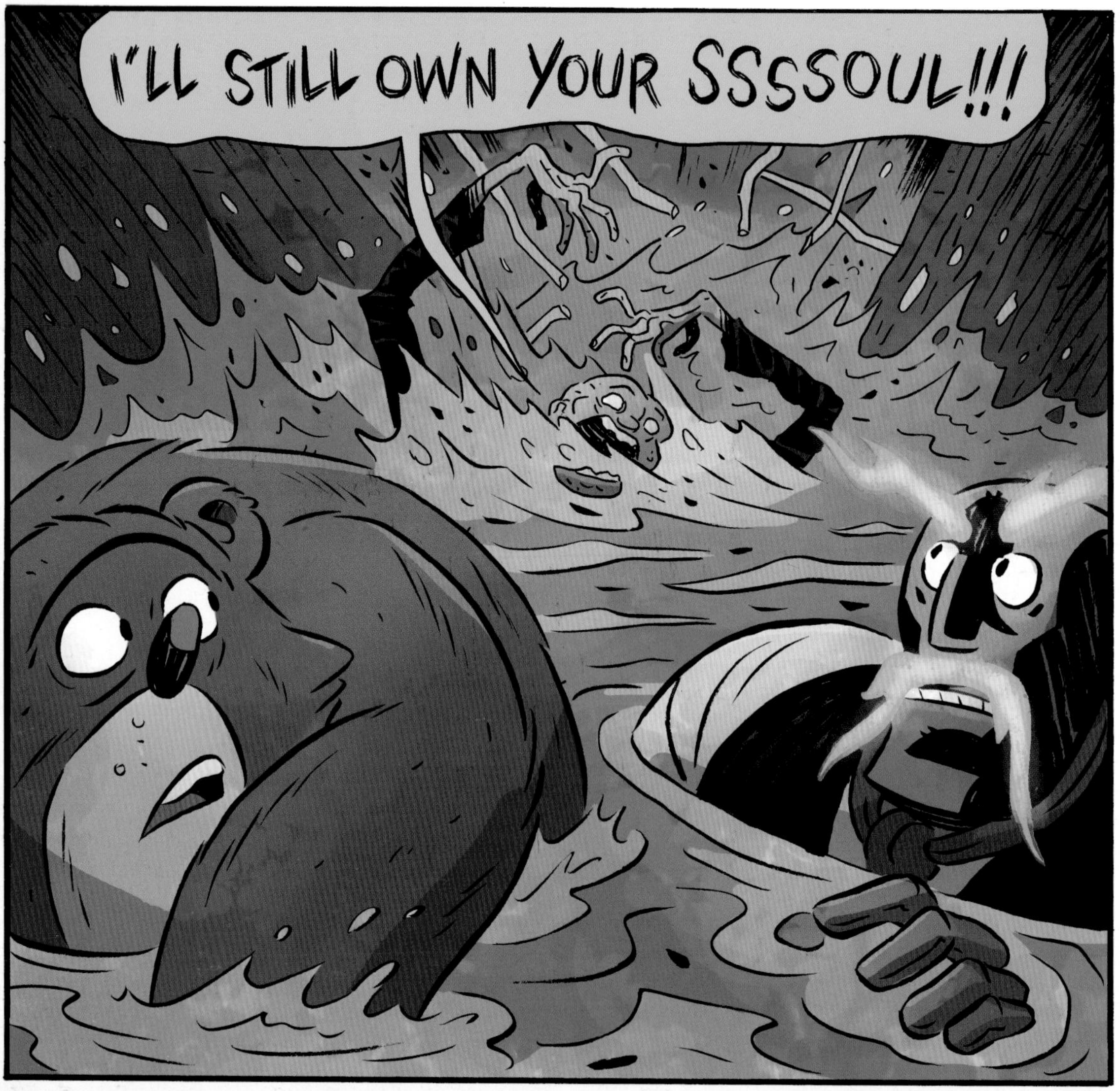
I'LL STILL OWN YOUR SSSSOUL!!!

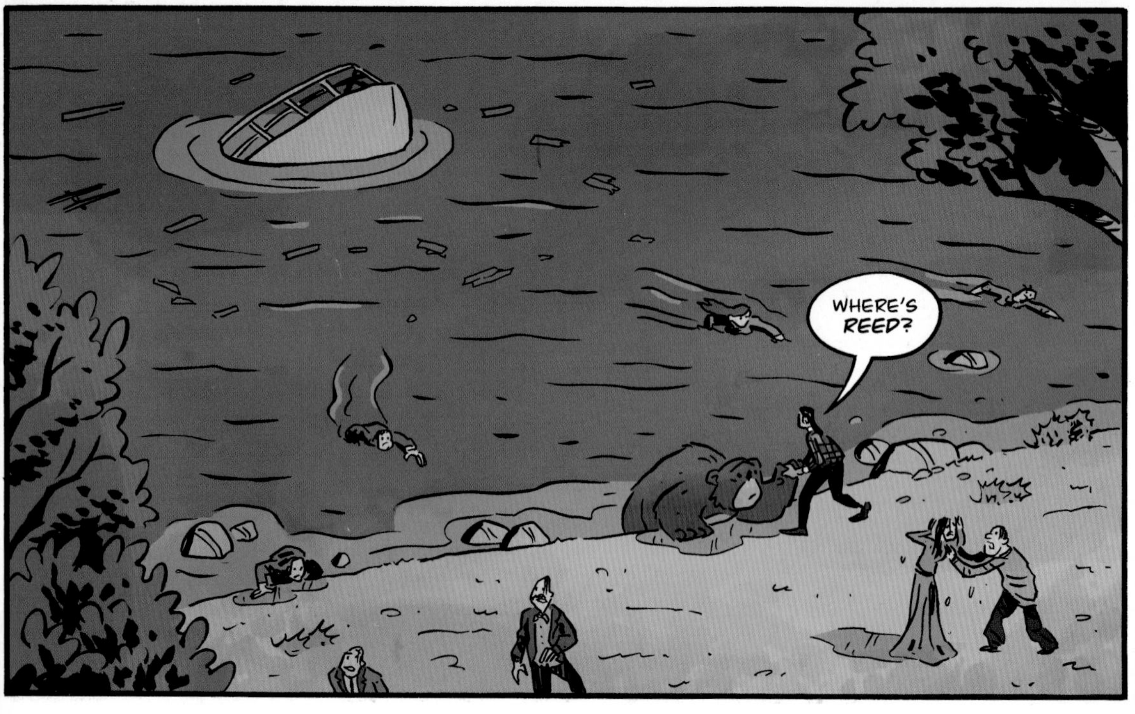
WHERE'S REED?

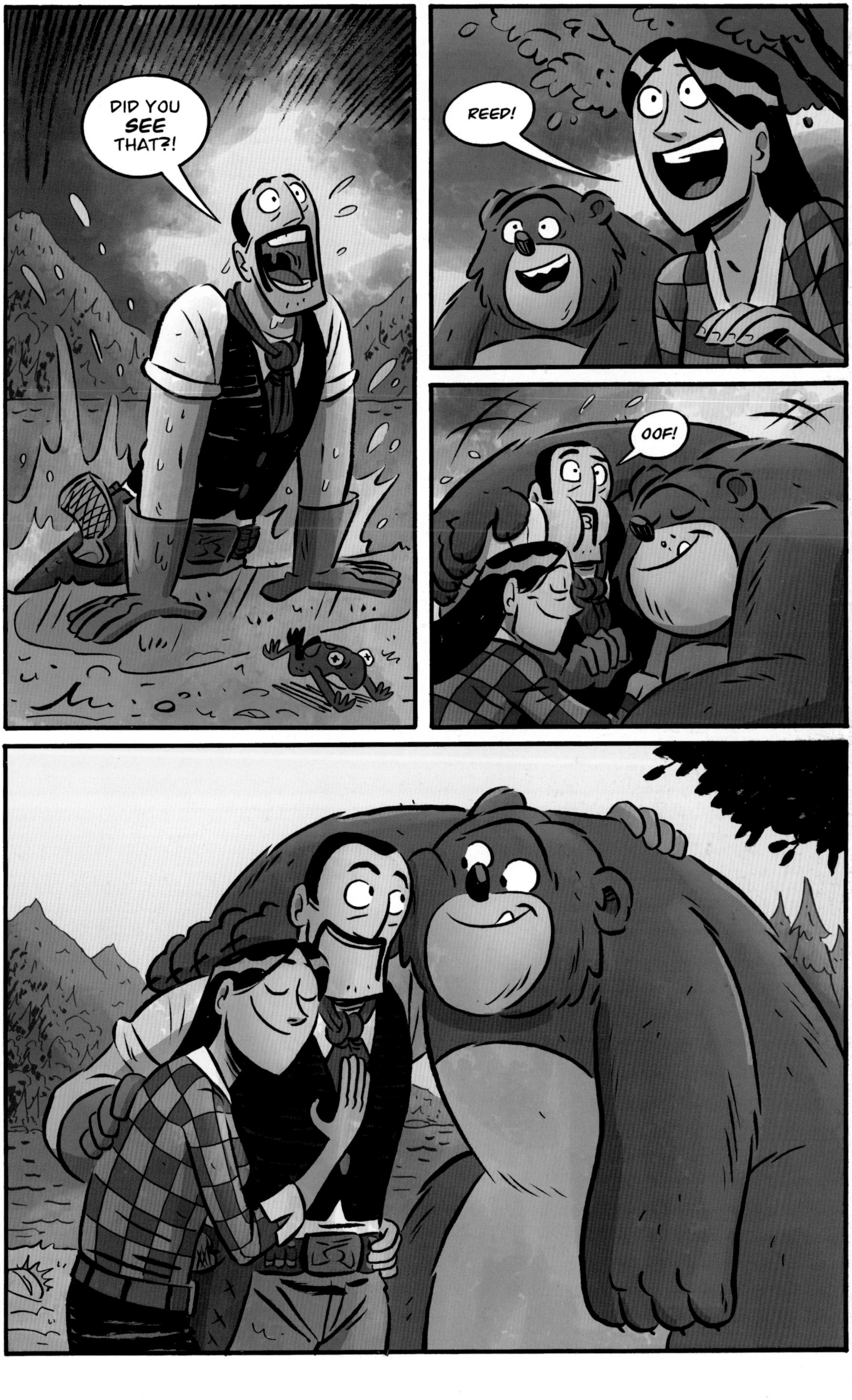
DID YOU SEE THAT?!
REED!
OOF!

HEY! THOSE ARE THE ONES WHO SUNK OUR SHIP!
HE'S RIGHT!
URP.
LET'S RIDE, STERLING!
THINK YOU CAN STILL GET US AWAY FROM THAT MOB STERLING...
...EVEN WITH ALL THIS ADDED WEIGHT?! *SNICKER*
YOUCH! I WAS JUST KIDDING, STARLA!
OUCH! WOW THAT MACHETE IS SHARP!
FRIENDS FOREVER

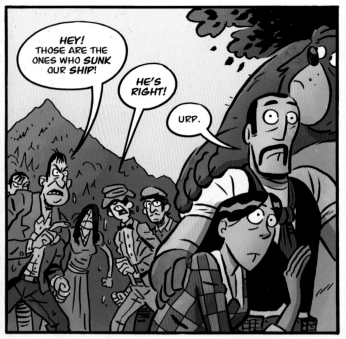

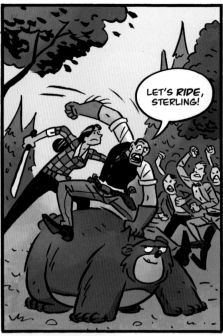

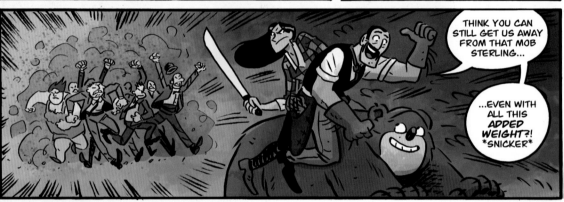

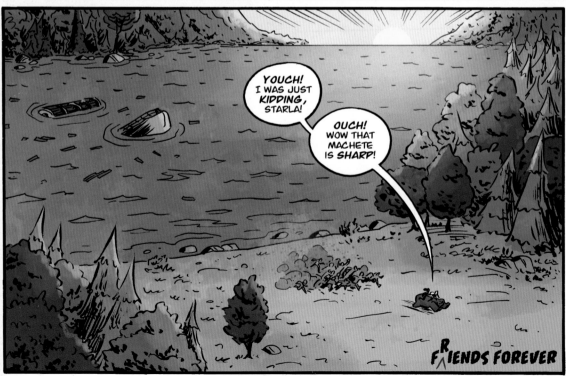

THE END

REED GUNTHER

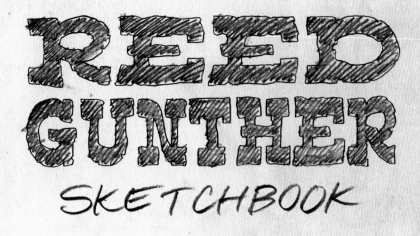

SKETCHBOOK

CHRIS: THERE WAS A LOT OF FUN STUFF TO DESIGN FOR THIS BOOK. SHANE'S IDEA FOR AN ORIGIN STORY FEATURING REED AND STERLING AS KIDS IS HILARIOUS. THINKING ABOUT HOW REED SHOULD LOOK AS A SCRAPPY KID WAS CHALLENGING BECAUSE REED'S DEFINING TRAIT IS HIS MUSTACHE, AND KIDS (BESIDES THAT ONE GUY IN 3RD GRADE) DON'T NORMALLY HAVE MUSTACHES. LUCKILY, SHANE CAME UP WITH A GREAT SOLUTION FOR THAT.

SHANE: A COUPLE OF FUN SECRETS ABOUT THIS STORY: ALTHOUGH ONLY SPOKEN ALOUD ONCE IN THE COMIC, REED'S MOM IS NAMED AFTER OUR ACTUAL GRANDMA, DOLORES. ALSO, REED'S PA, RICHARD, IS OUR ACTUAL DAD'S MIDDLE NAME.

CHRIS: ...AND THE SCAREDY CAT ON THE COVER FOR THIS ISSUE IS MY CAT, SIMON!

big eyes: sheep h—
friendly.

nose: shorter, wide

SHANE: I DON'T THINK WE EVER USED MR. HILL'S FIRST NAME IN THE COMIC BUT IN THE SCRIPT HE'S LISTED AS "JOE HILL" AFTER THE WRITER OF ONE OF MY FAVORITE COMIC BOOK SERIES, LOCKE AND KEY.

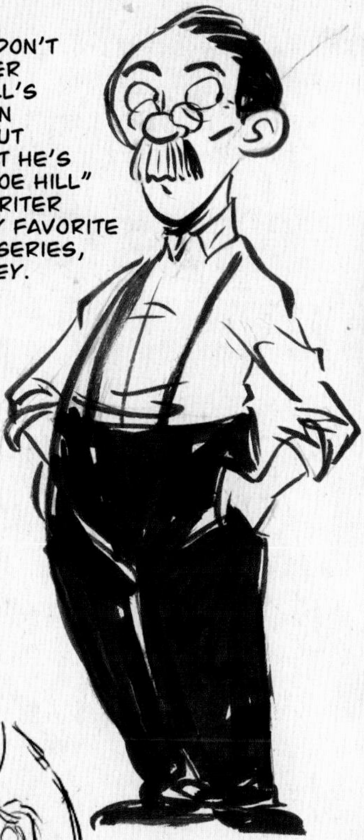
JOE

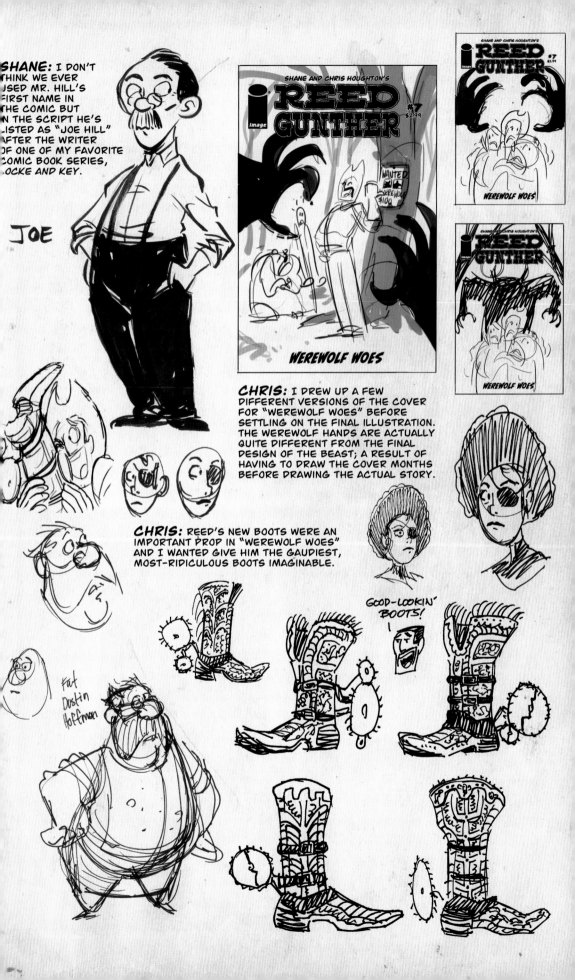

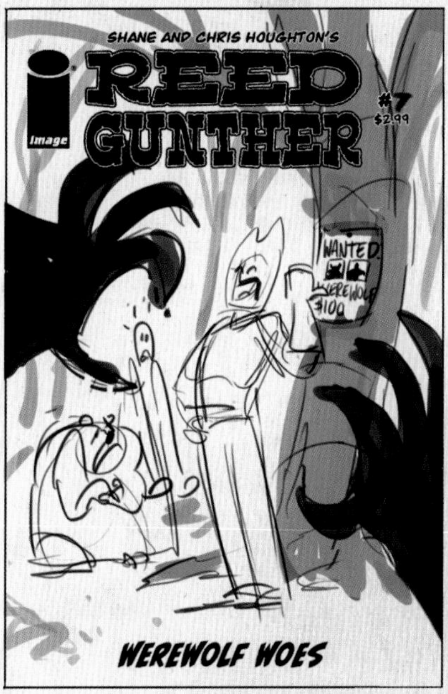
SHANE AND CHRIS HOUGHTON'S
image
REED GUNTHER
#7
$2.99
WANTED
WEREWOLF
$100
WEREWOLF WOES

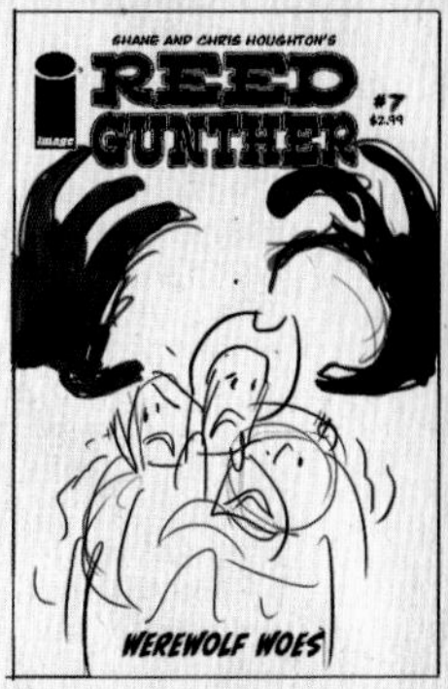
SHANE AND CHRIS HOUGHTON'S
REED GUNTHER
#7
$2.99
WEREWOLF WOES

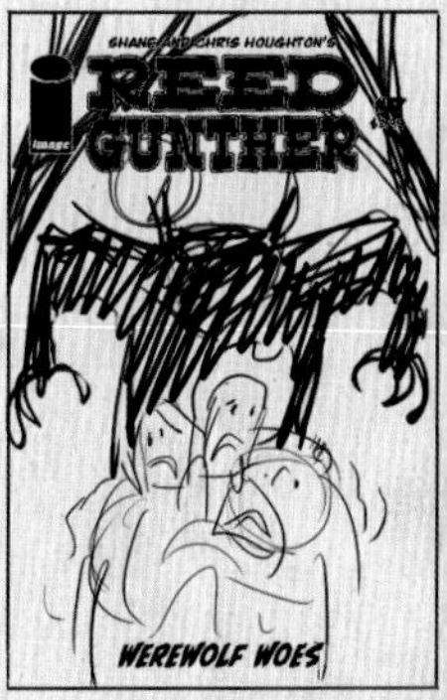
SHANE AND CHRIS HOUGHTON'S
REED GUNTHER
WEREWOLF WOES

CHRIS: I DREW UP A FEW DIFFERENT VERSIONS OF THE COVER FOR "WEREWOLF WOES" BEFORE SETTLING ON THE FINAL ILLUSTRATION. THE WEREWOLF HANDS ARE ACTUALLY QUITE DIFFERENT FROM THE FINAL DESIGN OF THE BEAST; A RESULT OF HAVING TO DRAW THE COVER MONTHS BEFORE DRAWING THE ACTUAL STORY.

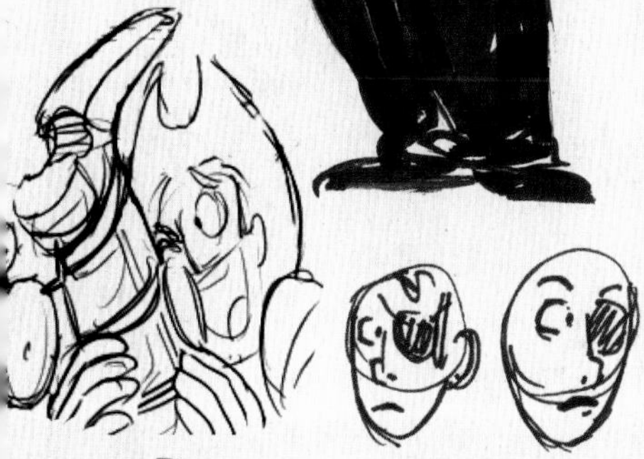

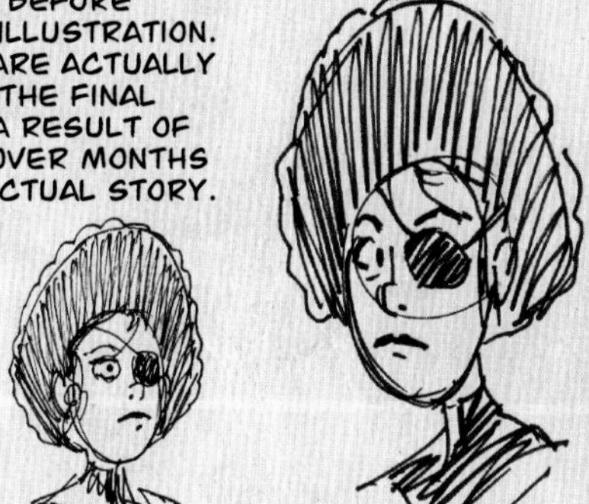

CHRIS: REED'S NEW BOOTS WERE AN IMPORTANT PROP IN "WEREWOLF WOES" AND I WANTED GIVE HIM THE GAUDIEST, MOST-RIDICULOUS BOOTS IMAGINABLE.

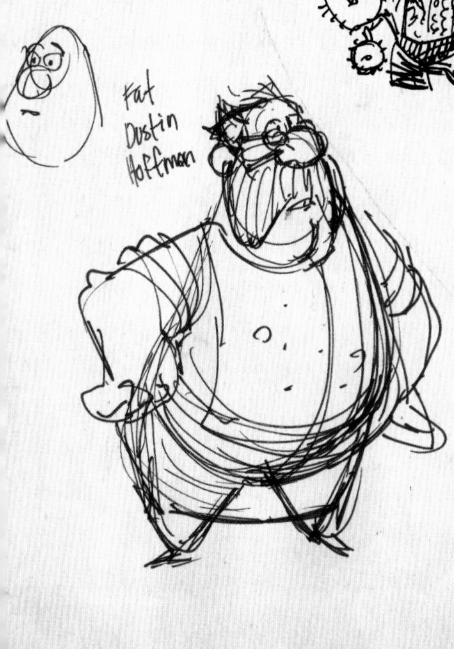
Fat
Dustin
Hoffman

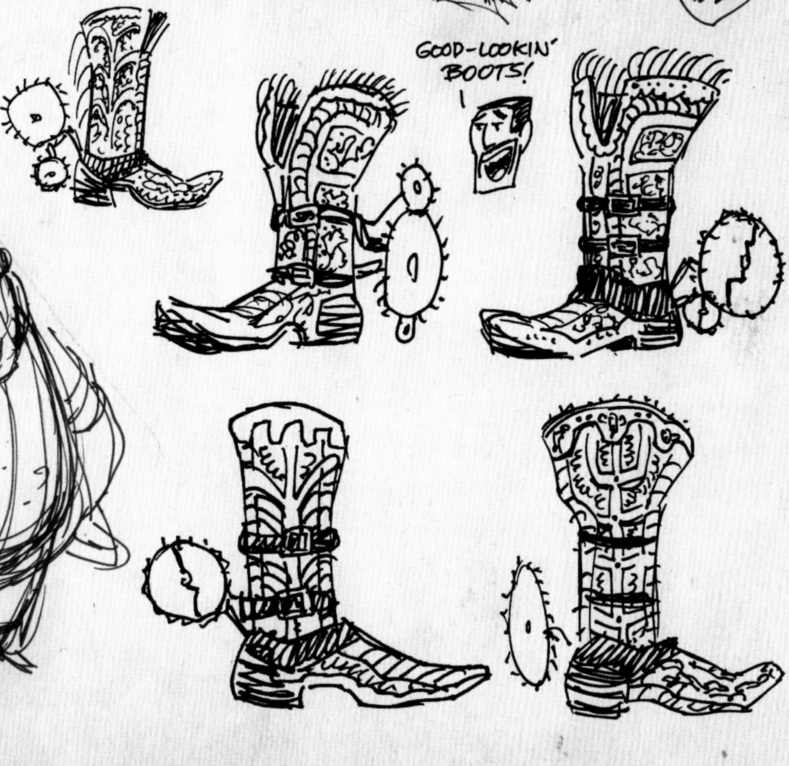
GOOD-LOOKIN' BOOTS!

CHRIS: SHANE ALWAYS HAD AN IDEA FOR AN ISSUE THAT WOULD FEATURE A REVERSE WEREWOLF. IT'S A GREAT IDEA; A WEREWOLF THAT ONCE A MONTH TURNS INTO THE TRUE MONSTER: A HIDEOUS, AWFUL MAN.

THE MAN NEEDED TO BE VERY INTIMIDATING, DIRTY, AND A BIT MYSTERIOUS. WE ALSO WANTED THE WOLF TO BE A LITTLE SCARY IN HIS APPEARANCE AS TO NOT GIVE AWAY THE TWIST ENDING UNTIL THE LAST FEW PAGES OF THE STORY.

I ALSO GAVE THE OLD HERMIT MAN IN THE WOODS POPEYE ARMS BECAUSE WHO DOESN'T WANT POPEYE ARMS?

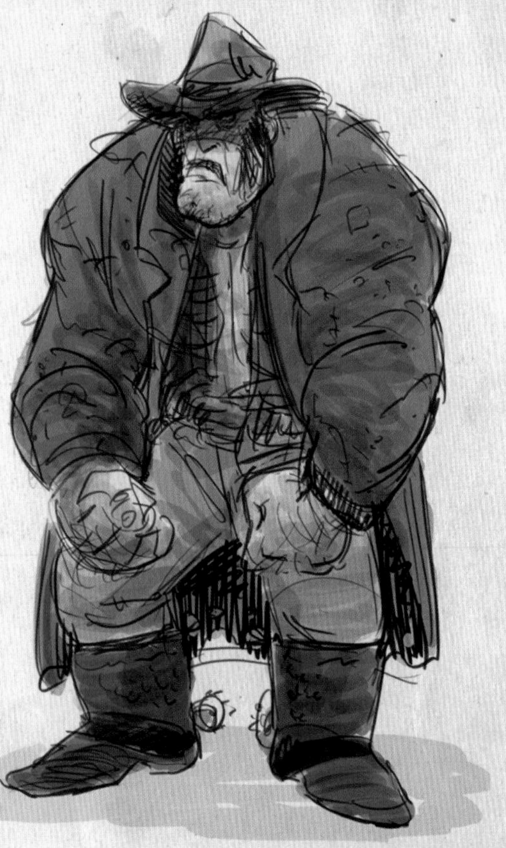

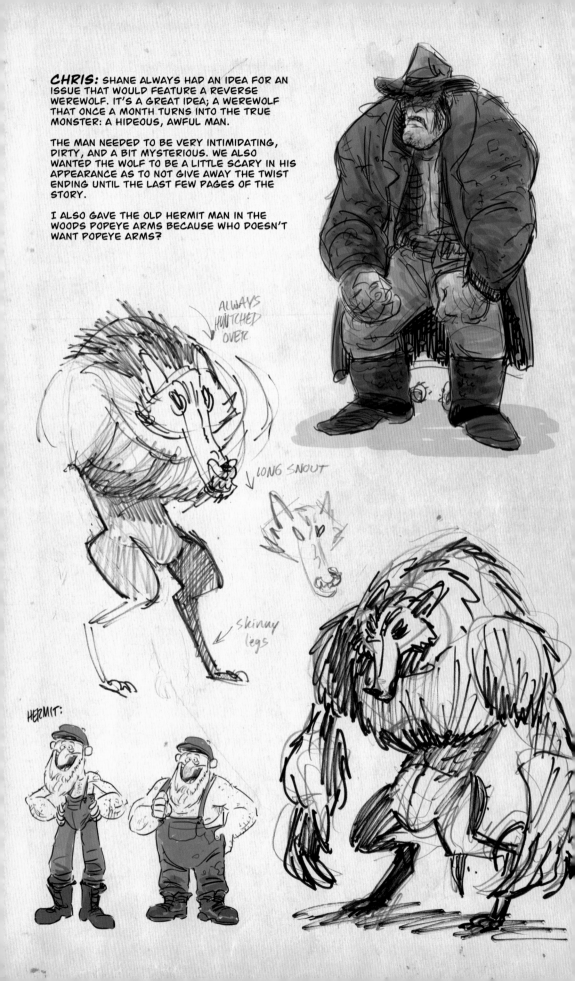

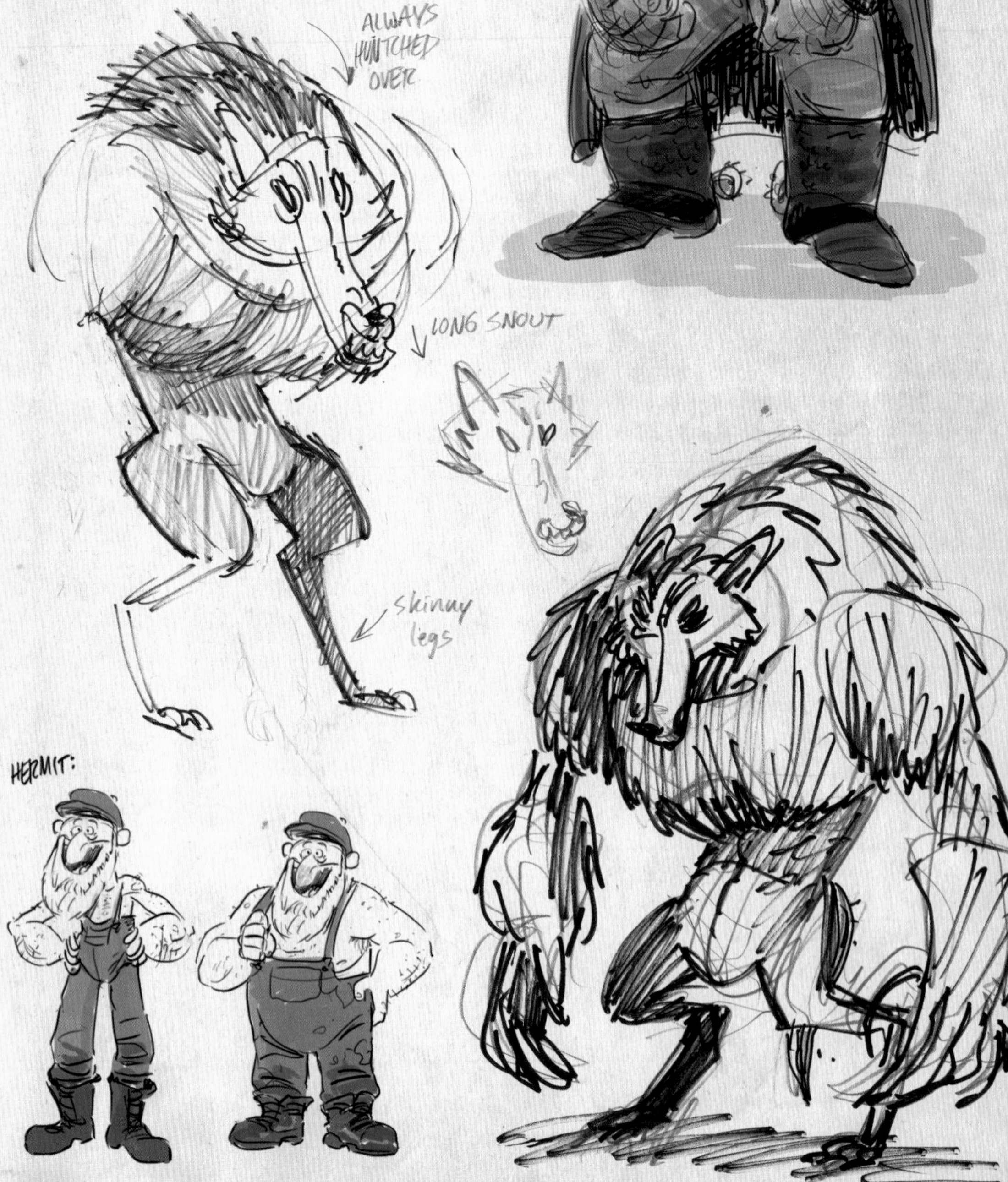
ALWAYS HUNCHED OVER
LONG SNOUT
skinny legs
HERMIT:

CHRIS: I KEPT BUGGING SHANE TO WRITE A STORY THAT FEATURED NATIVE AMERICAN MUMMIES. SINCE HE'S A GOOD BROTHER HE FINALLY CAVED TO MY REQUEST. BUT MONSTERS ARE NEVER THE MAIN FOCUS IN REED GUNTHER STORIES; THE CHARACTERS ARE. THE MUMMIES IN "REAL LADIES PUNCH HARDER" WERE ONLY A SMALL SUPPORTING ROLE TO MUCH MORE IMPORTANT AND INTERESTING THEME.

SHANE: STARLA IS SUCH AN IMPORTANT PART OF REED'S GROUP, AND I REALLY WANTED TO FEATURE HER IN A STORY CENTERED AROUND HER. STARLA IS A VERY PROGRESSIVE LADY FOR HER TIME PERIOD. I ALWAYS DISLIKED THE HOITY-TOITY HIGH CLASS LADIES THAT SEEM TO SURVIVE IN HISTORY BOOKS. BUT REAL LADIES LIKE STARLA ARE THE ONES THAT INTEREST ME.

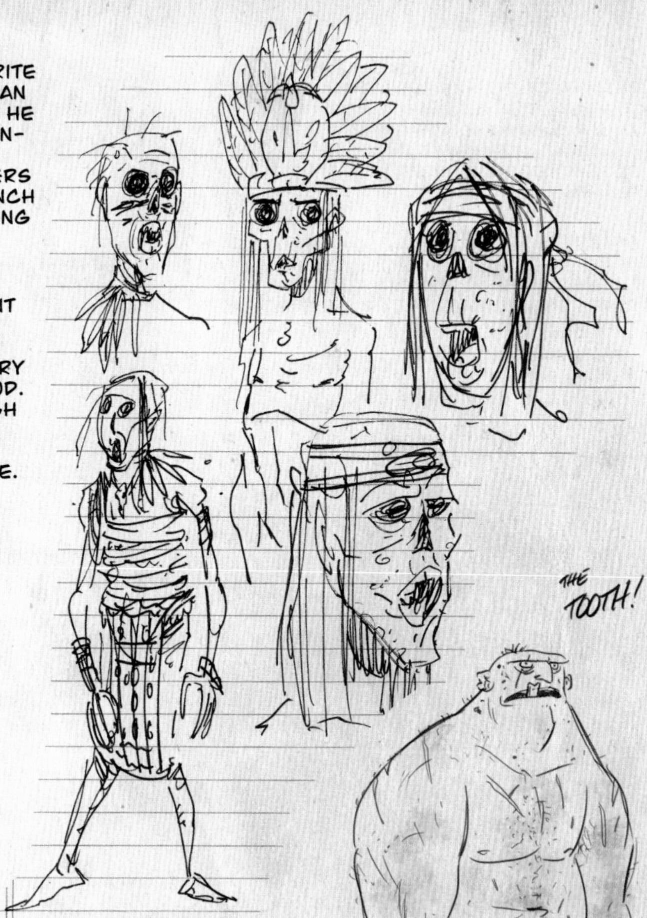

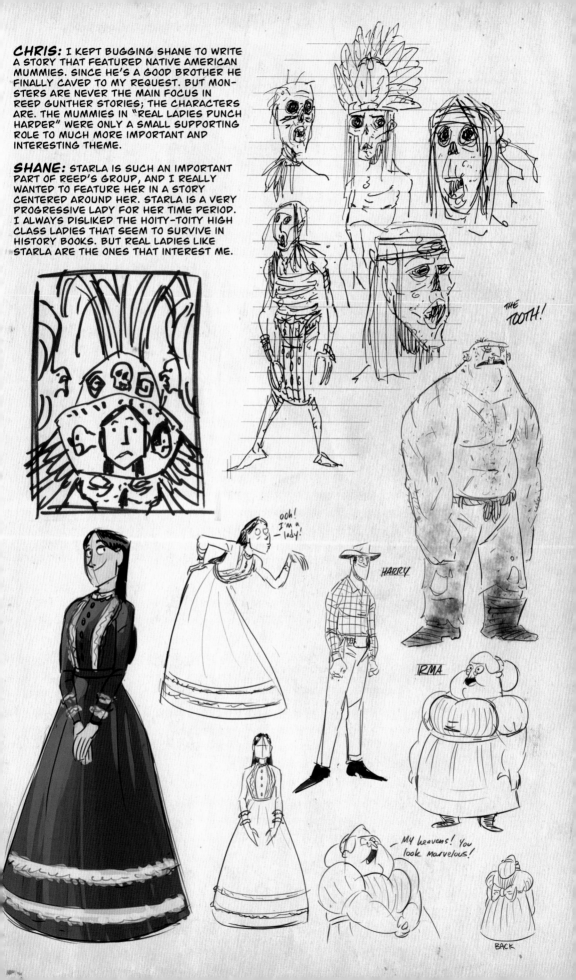

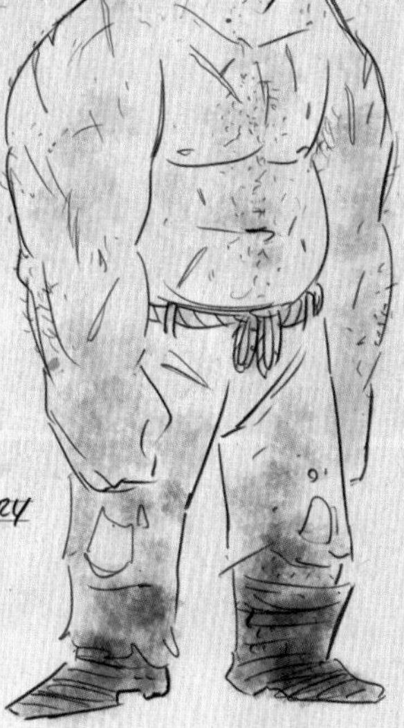
THE TOOTH!

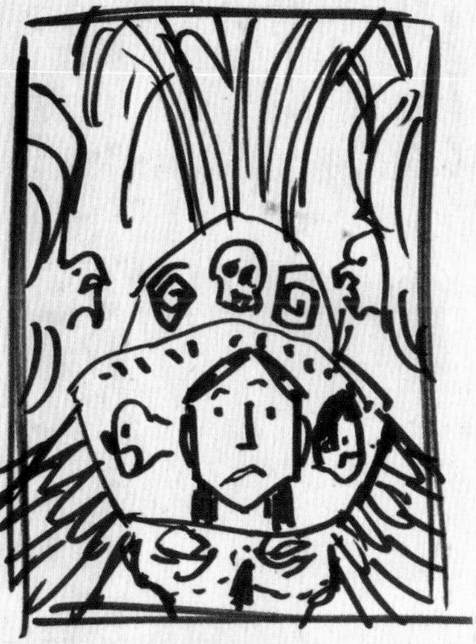

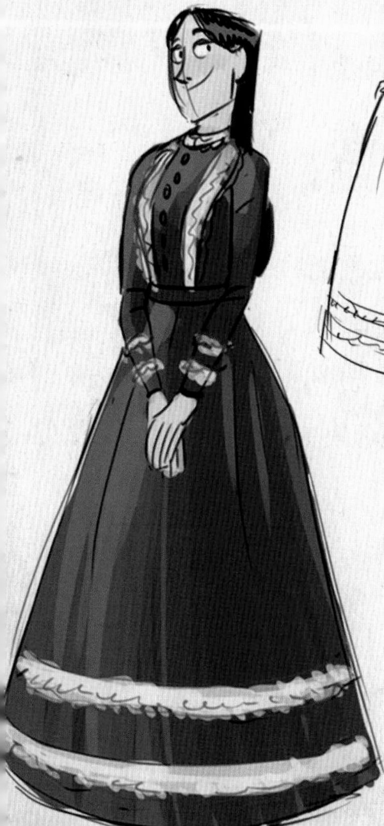

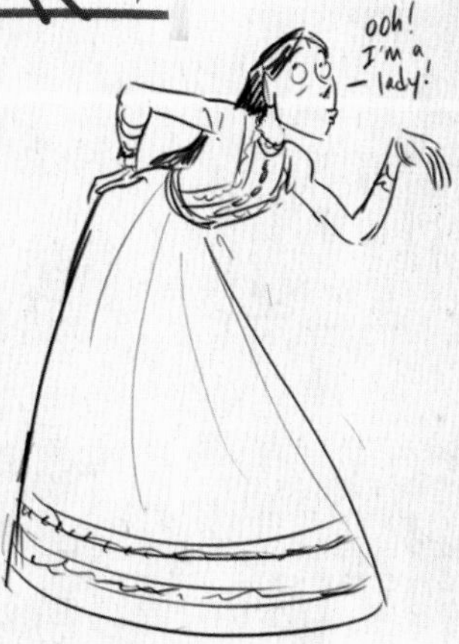
ooh! I'm a lady!

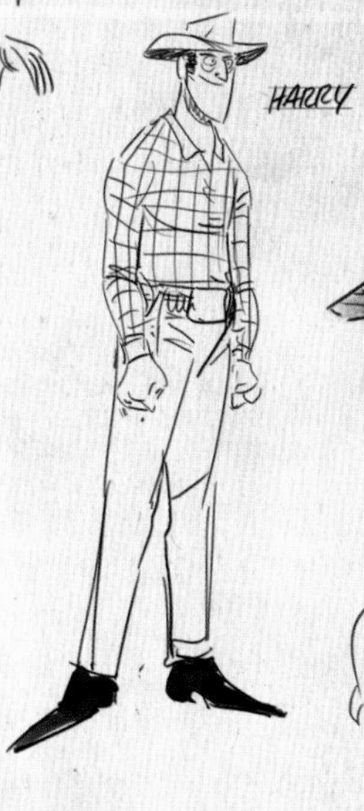
HARRY

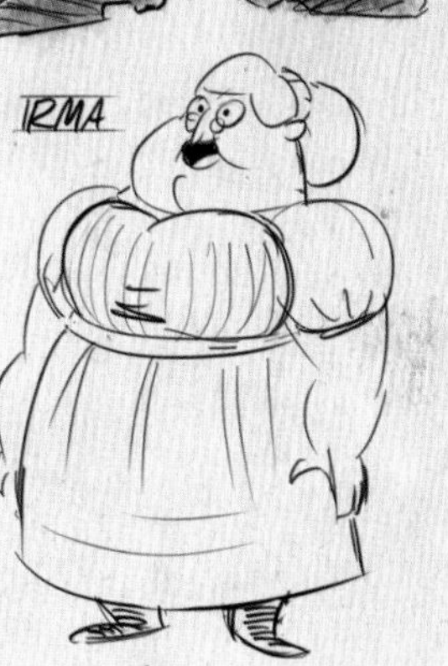
IRMA

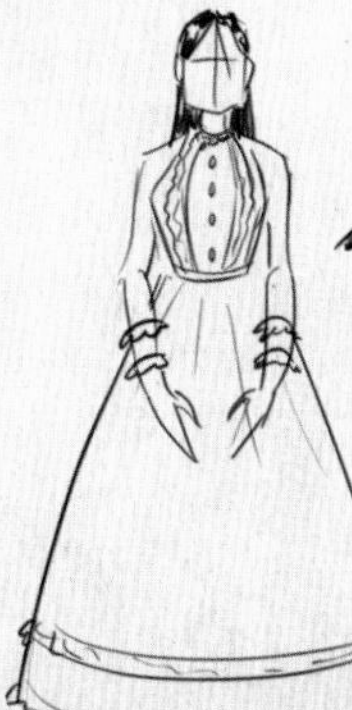

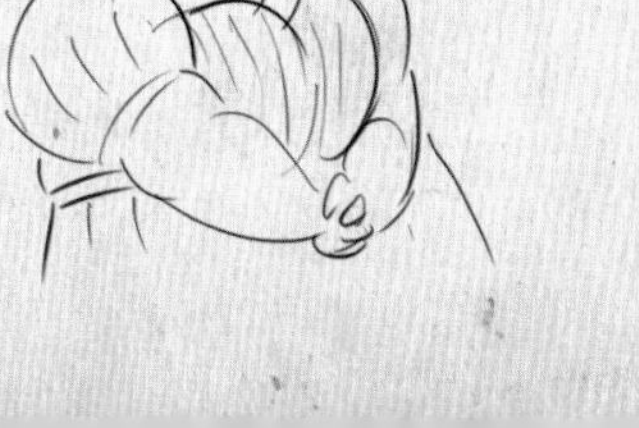
My heavens! You look marvelous!

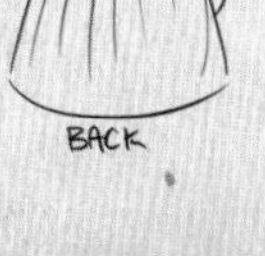
BACK

CHRIS: I HAD AN ABSOLUTE BLAST DRAWING REED POSSESSED BY MR. TODD. THE REAL FUN WAS WHEN REED FINALLY TAKES CONTROL OF THIS BODY. AS OUR COLORIST, JOSH SAID, "I'M GLAD REED GETS TO SPEND SOME TIME WITH THE FLAMING MUSTACHE!"

SHANE: MOST COMIC BOOK HEROES ARE OFTEN SEEN FIGHTING EVIL VERSIONS OF THEMSELVES. WE WANTED TO DO A STORY THAT FEATURED AN EVIL OR BIZARRO-LIKE REED BUT WITH OUR OWN UNIQUE TWIST.

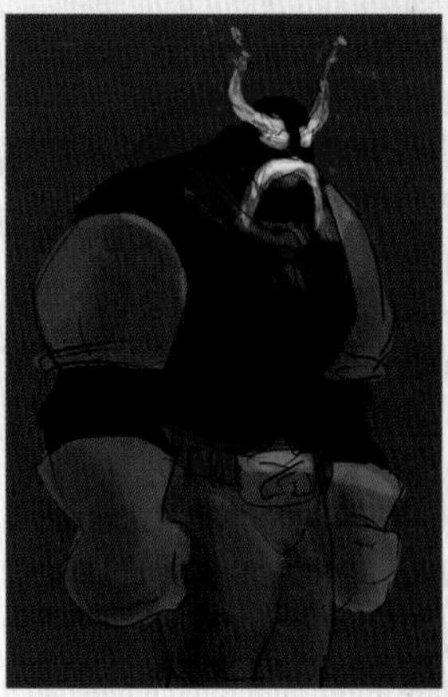

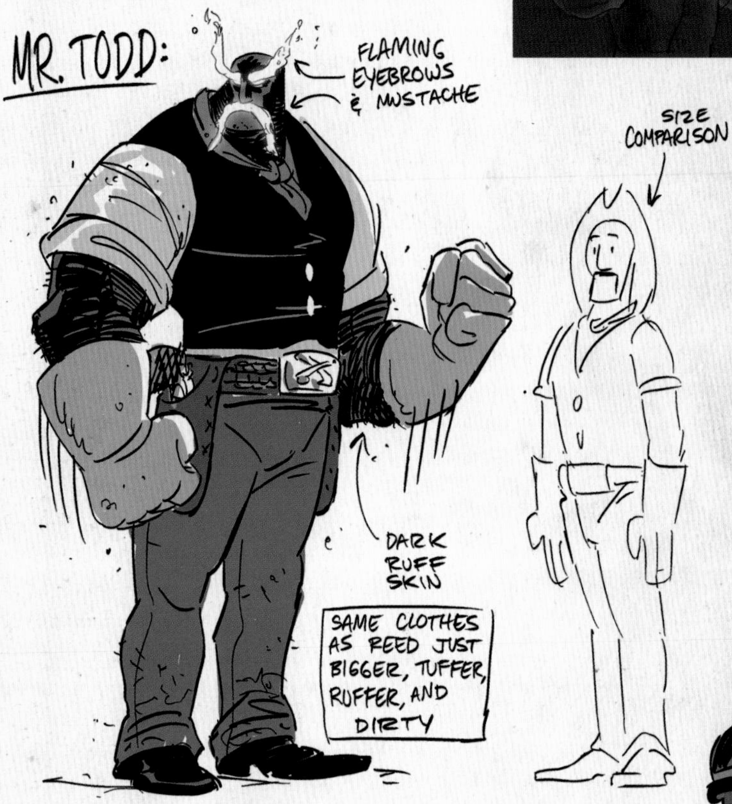
MR. TODD:
FLAMING EYEBROWS & MUSTACHE
SIZE COMPARISON
DARK RUFF SKIN
SAME CLOTHES AS REED JUST BIGGER, TUFFER, RUFFER, AND DIRTY

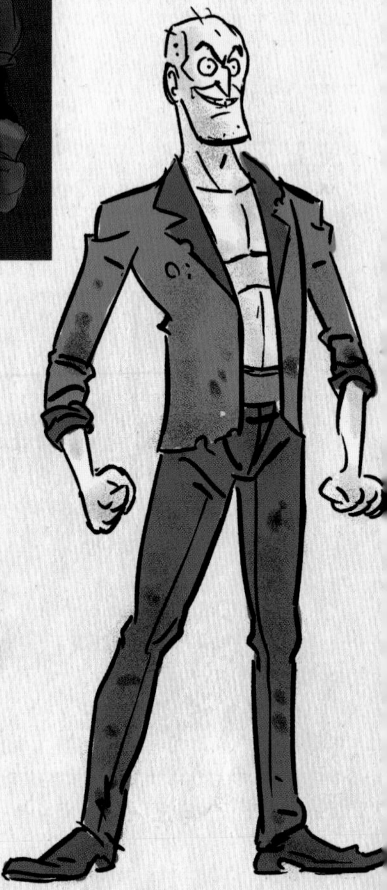

SHANE: AT THE END OF "FIENDS FOREVER PART 2" CHRIS AND I HAD A BRIEF CAMEO AS A REPORTER AND SKETCH ARTIST FOR A LOCAL NEWSPAPER.

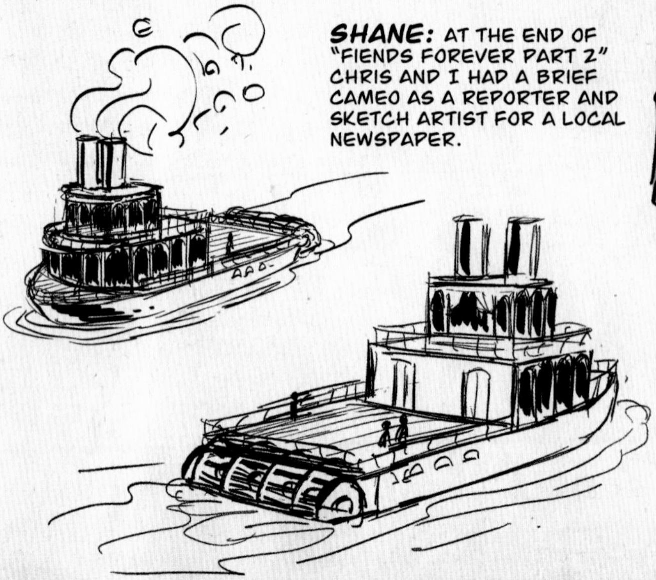

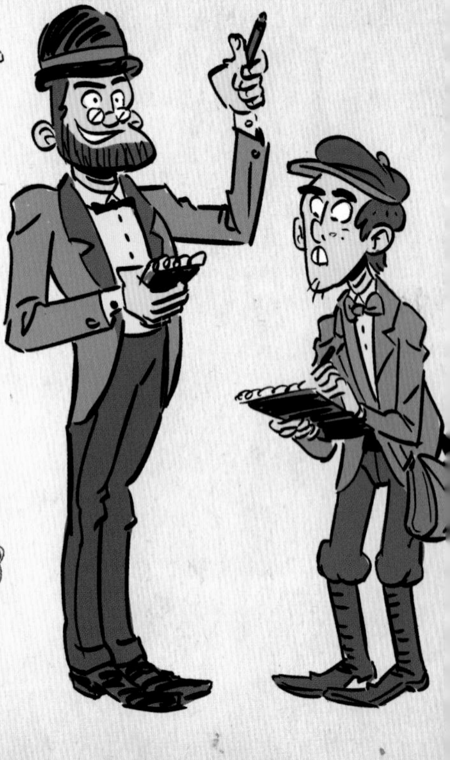

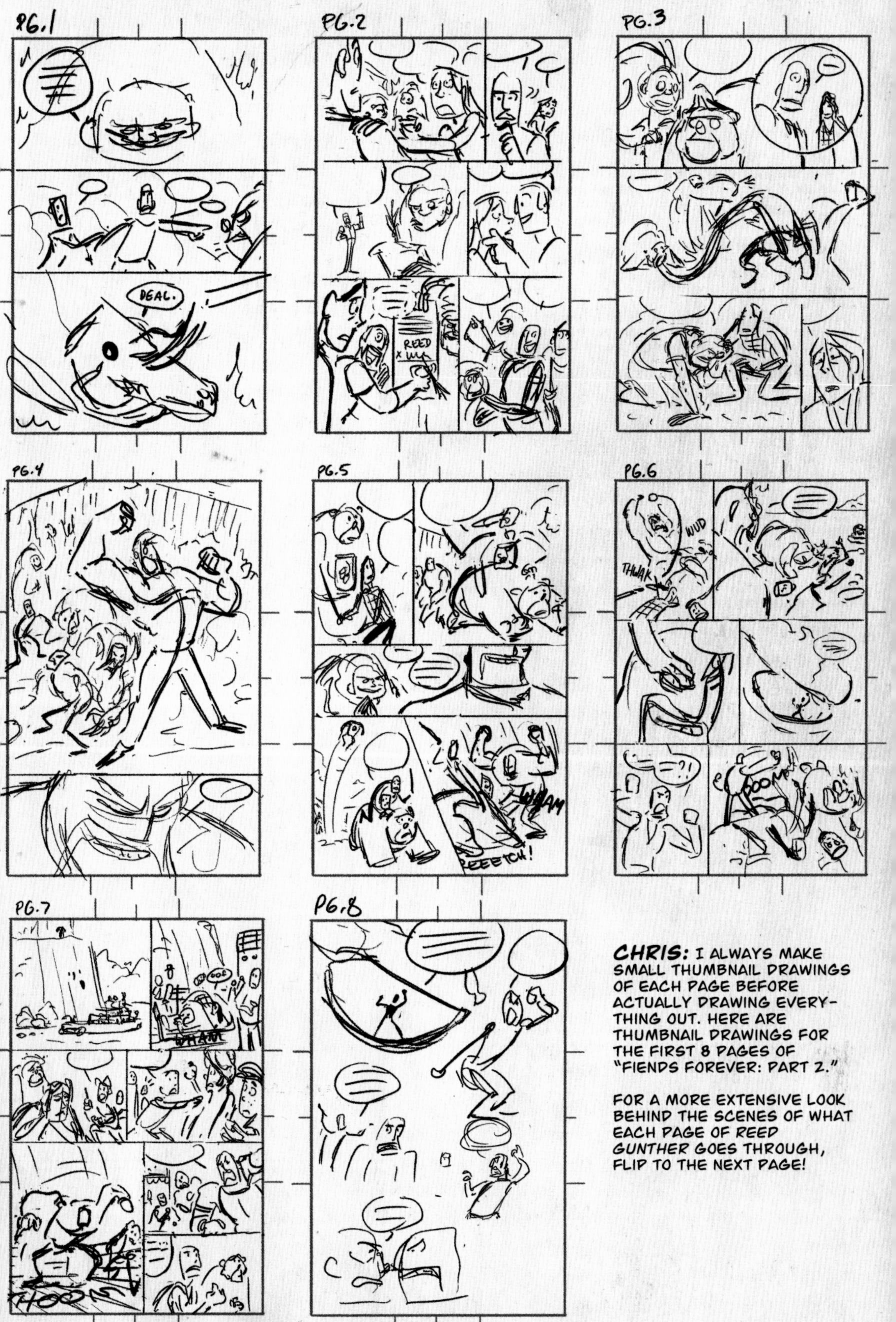
PG.1
DEAL.
PG.2
REED
PG.3
PG.4
PG.5
WHAM
REEEETCH!
PG.6
WUD
THWAK
PG.7
WHAM
PG.8

CHRIS: I ALWAYS MAKE SMALL THUMBNAIL DRAWINGS OF EACH PAGE BEFORE ACTUALLY DRAWING EVERYTHING OUT. HERE ARE THUMBNAIL DRAWINGS FOR THE FIRST 8 PAGES OF "FIENDS FOREVER: PART 2."

FOR A MORE EXTENSIVE LOOK BEHIND THE SCENES OF WHAT EACH PAGE OF REED GUNTHER GOES THROUGH, FLIP TO THE NEXT PAGE!

PROCESS: FROM SCRIPT TO FINAL PAGE

1 SCRIPT

PAGE 1 - Three Panels

Panel One
Sterling and Starla look into the camera. There is a riot going on in front of them (that we can't see just yet) that they are not a part of. They look like they're watching a car wreck on TV in slow motion. They're not worried or scared about what they see, just kind of intrigued.

STARLA: Come on, Reed...

SFX: WHAM, BANG, CRUNCH

Panel Two
Wide establishing shot. We flip around and see Sterling and Starla stand in front of a General Store that looks like it's getting torn apart from the inside. Men crowd the main door, and through the window, we see men fighting over tools and supplies.

The roof rattles with all the commotion inside. A window breaks.

The title of the issue can go on this page.

SFX: THUD, WHACK, CRASH

Panel Three
WHAM! Reed Gunther kicks the front door of the General Store wide open, blasting it off its hinges. The kick is so powerful he even kicks a few of the men who were crowding the door out of the way.

Where did Reed get all this kicking power? At the ends of his legs, Reed wears brand new, super fancy leather boots with cacti and cow skulls pressed into the leather. However, perhaps the most prominent part of these new boots are the SPURS.

These spurs are giant, long, and SHARP. The fanciest and most dangerous looking spurs yet they are elegant and a sign of high class.

REED: Out of the way, string beans! New boots *comin' through*!

SFX: WHAM

2 THUMBNAIL DRAWING

3 PENCILS

GENERAL STORE

4 INKS

5 COLORS & LETTERING

COME ON, REED...
KRSH
GENERAL STORE
BAM
BANG
OUT OF THE WAY STRING BEANS! NEW BOOTS COMIN' THROUGH!

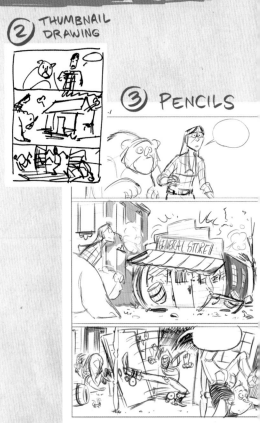

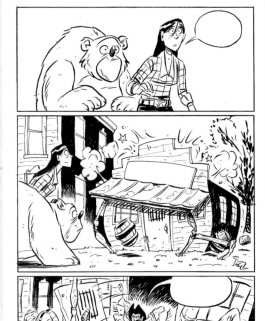

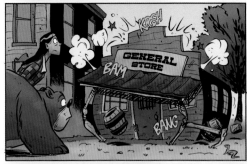

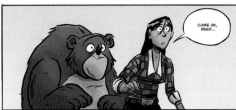

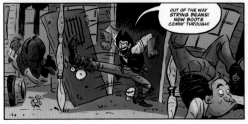

REED GUNTHER

short stories

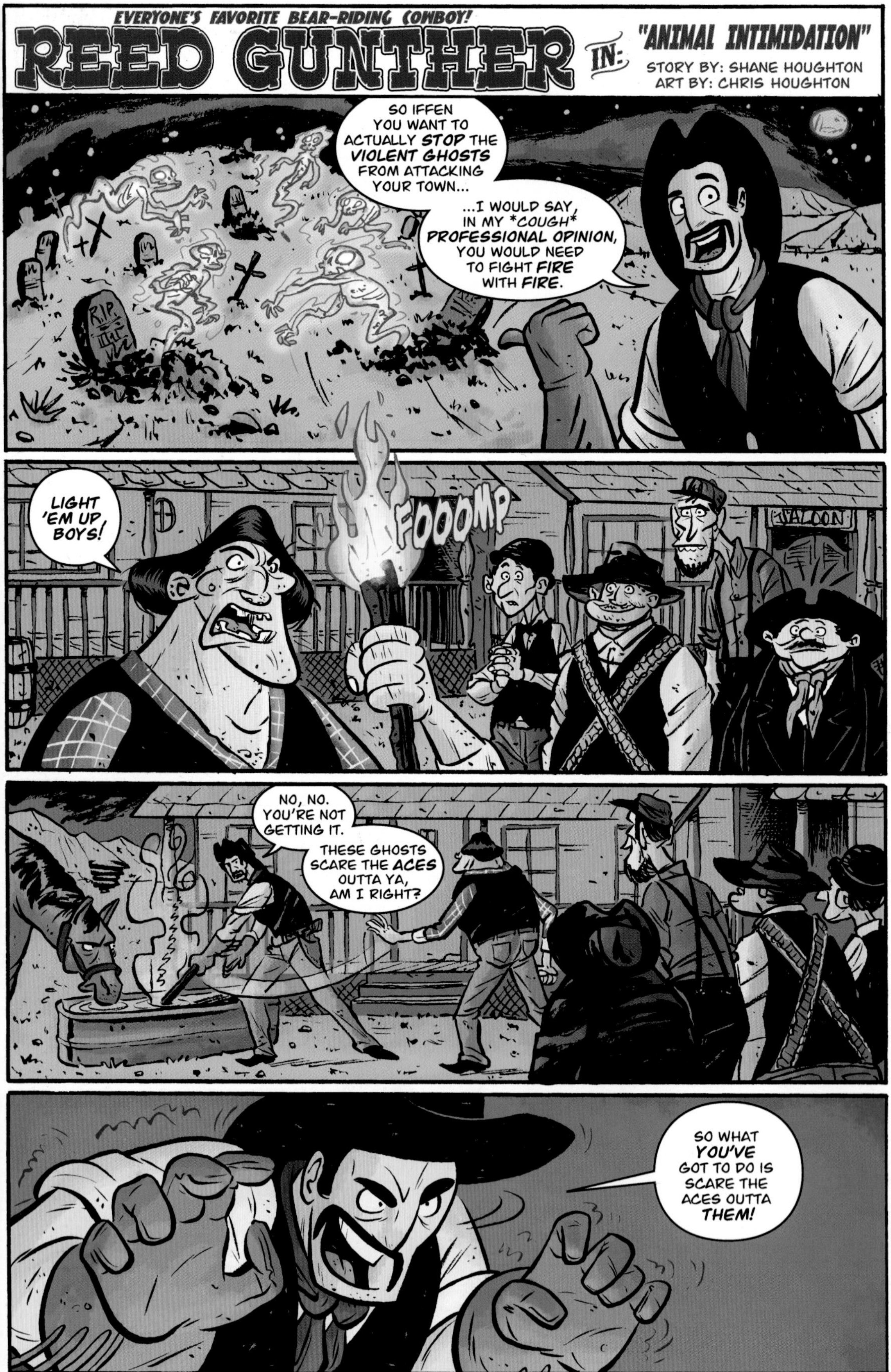
EVERYONE'S FAVORITE BEAR-RIDING COWBOY!
REED GUNTHER IN: "ANIMAL INTIMIDATION"
STORY BY: SHANE HOUGHTON
ART BY: CHRIS HOUGHTON
SO IFFEN YOU WANT TO ACTUALLY STOP THE VIOLENT GHOSTS FROM ATTACKING YOUR TOWN...
...I WOULD SAY, IN MY *COUGH* PROFESSIONAL OPINION, YOU WOULD NEED TO FIGHT FIRE WITH FIRE.
R.I.P.
LIGHT 'EM UP BOYS!
FOOOMP
SALOON
NO, NO. YOU'RE NOT GETTING IT.
THESE GHOSTS SCARE THE ACES OUTTA YA, AM I RIGHT?
SO WHAT YOU'VE GOT TO DO IS SCARE THE ACES OUTTA THEM!

WWW.REEDGUNTHER.COM

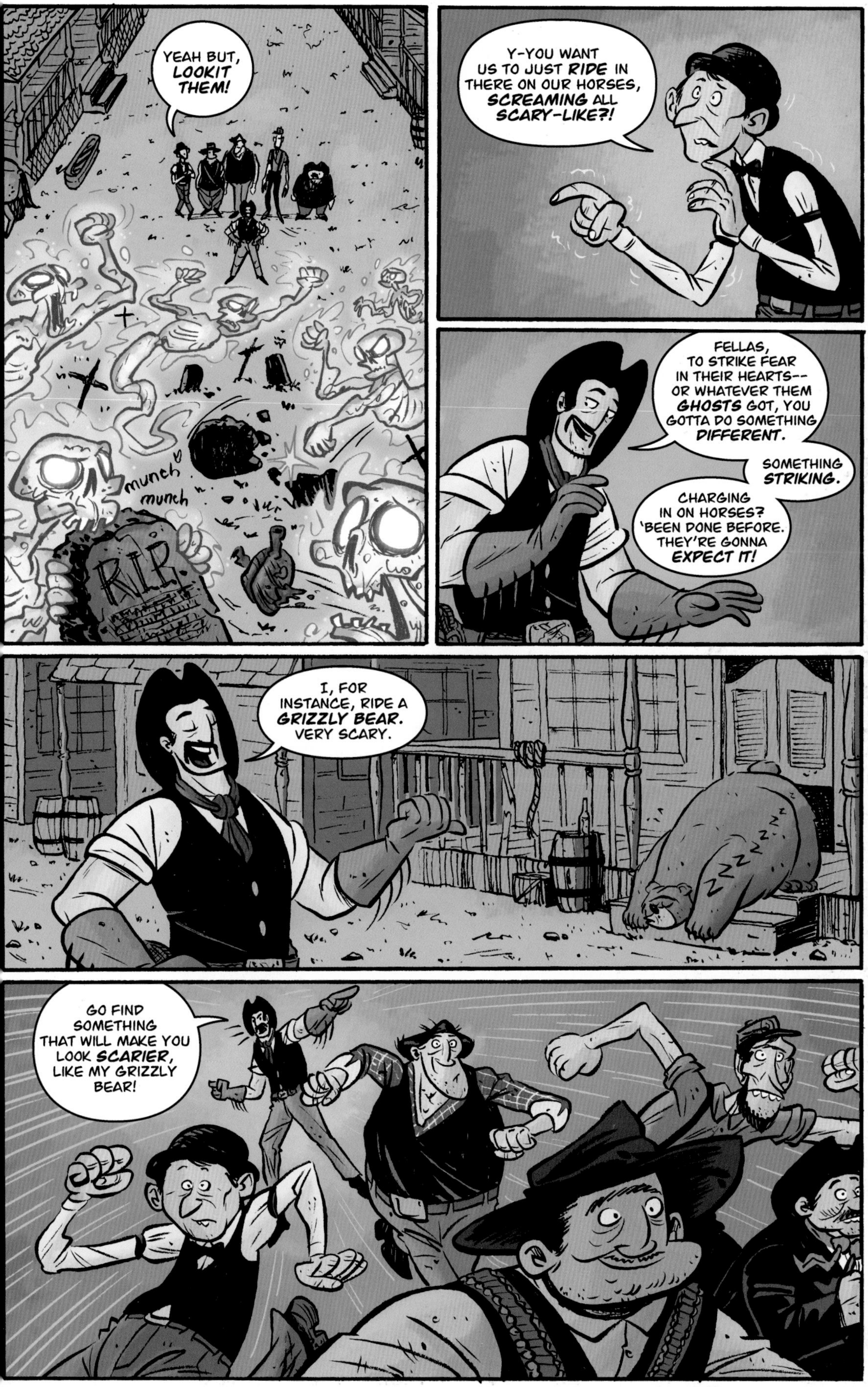
YEAH BUT, LOOKIT THEM!
munch munch
Y-YOU WANT US TO JUST RIDE IN THERE ON OUR HORSES, SCREAMING ALL SCARY-LIKE?!
FELLAS, TO STRIKE FEAR IN THEIR HEARTS-- OR WHATEVER THEM GHOSTS GOT, YOU GOTTA DO SOMETHING DIFFERENT.
SOMETHING STRIKING.
CHARGING IN ON HORSES? 'BEEN DONE BEFORE. THEY'RE GONNA EXPECT IT!
I, FOR INSTANCE, RIDE A GRIZZLY BEAR. VERY SCARY.
GO FIND SOMETHING THAT WILL MAKE YOU LOOK SCARIER, LIKE MY GRIZZLY BEAR!

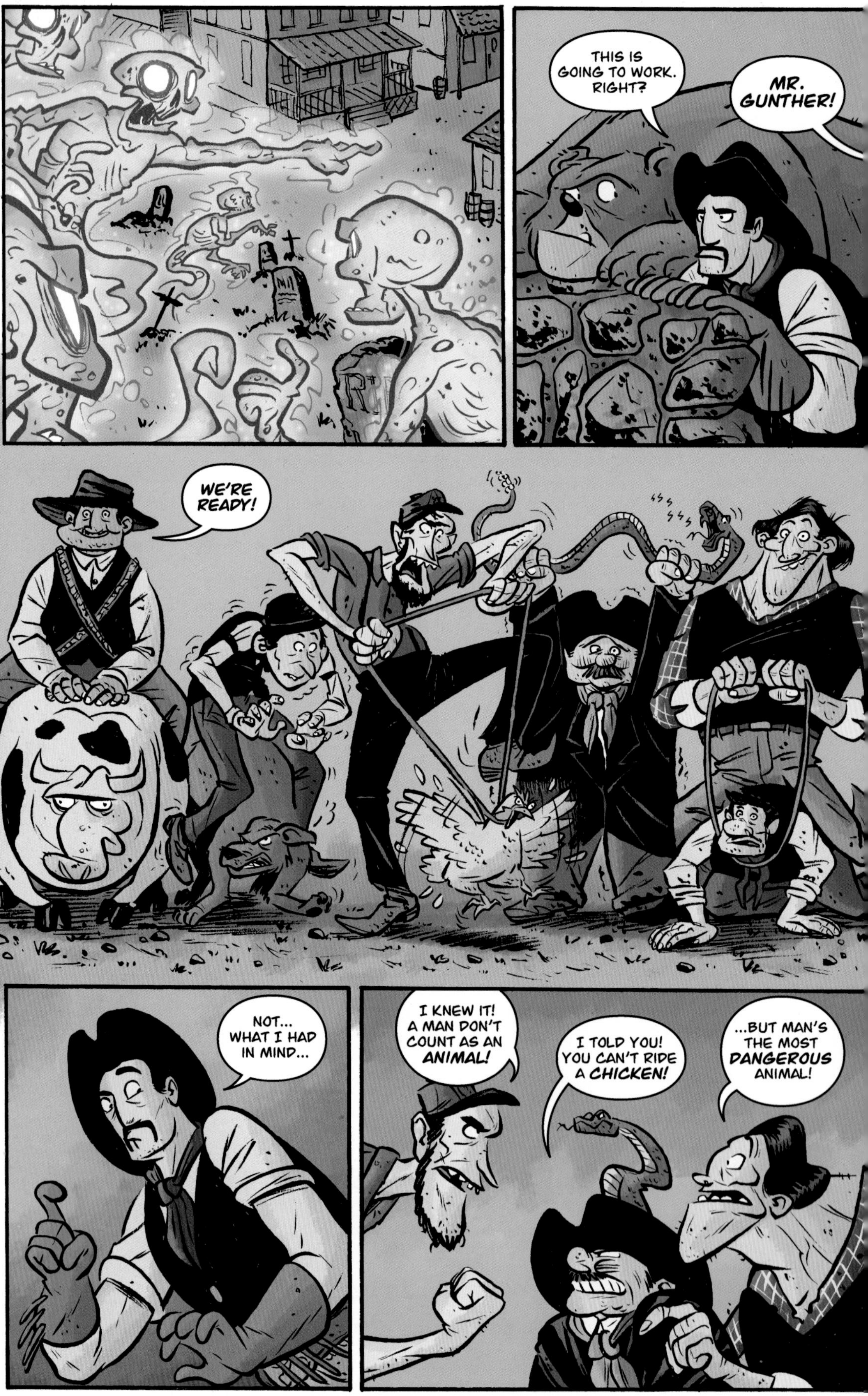
THIS IS GOING TO WORK. RIGHT?
MR. GUNTHER!
WE'RE READY!
NOT... WHAT I HAD IN MIND...
I KNEW IT! A MAN DON'T COUNT AS AN ANIMAL!
I TOLD YOU! YOU CAN'T RIDE A CHICKEN!
...BUT MAN'S THE MOST DANGEROUS ANIMAL!

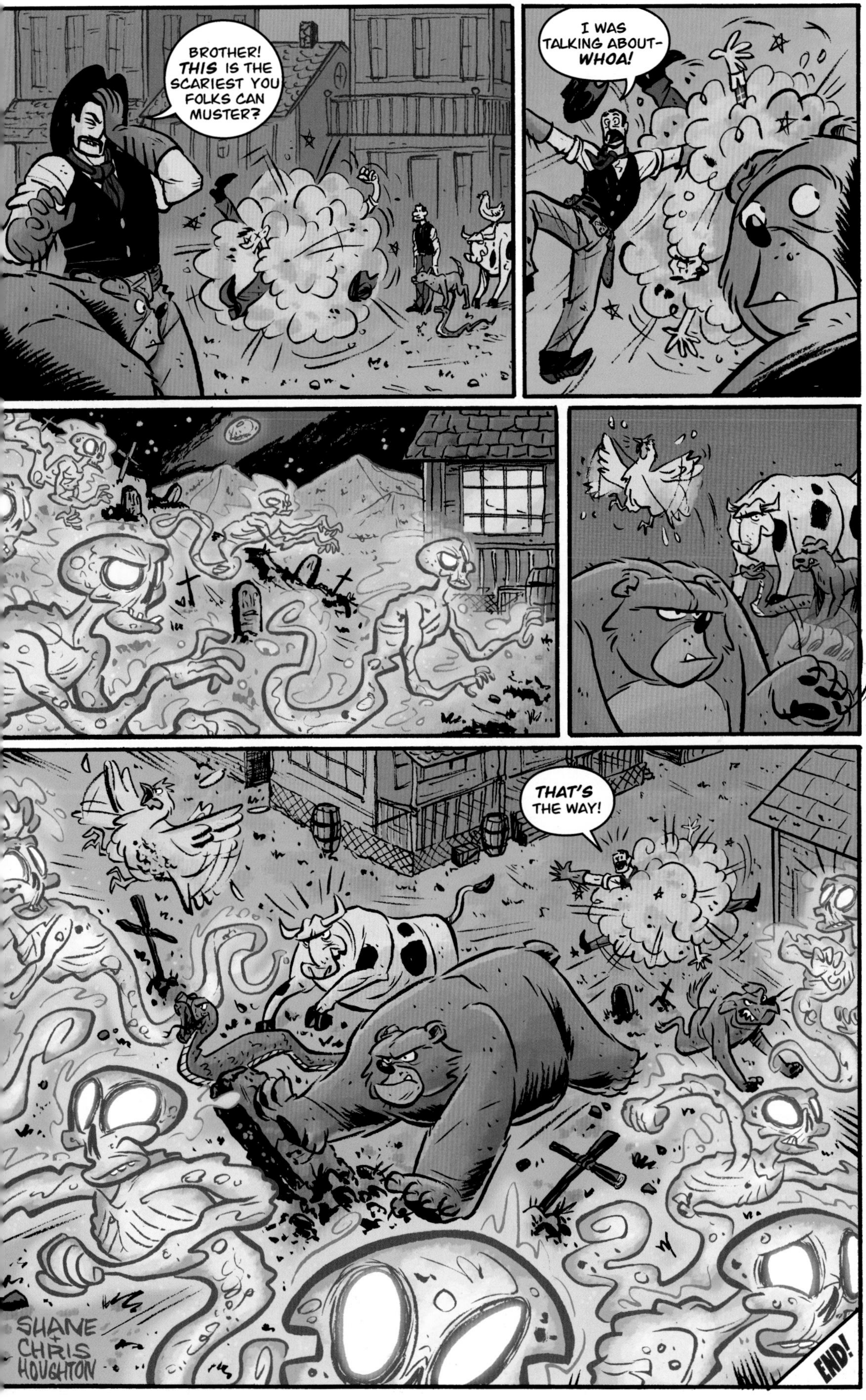
BROTHER! THIS IS THE SCARIEST YOU FOLKS CAN MUSTER?
I WAS TALKING ABOUT- WHOA!
RIP
THAT'S THE WAY!
SHANE + CHRIS HOUGHTON
END!

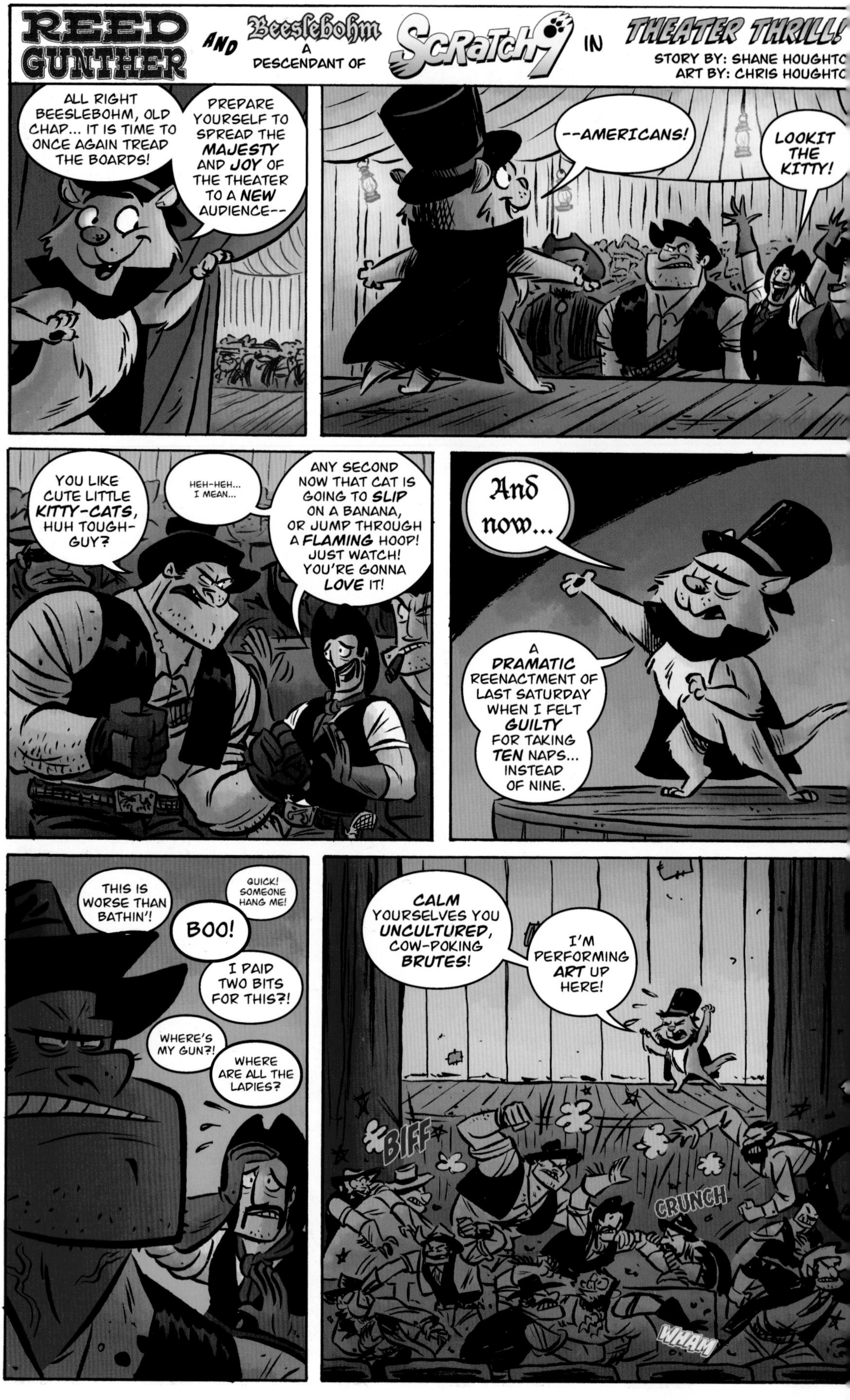
REED GUNTHER
AND
Beeslebohm
A DESCENDANT OF
SCRATCH9
IN
THEATER THRILL!
STORY BY: SHANE HOUGHTO
ART BY: CHRIS HOUGHTO
ALL RIGHT BEESLEBOHM, OLD CHAP... IT IS TIME TO ONCE AGAIN TREAD THE BOARDS!
PREPARE YOURSELF TO SPREAD THE MAJESTY AND JOY OF THE THEATER TO A NEW AUDIENCE--
--AMERICANS!
LOOKIT THE KITTY!
YOU LIKE CUTE LITTLE KITTY-CATS, HUH TOUGH-GUY?
HEH-HEH... I MEAN...
ANY SECOND NOW THAT CAT IS GOING TO SLIP ON A BANANA, OR JUMP THROUGH A FLAMING HOOP! JUST WATCH! YOU'RE GONNA LOVE IT!
And now...
A DRAMATIC REENACTMENT OF LAST SATURDAY WHEN I FELT GUILTY FOR TAKING TEN NAPS... INSTEAD OF NINE.
THIS IS WORSE THAN BATHIN'!
QUICK! SOMEONE HANG ME!
BOO!
I PAID TWO BITS FOR THIS?!
WHERE'S MY GUN?!
WHERE ARE ALL THE LADIES?
CALM YOURSELVES YOU UNCULTURED, COW-POKING BRUTES!
I'M PERFORMING ART UP HERE!
BIFF
CRUNCH
WHAM

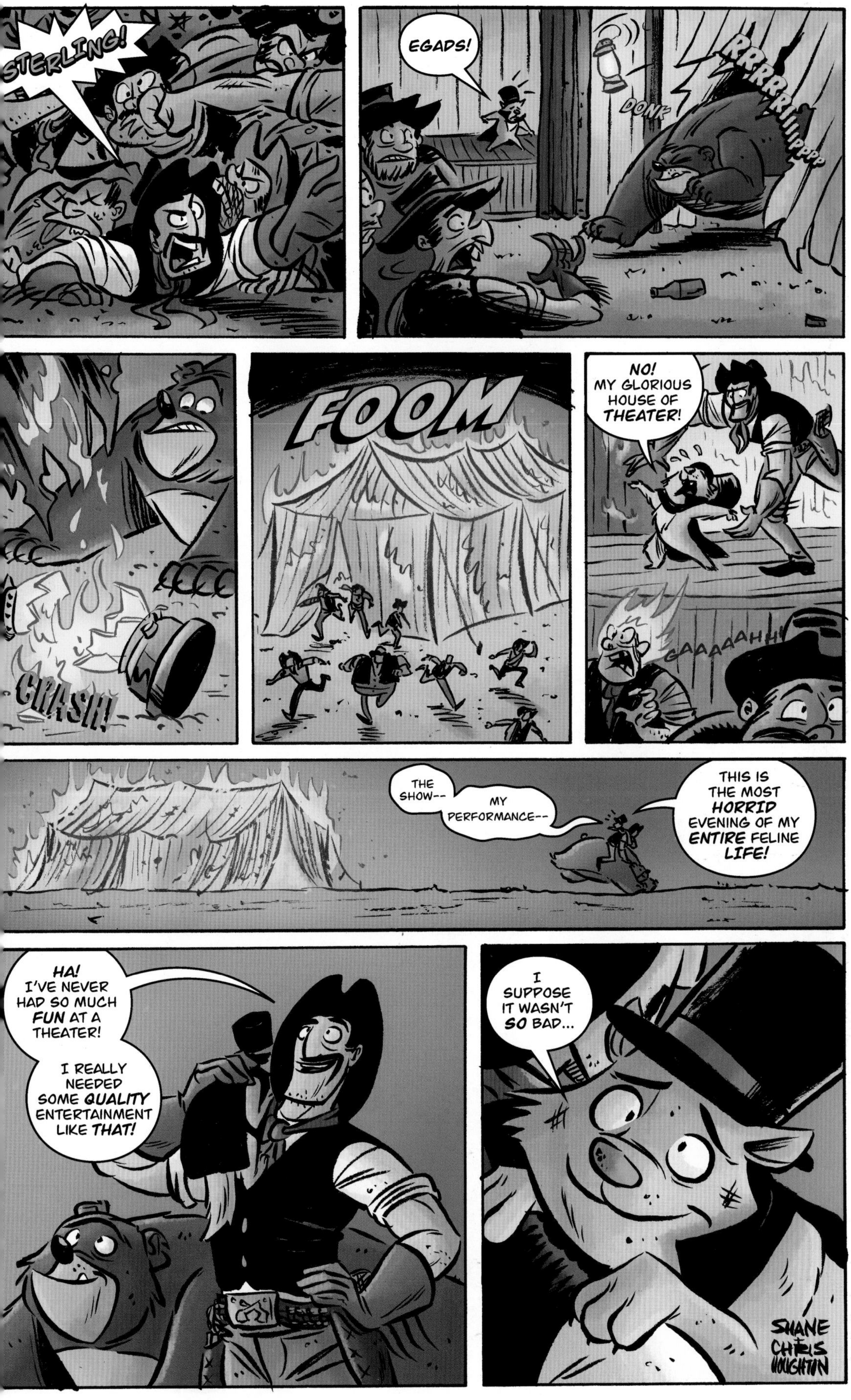
STERLING!
EGADS!
DONK
RRRRRrrrrippppp
CRASH!
FOOM
NO! MY GLORIOUS HOUSE OF THEATER!
GAAAAAHH
THE SHOW--
MY PERFORMANCE--
THIS IS THE MOST HORRID EVENING OF MY ENTIRE FELINE LIFE!
HA! I'VE NEVER HAD SO MUCH FUN AT A THEATER!
I REALLY NEEDED SOME QUALITY ENTERTAINMENT LIKE THAT!
I SUPPOSE IT WASN'T SO BAD...
SHANE CHRIS HOUGHTON

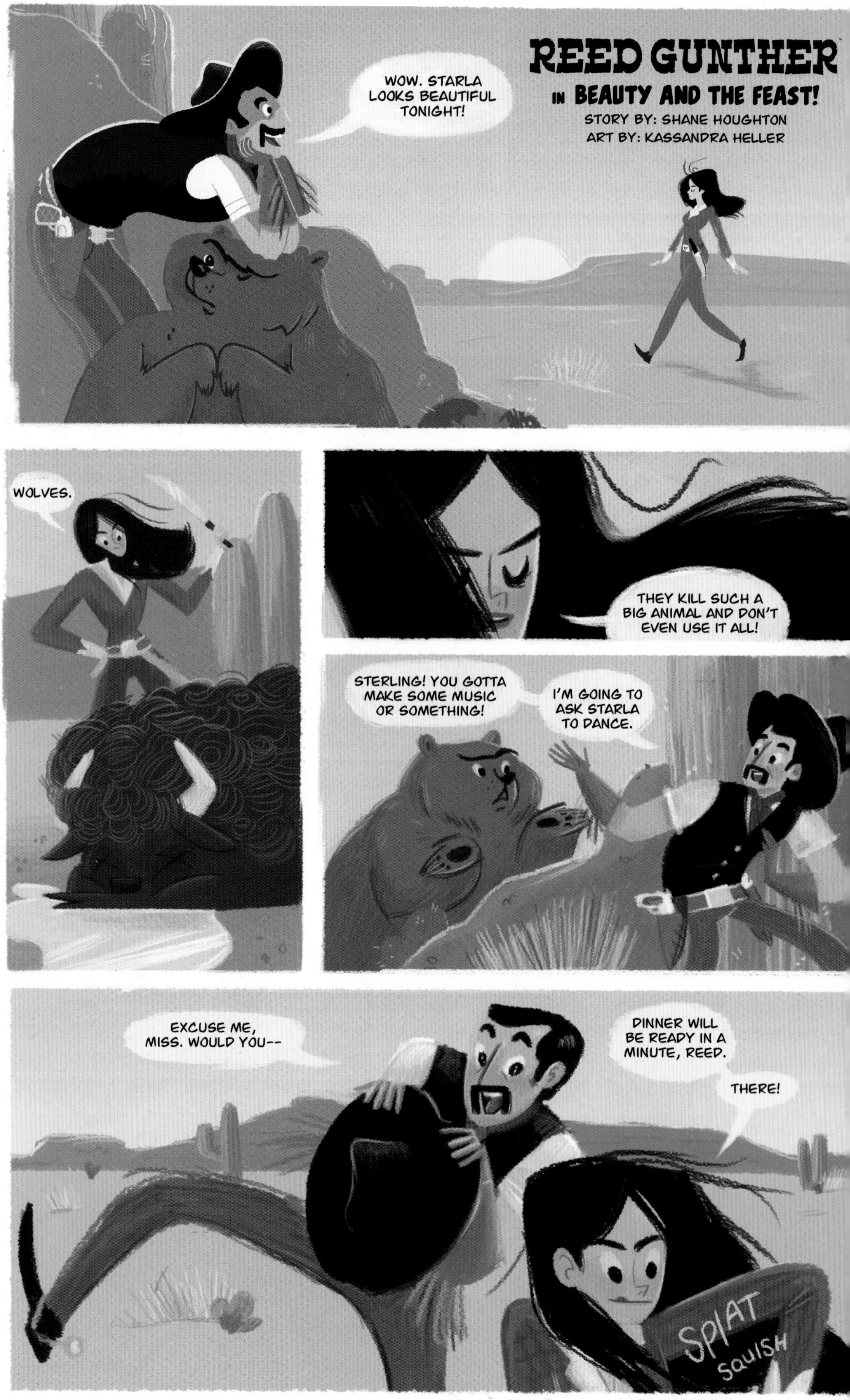
REED GUNTHER
IN BEAUTY AND THE FEAST!
STORY BY: SHANE HOUGHTON
ART BY: KASSANDRA HELLER
WOW. STARLA LOOKS BEAUTIFUL TONIGHT!
WOLVES.
THEY KILL SUCH A BIG ANIMAL AND DON'T EVEN USE IT ALL!
I'M GOING TO ASK STARLA TO DANCE.
STERLING! YOU GOTTA MAKE SOME MUSIC OR SOMETHING!
EXCUSE ME, MISS. WOULD YOU--
DINNER WILL BE READY IN A MINUTE, REED.
THERE!
SPLAT
SQUISH

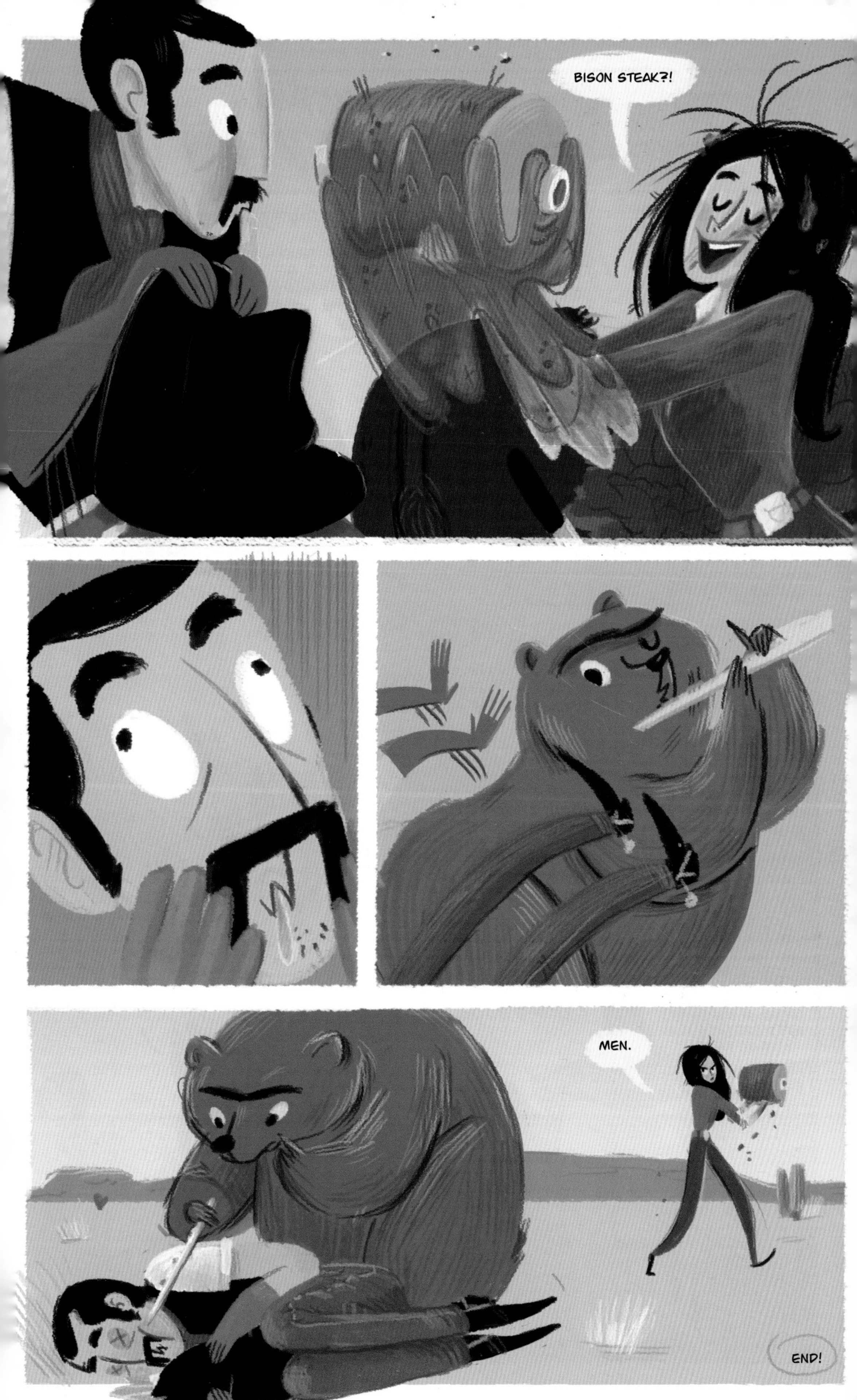
BISON STEAK?!
MEN.
END!

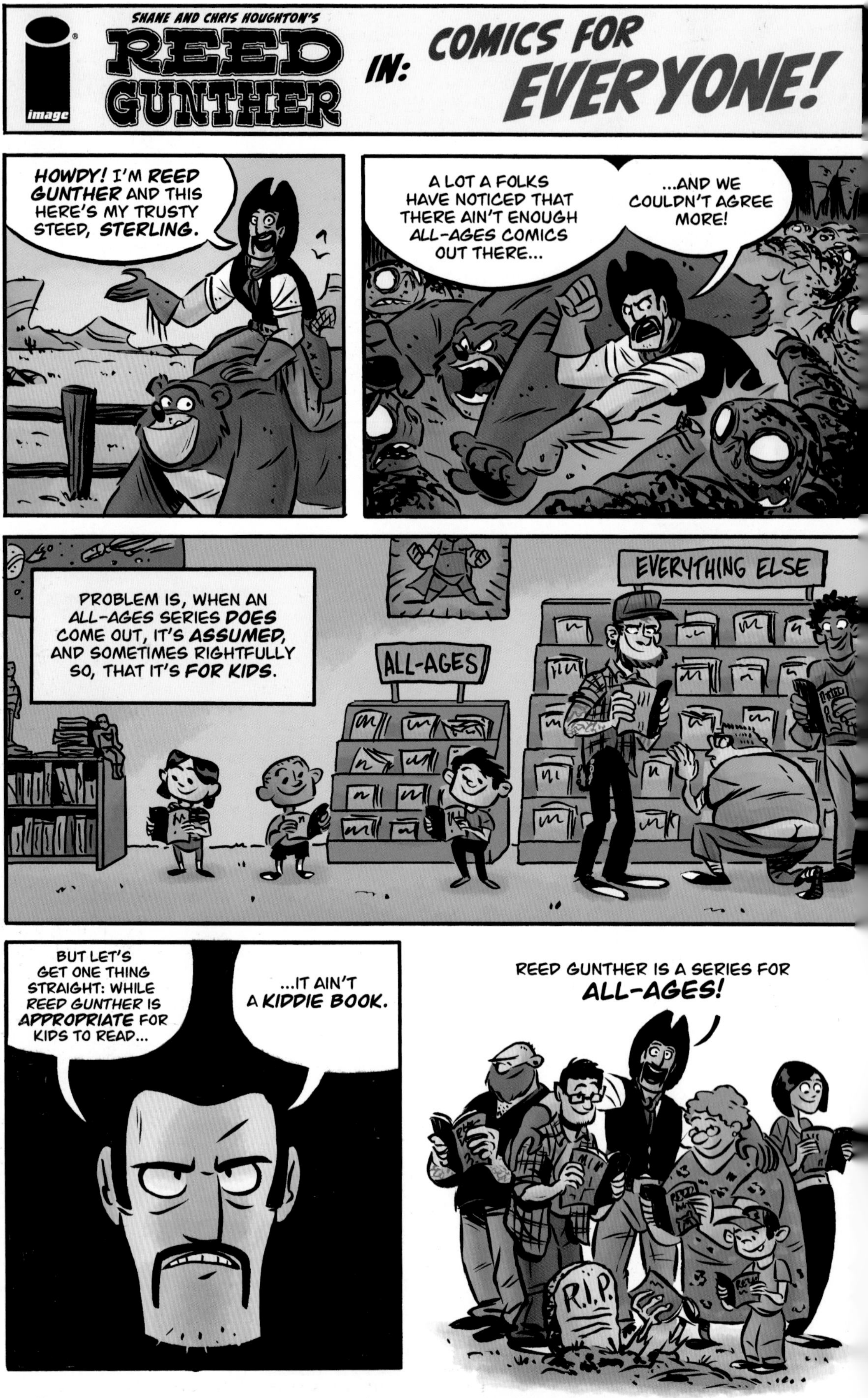
SHANE AND CHRIS HOUGHTON'S
image
REED GUNTHER
IN: COMICS FOR EVERYONE!
HOWDY! I'M REED GUNTHER AND THIS HERE'S MY TRUSTY STEED, STERLING.
A LOT A FOLKS HAVE NOTICED THAT THERE AIN'T ENOUGH ALL-AGES COMICS OUT THERE...
...AND WE COULDN'T AGREE MORE!
PROBLEM IS, WHEN AN ALL-AGES SERIES DOES COME OUT, IT'S ASSUMED, AND SOMETIMES RIGHTFULLY SO, THAT IT'S FOR KIDS.
ALL-AGES
EVERYTHING ELSE
BUT LET'S GET ONE THING STRAIGHT: WHILE REED GUNTHER IS APPROPRIATE FOR KIDS TO READ...
...IT AIN'T A KIDDIE BOOK.
REED GUNTHER IS A SERIES FOR ALL-AGES!
R.I.P.

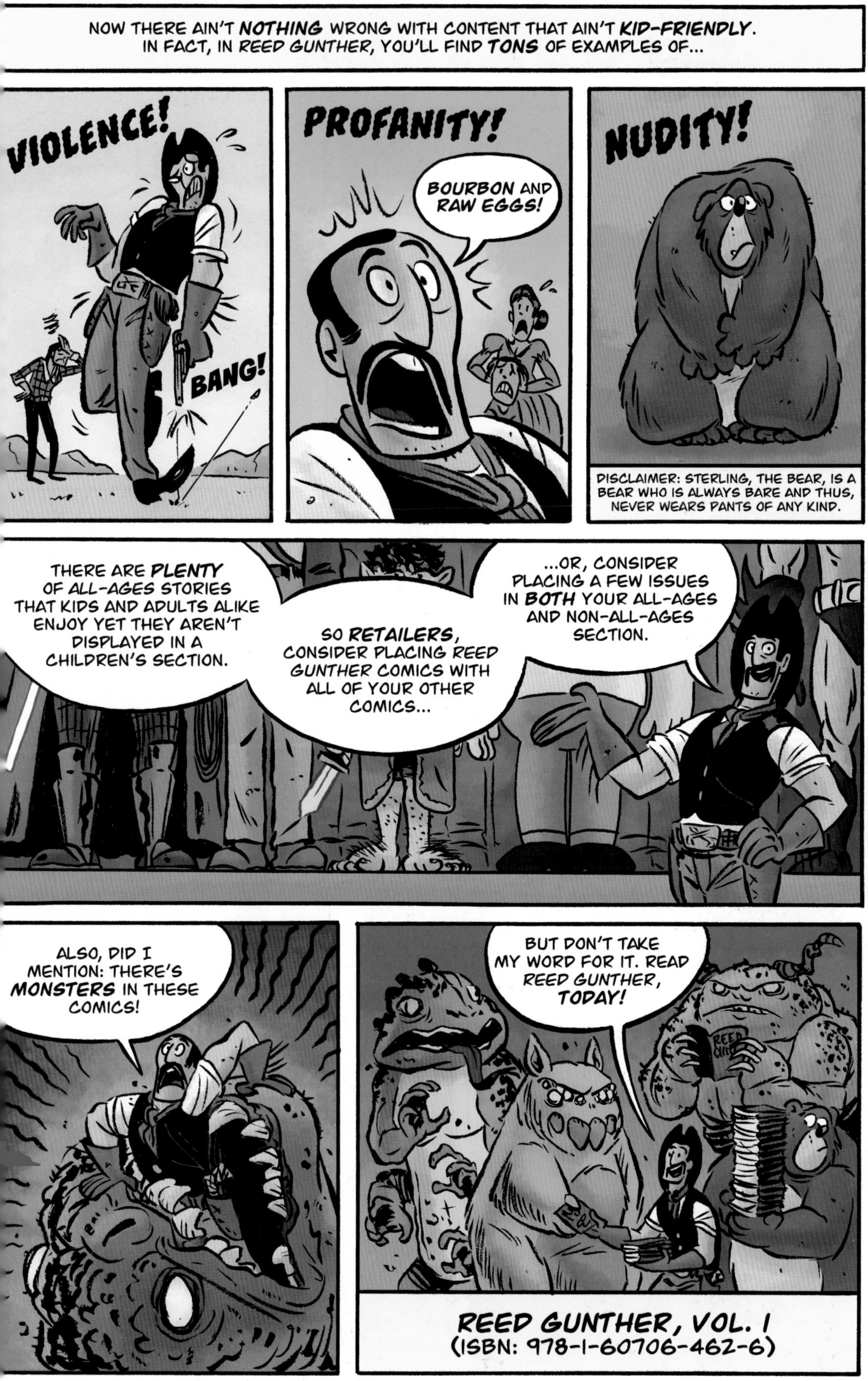
NOW THERE AIN'T NOTHING WRONG WITH CONTENT THAT AIN'T KID-FRIENDLY.
IN FACT, IN REED GUNTHER, YOU'LL FIND TONS OF EXAMPLES OF...
VIOLENCE!
BANG!
PROFANITY!
BOURBON AND RAW EGGS!
NUDITY!
DISCLAIMER: STERLING, THE BEAR, IS A BEAR WHO IS ALWAYS BARE AND THUS, NEVER WEARS PANTS OF ANY KIND.
THERE ARE PLENTY OF ALL-AGES STORIES THAT KIDS AND ADULTS ALIKE ENJOY YET THEY AREN'T DISPLAYED IN A CHILDREN'S SECTION.
SO RETAILERS, CONSIDER PLACING REED GUNTHER COMICS WITH ALL OF YOUR OTHER COMICS...
...OR, CONSIDER PLACING A FEW ISSUES IN BOTH YOUR ALL-AGES AND NON-ALL-AGES SECTION.
ALSO, DID I MENTION: THERE'S MONSTERS IN THESE COMICS!
BUT DON'T TAKE MY WORD FOR IT. READ REED GUNTHER, TODAY!
REED GUNTHER, VOL. 1
(ISBN: 978-1-60706-462-6)

REED GUNTHER IN: "WESTERN WIT"

BY SHANE & CHRIS HOUGHTON

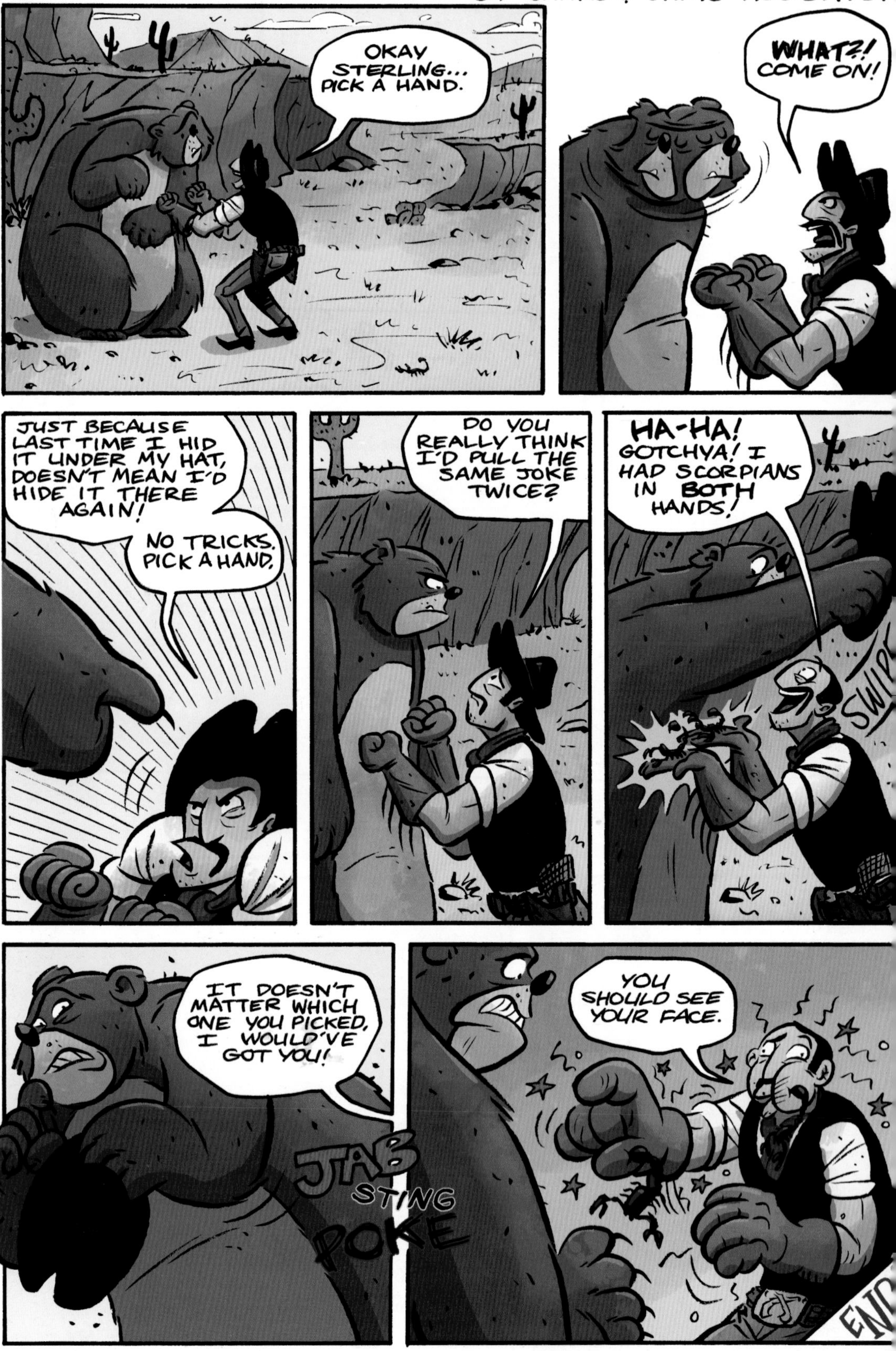
OKAY STERLING... PICK A HAND.
WHAT?! COME ON!
JUST BECAUSE LAST TIME I HID IT UNDER MY HAT, DOESN'T MEAN I'D HIDE IT THERE AGAIN!
NO TRICKS. PICK A HAND.
DO YOU REALLY THINK I'D PULL THE SAME JOKE TWICE?
HA-HA! GOTCHYA! I HAD SCORPIANS IN BOTH HANDS!
IT DOESN'T MATTER WHICH ONE YOU PICKED, I WOULD'VE GOT YOU!
JAB
STING
POKE
YOU SHOULD SEE YOUR FACE.

REED GUNTHER:
The Beginning

In the summer of 2007, Chris submitted a short story about a bear-riding cowboy to Comics Obscura, a small Michigan-based comic book anthology. The third issue of Comics Obscura was the first ever appearance of Reed Gunther, written and drawn by Chris when he was just starting art school. Originally planned as a three part story, Comics Obscura stopped being published after the fourth issue, leaving Chris's original Reed Gunther story without an ending. Chris shelved the idea of a bear-riding cowboy and moved onto other work.

That is, until Shane wrote a script using Chris's characters and created their first comic collaboration, "Reed Gunther and the Steak Snacking Snake!" The collaboration led to many more adventures with Reed and Sterling, but still, Chris's original Reed Gunther story remained incomplete... until now.

Five years after its humble beginning, Shane and Chris teamed up to complete the third and final chapter of Reed Gunther's true origin, presented here along with the original first two chapters.

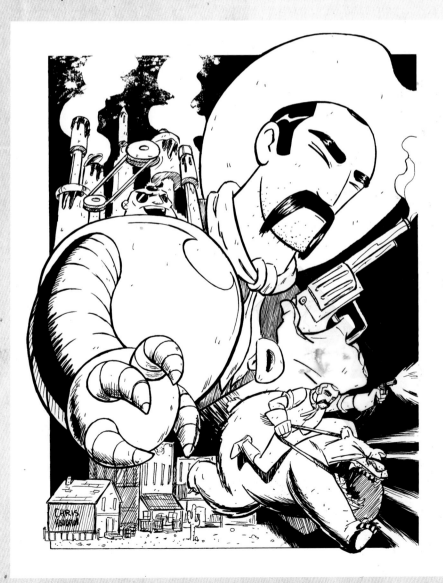

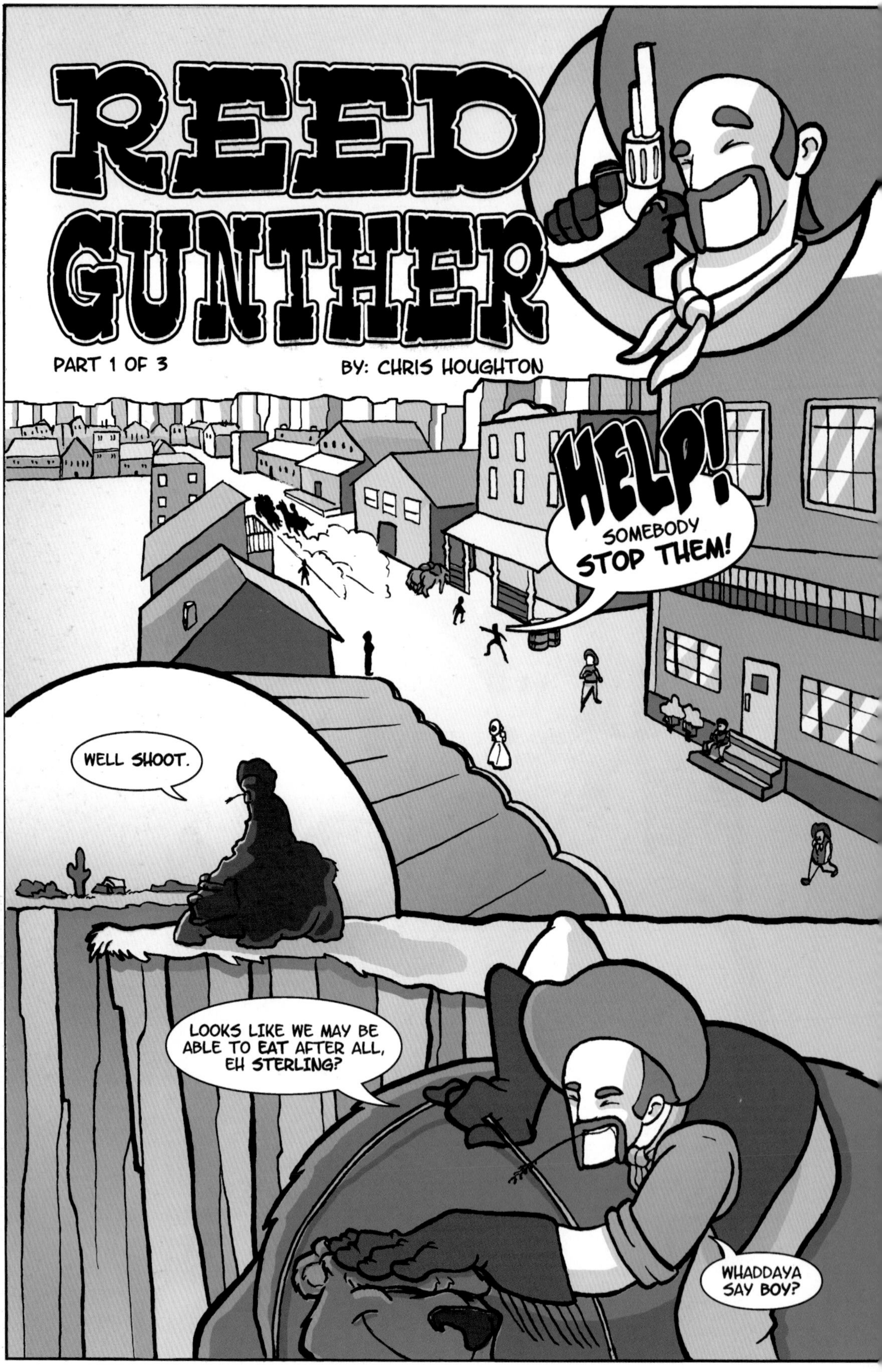
REED GUNTHER
PART 1 OF 3
BY: CHRIS HOUGHTON
HELP! SOMEBODY STOP THEM!
WELL SHOOT.
LOOKS LIKE WE MAY BE ABLE TO EAT AFTER ALL, EH STERLING?
WHADDAYA SAY BOY?

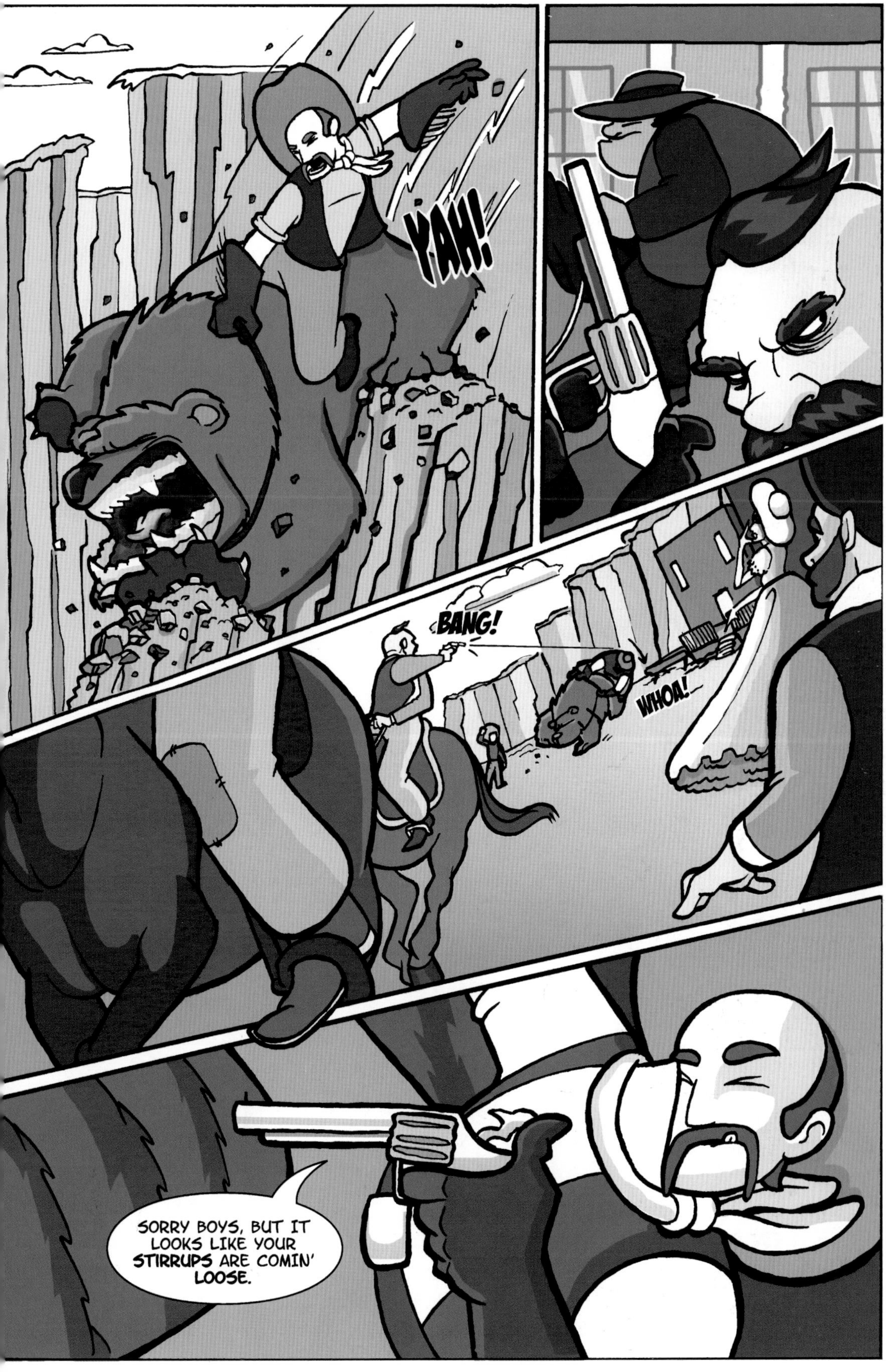
YAH!
BANG!
WHOA!
SORRY BOYS, BUT IT LOOKS LIKE YOUR STIRRUPS ARE COMIN' LOOSE.

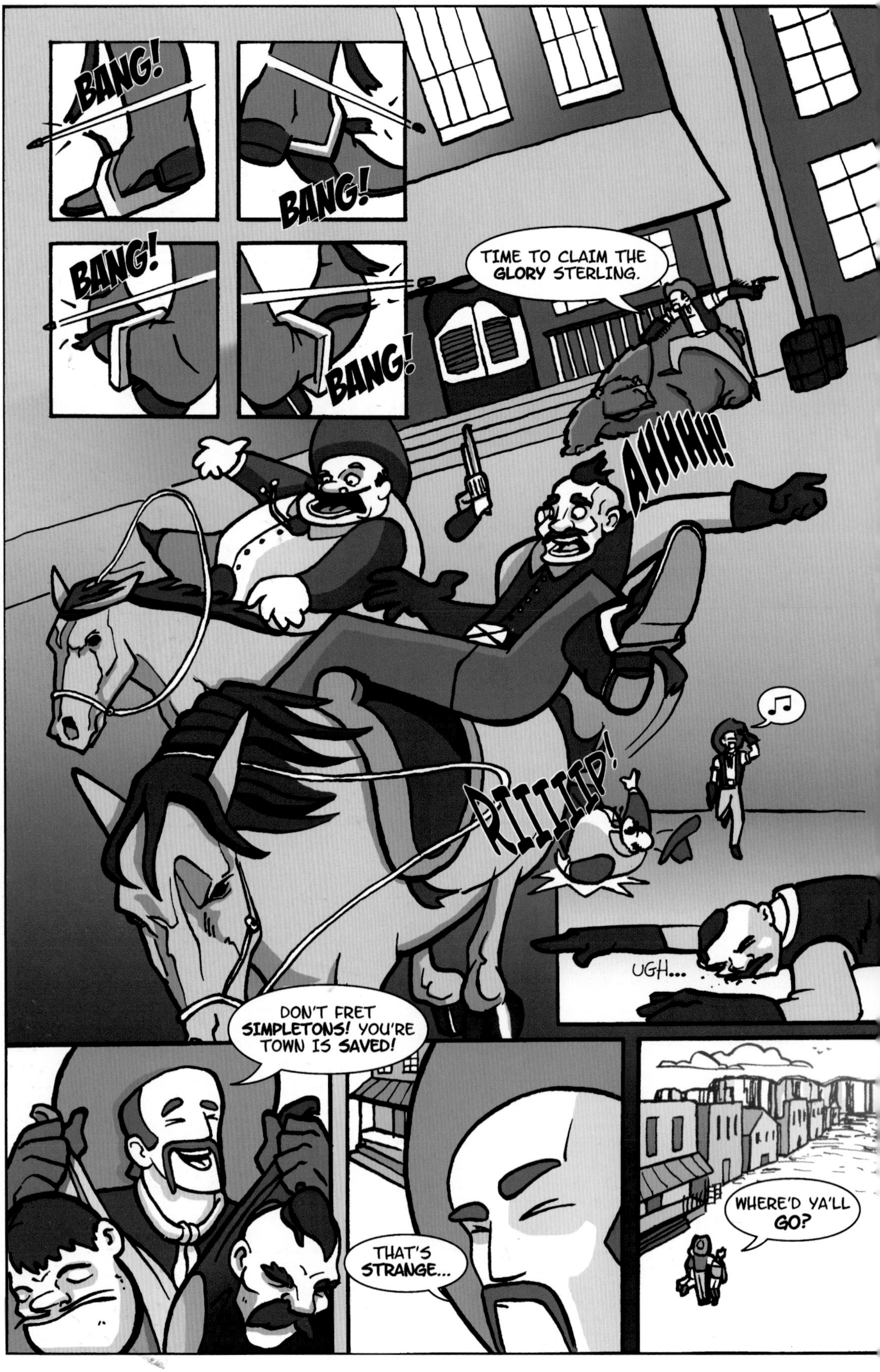
BANG!
BANG!
BANG!
BANG!
TIME TO CLAIM THE GLORY STERLING.
AHHHH!
RIIIIIP!
♫
UGH...
DON'T FRET SIMPLETONS! YOU'RE TOWN IS SAVED!
THAT'S STRANGE...
WHERE'D YA'LL GO?

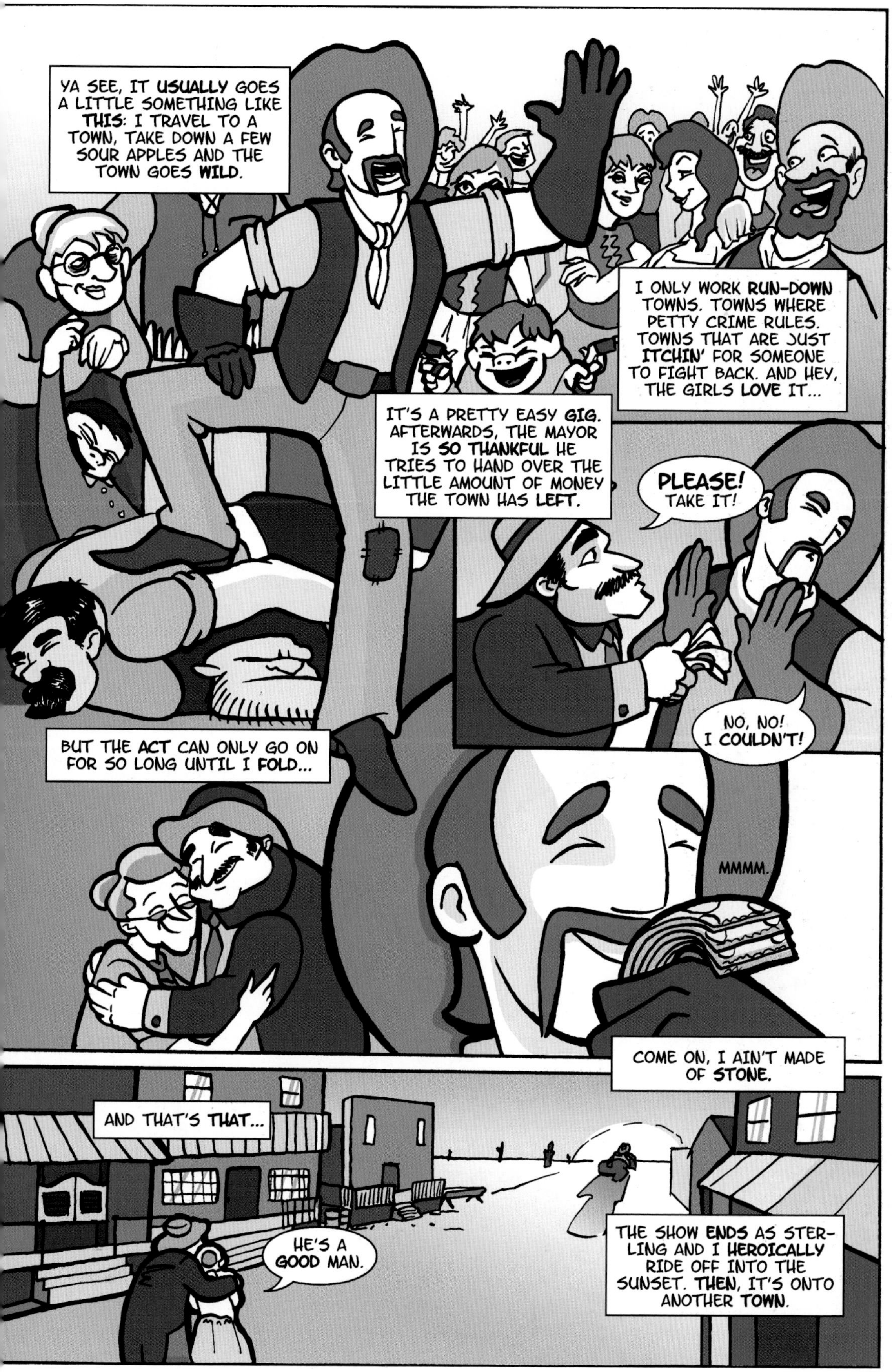
YA SEE, IT USUALLY GOES A LITTLE SOMETHING LIKE THIS: I TRAVEL TO A TOWN, TAKE DOWN A FEW SOUR APPLES AND THE TOWN GOES WILD.
I ONLY WORK RUN-DOWN TOWNS. TOWNS WHERE PETTY CRIME RULES. TOWNS THAT ARE JUST ITCHIN' FOR SOMEONE TO FIGHT BACK. AND HEY, THE GIRLS LOVE IT...
IT'S A PRETTY EASY GIG. AFTERWARDS, THE MAYOR IS SO THANKFUL HE TRIES TO HAND OVER THE LITTLE AMOUNT OF MONEY THE TOWN HAS LEFT.
PLEASE! TAKE IT!
NO, NO! I COULDN'T!
BUT THE ACT CAN ONLY GO ON FOR SO LONG UNTIL I FOLD...
MMMM.
COME ON, I AIN'T MADE OF STONE.
AND THAT'S THAT...
HE'S A GOOD MAN.
THE SHOW ENDS AS STERLING AND I HEROICALLY RIDE OFF INTO THE SUNSET. THEN, IT'S ONTO ANOTHER TOWN.

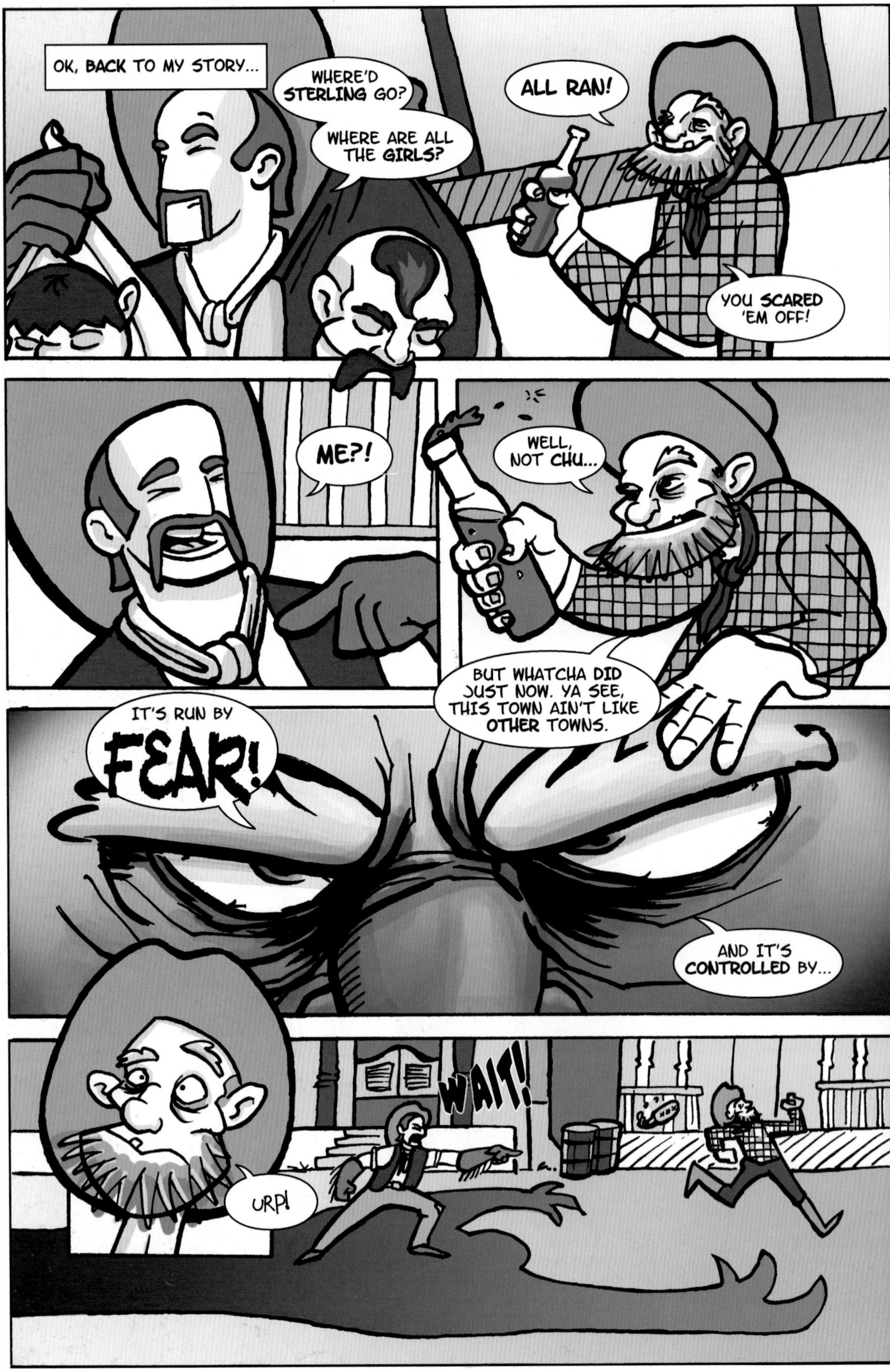
OK, BACK TO MY STORY...
WHERE'D STERLING GO?
WHERE ARE ALL THE GIRLS?
ALL RAN!
YOU SCARED 'EM OFF!
ME?!
WELL, NOT CHU...
BUT WHATCHA DID JUST NOW. YA SEE, THIS TOWN AIN'T LIKE OTHER TOWNS.
IT'S RUN BY FEAR!
AND IT'S CONTROLLED BY...
URP!
WAIT!

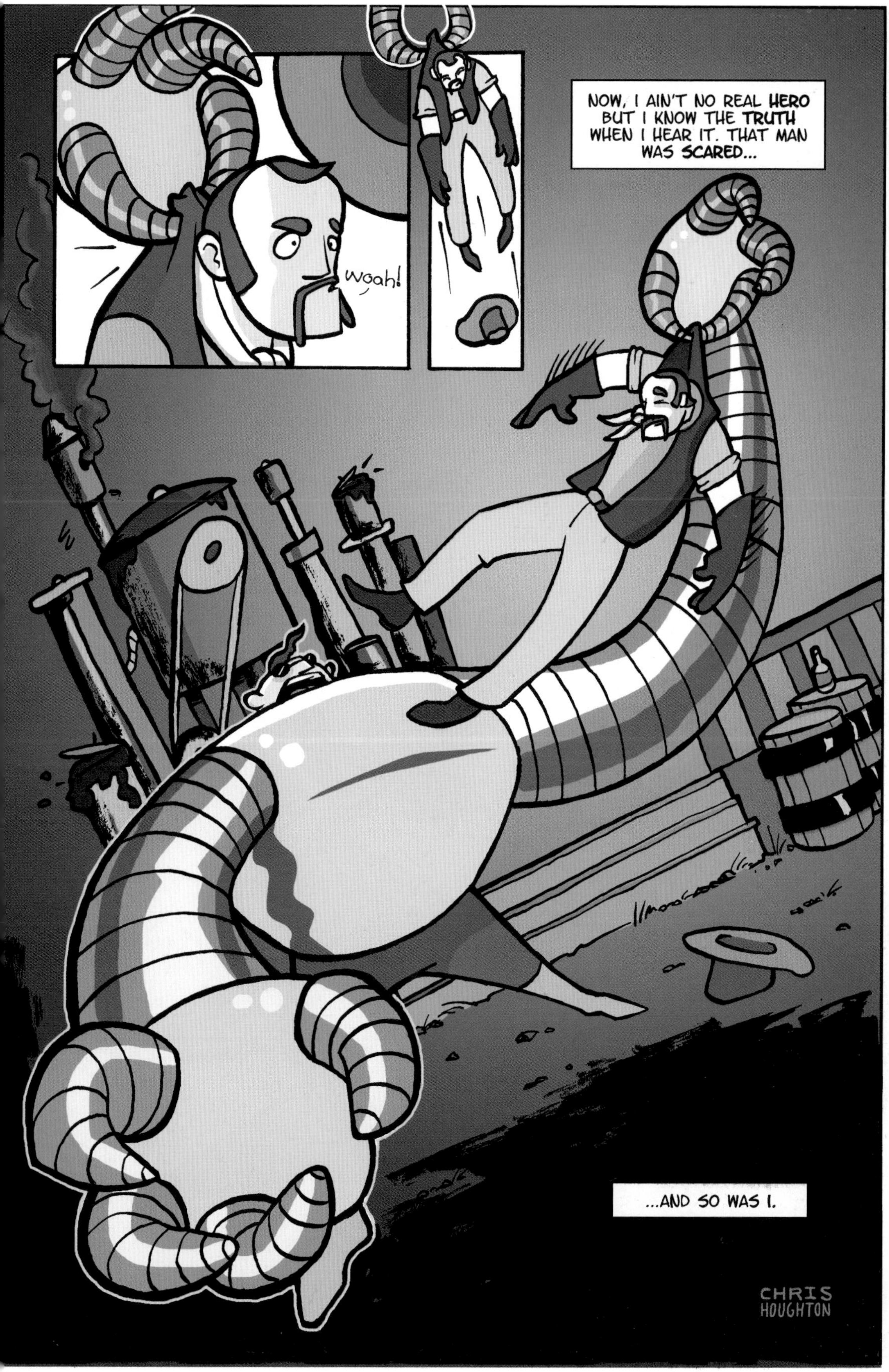
woah!
NOW, I AIN'T NO REAL HERO BUT I KNOW THE TRUTH WHEN I HEAR IT. THAT MAN WAS SCARED...
...AND SO WAS I.
CHRIS HOUGHTON

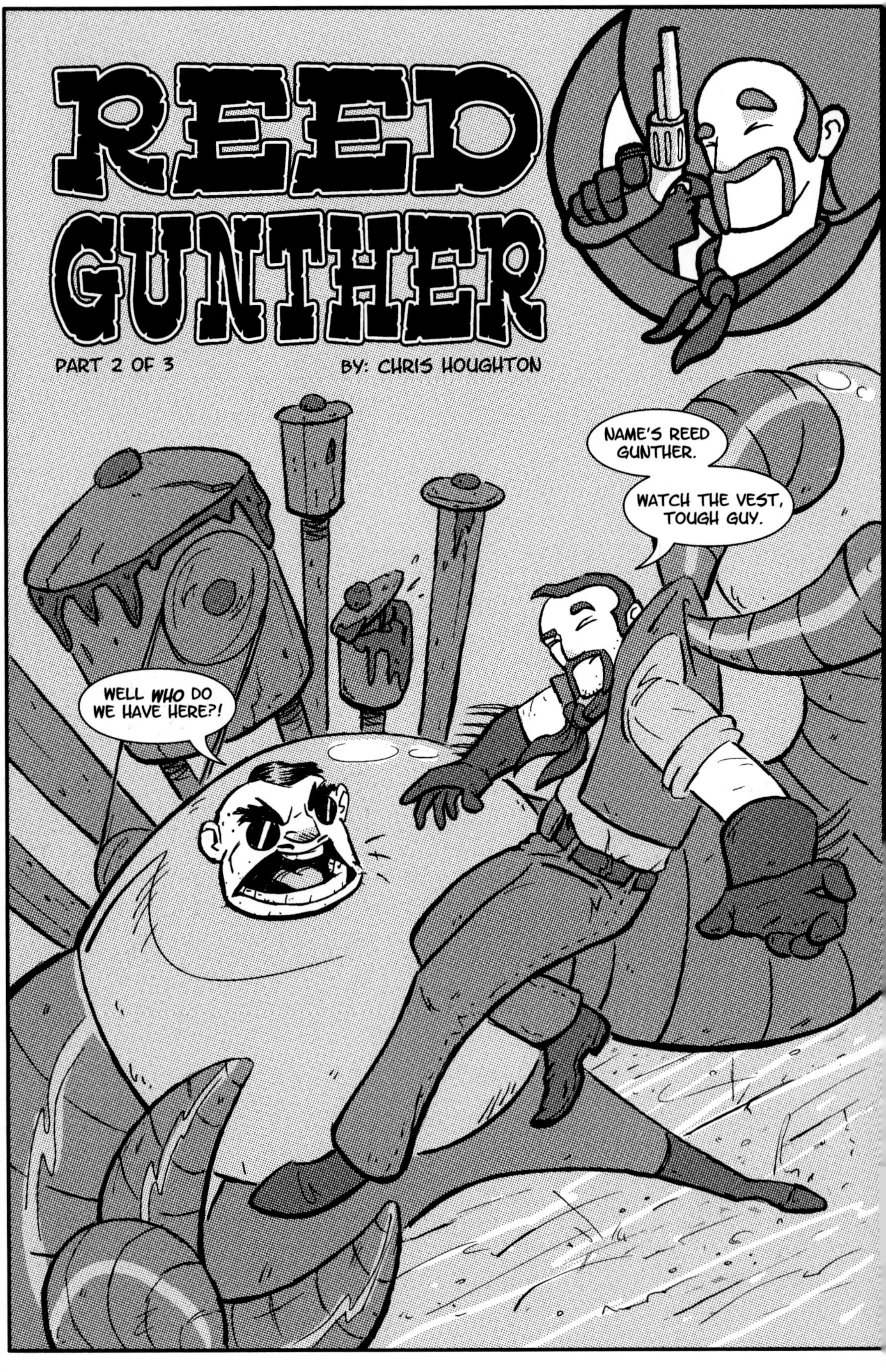
REED GUNTHER
PART 2 OF 3
BY: CHRIS HOUGHTON
NAME'S REED GUNTHER.
WATCH THE VEST, TOUGH GUY.
WELL WHO DO WE HAVE HERE?!

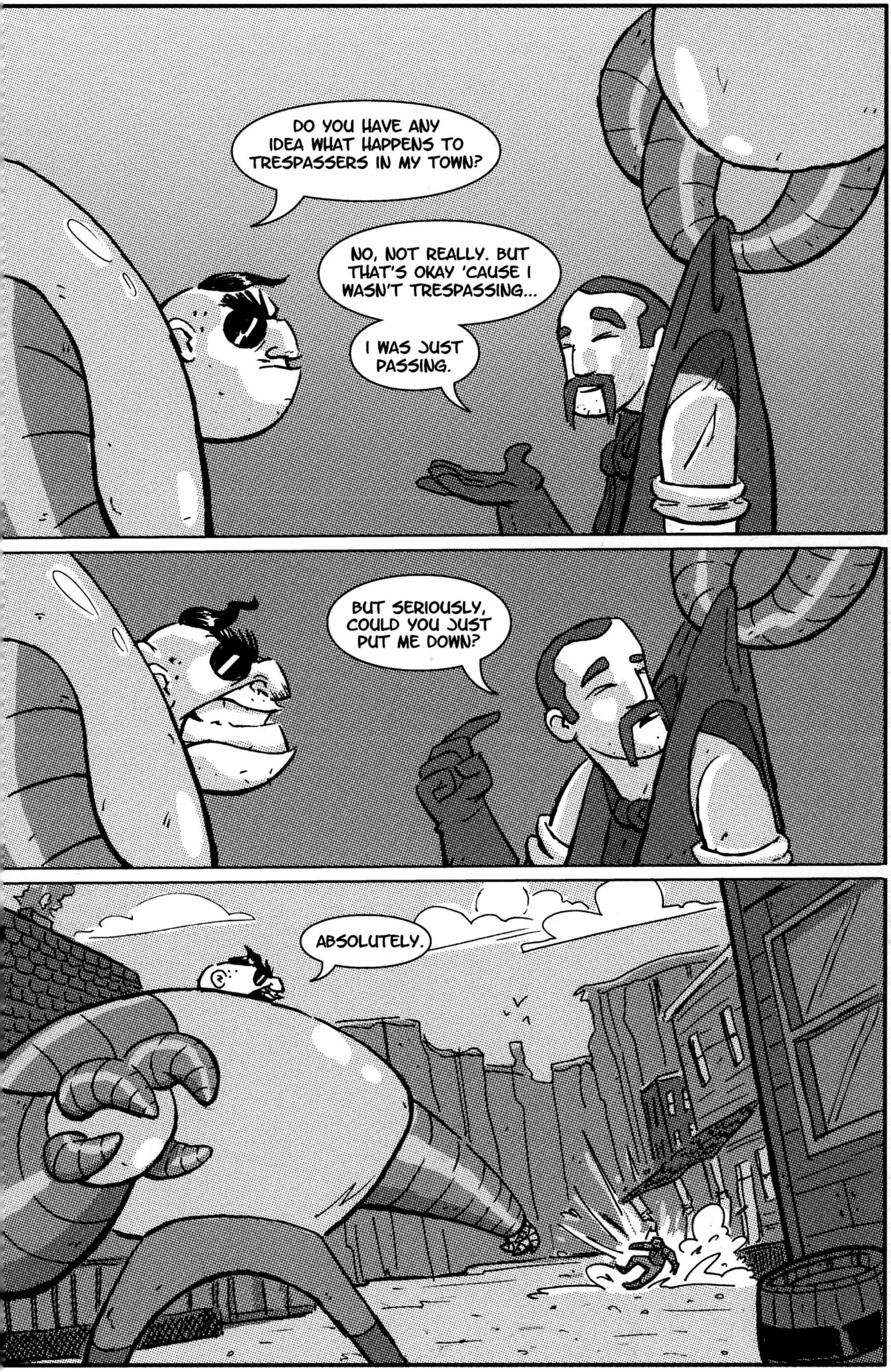
DO YOU HAVE ANY IDEA WHAT HAPPENS TO TRESPASSERS IN MY TOWN?
NO, NOT REALLY. BUT THAT'S OKAY 'CAUSE I WASN'T TRESPASSING...
I WAS JUST PASSING.
BUT SERIOUSLY, COULD YOU JUST PUT ME DOWN?
ABSOLUTELY.

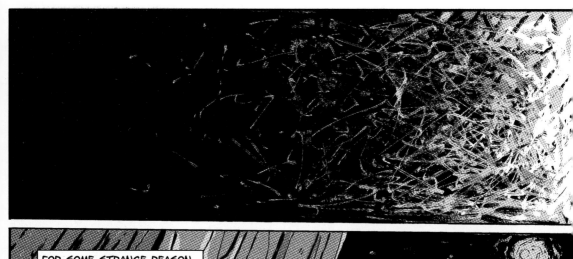

FOR SOME STRANGE REASON, WHENEVER I'M OUT COLD, I SEE THE SAME STUFF.

JUST ME AN' STERLING, THE BIG GOOF. COULDN'T HURT A *FLY*.

WHERE *IS* STERLING?

THIS *CAN'T* BE GOOD.

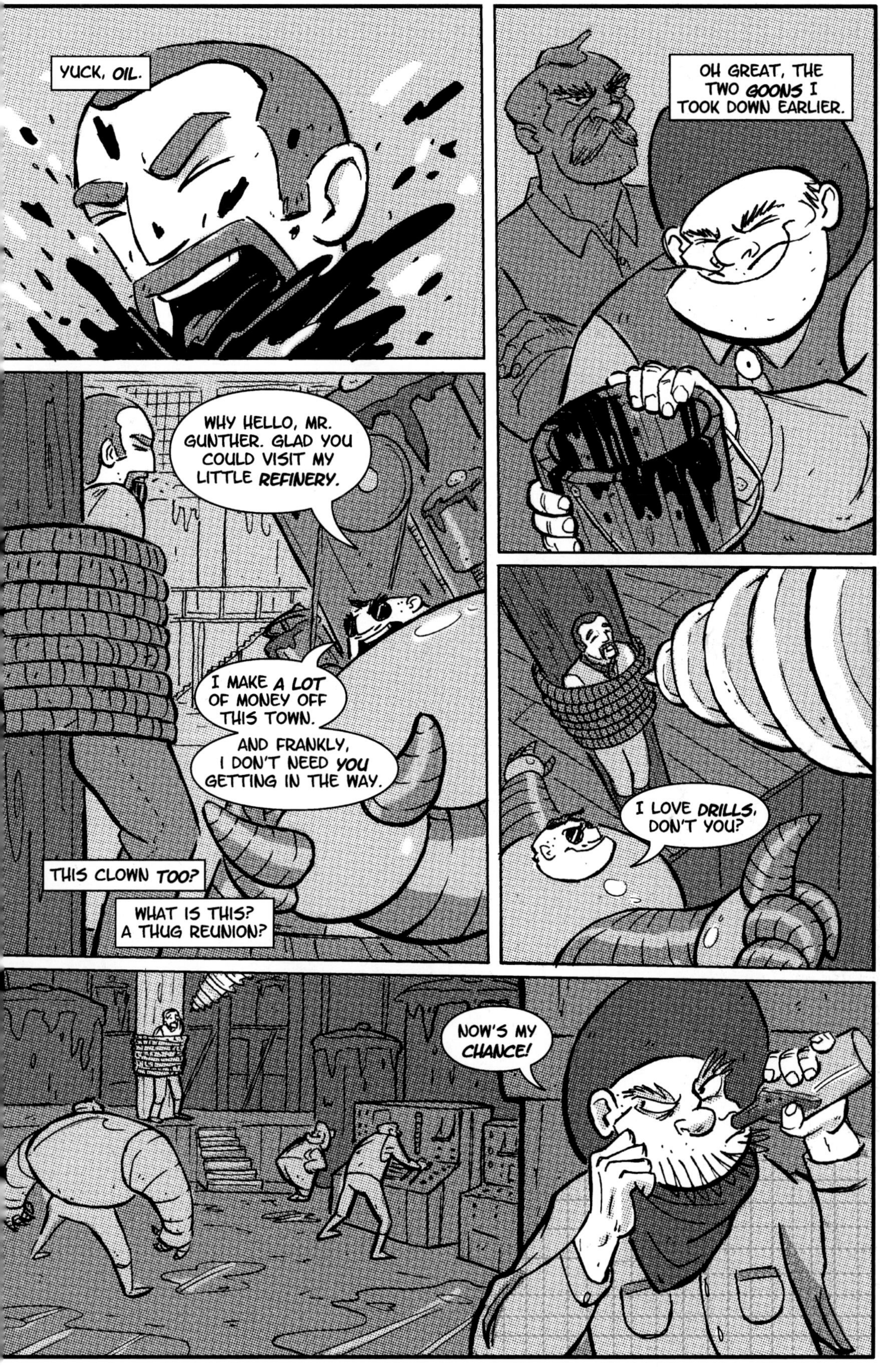
YUCK, OIL.
OH GREAT, THE TWO GOONS I TOOK DOWN EARLIER.
WHY HELLO, MR. GUNTHER. GLAD YOU COULD VISIT MY LITTLE REFINERY.
I MAKE A LOT OF MONEY OFF THIS TOWN.
AND FRANKLY, I DON'T NEED YOU GETTING IN THE WAY.
THIS CLOWN TOO?
WHAT IS THIS? A THUG REUNION?
I LOVE DRILLS, DON'T YOU?
NOW'S MY CHANCE!

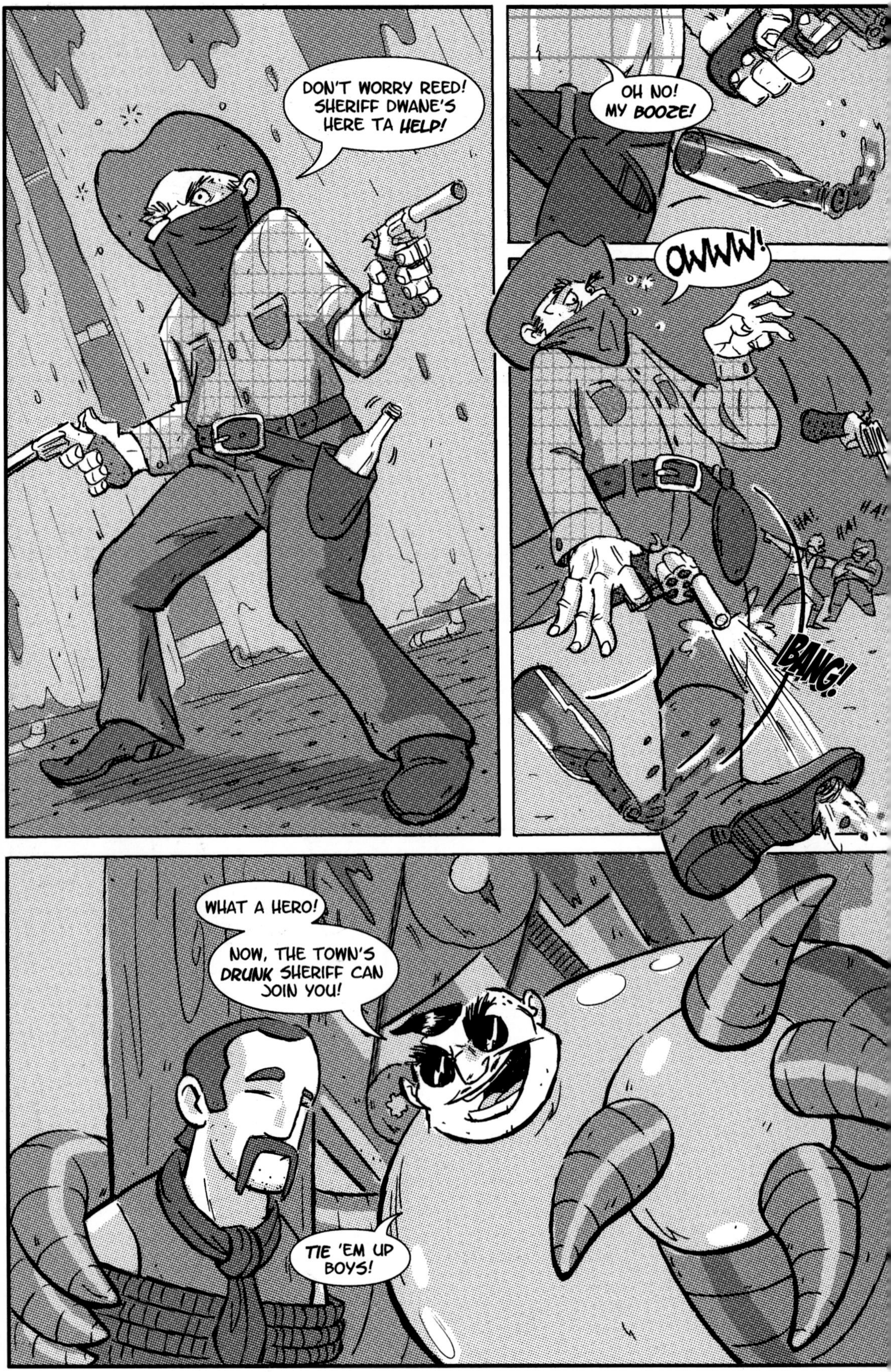

DON'T WORRY REED! SHERIFF DWANE'S HERE TA HELP!
OH NO! MY BOOZE!
OWWW!
HA! HA!
BANG!
WHAT A HERO!
NOW, THE TOWN'S DRUNK SHERIFF CAN JOIN YOU!
TIE 'EM UP BOYS!

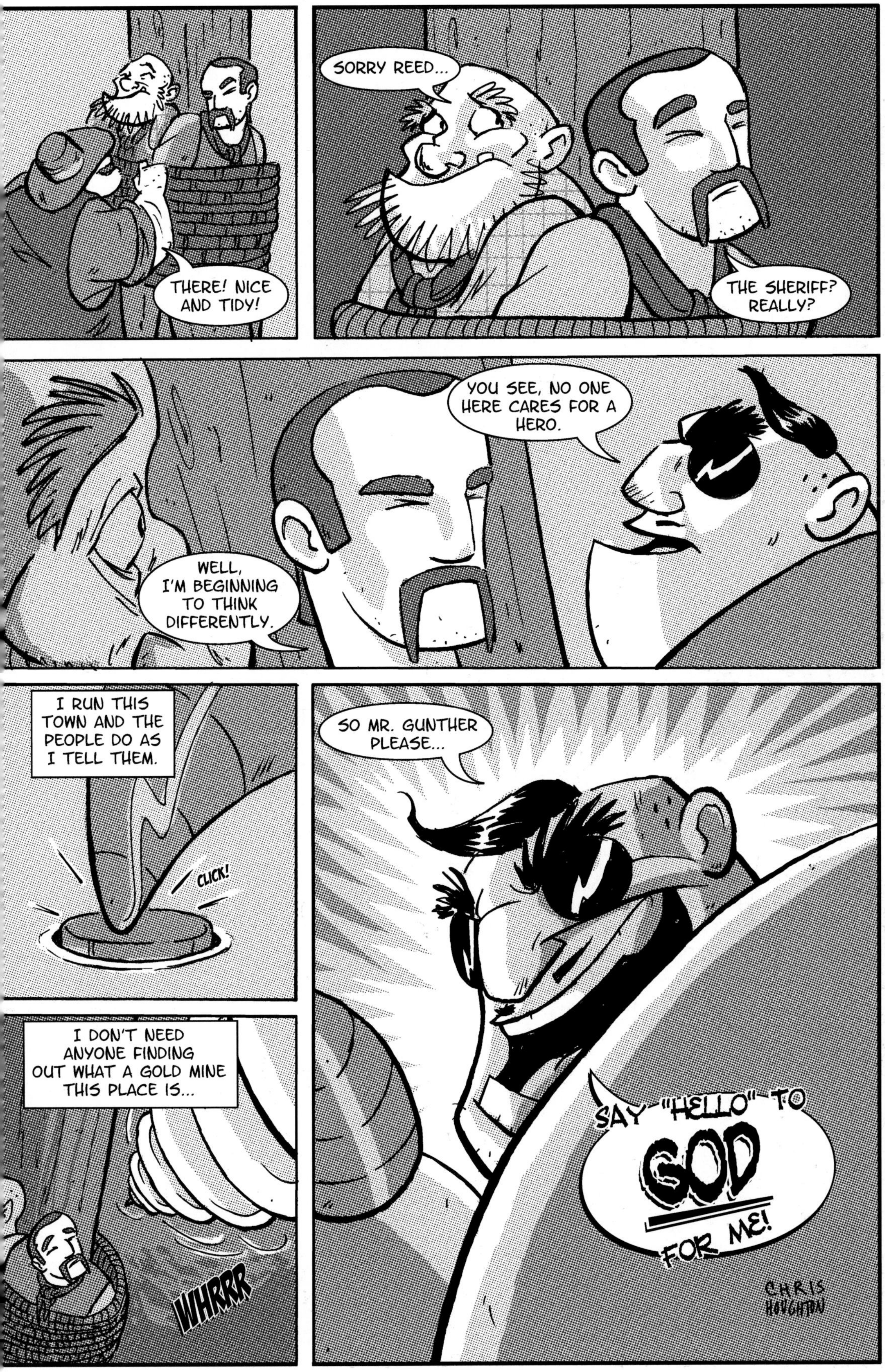
THERE! NICE AND TIDY!
SORRY REED...
THE SHERIFF? REALLY?
YOU SEE, NO ONE HERE CARES FOR A HERO.
WELL, I'M BEGINNING TO THINK DIFFERENTLY.
I RUN THIS TOWN AND THE PEOPLE DO AS I TELL THEM.
CLICK!
I DON'T NEED ANYONE FINDING OUT WHAT A GOLD MINE THIS PLACE IS...
WHRRR
SO MR. GUNTHER PLEASE...
SAY "HELLO" TO GOD FOR ME!
CHRIS HOUGHTON

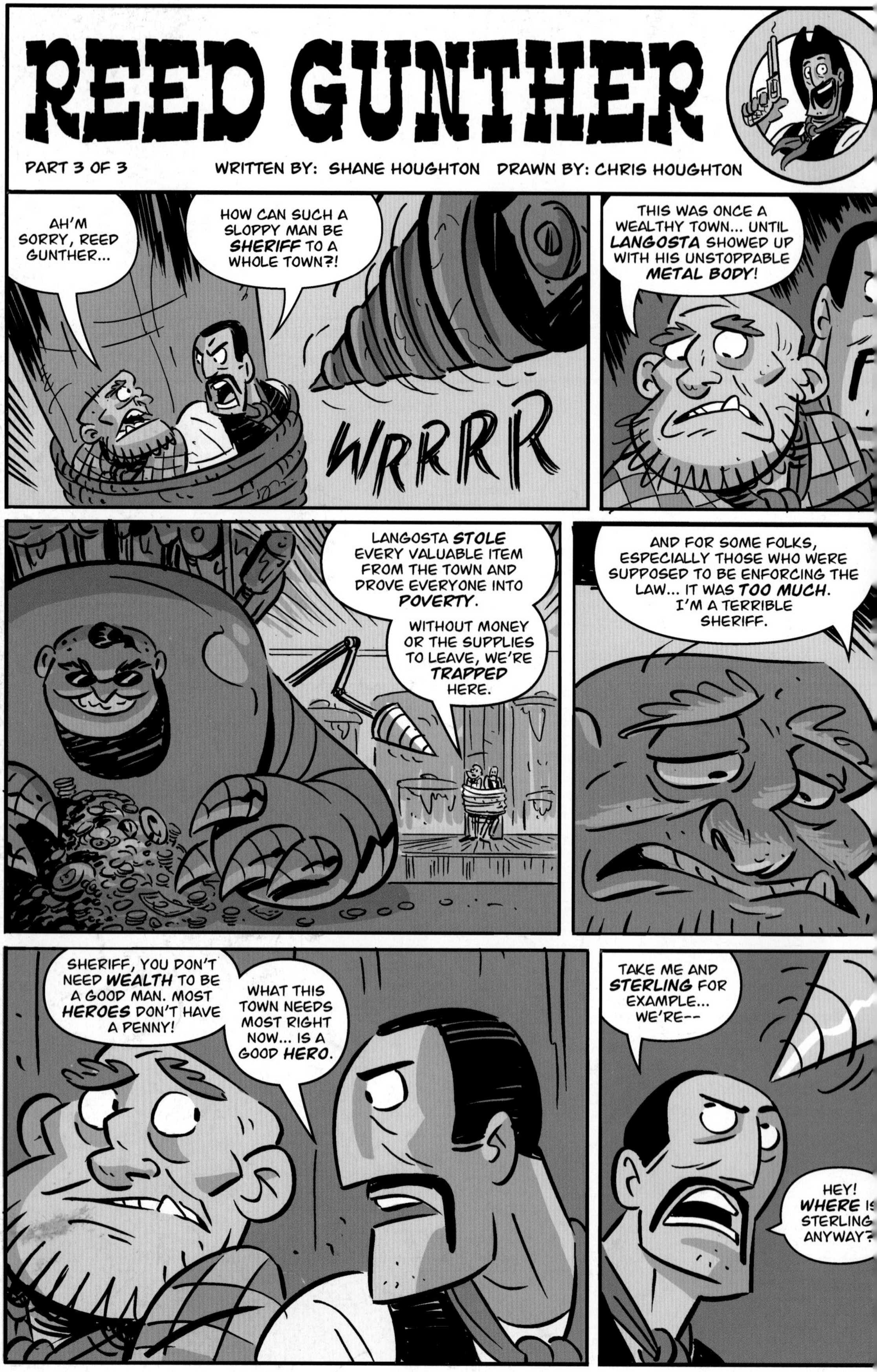
REED GUNTHER
PART 3 OF 3
WRITTEN BY: SHANE HOUGHTON
DRAWN BY: CHRIS HOUGHTON
AH'M SORRY, REED GUNTHER...
HOW CAN SUCH A SLOPPY MAN BE SHERIFF TO A WHOLE TOWN?!
WRRRR
THIS WAS ONCE A WEALTHY TOWN... UNTIL LANGOSTA SHOWED UP WITH HIS UNSTOPPABLE METAL BODY!
LANGOSTA STOLE EVERY VALUABLE ITEM FROM THE TOWN AND DROVE EVERYONE INTO POVERTY.
WITHOUT MONEY OR THE SUPPLIES TO LEAVE, WE'RE TRAPPED HERE.
AND FOR SOME FOLKS, ESPECIALLY THOSE WHO WERE SUPPOSED TO BE ENFORCING THE LAW... IT WAS TOO MUCH. I'M A TERRIBLE SHERIFF.
SHERIFF, YOU DON'T NEED WEALTH TO BE A GOOD MAN. MOST HEROES DON'T HAVE A PENNY!
WHAT THIS TOWN NEEDS MOST RIGHT NOW... IS A GOOD HERO.
TAKE ME AND STERLING FOR EXAMPLE... WE'RE--
HEY! WHERE IS STERLING ANYWAY?

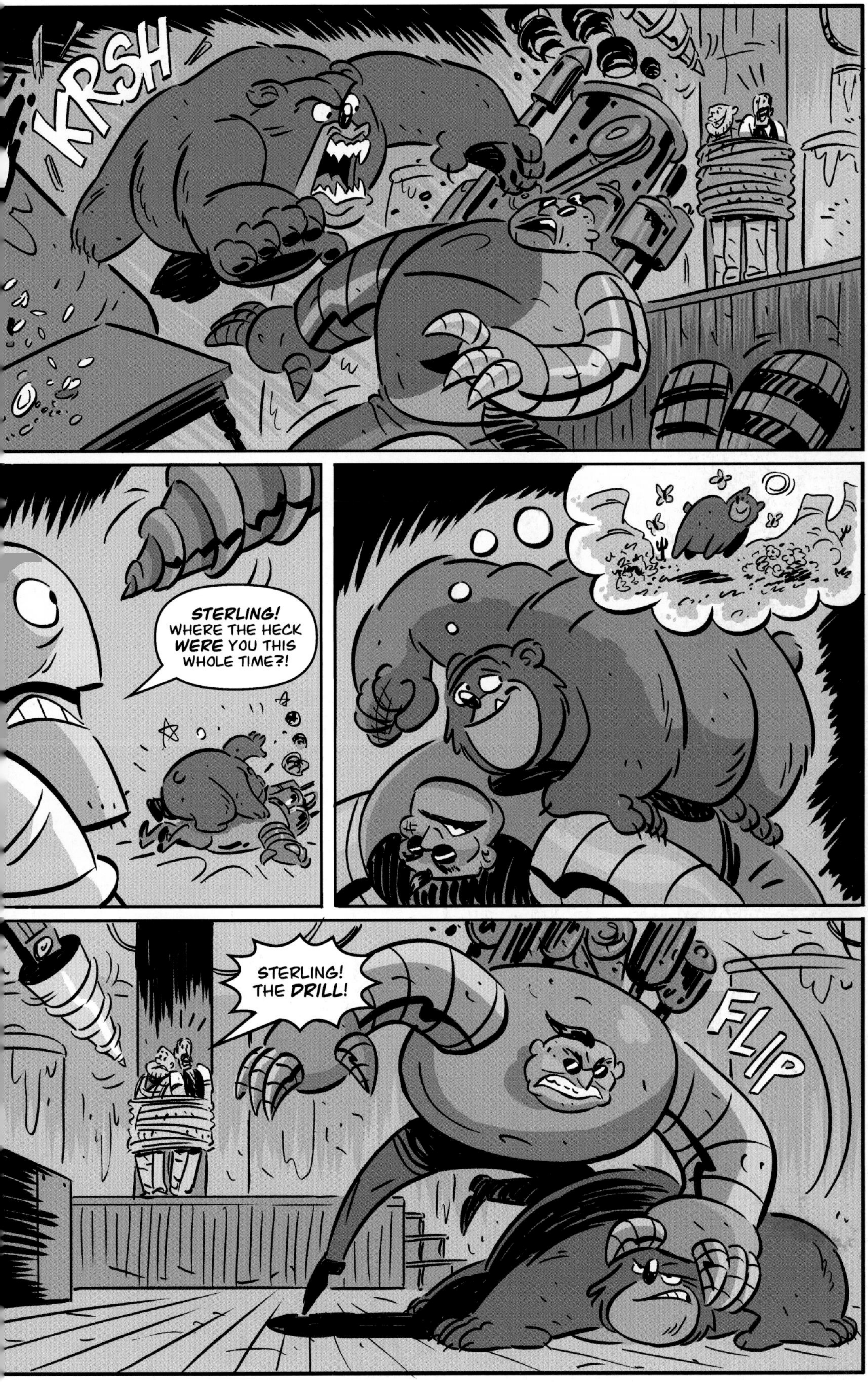
KRSH
STERLING! WHERE THE HECK WERE YOU THIS WHOLE TIME?!
STERLING! THE DRILL!
FLIP

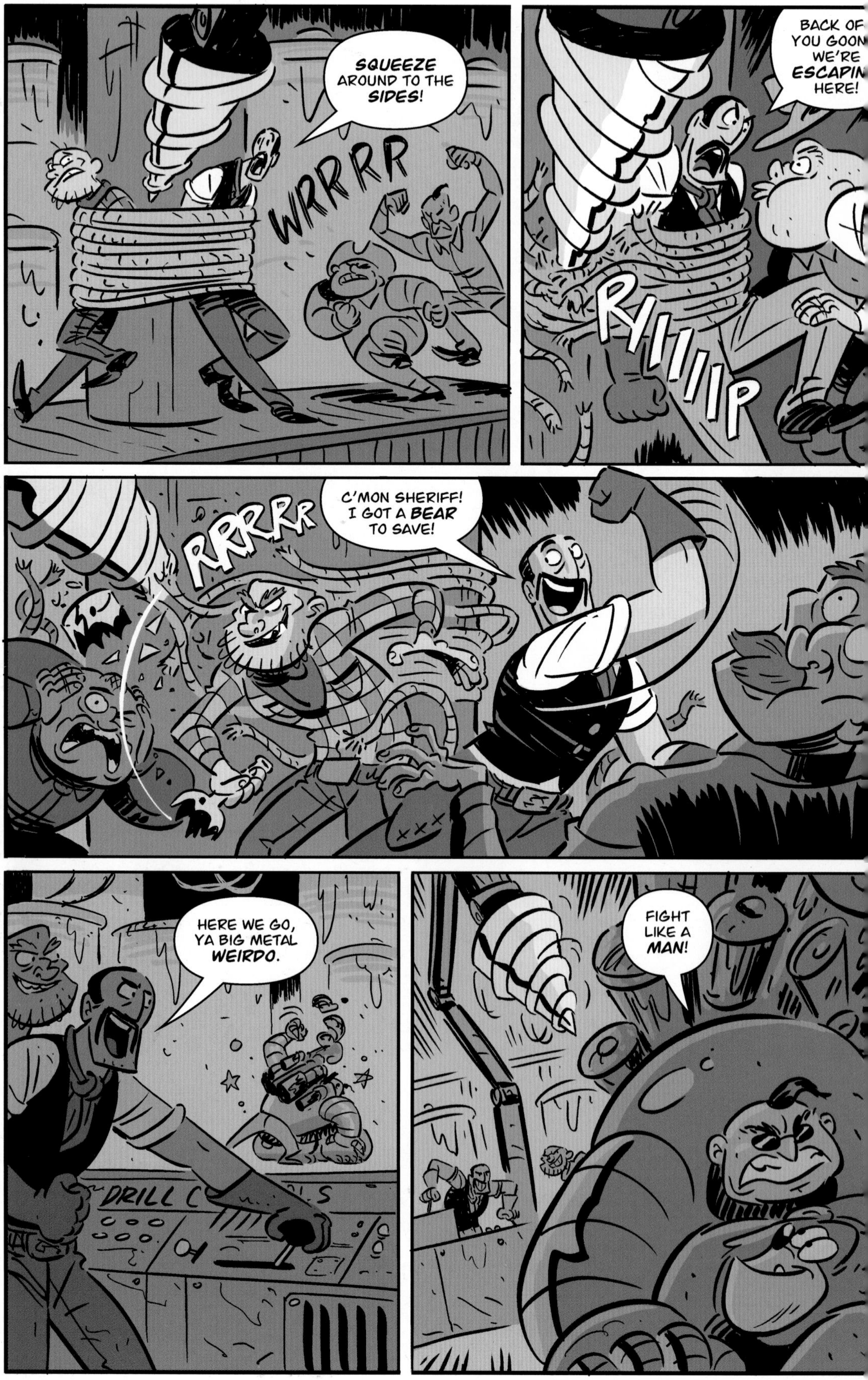
SQUEEZE AROUND TO THE SIDES!
WRRRRR
BACK OF YOU GOON WE'RE ESCAPIN HERE!
RIIIIIP
RRRRR
C'MON SHERIFF! I GOT A BEAR TO SAVE!
HERE WE GO, YA BIG METAL WEIRDO.
DRILL C
FIGHT LIKE A MAN!

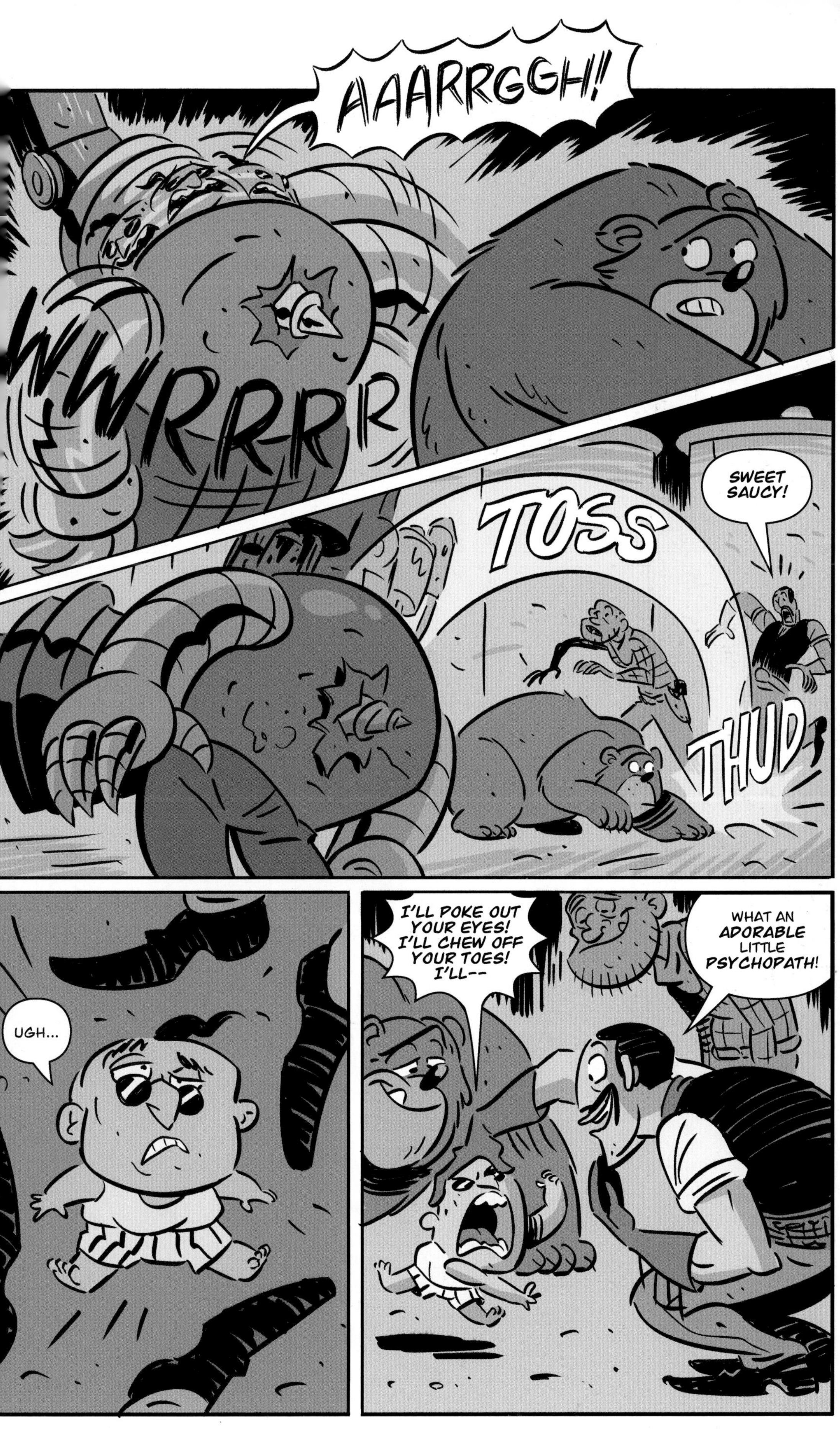
AAARRGGH!
WWRRRRR
SWEET SAUCY!
TOSS
THUD
UGH...
I'LL POKE OUT YOUR EYES! I'LL CHEW OFF YOUR TOES! I'LL--
WHAT AN ADORABLE LITTLE PSYCHOPATH!

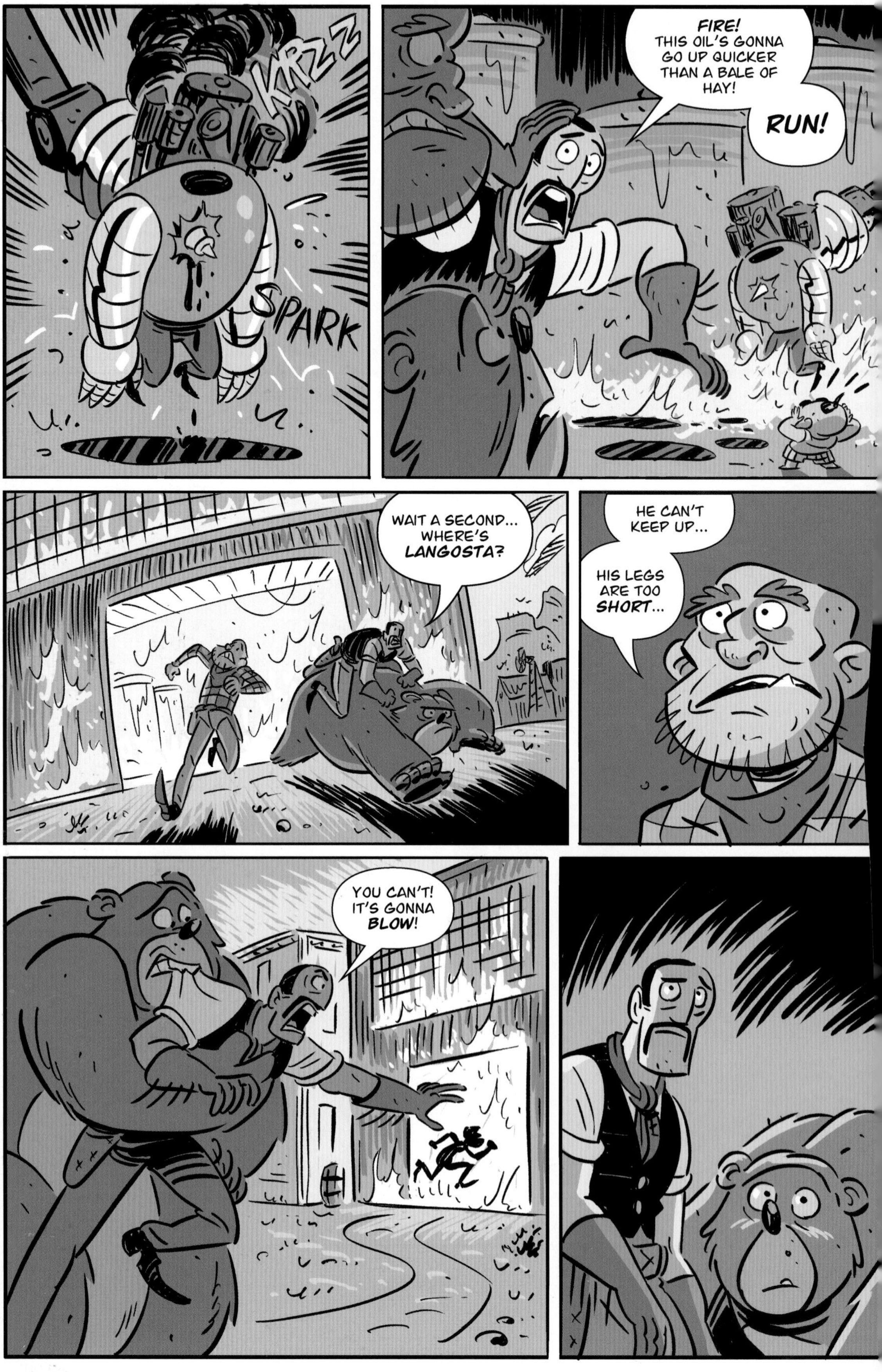
KRZZZ
SPARK
FIRE! THIS OIL'S GONNA GO UP QUICKER THAN A BALE OF HAY!
RUN!
WAIT A SECOND... WHERE'S LANGOSTA?
HE CAN'T KEEP UP...
HIS LEGS ARE TOO SHORT...
YOU CAN'T! IT'S GONNA BLOW!

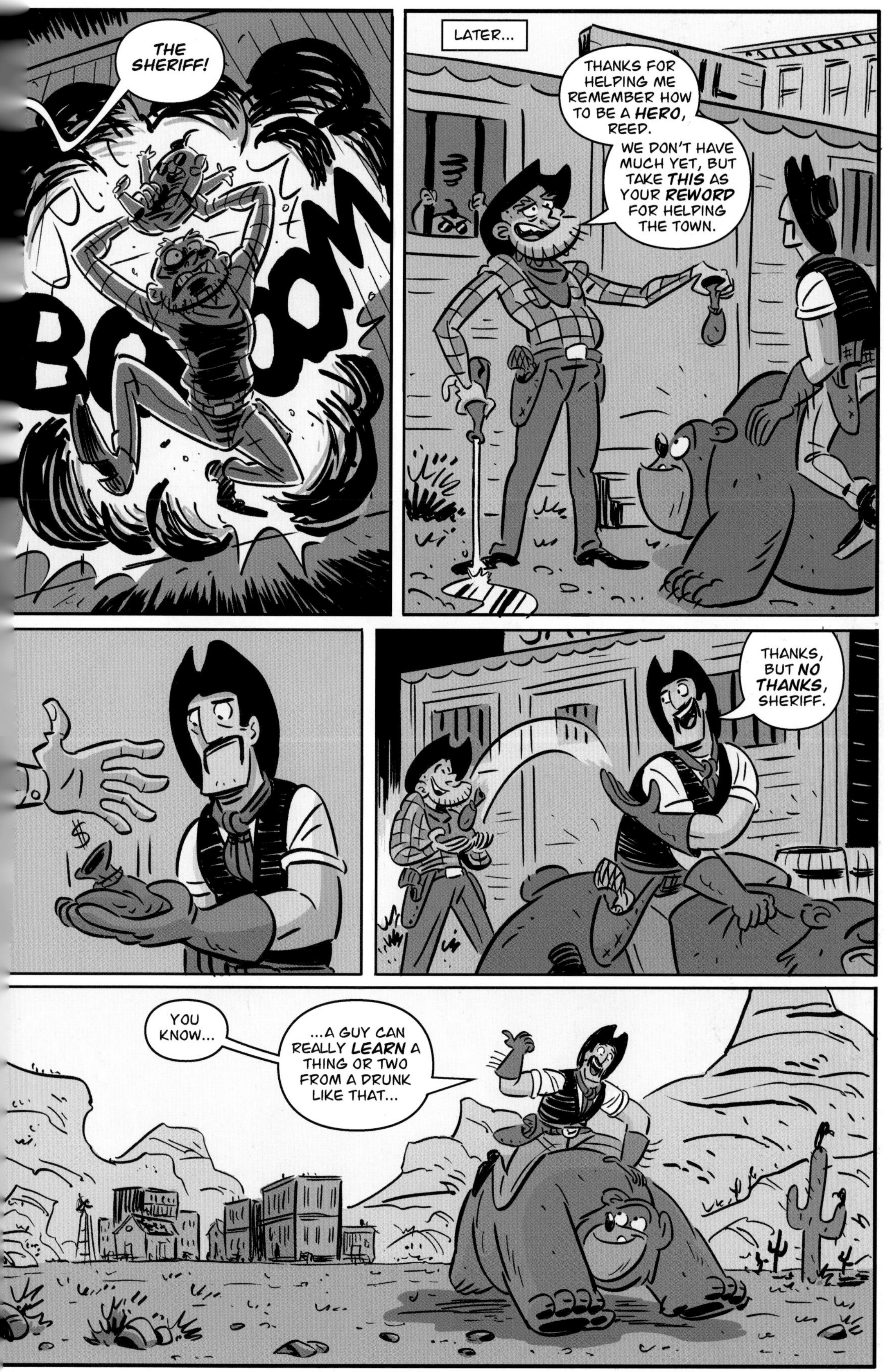
THE SHERIFF!
BOOM
LATER...
THANKS FOR HELPING ME REMEMBER HOW TO BE A HERO, REED.
WE DON'T HAVE MUCH YET, BUT TAKE THIS AS YOUR REWORD FOR HELPING THE TOWN.
THANKS, BUT NO THANKS, SHERIFF.
YOU KNOW...
...A GUY CAN REALLY LEARN A THING OR TWO FROM A DRUNK LIKE THAT...

THE END

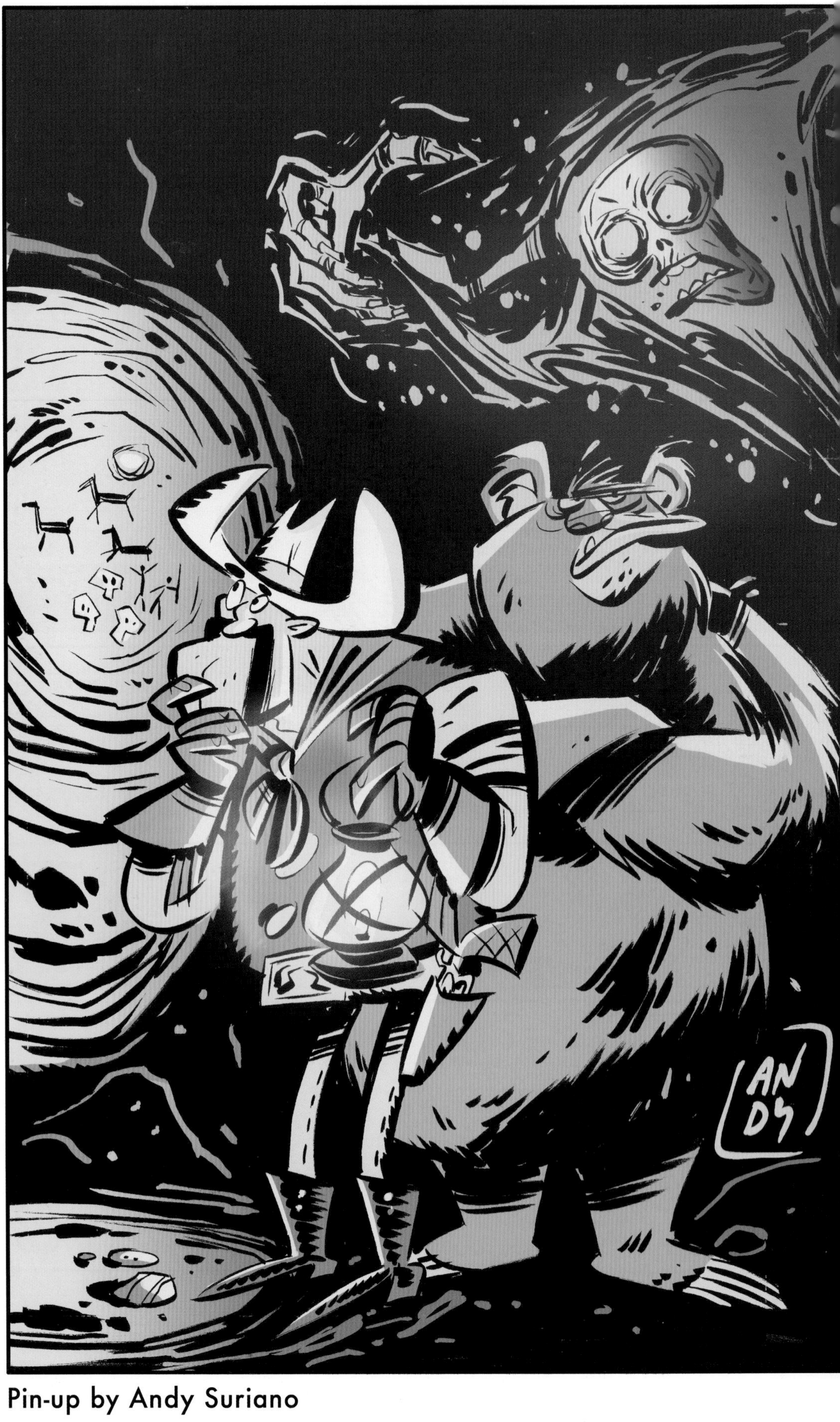
AN
DY
Pin-up by Andy Suriano

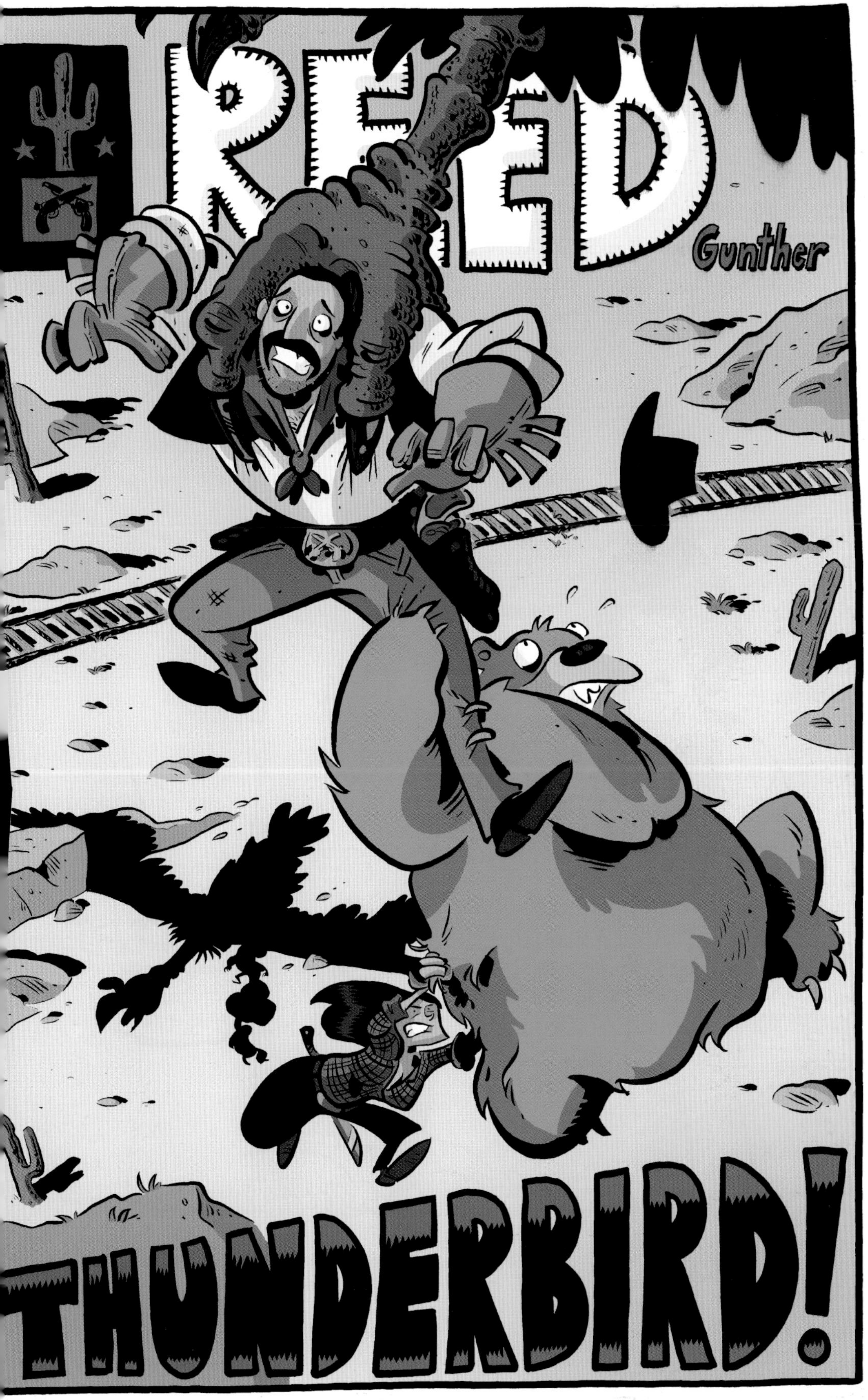
REED
Gunther
THUNDERBIRD!

Pin-up by Chris Schweizer

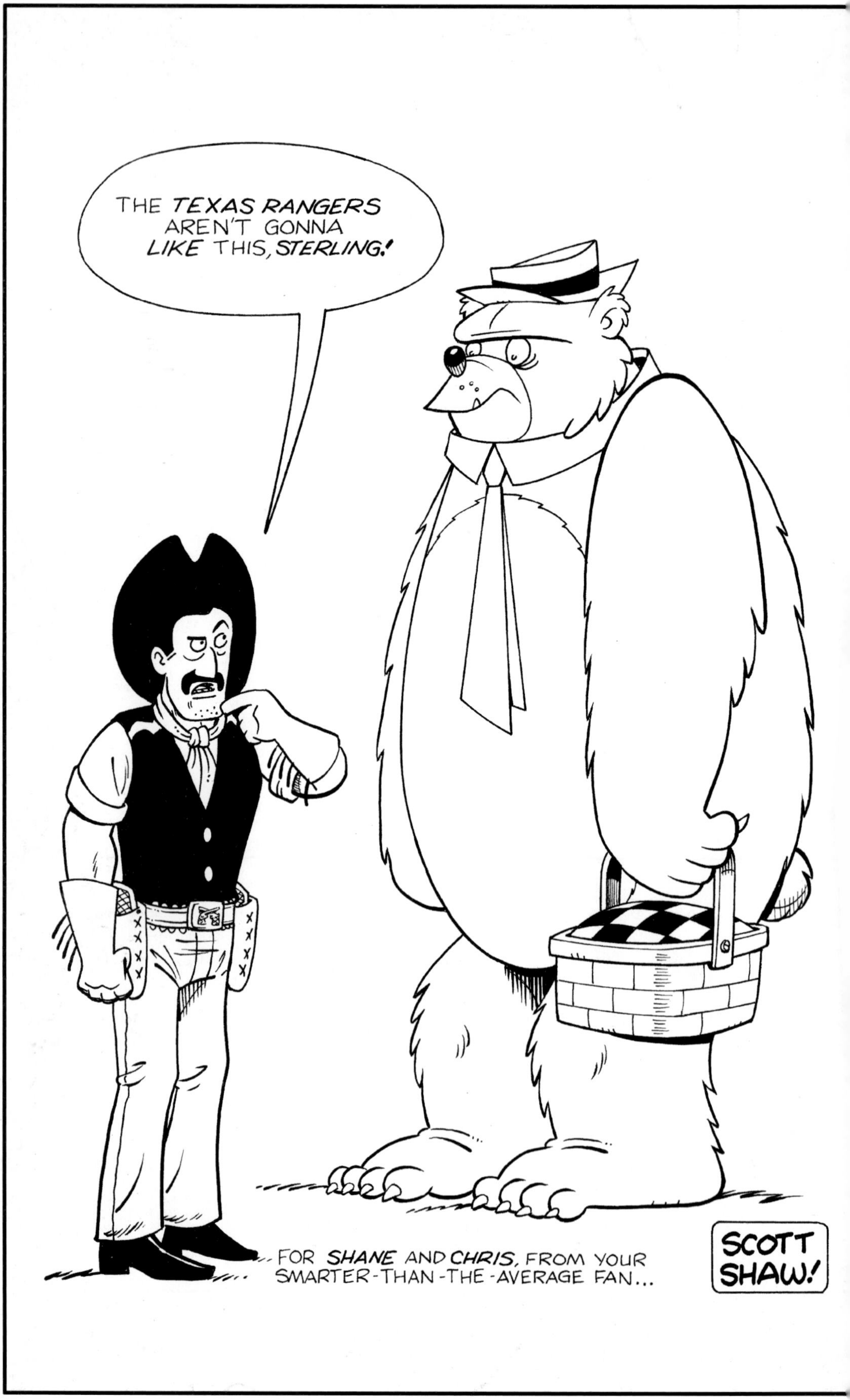
THE TEXAS RANGERS AREN'T GONNA LIKE THIS, STERLING!
FOR SHANE AND CHRIS, FROM YOUR SMARTER-THAN-THE-AVERAGE FAN...
SCOTT SHAW!

Pin-up by Scott Shaw!

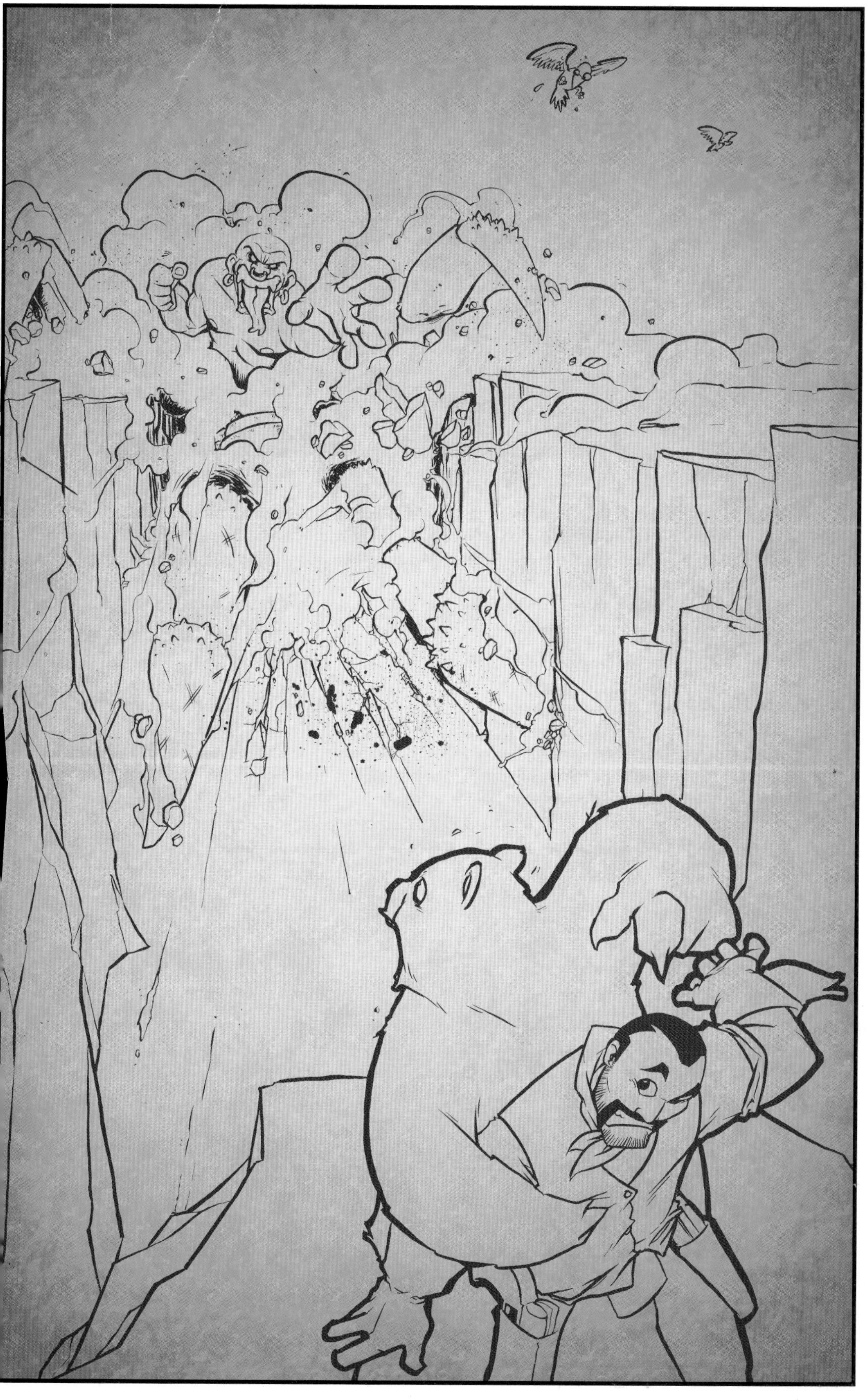

Pin-up by Vincent Kukua

CHRIS

SHANE

(BROTHERS)

Shane Houghton is the writer and co-creator of Reed Gunther. Shane attended the Florida State University Film School where he worked on many short films. Shane's other comic writing credits include *Peanuts* and *Casper's Scare School*. When not writing comics, Shane freelances as a filmmaker and has worked on Comedy Central webseries, Funny or Die sketches, and has edited reality television shows for HD Net and TLC. Shane live in Los Angeles with his fiancé, Katie, where he eats lots of burritos.

Chris Houghton is the artist and co-creator of Reed Gunther. He has also contributed work to the comic book series *Adventure Time*, *Atomic Robo*, and *Kung Fu Panda*. When not working in comics, Chris works in the animation industry and has worked as a storyboard artist and character designer at Nickelodeon and Disney. He is a member of the National Cartoonists Society and lives in Los Angeles with his wife, Kassandra, and wonder cat, Simon.

Josh Ulrich is the colorist for the very book you are reading! He has been coloring Reed Gunther since issue six, and this represents the first printed collection that he has worked on. Josh resides in Houston, Texas where he works at his computer twelve hours a day, hidden away from the burning light of the sun. On occasion, Josh is known to write various paragraphs about himself in the third person. When he's not coloring bear-riding cowboys, he draws a comic about a red headed girl adventurer named Jackie Rose, which you can find over at www.jackie-rose.net. Want to talk? Write me at josh@joshulrich.net